French PROPERTY

BUYING, SELLING & LETTING GUIDE

2004

THE ULTIMATE GUIDE TO BUYING A FRENCH PROPERTY

OVER 1,200 PROPERTIES FEATURED

French
PROPERTY

2004

THE ULTIMATE GUIDE TO BUYING A FRENCH PROPERTY

OVER 1,200 PROPERTIES FEATURED

guide

A few thoughts on buying in France.........

"I am writing to **congratulate** you on creating a truly superb company! The **professionalism** of all your staff at every level has been a joy to someone who has just ventured into the world of purchasing a second property abroad. I wish I had discovered VEF right from the start!"

R.Hanwell, Berkhamsted

"Please convey a **special thank you** to your teams in London and France for their professionalism and **efficiency**; this was greatly appreciated. I look forward to spending many holidays in my new home."

R.Thompson, Lincoln

"I felt that we had to write to you to say a big "**Thankyou**" to everyone for all their effort. It has been a time of great **enjoyment** for us, made all the more enjoyable because everything went so **smoothly**, due to all the team at VEF."

L&A Muir, Manchester

www.vefuk.com
020 7515 8660

 | french property

French Property 2004

BUYING, SELLING & LETTING GUIDE

Compiled, edited and designed by
Merricks Media Ltd
Cambridge House South
Henry Street
Bath BA1 1JT
Tel: 01225 786800
m.guides@merricksmedia.co.uk

Managing Director Lisa Doerr
Sales Director Keith Burnell
Publisher Simon Stansfield
Advertising Manager Julie Stagg
Sales Executives Ruth Leishman, Najat Taibi
Consultant Editor Rebecca Spry
Editor Rowena Medlow
Senior Production Editor Emma Gypps
Production Editor Leaonne Hall
Art Director Jon Billington
Art Editor David Eachus
Advertisement Design Maya Crowe, Becky Hamblin, Steve Mallinson

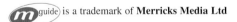 is a trademark of **Merricks Media Ltd**

Cover image © **Justin Postlethwaite, French Magazine and Comite Regional du Tourisme Languedoc–Roussillon**
Many thanks to the following who have provided the majority of the images for this guide, as well as the various individuals who have been credited throughout where applicable:
Justin Postlethwaite, French Magazine and The Touraine Tourism Department
Regional maps by Jamie Symmonds © **Merricks Media Ltd**

Printed and bound in Slovenia by Mladinska knjiga tiskarna d.d.
First published in the United Kingdom in 2004 by Merricks Media Ltd

French Property 2004
BUYING, SELLING & LETTING GUIDE

This fully updated and revised edition of the **French Property Guide** owes a great deal to the dedication, hard work and research and organisational skills of Emma Gypps and Leaonne Hall. A special thanks to David Eachus for his insight and design and to Rebecca Spry for overseeing the project. Many thanks also to Marie Crosnier and Sylvie Saunders for their invaluable input.

Many thanks to the experts who gave their time and knowledge to ensure that the hotspots featured in this book reflect the centres of economic activity in France and that the information on the French property market, law and finance is thorough and up to date. Particular mention must go to:

STEPS TO BUYING AND FRENCH LAW:
Stephen Smith, Stephen Smith (France)
Claire Ingleby, MB Law
Paris Séjour Réservation
French Property Market:
Adam Lister, Communications Manager, Barclays Bank
Alan White, Private Clients PR Manager, Barclays Bank
Barclays Bank France
Nick Clarkson, HSBC
Edwin Cottey, EJC French Property
Philip Winter-Taylor, Winter Taylors' French
Lettings Market:
Matthew Broadbent, Vacances en Campagne
Paris Séjour Réservation
Abbey National France
Liliane Levasseur-Hills

HOTSPOT RESEARCH:
Philip Mason at Coast and Country St Tropez and Var
Simon Malster at Investors In Property
Chris Slade at A House In Brittany Ltd
Nicholas Laletin at Coast and Country
Rhona Booth at VEF Normandy
Shirley de Wallens, Director at Sunshine Properties France
Sarah Francis, Director at Sifex Ltd
Edwin Cottey, Solicitor and Estate Agent at EJC French Property - Provence, Var, Cote d'Azur
Astrid Najar at Agence la Galere
Christine Hilton, Joint Proprietor at La Résidence

Thanks also to officials from the following authorities, who were extremely kind and helpful in providing information on the French economy and general information:

Gregory Chitiac and Mary, The French Embassy
Micette Hercelin, IAURIF
Touraine Tourist Department

The independent experts and tourist offices that ensured the hotspot property markets featured in this book are thorough, accurate and up-to-date are thanked at the end of each area's chapter.

guide

Editor's Introduction

Whether it is for a change of lifestyle or to take advantage of the reasonable price of homes in France today, buying a home in France, it seems, has never been more popular. Coupled with a buoyant market for commercial property, this is translating as a surge of interest in the more traditional areas for overseas buying activity, such as the Côte d'Azur, Paris and the Alps. The augmented demand for French residential property is also leading to the house-hunting net to be cast ever wider over the Gallic countryside. In this guide, we will be pinpointing the most popular areas for both the French and foreign buyers, both the traditionally and newly attractive.

We have chosen from all the corners of France almost 100 hotspots, where the world most wants to own homes. These range from famous cities to exclusive seaside and ski resorts and fashionable rural enclaves. The choice has been quite a challenge, as new areas are gaining heated interest all the time. But, through rigorous guidelines, including sustained interest, high turnover and price levels, we have named the best.

The revelation of France's hotspots is not, however, in an attempt to dissuade anyone looking to buy in France from journeying further afield in their search. It is simply, in homage to the mantra 'location, location, location,' to indicate where is hot in France, to provide the buyer with an understanding of the price differentials in property across France and help guide investment choices. If you are looking for a bargain buy, and cannot find a suitable property in any of the hotspots featured in this guide, take a look in the surrounding countryside or neighbouring towns and villages of any area that attracts you, where the perfect property may be uncovered.

To help you decide which area or property style best suits you and your budget, each hotspot comes with both a detailed description and a list of example properties, with actual asking prices. With activity as strong as it has been over the past handful of years, it can be presumed that this is a fair guide to the realised sales price. It is always good to make an offer, but buyers must be aware that in the hotspots and less known French locations, they will almost always encounter competition.

For the benefit of the foreign buyer, who, more often than not, find the paperwork and idiosyncrasies of the French property buying legal system something of a minefield, this guide is completed by a guide to buying. In no way attempting to include every eventuality, which only expert advice can provide, in compiling the buying guide we have outlined the steps the buying and selling process follows, pointing out the potential pitfalls that unwitting buyers can come across and ways buyers can protect their interests.

This section of the guide also provides hints and tips for those looking to rent out property in France, either in the city, in a resort or in the middle of the countryside. Together with this is useful information for anyone looking to move to France permanently, to retire, or simply give the French lifestyle a go. And bringing this subject to life, our case studies (pages 52 and 54) should provide inspiration to anyone who is contemplating living out their dream of a new life in France.

Rowena Medlow
French Property Buying Guide Editor

MERRICK'S MEDIA

Rowena Medlow has spent many years in France, first as a child in the Dordogne, then as a student in Paris. She edited French Magazine for three years

> 'The revelation of France's hotspots is not to dissuade people from journeying further afield... but simply a homage to the mantra 'location, location, location'

CONTENTS

The Nord-Pas-de Calais' Chartreuse Museum in the town of Douai helps attract would-be francophiles

Contents

French Property Market 2004   12
How To Use This Book   14
Map of France   16
Touring Map of France   18
France 2004   20
Transport 2004   22
Buying and Selling in 2004   24
Letting in 2004   26
Your Purchase in 2004   28

The Buying Guide   30
Steps To Buying   32
Living and Working In France   41
Taxation   45
Letting French Property   48

Buying Case Study   52
Business Case Study   54

Property Guide   56
How To Use This Guide   58

Brittany Property Hotspots (and Price Guide)   61
Normandy Property Hotspots (and Price Guide)   81
Nord-Pas-De-Calais Hotspots (and Price Guide)   101
Ile-De-France Property Hotspots (and Price Guide)   117
Champagne-Ardenne Property Hotspots (and Price Guide)   137
Alsace, Lorraine and French-Comté (and Price Guide)   151
The Loire Property Hotspots (and Price Guide)   167
Burgundy Property Hotspots (and Price Guide)   185
Poitou-Charentes Property Hotspots (and Price Guide)   201
Limousin and The Auvergne Property Hotspots (and Price Guide)   217
The Rhône-Alps Property Hotspots (and Price Guide)   233
Aquitaine Property Hotspots (and Price Guide)   255
The Midi-Pyrenées Property Hotspots (and Price Guide)   271
Languedoc-Roussillon Hotspots (and Price Guide)   289
Provence, Côte D'Azur and Corsica (and Price Guide)   309

Buyer's Reference   332
House Cross-France Price Matrix   334
Apartment Cross-France Price Matrix   337
Letting Cross-France Price Matrix   339
Glossary   343
Directory Of Contacts   346
Index To Agents   358
Acknowledgements   364
Index   366
Index To Advertisers   370

French Property Market in 2004

Increasing interest from foreign buyers combined with French Government initiatives helping young, native purchasers have made for a blossoming French property market.

RESIDENTIAL

The overall market for French property is currently buoyant. Over the past three years, the average house price has risen by approximately six percent per annum. While the average price for a flat in France is around the 155,000 euros mark, the average house price is now approaching 110,000 euros.

The reasons for a continued increase in French house prices are manifold. Firstly, buyers taking out mortgages in France are borrowing more than ever before, principally because exchange rates have been coming down and resting at a 50-year low. The *prêt à taux zéro* (PTZ) (zero interest rate) government initiative rolled out in 1995 has enabled both younger and less well-off households to get a foot on the property ladder, which is helping to prop up the lower end of the market.

On top of this, a burgeoning interest in French properties from foreign nationals has been pushing prices even higher than the national average in some corners of France. A strengthening euro does not appear to have had a marked effect on an apparently insatiable demand from British and other foreign nationals for gîtes, villas, apartments and châteaux, and France remains a favourite with British people looking for a home abroad.

Recently, British interest has been fuelled by a lack of faith in pensions and by sustained growth in the domestic property equity. The former development is leading the younger generation to consider investing in French property as a way of supplementing pension funds while they carry on working in the UK, and the latter not only offers homeowners the opportunity to buy their dream holiday home, but is also encouraging a large number of British people to live permanently in France. Many buyers have sold their expensive homes back in the UK, purchased a similar-sized or even grander property in France and have still been left with a considerable sum on which to live comfortably. There has also been increased interest from buyers in their forties and fifties looking for a home in France for their retirement; a decision that is frequently driven by a perceived higher standard of living and the excellence of the French health service.

It must be said that, despite a strong market and marked increase in sale prices, property buyers in many French enclaves, at least, still acquire much more for their money in France than they do in other European countries. There are a number of contributing factors, such as the much-quoted tradition of renting in France and the fact that land is cheap because there is comparatively so much more of it to share around.

Traditional rural properties are priced lower than similar properties across the Channel, often because they have been neglected and need a good deal of work doing to them, and in recent years it has been rare for anyone but a passionate Francophile foreigner to bother resurrecting from their ashes the unloved phoenixes that lie dotted about the French countryside. Added to this is the fact that French families tend to prefer to live in and around towns where their

TOURAINE COMITÉ DÉPARTEMENTAL TOURISM

children go to school and they can feasibly return home during their one-and-a-half-hour lunch break. Older-style properties have, however, gained ground on the modern in terms of volume sold. Across the country, the sale of period buildings now represents about three-quarters of all purchases.

Anyone looking for a bargain buy in 2004 would do well to look in Limousin, where a two-bedroom stone house with 2,000 square metres of land can be bought for as little as 47,260 euros. Solitude comes as part and parcel of buying a property in this mid-western French region and may put some potential buyers off, but rural France rarely gets more real than this. If you are keen on Dordogne, but feel priced out of the local market, you would be well advised to scour the hamlets and villages of Charente for a property in a similar environment just across the border, but at a much more reasonable price.

The Loire's beautiful valleys and towns have spawned several major property buying hotspots, including Angers, Le Mans, and Nantes. Popular with Parisian second-home owners, and British purchasers, prices here remain keenly competitive

COMMERCIAL
In 2003, even though France's diplomatic relations with its European neighbours and the US might have looked somewhat strained around the time of the war in Iraq, politics did not dampen American and British investors' enthusiasm. North Americans and the British backed about a third of all acquisitions, and Germans have been investing heavily in the Parisian office market, accounting for a third of that sector's activity, surpassing even French investment. This bullish behaviour is a reflection of the sound investment that commercial properties across the board represent in France, in the face of a downturn in those markets in the rest of the European Union. Yields, though down, have been higher than residential returns and have been exceeding those of neighbouring countries. Office vacancy rates in Paris are reportedly only half of the level found in London. Middle Eastern investors are now joining the stalwart overseas investors, having contributed to the hundreds of millions of euros in the past couple of years - limitations on the expansion of office space in the capital have also helped keep the prices of commercial property on an upward trend similar to those of residential properties. ▪

'Anyone looking for a bargain buy in 2004 would do well to look in Limousin, where a two-bedroom stone house can be bought for as little as 47,260 euros'

PROPERTY 2004

Regions of greatest house price growth 2002/2003		
Region	**% Increase**	**Average Property Price** (2003)
Côte d'Azur	15%	€246,000 (£172,000)
Paris	12%	€179,000 (£125,000)*
Dordogne	12%	€161,000 (£113,000)
French Alps	9%	€224,000 (£157,000)

Source: Abbey National France *Average price for flats

How to use this Book

The book's three sections – a Buying Guide, Property Guide and Buyers' Reference – focus on 94 property hotspots, covering all the key areas in France

This guide is divided into three easily distinguishable sections:

■ **PART 1:** *Buying Guide provides the latest facts and information on the French economy and property market, and guides you through the legal and financial processes involved in buying and letting.*

■ **PART 2:** *Property Guide is a series of illustrated snapshots of France's key regions, giving up-to-the-minute analysis region by region of economic performance, facilities available, property styles and prices.*

■ **PART 3:** *Buyers' Reference features a cross-France property price matrix and useful contact details.*

HOW TO USE THE PROPERTY GUIDE

Following consultation with our panel of French property experts, the *Property Guide* has been divided into 15 regions, with an additional grouping of some neighbouring *départements*. These 15 are in turn sub-divided into a total of 94 'hotspots' – centres of population and areas that share a common economic status regarding property. For each hotspot you will find a profile of its property market, including where to find the best value for money, a fact box with details of taxes and local facilities, a property price matrix showing the average selling prices of a wide range of properties and photographs of a selection of properties within a series of price bands to demonstrate architectural styles and value for money. Turn to page 58 for more information.

FINDING ANSWERS TO YOUR QUESTIONS

The way you use this book will depend on your priorities when choosing a property. The major priorities are as follows:

■ *Investment and, as is the case with most people, your budget is limited: use the cross-France property price matrix on page 334 to see how much you can afford in which areas, then use the index to locate the profiles of your chosen area.*

■ *To find the right property for a private residence in a given area; turn straight to the chapter on your chosen region and use the property price matrix, profiles and fact boxes of the area's hotspots to find out which particular area suits you and where you can find the best value for money.*

■ *To find the right property for a private residence in a choice of areas read through all the profiles to see which may suit you. The index will help you find profiles for areas that meet your needs, for instance a property near the sea, near a major city or in the mountains.*

■ *Buying to let: turn to the letting property price matrix to see where you can hope for the best return on your investment, then use the index to locate the profiles of your chosen area.*

■ *Exchange Rate: An average exchange rate of 1.5 euros to the £1 is used.*

Location,
location,
~~location.~~ *currency*

Fluctuating exchange rates could put your dream property out of reach.

To minimise the risk of paying more when buying abroad, call us now and speak to one of our expert advisors, or visit our website.

"For efficiency and delivery, HIFX are one of the most impressive companies I have ever encountered"
Susan Reader, private client buying property in Spain.

 **HIFX** PLC

Tel: 01753 859159   www.hifx.co.uk

The French Regions

France is officially divided into nearly 100 départements, which are local administrative areas quite similar to the British counties. They, in turn, make up the official French regions. This guide has grouped the French regions and their départements into 15 sections under the headings and in the order outlined below (the names in brackets are the official French versions).

■ **BRITTANY (BRETAGNE)**
Côtes-d'Armor (22), Finistère (29), Ille-et-Vilaine (35), Morbihan (56)

■ **NORMANDY
(BASSE-NORMANDIE,
HAUTE-NORMANDIE)**
Calvados (14), Manche (50), Orne (61) (Basse-Normandie); Eure (27), Seine-Maritime (76) (Haute-Normandie)

■ **NORD-PAS-DE-CALAIS &
PICARDY (PICARDIE)**
Nord (59), Pas-de-Calais (62) (Nord-Pas-de-Calais); Aisne (02), Oise (60), Somme (80) (Picardie)

■ **ILE-DE-FRANCE**
Ville de Paris (75), Seine-et-Marne (77), Yvelines (78), Essonne (91), Hauts-de-Seine (92), Seine-Saint-Denis (93), Val-de-Marne (94), Val-d'Oise (95)

■ **CHAMPAGNE-ARDENNE**
Ardennes (08), Aube (10), Marne (51), Haute-Marne (52)

■ **ALSACE, LORRAINE &
FRANCHE-COMTE**
Bas-Rhin (67), Haut-Rhin (68) (Alsace); Meurthe-et-Moselle (54), Meuse (55), Moselle (57), Vosges (88) (Lorraine); Doubs (25), Jura (39), Haute-Saône (70), Territoire de Belfort (90) (Franche-Comté)

■ **THE LOIRE
(CENTRE, PAYS DE LA LOIRE)**
Cher (18), Eure-et-Loir (28), Indre (36), Indre-et-Loire (37), Loir-et-Cher (41), Loiret (45) (Centre); Loire-Atlantique (44), Maine-et-Loire (49), Mayenne (53), Sarthe (72), Vendée (85) (Pays de la Loire)

■ **BURGUNDY (BOURGOGNE)**
Côte-d'Or (21), Nièvre (58), Saône-et-Loire (71), Yonne (89)

■ **POITOU-CHARENTES**
Charente (16), Charente-Maritime (17), Deux-Sèvres (79), Vienne (86)

■ **LIMOUSIN & AUVERGNE**
Corrèze (19), Creuse (23), Haute-Vienne (87) (Limousin); Allier (03), Cantal (15), Haute-Loire (43), Puy-de-Dôme (63) (Auvergne)

■ **THE RHONE-ALPS
(RHONE-ALPES)**
Ain (01), Ardèche (07), Drôme (26), Isère (38), Loire (42), Rhône (69), Savoie (73), Haute-Savoie (74)

■ **AQUITAINE**
Dordogne (24), Gironde (33), Landes (40), Lot-et-Garonne (47), Pyrénées-Atlantiques (64)

■ **THE MIDI-PYRENEES**
Ariège (09), Aveyron (12), Haute-Garonne (31), Gers (32), Lot (46), Hautes-Pyrénées (65), Tarn (81), Tarn-et-Garonne (82)

■ **LANGUEDOC-ROUSSILLON**
Aude (11), Gard (30), Hérault (34), Lozère (48), Pyrénées-Orientales (66)

■ **PROVENCE, COTE D'AZUR &
CORSICA (PROVENCE-ALPES-
COTE D'AZUR, CORSE)**
Alpes-de-Haute-Provence (04), Hautes-Alpes (05), Alpes-Maritimes (06), Bouches-du-Rhône (13), Var (83), Vaucluse (84) (Provence-Alpes-Côte d'Azur); Corse-du-Sud (2A), Haute-Corse (2B) (Corse)

MAPS

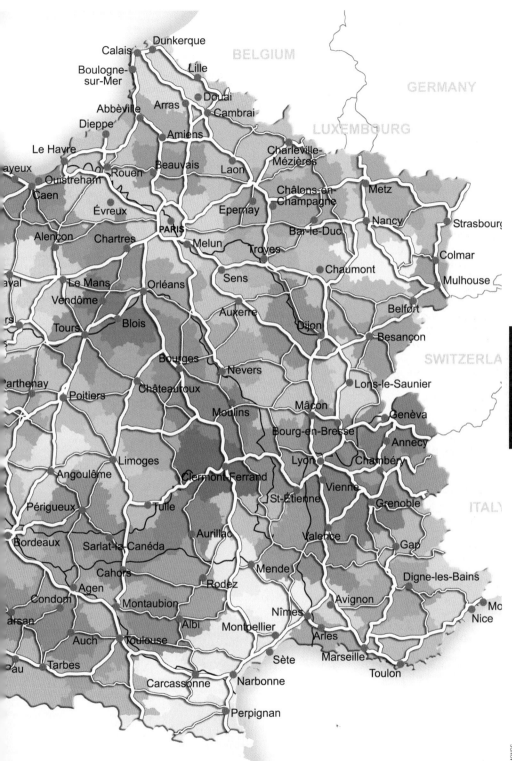

BELGIUM

GERMANY

LUXEMBOURG

SWITZERLA

ITALY

Dunkerque
Calais
Lille
Boulogne-
sur-Mer
Douai
Abbèville
Arras
Cambrai
Dieppe
Amiens
Le Havre
Charleville-
Mézières
ayeux
Rouen
Beauvais
Laon
Ouistreham
Châlons-en-
Metz
Caen
Champagne
Évreux
Epernay
Nancy
Strasbourg
Alençon
Chartres
PARIS
Bar-le-Duc
Melun
Colmar
Troyes
Chaumont
Mulhouse
Sens
aval
Le Mans
Orléans
Belfort
Vendôme
Auxerre
rs
Tours
Blois
Dijon
Besançon
Bourges
arthenay
Nevers
Lons-le-Saunier
Poitiers
Châteauroux
Moulins
Mâcon
Genève
Bourg-en-Bresse
Annecy
Limoges
Lyon
Chambéry
Angoulême
Clermont-Ferrand
Vienne
Périgueux
Tulle
St-Étienne
Grenoble
Aurillac
Valence
Gap
Bordeaux
Sarlat-la-Canéda
Mende
Digne-les-Bains
Cahors
Rodez
Agen
Avignon
Condom
Montaubion
Nîmes
Mo
arsan
Albi
Montpellier
Nice
Auch
Toulouse
Arles
au
Tarbes
Sète
Marseille
Carcassonne
Narbonne
Toulon
Perpignan

JAMIE SYMMONDS

Touring map

MAPS

France in 2004

Political and economic policies and trends, as well as less predictable global events have had an impact on the tourism and property markets. The repurcussions have affected the French economy and business community.

ECONOMIC REFORM

A centre-right government led by Prime Minister Jean-Pierre Raffarin has returned to power after five years of Socialist rule, with plans to roll out reforms aimed at liberalising the economy, promoting competitiveness and intensifying the appeal of France to foreign investors.

Over a five-year period the government aims to reduce income taxes by 30 percent and it has shown signs of a commitment to reforming pensions and the public sector, in particular calling a halt to public sector spending. The French government's budget deficit far exceeds euro rules, and it has long-term liabilities in certain public enterprises, along with unsustainable pension commitments. Its intention to solve this by privatising the huge public utility companies was thwarted by the poor state of the stock market, and that strategy was therefore postponed.

A recent statement by Raffarin announced the intention of the French government to sell off office space over the next three years to the tune of 1.5 billion euros. Selling off parts of France's huge public estate would certainly boost economic activity by releasing vast tracts of real estate that until now have been inefficiently used.

STATE OF THE FRENCH ECONOMY

So far, the French government has resisted EU pressure to reign in its budget deficit, in spite of threats of EU sanctions in which France could face penalties of up to 0.5 percent of GDP, as its budget deficit soars past the stability pact ceiling, tax cuts combined with low Eurozone interest rates are aimed at reviving economic activity.

The European Central Bank cut interest rates to 2.5 percent – the lowest in almost three-and-a-half years – amid concerns that the region's economy was heading for recession, in an effort to weaken the euro, a major cause of lack of investment and weak export figures in the Eurozone. In the spring, for example, as the euro continued its strong run against the US Dollar, rising 25 percent against the Dollar over the previous year, French export orders fell to the lowest level in almost seven years.

Other negative indicators within the economy in 2003 included the high rate of unemployment, which reached its highest level in more than two years. Over the course of the year, jobless figures grew to almost 10 percent.

To counter the signs of stagnation that have been observed over the past year, the French economy is predicted to grow more strongly than the EU average. For example, job creation in Ile de France is forecast to increase this year and next year. In addition, for 2004, a growth in both gross domestic product (GDP) and foreign investment is expected, which is testimony to

favourable government policies, including an array of investment subsidies and tax incentives.

THE EFFECT OF WORLD EVENTS

France's tourism industry, one of the most significant contributors to the country's GDP, was strongly affected by world events in 2003. The threat of international terrorism had a particularly dramatic affect on the confidence of other nations to travel to France.

Added to this was the international reaction to France's stance on the war in Iraq. While relations between the governments of coalition countries and that of France, which made clear its opposition to war, became strained, reports abroad of strong public antipathy for the actions of George Bush and Tony Blair and hostility towards the coalition nations, made some travellers think twice about making a trip to France. After France had declared its opposition to the war, tourism figures showed a significant drop in the number of Americans visiting the country.

The downward trend in visitors to France was not, however, reflected in the property markets. Neither American nor British investors in French property appeared to have allowed political issues to diminish their enthusiasm, and the buoyancy of the residential market showed no signs of subsiding.

POPULATION SHIFTS

While a huge strain has been put on government coffers by the result of a high percentage of the French population now being of a pensionable age, many British nationals are now choosing to relocate across the Channel to retire in France themselves. This is often in the expectation that they will benefit not only from more clement weather, but also from an unrivalled health service and an altogether better standard of living, derived from cheaper house prices, and quality food and wine, which they can find at reasonable cost on their doorstep.

As more of the British of all ages fall for the charm of French country life, certain enclaves have become what some describe as 'ghettos'. And this is not solely in the case of regions traditionally popular with British buyers, such as Provence in the South of France and Dordogne in the Southwest, where there are so many English homeowners that villages are known to have their own cricket teams. A positive rush on buying a dream home in France has led to British buyers moving en masse in areas once rather overlooked, such as Gard, which lies to the west of Provence in the increasingly popular Languedoc-Roussillon. ∎

To counter concerns that France was heading towards a recession, the European Central Bank cut interest rates to 2.5 percent last year, despite the French economy having a stronger predicted growth than the EU average

'As more of the British of all ages fall for the charm of French country life, certain enclaves have become what some describe as 'ghettos'

Transport in 2004

New developments
in France's cutting-
edge transport
infrastructure are
set to make getting
to and around the
country even easier.

TGV OVERVIEW

With a state-of-the-art transport infrastructure including the fast TGV train network linking Paris to Britain and Brussels and cutting a definite artery from the north to the south of France, it's no surprise that France continues to look forward in its transport infrastructure, to faster, easier links.

The existing TGV network links the capital to Lyon and Marseille and services Bordeaux, by its route to Vendôme, and both relocators and buyers-to-let, will be excited by the forthcoming plans to improve all forms of transportation into and within France.

NEW TGV LINKS

The most exciting developments for house hunters/holders in France must surely be the planned routes due for completion in the next couple of years, including an exciting link between Paris and Metz, bringing the Champagne-Ardenne closer for UK travellers. Antwerp's link to Amsterdam in the Netherlands, in 2005, will open up possibilities for those wanting to commute to Belgium from Lille and new track on the Channel Tunnel rail link between Britain and France is set to be constructed in 2007.

By 2020, France's TGV routes are set to include a new easterly route to Strasbourg, stopping at Reims, Metz and Nancy en route. A new branch of track to the east from Brussels will link to Köln in Germany, providing fantastic links for relocators hoping to work in Brussels and Germany. This will also open up a potential lettings market in Köln.

CHANNEL TUNNEL DEVELOPMENTS

The second phase of construction on the Channel Tunnel Rail Link (CTRL2) is underway and due for completion in 2007 (the first phase of the 74 kilometre new line – CTRL 1 – from the channel entrance into Kent was opened by Tony Blair last year) and has already cut the journey time to Paris by 20 minutes. Designed to give Eurostar double the capacity it has had at peak journey times, CTRL 2 should reduce journey times from London to Brussels by 15 minutes, decreasing the time to around two hours. (Eurostar began offering discounted fares from October 2003.)

This year, Eurostar's weekly direct summer services from London to Avignon (launched in 2002) are set to run from July 10 to September 18.

ROAD AND RAIL DEVELOPMENTS

Following the update to the Paris metro service via the *Meteor* project - named after the city's Es-Ouest Rapide project, Line 14, which runs between Gare de Lyon and Châtelet – alternative transportation to 8,000 passengers an hour has been provided since December 2003.

New and
dropped air
routes will
affect the
accessibility
to some off-
the-beaten
track areas
of France

Recent additions to the road network include the arterial A20 from Paris which cuts a link through the heart of France to the Midi-Pyrenees, and has recently opened up the south. (There are also the new Ryan air flights into Rodez airport which has added to the area's accessibility.)

To be completed in 2005, the future A75 route extending from Paris to the Languedoc will make Beziers a logistic centre for industry and commerce. Elsewhere, more motorways are planned for the Clermont Ferrand area of Limousin and the Auvergne department.

NEW AIR ROUTES

Perhaps the biggest news for relocators who depend on cheap and speedy flights to any of the 19 areas serviced by budget airline Ryanair, is its threat to suspend flights to airports that do not prove cost-effective. However, the bad news for potential relocators to more off-the-beaten track parts of France, has to be the airline's lost legal fight to sustain subsidised airport payments from Strasbourg's publicly owned airport. Judged to give the airline an unfair advantage in its budget flight prices, Ryanair's Stansted to Strasbourg route ceased in September 2003.

Still under European Commission investigation for their right to continue with subsidised Ryanair services to localised, publicly owned airports, including Limoges, Carcassonne and Reims could be under threat. The airline has cancelled services to Belgium's Charleroi airport and could be pushed into dropping services to airports that no longer prove profitable.

Relocators relying on cheap flights to off-the-beaten track airports might be sensible to cost in alternative routes/transport as Ryanair's seeming monopoly on cheap fares has come into question this year. Bordeaux, (from East Midlands and Manchester) is the new destination added to bargain flight operator, Bmi Baby's routes for 2004. Manchester to Paris is the company's other new route. Flybe's routes to France have expended widely this year with new routes from Bristol to Bordeaux and Bergerac, Birmingham to Perpignan, and Southampton to La Rochelle, Limoges and Perpignan added to its existing service of Birmingham to Toulouse.

France's extensive TGV route is set to expand further over the next few years

A new service to Berlin from Paris Orly via Easyjet flies twice daily from May 25 2004. (Flights to Toulouse and Marseille from London Gatwick began in October 2003.) Routes between Berlin to Nice are also set to take off. Flights from Gatwick to Marseille and Toulouse began on October 26 2003.

Limousin and the Auvergne are set to become more accessible via a new airport planned for the town of Brive – although it's not due to be built until 2021. British Airways recently reduced fares of £89 to Montpellier and Nantes and Toulon from London Gatwick. My Travel Lite's Birmingham to Paris route was recently cancelled. British Airways franchise, GB Airways new weekly service to Corsica's Bastia Airport, flying on a Sunday from £129 is opening up the previously limited flight portfolio of limited flights to keep the island unspoilt - good news for potential home owners. Lyddair's new summer routes to France are to be confirmed this year.

NEW SEA ROUTES/DEVELOPMENTS

P&O Ferry's two new routes include the 'sea-cat' service from Portsmouth to Caen in around three and a half hours (it comes with the boast of a reduced journey time by up to four hours compared to other operators) and Portsmouth to Cherbourg. Available from April 2 2004, both routes will run each year from April until mid-November. Transmanche Ferries have run a new route from Newhaven to Dieppe.

No new routes are planned for Condor Ferries, which launched their Poole to Saint Malo service in 2003. Corsica Ferries, Hoverspeed and Norfolkline have no new routes planned, either.

Speed Ferries' new Dover to Boulogne service via its new catamaran vessel, SpeedOne, is due to transport 200 cars and 800 passengers to Boulogne across the Dover strait in 50 minutes. Travellers will have quick access to the new A16 motorway into France. Seafrance is another operator launching a new ship, with the Saint Nazaire Chantiers de Atlantique ship yard commissioned to build the new Seafrance Rodin, a 185 metre-long ferry designed to service the Dover to Calais route. Able to carry around 1,900 passengers, Seafrance boast that it will be the quickest vessel on the route, travelling at up to 25 knots and making the journey in 50 minutes. Residents in Boulogne are set to benefit from a new 320 boat mooring development, due to be installed as part of the new Boulogne harbour revamp. ∎

Buying and Selling in 2004

New transport links have contributed to the rising popularity of key regional areas, especially those with holiday letting potential, making France very much a seller's market in 2004. So once you have found that dream property, it's essential to move quickly.

USEFUL CONTACTS

MAGAZINES
French Magazine (UK-based, bi-monthly)
French Property News (UK-based, fortnightly)
Living France (UK-based monthly)
Maisons Secondaires (French monthly)

WEBSITES
www.french-connections.com
www.french-property-news.co.uk
www.entreparticuliers.com
www.pap.fr

PROPERTY FAIRS
French Property Exhibition
This exhibition is held in London Olympia, as well as Birmingham and other towns in the UK. For information about forthcoming exhibitions, call 020 8543 3113 or visit www.french-property-news.com.

Hamptons International Property Exhibitions
In its Overseas Property Exhibition Centre in Knightsbridge, London, and at a number of its offices across the country, estate agent Hamptons International holds exhibitions of property in France and other countries. For details, call 020 7589 8844 or visit www.hamptons.co.uk.

OVERVIEW

Over the past year, changes in air travel to France have had a significant impact on both buyers and sellers of French property. These changes, particularly the operations of budget airlines in responding to the need for improved and more affordable access to French regions, affected how – and how often – people travel to France. New routes came on stream, while the apparently ephemeral nature of others has resulted in some of last year's potential hotspots turning into this year's has-beens.

In 2002 and 2003, there was a great deal of excitement over the introduction of budget flight routes into parts of France that other airlines had not previously serviced. It was widely believed that these routes would open up areas little known to tourists and house hunters, and that property in these areas could prove a wise purchase, either for personal use or as an investment. However, anyone who rushed to buy in areas now easily accessible from other European countries may be regretting that decision, and buyers should bear in mind that choosing a location because it is served by a less-established route is not always prudent.

Low-fare routes such as London-Stansted to Strasbourg or Bordeaux have been discontinued, either because they proved unprofitable or because courts ruled that incentive payments to encourage budget airlines to fly into these airports were illegal. If more routes are terminated this year, it will prevent you making the most of your French home, and may also make it more difficult to rent out.

Terrestrial travel routes could also affect the buying and selling of property in 2004. Although still only on the drawing board, the official go-ahead has been given to extending the TGV rail service from Paris through Provence and the Côte d'Azur. High-speed rail connections to Europe's towns and cities will no doubt add extra cachet to properties near new TGV destinations in this southeastern corner of France. It's not all good news though: work on the tracks and indeed, the tracks themselves, may not be too appealing to those living in or renting property nearby.

In France today, apart from travel considerations, it is very much a seller's market. So much so that properties, especially in areas popular with foreign buyers looking to invest, are frequently sold within hours of them appearing on the market, sometimes even before there has been time to print particulars. This has made finding an apartment in the resorts popular with international skiers – in the Savoie and Haute-Savoie départements of the French Alps, for example – exceedingly difficult.

It should be particularly easy in 2004 for vendors to find a buyer through agents – whether estate agents in the UK, or French agents, *immobiliers* and *notaires* – with a web presence and an international outlook. Well-targeted advertising opportunities in the classified sections of specialist magazines and national newspapers, both in France and abroad, are increasingly available for sellers who can advertise directly or through the agents who are marketing the property. Sellers can also advertise their property direct on websites dedicated to overseas properties. Alongside the development of marketing opportunities on- and off-line, there is a growth in French property fairs in and outside France.

The increasing number of publications and websites advertising French property makes it easier both for owners to find buyers and for buyers to find their ideal home, especially if they are searching from far afield. Surprisingly perhaps, less than half the 600,000 annual property sales are handled by estate agents, with the remainder arranged either privately or by the notarial profession.

Whether you choose to buy through an estate agent or not, with properties

changing hands as swiftly as they are at the moment, you could find yourself pressurised into buying without checking on the property and its area thoroughly. If you do need to proceed rapidly with a sale in order not to miss what you believe is a perfect opportunity, make sure you do so subject to a contract. The contract should be one that provides you with the opportunity to 'get out' if you discover problems after you have signed and handed over your deposit.

Checking the internet for *immobiliers*, or British estate agents with an international outlook, is essential in your search for that ideal French home

CAPITAL GAINS TAX ON PROPERTY

The declaration of capital gains on French property has been simplified for 2004, off-loading the burden of declaration from the vendor. From January 1, 2004, the *notaire* in charge of the sale will be responsible on behalf of the client for progressing the calculation and payment of capital gains tax during the registration of the sale.

The calculation itself will be simplified by the granting of a fixed allowance of 15 per cent on the sale price, to take into account works that have been carried out on the property. There will also now be no capital gains tax levied on a property that has been owned for 15 years or more, instead of the 22 years previously. After the fifth year, capital gains will also be reduced by 10 per cent every year, instead of using the *coefficient d'érosion monétaire* (monetary depreciation coefficient).

Other changes to the regime include the exemption of property under 15,000 euros from this tax and a fixed reduction of 1,000 euros on the total capital gains due. The vendor will also now be taxed at the time the buyer transfers the balance of the purchase price to them, with the tax payable being taken from the sum transferred, instead of waiting more than a year to pay when the income tax for that tax year is due. ■

'From 1 January, 2004, the notaire in charge of the sale will be responsible on behalf of the client for progressing the calculation and payment of capital gains tax'

Letting in 2004

The French letting market has long been popular with French, British, German and Dutch landlords, and despite a dip last year, it remains a strong investment source for canny buyers-to-let. In this chapter, we look at the short- and long-term markets and legal details that should be taken into account by potential landlords.

FINDING TENANTS

There are currently a variety of ways to find tenants for French rental properties. You can advertise directly through French, British and other European publications and on websites dedicated to those markets; alternatively, you can leave the property in the hands of local lettings agents; or, in the case of holiday homes, market the property through a French or international lettings company specialising in French holiday gîtes and villas. In Paris, as well as in popular ski and coastal resorts, short-term lettings agents will not only find tenants for you, but also manage the changeovers and maintenance of the property in your absence.

SHORT-TERM LETS

Although France has more than 70 million visitors a year and remains a leading destination for holidaymakers, over the past year, it saw a downturn in visitor numbers from several nations. After the war in Iraq, some lettings companies saw both the US and Australian markets drop by as much as 50 per cent, but in the ensuing months, the US market recovered to a level 35 per cent below what it had been the previous year, while Australian interest recovered almostcompletely.

The German market may not recover so rapidly, however, as the cause here was not the war, but a general downturn in the economy. France is as popular as ever with UK holidaymakers and, since Great Britain is one of the key markets for French tourism, its continued buoyancy should be a good indication that there will be a healthy holiday rental market in 2004. Nevertheless, anyone letting a gîte or villa should remember that the British are becoming more demanding. While in the past a simple rustic cottage would have appealed, today British holidaymakers are often not satisfied with holiday cottages smaller than their own homes, and expect all the comforts they are used to at home as well, not to mention that increasingly important swimming pool.

The length of the season currently averages out at 10 weeks in the height of summer, when occupancy is almost guaranteed, and the highest rents can be charged. In certain regions, the summer letting period can last up to 20 weeks, although prices do not plateau for the whole season; prices can dip as well. In some areas, landlords expect two distinct seasons: the Provençal Alps and the Pyrenees, for instance, attract both skiers in the winter and outdoor enthusiasts in summer. The Parisian short-let scene is quite the opposite from the rural market; quiet in August, but busy in spring, autumn and Christmas. In Paris, the 1st *arrondissement* is popular with both tourists and people on business trips, as it is conveniently located near significant monuments, museums, the opera and the main banks. American interest has traditionally buoyed up the market for holiday apartments in Paris, yet Europeans have been showing increasing interest in renting apartments over the past year.

An up-and-coming rental area is the town of Pantin, on the outskirts of the capital. Prices for apartments here are well below the Parisian average, and although the area still has some way to go in the desirability stakes, it is a growing business district for which the new mayor has a bullish development plan. The local métro station, Hoche, gives access to the centre of Paris in 15 minutes, and leaseback schemes, which guarantee a rental income, are currently being offered in this area.

In rural France, the Loire Valley, with its fine châteaux and famous wines, is currently the most popular destination for Americans outside Paris, while Dordogne and Provence are favourites with the British, Germans and Dutch. Each region has its share of tourist attractions – Futuroscope near Poitiers is a case in point – that guarantee the surrounding areas more interest from holidaymakers. Increasing competition from foreigners starting up gîte businesses is, however, affecting the profitability of letting in even the most popular areas.

USEFUL CONTACTS

PUBLICATIONS
French Magazine (UK-based bi-monthly)
Holiday Villas Magazine (UK-based bi-monthly)
Chez Nous (UK-based annual publication)
De Particulier à Particulier (French newspaper)

WEBSITES
www.french-connections.com
www.holidaylets.net
www.holidayvillasmagazine.co.uk
www.pap.fr

LETTING AGENTS
Gîtes de France (+33 1 49 70 75 75;
www.gites-de-france.fr)
Vacances en Campagne (0870 077 1771;
www.indiv-travellers.com)

Being close to tourist attractions can be critical for ensured letting success

RECENT FRENCH LEGISLATION

• France has noise 'zones', classified A to D, which will appear on the *plan d'exposition au bruit*, of which *préfectures* hold the details. Landlords must provide the official noise category of the area in which they are lettingproperty. This is particularly important if the property is situated near a civil or military airport.

• Any UK resident letting a French property should take note of the UK Data Protection Act 1998, which aims to ensure the privacy of individuals in relation to any processing of their personal data. It does this by imposing numerous obligations on data controllers, including accommodation suppliers, and by giving relatively wide rights to the individuals to whom that data relates.

• 'Personal data' is data from which it is possible to identify a living individual and includes names, postal and e-mail addresses, and photographs.

• 'Processing' is widely defined and covers activities such as collecting and booking details from consumers, supplying those details to suppliers, using or storing those personal details for direct marketing purposes, or using consumers' photographs in promotional material. Before processing any personal data, data controllers must notify the Information Commissioner.

* Source: Investment Property Databank France

LONG-TERM LETS

By all accounts, the French long-term lettings market is proving resilient. However, the total return on rental properties – commercial as well as residential – has dropped slightly. In 2002, it had slipped to 8.6 per cent, having reached 9.8 per cent in 2001*.

Although home ownership has recently overtaken renting in popularity, many French families, couples, young professionals and students still consider taking on long leases. Cities are prime locations for prospective tenants looking for long lets. In Paris, the 6th and 7th *arrondissements* command some of the highest rents, having been at the luxury end of the market for some time and enjoying long-term popularity with wealthier tenants. But other areas, such as Le Marais, are becoming increasingly sought after, and rents there are gaining ground on traditionally coveted areas. Commercial properties in Paris have been producing higher yields than residential properties, with retail outlets achieving the highest returns, and industrial properties and offices coming second and third. Paris is still seen as the investment capital of Europe. New offices are a rare find, and although a handful of developments are in the pipeline, a limited supply has protected the French capital from the slump in office rents suffered in other European countries.

Owners of holiday properties should consider letting on long leases out of season to keep the properties earning money throughout the year. Older British couples are particularly interested in these off-season lets, as are other foreign buyers looking for their dream home in France; they may want to take time to get to know the areas they are interested in. Rents for holiday homes let on a long-term basis out of season will, naturally, be considerably lower than weekly rentals in high season.

NEW LAWS AFFECTING LANDLORDS

To ensure contracts, terms and conditions, and practices comply with the laws of the countries governing the letting of an individual property — this can be UK law as well as French, if both landlord and tenant are British residents — it is advisable to have them reviewed on a regular basis by specialist legal advisors. Up-to-date, off-the-peg agreements, and schedules of condition can be downloaded from French website www.jurimodel.com. ∎

'Owners of holiday properties should consider letting on long leases out of season to keep the property's earning money throughout the year.'

Your Purchase in 2004

Many of the potential pitfalls involved in buying a French property can be avoided by not rushing into a purchase, seeking independent advice and having the building thoroughly checked over. This chapter is essential reading for anyone considering making that all-important purchase this year.

INITIAL CHECKS

■ Check that where the agent's fee appears in the sales contract, it is accompanied by a note explaining that this figure is the commission paid to the estate agent. Should a phrase such as *'commission de l'agence immobilier à la charge de l'acquéreur'* appear, you will only pay duties on the price the vendor receives. On a property sale of 1,908,000 euros, including a six per cent agency commission of 108,000 euros, not paying duties on the commission would save the buyer 5,280 euros.

■ Commission fees are a potential hidden cost which you should also take steps to avoid paying duties on when buying a French property through an estate agent.

DRAINAGE TIPS

■ If a proper septic tank is not in place, nor mains drainage, and the local *commune* has not already carried out a general survey of the area, the buyer will also be required to have an *étude du sol* (soil test) carried out by a registered inspection service, which will state exactly how and where a septic tank can be installed.

■ This test should be carried out before completion of the purchase and will add approximately 400 euros to your costs. Local town halls can help by pointing buyers in the right direction. Anyone installing a septic tank must now follow the guidelines provided by this type of report, or by the survey for the area. As work progresses, the local water authorities will need to inspect the site to ensure that it complies with regulations.

OVERVIEW

Foreign purchasers can be all to easily persuaded to sign a sales contract before properly protecting their interests, and to buy what they assume will be a dream home without calculating the full cost of repair or renovation work.

Involving both an independent legal advisor and a qualified buildings surveyor in the purchase, although still not common practice in France, is to be highly recommended as a way of avoiding setbacks.

If you are considering buying a home in France but cannot quite afford your dream property, you could group together with like-minded friends or families to make the purchase attainable. If you do consider this option — sensible if you do not anticipate spending more than a handful of weeks there each year — it is wise to seek advice on how best to structure the purchase of the property. An increasingly popular option is to use a civil company or *société civile immobilière* (SCI) to buy the property. Owning through an SCI can incur extra legal costs at the outset, as well as accounting costs and substantial amounts of paperwork each year, but it can make ownership more manageable by simplifying the disposal of shares in the property without recourse to a *notaire,* and by saving owners a great deal in inheritance tax.

Another way to make a holiday property more affordable is to participate in a leaseback scheme. These are set up by developers, who pass on government tax breaks in the form of a TVA (French VAT) rebate to the buyers and who manage the property as a rental investment for a number of years; the VAT rebate is currently 19.6 per cent. But also, provided they keep it on for a certain period (typically nine years), users can enjoy the property for several weeks of the year and earn a guaranteed net return on their investment of between three and seven per cent. In addition, the owners' holiday home and changeover days are managed in their absence.

Although these schemes are only available in the main tourist areas, if the development has been awarded tourist class, or *résidence de tourisme,* status, they can be found in a great variety of French regions, from Ile-de-France to the Pyrenees.

BUYER BEWARE

If you are planning to buy a home in the country, you should also be aware of some of the current issues involving rural properties that may not be pointed out during your search. One such issue is foul drainage. By law, all homes must either be on mains drainage or have a self-maintaining septic tank system by 2006, when a new inspectorate will have been set up. Even if a property does have a septic tank in place, it may not necessarily comply with the new regulations. If a property you are considering does not have an approved drainage system, you should take into consideration the cost and time required to have one installed.

An approved septic tank or *fosse septique* can cost between 3,500 and 4,500 euros, and on top of that you will need to set money aside for the installation. There is another cost to take into account which, although it is minimal by comparison, is another addition to the mounting cost of the purchase. If there is neither a proper septic tank in place, nor mains drainage, and the local *commune* has not already carried out a general survey of the area, the buyer will also be required to have an *étude du sol* (soil test) carried out by a registered inspection service, which will state exactly how and where a septic tank can be installed. This test should be carried out before completion of the property purchase, and will add approximately 400 euros to your costs. Local town halls can help by pointing buyers in the right direction. Anyone installing a septic tank must now follow the guidelines provided by this type of report, or by the survey for the area. As work progresses, the local water authorities will need to inspect the site to ensure that it complies.

While not everyone will need to improve their drainage system immediately, the new regulations will have an immediate impact if you need to obtain planning permission for any alterations to a property. Applications for planning permission will only be accepted if your property either has a foul drainage system that complies with these new regulations or if there is the means to connect to a mains system or sufficient land to accommodate a new septic tank.

Barn conversions are another problem area since legislation, brought in to protect agricultural buildings, came into place in 2000. As a result of this legislation, local planning offices are being much stricter about planning applications, and the worst case scenario is that you could find yourself buying a heap of bricks in a field that you will not be able to turn into a home. The only way you can be confident of being able to convert an agricultural building into a house is to ensure that a *certificat d'urbanisme* (planning permission certificate) is in place before you buy the property.

Buyers should also be aware of new legislation concerning swimming pools in order to avoid incurring hefty fines and curtailed lettings. From January 1 2004, private swimming pools built into the ground will need a fence or similar device to enclose the pool, as a safety feature. With swimming pools built before January 1 2004, owners have until January 1 2006, to take appropriate security measures. However, if the pool belongs to a rental property, the deadline remains January 1 2004. ■

With proper planning, legal checks and preparation, purchasing your French home can be easy

Buyers should be aware of new legislation concerning swimming pools in order to avoid hefty fines and curtailed lettings

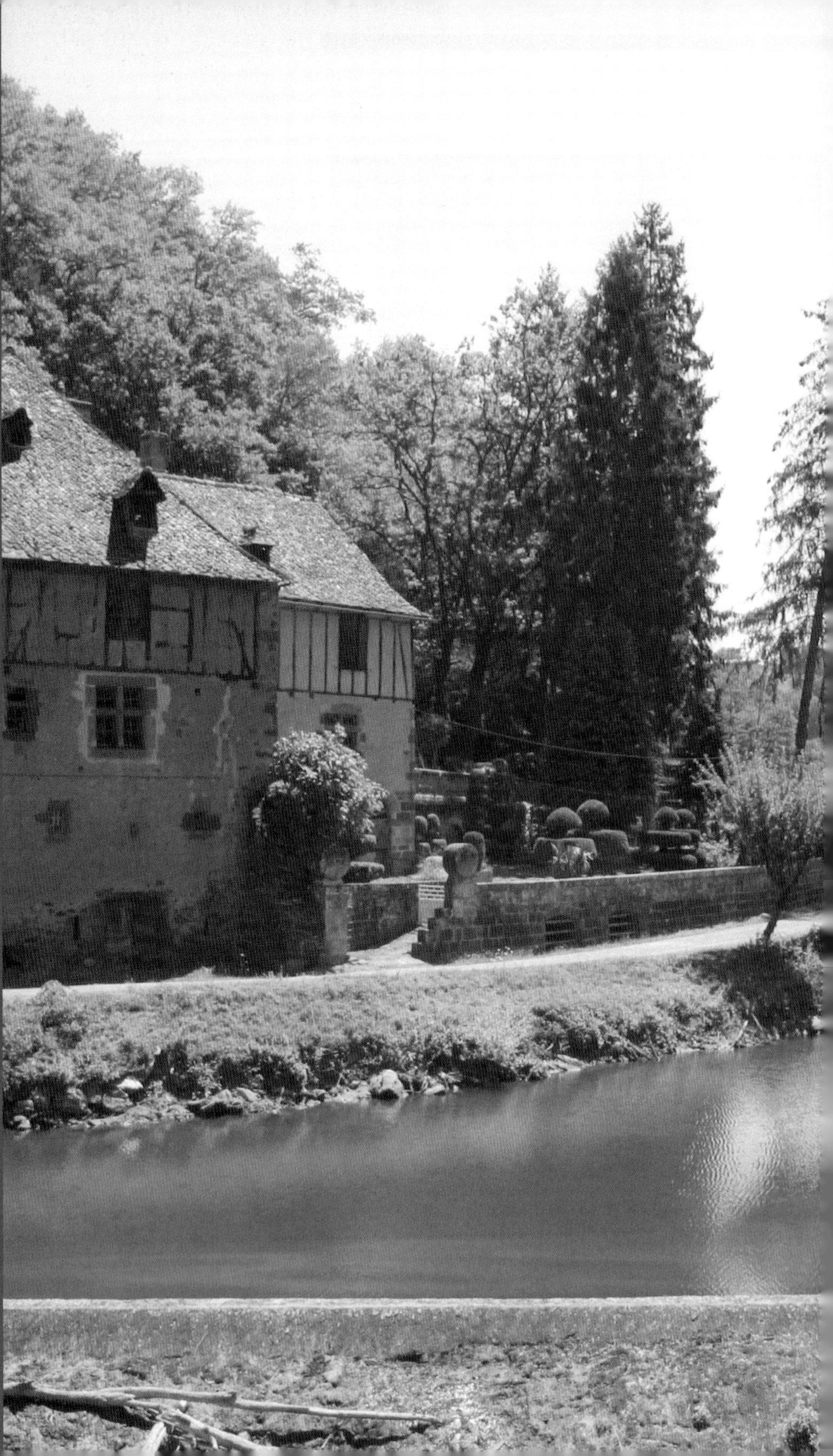

JUSTIN POSTLETHWAITE

Cost of Purchase
Steps to Buying
Case Studies

Buying
Guide

Steps To Buying 32
Buying Case Study 52
Business case study 54

The Aveyron
region is becoming
increasingly
popular with the
foreign buyer

Steps to Buying and Letting

Buying a property in France can seem complex. This section gives a comprehensive breakdown of what's involved, expert tips on how to avoid any pitfalls, and advises on the tax system and healthcare provision for EU citizens in France.

THE PURCHASE

Buying a property abroad is not a decision to be taken lightly, nor is it a decision that should be made on impulse, even when the turnover of properties in your area of choice is swift. Buying a house you fall in love with at the end of a holiday, for example, can be a recipe for disaster. In a foreign country in particular, there are legal, cost and other practical issues that you must take into consideration before embarking on house purchase.

One of the first questions to ask yourself is how much you can really afford to spend. When you know how much you can raise, consider the purchasing costs, then set yourself a realistic price limit. Once you've set your budget, you will know whether you should be looking for a stone *fermette* (a small farmhouse), a town house or a much grander *manoir* (a manor house).

In some regions, a manor house can cost the same as a farmhouse does in others. By taking a look at property in areas you may not have considered before, simply because your travels have not taken you there yet or because it is not an area that people tend to talk about, you can open up your options. This is particularly important in today's climate, as budget flight routes and high-speed train links have made areas that were once inconceivable to visit for a long weekend, for example, easily accessible from the UK.

FINDING THE RIGHT PROPERTY

Buying a home abroad can be an emotive business, but it's important that buyers are practical when choosing a property. An isolated farmhouse can be perfect for escaping the bustle of city life, but if you need medical assistance close at hand, or would like neighbours to look after your property when you are away, you should think of buying somewhere within easy reach of other households and village amenities. You should also spend time getting to know the locality properly, seeing it in winter as well as summer if possible, before you take the plunge. If, for instance, you find your dream location off-season, it may be spoilt by hordes of tourists in the summer and, although in summer it appears an idyll, winter gales may make it feel inhospitable.

There are several different routes buyers can follow to find their dream French home today. You can simply trail around the region of your choice, hunting out *à vendre* (for sale) signs and looking in the windows of *agents immobiliers* (estate agents) and *notaires* (public notaries), but you don't have to rely on this method to track down your dream home. A good way to start is by searching through specialist magazines and websites, as well as attending the growing number of overseas property fairs held outside of France.

It may be even more convenient to work with a property search agent, or 'homefinder'. Based in France or even the UK, they can cut the legwork out of finding your property and present a select range of properties for you to view. These could be on the books of local estate agents, selected from forthcoming auctions or even private sales.

Whichever intermediary you choose, at some point you will have to organise a trip to France to arrange viewings of your shortlist of properties. Narrow the final list down as much as you can before you go. The details intermediaries provide on French properties are rarely as exhaustive as the particulars produced by UK agents. Quite often, for example, details such as room measurements or fixtures and fittings will not be included unless you ask, so make sure you request extensive details and see as many pictures of the properties as possible before taking time to visit them.

NEW BUILDS

While foreigners moving to France or looking for a holiday home there are

Working with legal experts when buying your French property is vital for the safeguarding of your interests

WHO TO BUY A FRENCH HOME FROM

Every town in France should have at least one estate agent and there is an increasing number of UK-based agents specialising in French properties who have a network of French agents providing them with local knowledge and property details. These agents understand the needs of foreign buyers, and, of course, they offer an English-speaking service.

All French estate agents should have a *carte professionelle*, proving that they have the correct professional qualifications and are backed by a financial guarantee and professional liability insurance, and also that they are members of a regulatory body such as the Fédération nationale des agents immobiliers et mandataires, or FNAIM.

Estate agents' fees are normally included in the sale price, so buyers do not usually have to worry about raising extra money to pay them. Mortgage providers usually lend only a percentage of the actual sale price and do not take additional costs into consideration. However, if an estate agent's commission is included in the price, the buyer may end up paying purchase duties on this fee as well as on the property itself.

To avoid paying more duties than necessary, ensure the contract includes the statement *'commission de l'agence immobilier à la charge de l'acquéreur'* (agent's commission paid for by the buyer). For a list of estate agents in France, contact the FNAIM (see Directory of Contacts on page 346).

often keen to find a charming period house, building a home in the right location can prove to be good value and a practical alternative. Many French families opt to buy a plot of land on which to have a house built, as in France building land is cheaper and more readily available than in other countries, particularly in the countryside. When it comes to buying a home, the French tend to consider practicalities and convenience before heritage issues and new homes can provide more comfort from day one, and be more conveniently located for schools and workplaces than the traditional rural buildings that were typically inhabited a century or more ago.

A newly-built home is often easier to look after - a particularly important consideration if it is to be let out - and is usually much less expensive to buy. For this reason, new-builds can also make a sensible holiday rental investment, although there is a significant disadvantage to buying a property under five years old that is being sold for the first time: VAT, or TVA as it is known in France, is normally charged on the sale, but there is a way of avoiding it. A new property leased back immediately to the developers, who then rent the property to holidaymakers over a period of about nine years, is usually exempt from VAT. Owners can expect to earn a net return of around six percent, as well as save on the initial cost of their purchase. Leaseback schemes are only found in areas popular with tourists, and are only available if the property is accepted as tourist standard by the local authorities. This is a government initiative to encourage the development of tourist accommodation, as tourism is a key contributor to France's economy. Tax breaks are given to developers building tourist accommodation, and the VAT refund is passed on to buyers, to encourage them to participate in the scheme.

If you are interested in new-builds and are considering buying a building plot on which to have a home built, plots of land or *parcelles* can be found through estate agents or specialist publications and websites such as www.terrain-a-batir.com and www.frenchland.com. Should you choose this option, it is best to scrutinise the *plan local d'urbanisme* held at the local town hall and the related *coefficient d'occupation des sols*. Used in combination, these can confirm whether or not the land can be built on and can provide a reasonably accurate picture of the size of building that could be constructed there. Note also that the granting of planning permission will depend on access to roads and utilities. (See also Building a New Home.)

JUDGING THE REAL PRICE

As a rule of thumb, to roughly calculate the total cost of buying a French property, add another 10 percent on top of the actual purchase price. In reality, however, the total can be much higher than this. One of the main costs is the sales commission, which is normally about five or six percent but, particularly in the case of less expensive properties, can reach up to 20 percent. You must therefore check whether or not the fee is included in the advertised price and also whether VAT has been added. Phrases like *'toutes taxes comprises'* or *'TVA comprise'* should indicate that it has been.

Although it is sometimes the vendor who pays the agent's commission, the buyer is always responsible for paying the conveyancing fees to the *notaire*. The *notaire*'s fees are fixed by law, and are a percentage based on a sliding scale, depending on the age and purchase price of the property. They can range from around three percent for a property less than five years old to about 10 percent for a property more than five years old. If two *notaires* are appointed, one by the buyer and one by the vendor, this does not increase the fee paid, as it is simply divided between them.

On top of their own fee, the *notaires* will collect various duties and fees,

FINANCE

including stamp and transfer duties, land registry fees, taxes and disbursements, all of which depend on the location, type, age and value of the property. When a mortgage is taken out on a property, there will also be a charge payable to the *notaire* that is usually between one and three percent of the mortgage value. This is for registering the charge of the lender with the relevant land registry, or *conservation des hypothèques*.

Exchange rate fluctuations can potentially increase the cost of financing if a borrower is converting sterling to make payments on a euro mortgage. However, fixing the exchange rate through a currency specialist over a long period of time can give the borrower peace of mind. If the property is being bought for cash, it can also be a good idea to fix the exchange rate at the beginning of the purchase process, so that the actual price of the property will not increase unexpectedly due to exchange rate fluctuations before the completion date.

Not everyone bears in mind from the outset that one of the biggest costs of buying an older property is renovation work. A would-be buyer may spot a derelict building in a field, for instance, and think it's a bargain, without giving due consideration to how much it will actually cost to restore. This can be at least as much as the price of the building itself and to prevent a dream home turning into a renovation project that was never completed, the potential buyer must calculate all the outlays before proceeding with a sale. To gain a realistic estimate of this cost, buyers should consider obtaining estimates (*devis*) from local builders before signing a contract. This is still, however, merely an approximate price for the work and materials.

THE SURVEY

Foreign buyers are not always aware of the local market prices of property, and can run the risk of paying inflated prices. A valuation by a local valuer, or *expert immobilier*, can help avoid this. They can also help estimate the cost of any renovation work to make the property habitable or to simply improve the living space.

Even an *expert immobilier* will not, however, provide a full structural survey. The survey, or *expertise*, that they carry out is, in effect, more like a valuation. The closest equivalent to a British structural survey is an *évaluation structurale*. The French do not have a professional equivalent to the British chartered building surveyor. They usually either turn to an *architecte* (an architect), who will normally provide only a very brief report on the condition of a building, or they rely on testimonies from local tradesmen, or *artisans*, to gauge a property's state of repair. Be careful when looking for an older property, as age often brings problems.

An older property may have been left for years without proper maintenance, for example, perhaps because it was part of an inheritance and not subsequently lived in. Others may never have been connected to mains electricity or had proper sewerage. The cost of renovating and connecting utilities can be onerous, and should be borne in mind when thinking about buying an old French building. One of the best ways to obtain a structural survey can be to instruct one of the growing number of properly qualified British building surveyors or architects who now live in France or who will travel across the Channel, to carry out such surveys.

British buyers of French property should also note the need to check certain details that would not necessarily require checking when buying a property in the UK. If a property is made up of a collection of buildings, for instance, it should be determined whether or not all the buildings are actually included in the sale. Boundaries can often be blurred too, especially if land has been split

NOTAIRES

Much of the property sold in France is still offered through *notaires*, who were the principal source of French property before estate agents set up in business. *Notaires* are highly-trained lawyers who oversee the purchase, and their sales commission will not normally be included in the price.

Properties sold through notaires can often be more reasonably priced than those sold through estate agents, as the latter are usually more aware of market trends. For details of regional *notaires*, contact *Notaires de France* (see Directory of Contacts on page 346).

DEVELOPERS

It's quite common in France to buy a property before it is completed – a *vente en l'état futur d'achèvement* – from a developer, or *promoteur constructeur*. This can be an apartment in a building, whether a villa, a town house on an estate, or a *lotissement*. French developers buy land, obtain planning permission and then try to attract buyers. You can obtain details of developers through the Fédération nationale des promoteurs constructeurs (see Directory of Contacts on page 346).

JOINING A USER GROUP

You can purchase a share in a new *multipropriété* or an existing one – resales do become available – set up by a group of individuals or a specialist company. Check out publications or newspaper sections advertising French property for announcements of the sale of shares in *multipropriétés*, or contact specialists like Owner Groups Company (www.ownergroups.com).

Properly qualified British building surveyors can be found in France, and will travel to give a survey

up into several *parcelles*, or if a wood obscures part of one of these. They can be checked against a *plan cadastral*, the official record of site boundaries, although this can sometimes be out of date. A land surveyor, or *géomètre*, can help verify such details.

FINANCING THE PURCHASE

Over recent years, it has become much easier for non-residents to raise a mortgage, or *prêt immobilier*, on a home in France. There are two basic ways to do this: by remortgaging a property in the UK in sterling with a UK lender or by taking out a euro mortgage with a French bank against the French property – since British and French banks cannot take first legal charge on a property outside their own countries, they do not offer mortgages on properties in any country apart from their own.

Although there can be a substantial initial exchange rate fee to pay when money is raised in a currency other than the euro, remortgaging in sterling can protect the British buyer against the effect of future exchange rate fluctuations on their repayments. Taking out a mortgage in euros on a French property will always, on the other hand, reflect the true euro value of the property, and the bank will have the first legal charge on the actual property being financed. The cost of the mortgage can also potentially be offset against any income received from letting the property.

There are many French lenders for overseas buyers to choose from if a mortgage is to be raised on a property in France, but one of the most interesting propositions today is offered by the French branches of UK banks. All the paperwork can be supplied in English, for instance, and although the mortgage will be in euros, the monthly payments can be made in sterling, straight from a British bank account. Remember, also, that a French bank usually asks for a life policy to be taken out on the life of the borrower, which require a medical and blood tests.

Repayment mortgages, or *prêts amortissables*, are most commonly offered by French banks to foreign buyers because they have been traditionally favoured above interest-only mortgages and endowment policies by the French. British buyers are usually lent money by a French lender for between five and 20 years. Rates can be fixed (*à taux fixe*), or variable (*à taux variable*). There are likely to be early redemption charges payable on the former, but not on the latter. French variable rates are linked to the EURIBOR (Euro Interbank Offered Rate), and for foreign buyers this is usually fixed for a period of 12 months, mainly for convenience. One main difference between UK and French variable interest rates is that, whereas in the UK the monthly payments are likely to fluctuate regularly, in France the rates tend to stay stable, and it is only the term of the loan that changes according to the EURIBOR rate change.

A deposit of at least 20 percent of the price of the property is usually required, and it is generally true that the higher the deposit, the better the interest rate. French lenders are usually obliged to prove that the borrower can afford the repayments, so they often insist that the monthly payments for all the borrower's mortgages and other fixed outgoings should not exceed 30 to 35 percent of their income.

Even if properties financed by a residential mortgage are to be let out for part of the year, lenders will not usually take into consideration the potential rental income when assessing the loan request. Neither will they lend money to cover the costs of buying a property, though subject to the approval of relevant estimates from builders or developers, mortgages can cover the cost of renovation or construction work.

Note that once a mortgage offer is received, the borrower must wait at least

10 days, but no longer than 30, before signing and accepting it. This is in order to comply with French financial legislation. On the acceptance of a French mortgage offer, an arrangement fee of between one and two percent of the loan value will usually be payable. Borrowers are also obliged to take out a life insurance policy so that, in the event of death or disability, the outstanding loan value will be repaid.

French banks pay the sum of money being lent directly to the *notaire*. The portion covering renovation or construction costs, however, is paid directly to the contractor on presentation of invoices (duly authorised for payment by the customer) and after the customer's personal contribution has been paid. As a general rule, you should allow two months between the receipt of the completed mortgage application and the mortgage offer.

THE LEGAL PROCESS

The French legal system can be a minefield for foreign buyers. Never does the expression 'take independent advice' ring more true than in the case of buying a property abroad. There are numerous pitfalls that the unsuspecting buyer can encounter when buying a home in France and there are also ways that a legal advisor can help the buyer best structure their purchase.

A French property can either be purchased by individuals, in single, joint or multiple names, or through a French property-holding company, a *société civile d'immobilière* (SCI), whose shares are held by the buyers. Although an SCI can can cost between £1,000 and £3,500 to set up, and annual accounts must be prepared for the company, this purchase structure should be considered in many cases, as it can have tax advantages and make it easier for owners to dispose of their share of the property. It can also overcome some of the restrictions of France's succession law. French law dictates that upon the death of a homeowner, the property is divided up equally between the surviving spouse and any children. Shares in a company, however, are easier to distribute than immovable property, thus enabling better management of inheritance and property transferring. (See also Taxation.)

THE POINT OF NO RETURN

In France you buy a property subject to contract. A contract, known as a *'compromis de vente'*, a *'promesse de vente'* or a *'sous-seing privé'*, is entered into early on in the process, and this commits the vendor and buyer to a deal they will conclude with a deed of sale, or conveyance. The agreement is normally drawn up either by an estate agent or a *notaire* and then handed to the *notaire* who will be overseeing the completion of the sale together with the deposit to conduct the sale. Under no circumstances should the deposit be paid direct to the seller, nor should the buyer agree to any side payments, or *dessous la table*.

Unless special arrangements have been made, the conveyancing on the sale will be conducted by the *notaire* appointed by the seller of the property. The buyer may if he wishes appoint his own notary to protect his interests. The contract gives the details of the parties and the property, and the price and the completion date when the signing of the final deed of sale takes place. It will also include details of the *notaire* or *notaires* overseeing the transaction and of where the deed that completes the conveyancing, the *acte de vente* - sometimes referred to as the *'acte authentique'* or even the *'acte authentique de vente'* - will be signed. At this stage, a deposit of 10 percent of the purchase price is paid by the buyer to the *notaire* or the estate agent, backed by a financial guarantee and a professional liability insurance. Under no circumstances whatsoever should money be paid directly to the vendor at this or any other

FINANCE

'Euro mortgages can be repaid to French branches of UK banks in Sterling, direct from UK accounts'

BUYING AT AUCTION

Auctions can be a source of real bargains, as here properties are often sold as a result of inheritance disputes or mortgage defaults, and consequently are priced keenly for a swift sale. At an auction, or *vente aux enchères*, a *notaire* must usually bid on behalf of the buyer.

Written authorisation, in the form of a *mandat* to bid up to a certain value, must be given to the *notaire* before they attend the sale. Be prepared also to pay 20 percent of the highest price you are prepared to bid to them in advance. The balance of a successful bid must be paid between one and three months after the sale date. Note that there is no prospect of including get-out clauses in the sale agreement, so care must be taken to examine carefully the property and details such as third party rights of way over it, and in addition, any loans should be in place before the sale.

Auction details will appear in local newspapers, in national publications such as the bi-monthly *Le Journal des Enchères* and *Les Ventes aux Enchères des Notaires*, and on websites like www.encheres-paris.com and www.ventes-judicaires.com. Both estate agents and *notaires* should also have details of properties up for auction in their area.

BUYING DIRECT

Homes in France can also be bought direct from the owner. Private sales are advertised in specialist magazines and on websites based in France itself and in many other countries. If you buy from an owner, do not be pressurised into handing over a deposit to the owner themselves. There may be no guarantee that they will return it if either party withdraws from the sale for valid reasons. Deposits should be handled by the *notaire* in charge of overseeing the sale. It is also preferable not to hand over any deposit without seeking independent advice, as it may prove to be non-refundable.

point in the process. There is a seven-day 'cooling-off' period from the day the buyer receives a copy of the contract, countersigned by the vendor. During this period, the buyer can withdraw from the sale and not be liable for any penalties. If the buyer withdraws from the purchase after this cooling-off period, however, they will probably lose their deposit and may be liable for penalties. If a penalty clause is included in the contract, it will stipulate the amount payable in case of withdrawal. Should the vendor withdraw, the deposit will normally be refunded and the vendor must pay any damages stipulated in the contract.

If the contract contains what are called '*clauses suspensives*' (get-out clauses), which lay out conditions to be met during the sale process, the buyer may, in some circumstances, be able to withdraw from the purchase without the risk of losing the deposit and having to pay penalties. The sale can be made conditional upon a number of factors, such as the offer of a mortgage, the absence of rights of way across the property, planning restrictions affecting potential future development or a *droit de préemption* (right of pre-emption) that gives a local authority, land commission or another third party the right to buy the property or its land.

In the case of properties whose construction has not yet been completed, a *contrat de réservation* precedes the conveyance. The contract should preferably provide a full description of the property to be built, an approximate surface area or *surface habitable*, a floor plan and a proposed date for the completion of the construction. When this contract is signed, the buyer will need to pay the developer a non-interest-bearing deposit, or *réservation*, of up to five percent. If construction is due to be completed within a year of signing the contract, the deposit cannot exceed five percent; or two percent if within two years. No deposit is payable if the construction is not due for completion within two years.

COMPLETING THE SALE

When all the procedural formalities have been concluded, the *notaire* will summon the parties to his office for the signing of the final deed. The formalities usually take between two and three months. The completion date in the contract will be postponed automatically by the notary if any part of the administrative process remains outstanding. This should be borne in mind by the buyers who should not make any travel arrangements until a date has been given by the notary. They will ask for the balance of the purchase money and the costs to be sent direct to his bank. This process can take up to two weeks, so buyers are advised to pursue this as soon as they are given instructions by the *notaire* to do so.

Many buyers complete the purchase by proxy using a power of attorney drawn up by the notary. It is common practice for a member of the *notaire*'s staff to be appointed to sign the final deed on the buyer's behalf.

After completion, the notary will stamp and register the title deed which can take about six months. A certified copy of the purchase deed, or *expedition de vente*, is then sent to the notary by the land registry who usually keeps it on behalf of the buyer. This is the only evidence of ownership available. There are no title deeds. If a buyer requires evidence of his ownership, he can ask the notary for declaration to this effect (an *attestation de vente*).

On completion of the purchase of an unfinished property, ownership of the land and incomplete construction (if building work has commenced) passes to the buyer, though proprietorship of the rest of the building is only transferred as works proceed. Unlike in the case of completed buildings, the balance of the purchase price is payable in instalments as construction progresses, and not at the time of the signing of the conveyance. The instalments due are 35 percent on completion of the foundations, 35 percent on the building being made watertight and 25 percent on completion of the building. The final five percent is due when the property has been inspected by the buyer, who is in agreement that there are no faults with the construction.

EXPECTING THE UNEXPECTED

The *notaire* who oversees the sale of a property is primarily concerned with registering the sale, ensuring that the conveyancing is carried out according to the law and collecting the relevant taxes on behalf of the government. Although they are perfectly qualified to provide legal advice, *notaires* are not acting on behalf of either side so, to make sure that you are bound by favourable terms, it would be best to either employ a separate *notaire* in France or to employ a British lawyer familiar with conveyancing law in France from the very start of the legal process. There are now many UK-based solicitors who specialise in the buying and selling of French property.

Not only can a solicitors working on behalf of the buyer draw up any necessary get-out clauses in the contract, they can also advise on the best way to structure the purchase according to personal circumstances and recommend ways of minimising the effect of French inheritance law. The latter should be considered well before the conveyance is signed.

Special *assur'titre* insurance policies can be taken out to insure the title of a property against unknown title defects, such as unforeseen claims by third parties and the violation of planning regulations by former owners, as well as mistakes on behalf of the *notaire*. This policy gives the buyer protection against any costs or damages that may follow as a result of any claims from third parties or subsequent owners. Such policies are being offered increasingly by estate agents as part of their service, and are a good complement to the advice of an independent solicitor.

OWNERSHIP

Residential properties are usually bought freehold, or *en propriété libre*. Even owners of apartments normally have a share of the freehold. If a building is divided into apartments, the freehold of the various privately-owned parts is held by the respective co-owner, and all the common areas of this *copropriété*, such as walls, staircases and lifts, are usually owned by them collectively. Land can also be divided up into parcels (*parcelles*) on an estate or *lotissements*, and owned in a similar way. Co-owners must usually pay *charges de copropriété* (maintenance and service charges), which are usually set in proportion to the size of the individual apartment.

A *copropriété* or *lotissement* is managed by a co-ownership manager, or *syndic*, which represents the group of co-owners. General meetings attended by the co-owners are held when important decisions need to be made. Co-ownership regulations – *règlement de copropriété* or *règlement de lotissement* – drawn up by the co-owners set out the terms and conditions applicable to the privately owned and the commonly owned parts of the property. Any buyer who signs a preliminary agreement to purchase a *copropriété* apartment or *lotissement* is legally bound by this *règlement*. If you are looking to buy an apartment in a *copropriété* and let it out, you must ascertain before you sign that there are no restrictions which could make this difficult.

If you are planning to buy a French home solely for personal use and do not intend to occupy it for more than several weeks in any one year, you could consider sharing the ownership with family members or others. You can organise the sharing of a property (termed a '*multipropriété*') yourself, under the guidance

THE 10 STEPS TO BUYING
TIMESCALE: TWO MONTHS+

1) Calculate how much you can spend on the property, making allowances for the cost of the purchase itself, which can be around 10 percent of the sale price.

2) Decide on your requirements for the setting of your French home and select areas that match them.

3) Search for your for ideal property or building plot within areas you have chosen, either calling on the services of an estate agent, *notaire* or search or using specialist websites and magazines or local papers.

4) View a range of properties in your chosen areas and, if possible, research the neighbourhood and local amenities of any properties that interest you.

5) Make an offer on any property you think is right for you and negotiate the price if it is not accepted at first.

6) Sign the preliminary sales agreement, either in France at the office of the estate agent or *notaire* overseeing the sale, or in your own country if you are prepared to wait, preferably after seeking independent legal advice and possibly having engaged your own *notaire*, and pay a 10 percent deposit to the *notaire* overseeing the sale.

7) Have a survey carried out - a full building survey is best - and request an estimate of any potential building or renovation work.

8) Arrange for any necessary loan or mortgage application to be processed.

9) Transfer the outstanding balance of the purchase price to the *notaire*, as well as funds to cover their fees and disbursements.

10) Sign the conveyance and prepare to move in or for building work to commence.

FINANCE

'After working in France for three months, any EU citizen will need to obtain an EU resident's permit'

of a lawyer specialising in French property law. It is often advisable for a property with multiple owners to be bought through an SCI. (See also Who to Buy From.)

Location accession and *rente viagère* are two methods of buying property that are unique to France. In the former case, the purchaser rents the property for a given number of years and, in addition to rent, pays contributions towards the cost of the potential purchase before paying the balance of the purchase price, at which point the property is transferred to them. The initial sales contract will include an agreed time limit for the payment of the balance and a clause committing the owner to sell the property. For this clause to be made binding, a five percent deposit must first be paid to the vendor. In the case of *rente viagère*, the purchaser first pays the owner of a property a *bouquet* of 20 to 30 percent of the house price and then a monthly sum, in return for the transfer of the property to the purchaser on the owner's death. The owner may or may not live in the property until this time. Visit www.viager.fr for a list of properties available to buy in this way.

MOVING IN

The new owners of a French property are only allowed to take possession of it officially when the sale has been completed by the *notaire*. If the property is vacant, it may be possible to arrange an earlier removal date but solely for the purpose of installing furniture. Once the moving-in date is set, almost as much planning can be required at this stage as for the purchase itself.

After completion, the buyer will need to start paying for utilities that are connected, as well as for local services like rubbish collection. A *notaire* or estate agent will often help with this. Water is supplied by a range of private companies in France. When a property is not connected, an application should be made to the local supplier. New owners also have to contact Electricité de France (EDF) and Gaz de France (GDF) to read the meters and to change the name on the accounts. A connection charge is usually payable, as is a deposit if the owner is a non-resident. Mains gas is not always provided in rural areas, where inhabitants usually rely instead on cylinder gas.

Homeowners are also legally obliged to take out a third-party liability insurance policy on their property. A *notaire* will ask to see some proof that the buyer has adequate insurance cover from the day they take ownership of the property. The vendor's insurance can simply be transferred into the new owner's name. This can be part of a multi-risk household insurance policy or *assurance multirisques habitation*, which includes contents and buildings insurance. Contents and buildings insurance policies specific to holiday homes may be preferable for those who only intend to visit the property from time to time.

Although it is possible to pay utility bills and insurance premiums from across the Channel, if the French home is not going to be used as a main residence, it can be more convenient to pay by direct debit, or *prélèvement automatique*, from a French bank account. Not only does it simplify the process, but it also avoids supplies being cut off simply because letters and cheques never reached their destination. Opening a French bank account is easier now than it has ever been. Help is usually on hand as part of the service from estate agents, homefinders and even solicitors involved in the purchase, and today banks in France even have English-speaking branches, and non-resident as well as resident bank accounts. The main difference between the two is that non-resident bank accounts offer no overdraft facilities.

There are no restrictions on the importing of most furniture and other household goods into France by an EU citizen, provided they are for personal

use. However, the movement of antiques in and out of the UK can be more complicated than other items, and proof of their origin should be kept ready to be produced when they are moved between countries. These days, thanks to a new 'pet passport' scheme, pets are much freer to move between the UK and other EU countries, without the need for quarantine periods. To enter France, they must have a current Anti-Rabies Vaccination Certificate, and to get back into the UK they will need a pet passport and a microchip.

Various methods of buying a property through shared ownership exist including *multipropriété* through an SCI

LIVING IN FRANCE

EU nationals can spend up to three months in France before they need to apply for an EU resident's permit, or *carte de séjour de ressortissant de l'Union* . This can be done in France at either a local *préfecture* (town hall), or *commissariat de police* (police station). To obtain a *carte de séjour* you will need to produce a number of documents with passport-size photographs and be able to prove that you will not be a burden on the state – that is that you have a job, own a business or have independent means of support. (See Carte de Séjour Checklist.)

A resident's permit is valid for five years, and renewable for 10 or more years. The right of residence granted with the *carte de séjour* can be extended to the holder's spouse, dependant descendants under the age of 21, dependant ascendants and the spouse's ascendants.

'An E111 health form is needed before entering France, to gain free or reduced fee emergency care'

FINANCE

10 TIPS FOR BUYERS

1) Cast your net wider than the areas you already know.

2) Ask for detailed descriptions of properties before you view them, to help you cut down on wasted trips.

3) Do not buy simply on impulse - this is a major purchase that could have any number of hidden costs.

4) Visit the area in all seasons if possible.

5) Rent in the locality if you can to get to know the area before you buy.

6) Introduce yourself to the neighbours to get to know them and the neighbourhood before you commit yourself to a property.

7) Be prepared to negotiate the asking price, engaging a local *géomètre*, or valuer, to offer an independent opinion.

8) Seek independent legal advice before signing any contract and handing over any money, and consider instructing your own *notaire* who can oversee the sale alongside the *notaire* instructed by the vendor - there is no extra cost for this service.

9) Instruct a qualified buildings surveyor to provide a full survey and estimate the cost of any necessary repairs or building work.

10) Plan the move to the property as carefully as the purchase itself.

WORKING IN FRANCE

EU nationals from another country do not need a work permit or visa to gain employment in France. While nationals from Belgium, Italy, Luxembourg and the Netherlands need only produce their national identity card when seeking employment, British citizens must have a valid passport. After three months, however, any EU national residing in France while working there will need to obtain an EU resident's permit.

To be eligible to work in France, even on a temporary, paid or unpaid basis, non-EU nationals must obtain a work permit, called an *autorisation de travail*, before entering the country. It is the prospective employer who should apply for this permit, which is issued by the Office des migrations internationales, 14 rue Brague, 75015 Paris; Tel: +33 1 53 69 53 70.

Anyone working in France, either as an employee or self-employed, must be registered with the social security organisations, or '*caisses*', that cover their particular occupation and pay contributions called '*cotisations*' to the relevant '*caisses*'. Employers should automatically register anyone working for them and arrange for both employer and employee contributions to be paid to the '*caisses*'. The self-employed must organise the payment of their own contributions into the correct '*caisse*' for their profession.

RETIRING IN FRANCE

Anyone moving to France to retire should inform their Social Security office a number of weeks before their departure date, so that they can set the necessary administrative arrangements in motion. You can still receive a state pension from one country if you retire to another, but you must, for example, make sure that you pass on details of any new bank account.

If you work in France before you retire there and have made contributions to the French state pension scheme, you will probably be entitled to receive a French state pension in addition to one from any other country you have lived and worked in. The level of state pension you receive will depend on how long you contributed to the pension scheme of that particular country. In France, on reaching retirement age you should contact the Caisse nationale d'assurance vieillesse (CNAV). (See Directory of Contacts.) The overseas branch of the UK's Department of Social Security (see Directory of Contacts) can provide information about pensions for British citizens moving abroad.

HEALTH CARE

If you are an EU national and visit your French home solely for short periods, you will need to present a valid E111 form to receive free or reduced-cost state-provided emergency medical treatment when in France, The form should be obtained before you enter the country and is available at post offices in the UK. If you reside for periods of more than three months and are not working, you may be entitled to the same treatment and benefits as French nationals, up to a certain time limit. After this period, to cover much of the cost of your future medical treatment, you may be able to start contributing voluntarily to the state health insurance scheme – the Caisse nationale d'assurance maladie – or you will have to take out private medical insurance.

Once employed in France, you will be registered by your employers with France's Social Security, or *Sécurité sociale* – often referred to by the abbreviated term '*la Sécu*' – and you will be paying contributions automatically to the state health insurance scheme. While you are making these payments, the French state health insurance scheme will cover the majority of your healthcare costs. The same is true if you are self-employed and paying contributions to the C*aisse* for your profession.

If you are retiring in France and are in receipt of a state pension from another EU country, that country will usually cover the cost of your healthcare. Pensioners should request a form E121, which will enable them to register for free healthcare in France. If you also receive a French state pension, though, you will be treated as a French pensioner as far as healthcare is concerned, with the French state health insurance scheme taking responsibility for all healthcare costs.

If you will not be working in France, but are not yet eligible for a state pension, complete a form E106 in order to obtain medical cover for up to two years. After this date, you should consider paying voluntary contributions to the state healthcare system or taking out a private insurance. You may wish to take out private medical insurance in any case, of course, but the state system in France is renowned for its excellence.

British nationals can contact the Department of Social Security (see Directory of Contacts) for further information and for a copy of their leaflet SA29, entitled *Your Social Security, Healthcare and Pensions Rights in the European Community*. In France, your local health insurance office (*caisse primaire d'assurance maladie*) or local social security office (*caisse de sécurité sociale*) should also be able to offer advice and relevant forms.

Even when someone is living in France and has joined the state health insurance scheme, unless they fall into the 'low income' bracket or are suffering from a serious illness, the full cost of any consultation or medical treatment is not usually borne by the state health service. Consultations, treatments and prescriptions must usually be paid for upfront, before being reimbursed, in full or in part, by the relevant health insurance *caisse*. This applies unless treatment is carried out in an approved hospital, in which case the state will pay 80 percent of the cost of the treatment directly to the hospital. You must then pay the balance and any fixed daily hospital charge, or *forfait journalier*.

To apply for the refund of a prescription, attach the stamps, or *vignettes*, that come with the prescribed medicine to the form (*feuille de soins*) supplied by the doctor for this purpose, and send it along with the prescription to your health insurance office. To cover any expenses that the patient must bear, a private health insurance policy can be taken out through a *mutuelle*.

Patients do not have to be registered with a particular GP and can, in theory, visit any GP, specialist or dentist of their choice. What may limit your choice is the fact that some medical professionals and hospitals charge rates within the state health service's limits, while others do not and can charge much more. A doctor or dentist who is *conventionné* falls into the former category. Contact details of local doctors, dentists and hospitals can be obtained from a *gendarmerie* or by dialling 15 from any French telephone. Your local *caisse de sécurité sociale* can provide a list of the doctors who charge the official social security rate.

SOCIAL SECURITY BENEFITS

If you're entitled to unemployment benefit in another EU country, and have been claiming this benefit for at least four weeks, you may continue to receive it for up to three months while you seek some work in France. Unemployment benefit is the only transferable benefit, however. Foreign nationals who are aged over 25 years and possessing a *carte de séjour* are entitled to claim the *revenu minimum d'insertion* (RMI) or France's income support. If you work in France with your family, a family allowance will be paid after the birth of a second child and until the child is 20 years old. You may also be entitled to the family benefits of another EU nation if members of your family reside in that

CARTE DE SÉJOUR CHECKLIST

EU nationals will typically be asked to produce the following documents to obtain a *carte de séjour*:

● Valid passport

● Birth certificate or a marriage certificate

● Proof of accommodation

● Proof that you pay contributions to the French state health insurance scheme or have medical insurance that will cover you until you join it

● Three passport photographs

● Proof of employment or receipt of a state pension, or proof of enrolment with a French university, or, if you are married to a French national, a copy of your marriage certificate

FINANCE

Characterful French properties can be found with 'Se Vende' signs on exploring small towns and villages around France

country, provided you are insured in France. For enquiries about both unemployment benefit and income support, visit your local *caisse de sécurité sociale*, and for family allowance, contact your local *caisse des allocations familiales*.

When applying for benefits in France, you will need to provide a letter from your current Benefits Agency stating that you are no longer receiving benefits from another state. For more information about social security benefits in France available to foreign nationals and for a copy of the guide *Social Security in the European Union*, contact the overseas branch of the UK's Department of Social Security. (See Useful Contacts.)

EDUCATION

Any foreign child living in France has the right to join the French education system and can attend a local state school, a private school or one of the many bilingual schools – both state-run and private – depending on which establishment best suits their needs. Between the ages of three and five, children can join an *école maternelle* (a nursery). All six to 16-year-olds must first attend an *école primaire* (a primary school), then a *collège* (a secondary school). The last two years are spent at a *lycée*, where students either study for a *baccalauréat* or for vocational qualifications.

The French state education system has an excellent reputation, but if children have a poor command of the French language when they arrive in the country, they may be better off at a bilingual school rather than a local state school. Each region has one or sometimes two *académies* (education districts), managed by a *rectorat* (local education authority), which can provide details

'As direct taxes are not taken by a PAYE system, every individual must submit their own tax return'

of all the different schools and universities based in their locality.

TAXATION

A foreign homeowner only usually becomes a resident of France when they spend more than 183 days in the country, or if their permanent home is there. Even if they are not a tax resident, apart from the taxes paid to the *notaire* at the time of the property purchase, owners of French homes may also be liable at some time or another to pay a range of other taxes.

Both the tax offices of France and the country in which a foreign national resides will be interested in their annual income from activities in France, which could range from simply the interest from a French bank account to rental income from a French property. If this is above an official threshold, they must make an annual declaration of income in France. In theory, a tax resident of France could be liable for both French and UK taxes.

Fortunately for tax residents of both countries, there is a double tax treaty between France and the UK, which protects most British nationals with property in France from paying tax twice. Anyone planning to move permanently from the UK to France would be advised to notify the British tax authorities before leaving, and provide them with proof of new employment and property details.

It is also important to note that direct taxes are not deducted by means of a PAYE system in France. Instead, they are paid in the year following the tax year in question, which runs from January 1 to December 31. This is done either in three or 10 instalments, and taxation is always on a self-assessment basis. Residents' taxes are collected by the Direction générale des impôts, which is organised on a national and a regional level, while non-residents deal with the Centre des impôts des non-résidents in Paris. A tax return form, *a déclaration des revenus*, can be obtained from the local tax office, or *centre des impôts*, which can also help the uninitiated fill out their forms.

PROPERTY TAXES

Based on the average rental value of a property, there are two types of local tax payable by individuals. The *taxe foncière* is a property ownership tax paid by the owner, whether a resident in France or not; while the *taxe d'habitation* is a residential tax paid by the occupiers, who may or may not be the owners. Both are paid in the year following the rental period. Retired residents may be exempt from paying these taxes, as may owners of new houses or uninhabitable properties.

INCOME TAX

Income tax, or *impôt sur le revenu des personnes physiques* (IRPP), is levied on 'earned' income, and depends on the level of income. There are, however, a number of allowances. A tax on investment or 'unearned' income tax, named the *impôt sur les revenus de capitaux*, is payable on property and investment income, as well as interest paid on bank accounts. There is also a separate rental income tax called the *contribution sur les revenus locatifs*, which is levied on gross rental income.

WEALTH TAX

A wealth tax called the *impôt de solidarité sur la fortune*, is levied on net assets held in France that are valued above a certain threshold. The assets can include a property, a car and bank balances. Wealth tax can be minimised if you buy a property through an SCI and the net worth of the property can be reduced for tax purposes by way of debt.

'Careful planning when making your property purchase will lessen future inheritance tax liabilities'

FINANCE

TAX RATES*

INCOME TAX FROM 7.05% TO 49.58%
Taxable from 4,191 euros (£2,619)

RENTAL INCOME TAX
2.5%

SOCIAL CHARGES
On income derived from a professional activity
CSG 7.5%
CRDS0.5%

WEALTH TAX FROM 0.55% TO 1.80%
Taxable from 720,000 euros (£450,000)

CAPITAL GAINS TAX
Non-residents 331/3%

INHERITANCE TAX
From 5% to 60%

*Correct at time of going to press

FINANCE

'A French or British surveyor, project managing a new build can save absentee owners time and money'

CAPITAL GAINS TAX

There is no tax on any gain made from the sale of a principal home, but capital gains tax, or the *impôt sur les plus-values,* is levied on the profits of the sale of other property, as well as shares, subject to certain allowances.

SOCIAL CHARGES

All income and capital gains declared in France are subject to social contributions or charges, such as the CSG (generalised social contribution) and the CRDS (repayment of the social debt contribution).

INHERITANCE TAX

French inheritance law, which governs inheritance tax, and death and estate duties, decides who inherits a person's assets. It is probably quite unlike anything that a British buyer will have encountered previously. In theory, inheritance tax is paid on the global assets of a French tax resident. The beneficiaries pay a percentage of their inheritance, depending on the value of the estate and how closely they are related. Inheritance tax will also be due on any French property owned by a non-resident.

There are several ways to minimise an inheritance tax bill, however, and careful planning at the time of the house purchase is crucial. In certain circumstances, for example, changes to a marriage contract can help, as can buying through a property-holding company or SCI, of which the owners are the shareholders. An SCI can be a great advantage for foreign residents whose home inheritance tax is less onerous than the French one.

Usually the law of the country in which the property is located is applicable. If, however, it is owned by an SCI, the applicable law will be that of the deceased's last country of residence, as it is not immovable property, which is always subject to French inheritance law.

To benefit the surviving spouse, provisions can also be made in the French will of an owner to ensure that their husband or wife receives a lifetime interest in the property (*usufruit*) on their death. One of the most popular methods that couples opt for, however, is to put a clause called a '*clause tontine*' in the conveyance, which, in effect, suspends the ownership of the entire property until one or other of them dies. However, this does not necessarily make the property exempt from taxation.

RENOVATIONS AND BUILDING WORKS

If you buy a property with a view to making alterations, you should check for any planning restrictions that may affect any building plans you have. A certificate showing planning permission, a *certificat d'urbanisme*, will provide precise details of the rules regarding the potential development of an individual property. Each area has an official maximum planning density, the *coéfficient d'occupation des sols*, and some areas have no-build zones. Contact your local town hall for these. Buyers should also be aware that not all buildings can be improved and turned in to gîtes. Some buildings may be too small in the first place to do so. The maximum size for which smaller buildings can be increased should be checked under the planning regulations.

Some minor works require no formalities, but even before building a swimming pool, you may need to fill in a form called a *déclaration des travaux* at your local *mairie*. In the case of more extensive alterations to a French property, both planning permission and a building permit, called a *permis de construire*, must be applied for through the local *mairie*.

Once the application has been considered by the *mairie*, it is forwarded on to the local planning office, and following approval it is then passed back to the *mairie* for a final sign-off. The whole process usually takes approximately two months. Applications can be made by the owners themselves or through either a *notaire* or a surveyor, unless the net surface area to be built upon exceeds 170 square metres, in which case it should be made by an architect who is a member of the Ordre des architectes. A listed historical building, or a building that is situated near one will also require review by an *architecte des bâtiments de France*. The majority of planning applications in France also require an environmental declaration providing an assessment of the impact of the proposals on the local area. An architect will usually deal with this, for you.

It may be tempting to try to carry out renovation work without recourse to builders or architects, but anyone renovating or adding to a historic building must be competent in the use of the local wood and stone, and understand the regulations governing the use of building material in the area. French builders are not renowned for their punctuality, but they are known to do a good job. The local *chambre des métiers* (chamber of trade) can supply details of builders registered in the area.

Some British homeowners are more comfortable employing British builders, even though they will probably not be as knowledgeable about the local materials and planning regulations. There are plenty of British builders who live in France or will travel to France to work. It is essential, however, to check that the work of British builders, electricians, plumbers and other tradesmen complies with French standards.

When the owner cannot be on site to supervise the project, employing an architect or surveyor, French or British, to see the project through can end up saving you money as well as time. However you decide the project should be managed, when work has been completed, the owner will need to obtain a certificate, or *certificat de conformité*, proving that it complies with the planning permission. Most, but not all, residential building works and equipment installations come with a 10-year guarantee from the contractor who has carried out that work, provided that they are properly registered with the French authorities. The guarantee will be backed by the contractor's professional insurance.

What is rarely guaranteed, however, is the actual cost of the work itself. Estimates form the basis of a fixed price deal if the builder carrying out the works signs an estimate endorsed with the words '*prix global au forfeit*'. This binds them to completing the job for the price shown. Completion dates can also be hard to guarantee, but again there is a way to help fix the date. By inserting a few more words on the paperwork, such as '*le délai d'achèvement des travaux sera le 31 juillet 2004*' (building work will be completed on July 31 2004), the builder will feel obliged to stick to that date. A penalty clause can also be included in the agreement, such as 'avec une pénalité de 20 euros par jour de retard', in which case if completion is delayed, the bill will be reduced by 20 euros for each day's delay.

A nationwide organisation called the Conseil d'architecture, d'urbanisme et de l'environnement (CAUE), which has local branches in all of France's regions, can offer advice on renovating or extending traditional buildings. It is also well worth checking with a *mairie* to discover if the local council provides grants for restoring buildings in the area. Some offer particular help to anyone converting buildings into holiday accommodation, as part of a drive to attract tourism into the regions. The larger gîte rental companies are also known to offer money for this purpose, with the proviso that the agency will have the right to let out the property afterwards.

'If planning to let, it is vital to get your tenancy agreement checked by a legal expert for potential disadvantages'

FINANCE

'The UK Trade Descriptions Act 1968 makes it a criminal offence to misrepresent a property to potential tenants'

BUILDING A NEW HOME

If you buy a home to be constructed by a developer, they will oversee the construction of your new home, and your choice of architectural style may be limited by the designs drawn up for that particular development. If you are not buying from a developer, you can choose between hiring an architect to draw up plans or buying a ready-made plan from the builder you engage to construct it. If you choose the former option - which will give you the greatest scope for influencing the style of the building according to your personal tastes - you can either oversee the building of the property yourself, or engage a *maître d'œuvre* to do so. In any case, you will usually be expected to pay the cost in stages over the course of the construction.

In France, if you buy a new apartment or villa under construction which forms part of a development, you should be protected by the *code de la construction* (construction law) from the developer being made bankrupt during its construction, and from other possible pitfalls. By law, when the keys to your newly-built home are handed over, there will be a one-month guarantee against structural defects and a 10-year warranty against latent defects affecting the structure of the building. There will also be a two-year warranty against defects in equipment in the building, such as central heating.

MAINTAINING YOUR PROPERTY

When owners are away, they often turn to neighbours to help look after their property. Having someone clean the property and tend the garden in their absence makes visiting even more enjoyable. Specialist companies can also offer property checks, sending someone round regularly to see if there has been any damage to it and to check if any pipes are leaking, for example.

LETTING FRENCH PROPERTY

The letting of residential property can involve a mixture of both short and long-term lets. If you are questioning whether you should purchase a holiday home in France because you will not be able to make use of it for more than a handful of weeks each year, or you wish to spend some holidays in different regions or countries, it may be worth considering letting out your home to other holidaymakers, as well as friends and family. This can certainly help cover the cost of home ownership, help pay for your holidays elsewhere, and can also become a reasonably profitable business.

There are a number of rental options that the would-be landlord can weigh up. Depending on type and area, residential properties can be rented as short-term (for holidays or business trips) or long-term lets. The length of the holiday letting season differs greatly from region to region. In Paris, for example, apartments let to holidaymakers often remain empty in August, whereas family gîtes in Dordogne,could be booked two or three times over during the same month. There are also areas in France that have two distinct seasons, bringing landlords rental returns over more weeks of the year. The Provençal Alps, for instance, attract skiers in the winter and outdoor enthusiasts in the summer, many of whom will book holiday accommodation.

If you buy in a city, you may be able to let to travelling businessmen and holidaymakers for short periods, and in addition find tenants looking for long-term lets. As a general rule, cities yield the best rents and number of prospective tenants for long-term lets. Throughout France there are young professionals, students and families looking for homes to rent with easy access to offices, universities and schools. City living is popular partly because it is often feasible to go home at lunchtime, which is typically 90 minutes long and during which traditionally a substantial meal is served. Each city has different

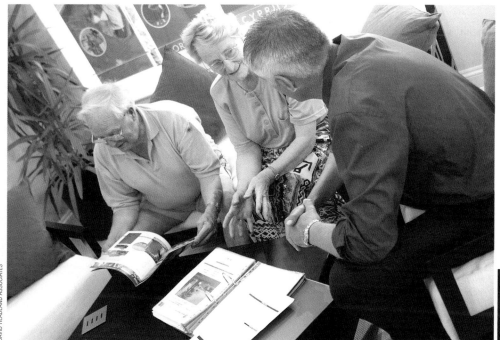

FINANCE

areas attracting different clients, and none more so than Paris, where each *quartier* has a unique ambience and range of amenities.

Working with an architect can give you greater freedom in the design of your French home

You should not necessarily rule out long-term lets off-season. Rents are lower out of season and the tenancy agreement is for a longer period, but there will be money coming in and having the property occupied can be a benefit to security.

If you are buying as a rental investment, issues such as lengths of seasons and popularity with different types of tenants and holidaymakers should be investigated thoroughly, if the business is to be a success. Talk to estate agents who are already renting property in the area and read letting advertisements in the press to gather market knowledge. Do not overlook commercial property as an investment both for the short and long term. Yields on commercial properties can often be higher than those for residential property, and a strong interest from the international corporate investor is a testimony to the soundness of speculation in this type of property.

FINDING TENANTS

Owners of French property have a range of options when it comes to finding tenants and managing. If you choose to let privately, and want to attract holidaymakers rather than your friends and family, you can place an advertisement in a specialist publication with lettings advertisements in France and in the home country of your target audience, or on specialist websites. In France, local papers have listings sections of properties for rent. To advertise holiday lets to a foreign audience, place an advertisement in publications distributed in the relevant countries.

If you prefer to relinquish the responsibility of marketing your property yourself you can, for a certain percentage of the rent, do it through a local estate agency or holiday lettings specialist, or, in the case of new-builds

'The French tax authority can take payments up to three years in arrears after its due date'

BUYING A PROPERTY:
THE COST
(FROM BARCLAYS)

Property prices in the south of France: at least 200,000 euros for an apartment, and at least 450,000 euros for a villa.

NOTARY FEES:

Depending on the construction period:

For a construction less than five years old, the charges should amount to between 2% and 4% of the purchase price; for a property over five years old, the charges can represent between 6% and 8% of the purchase price (on a sliding scale).

COST OF SURVEY:

A survey is not obligatory if the property is valued at less than 762,000 euros, or if you pay in cash.

A survey with photographs and with an expert valuation should cost between 0.3% and 1%, depending on the expert, the type of property, and its surface.

LEGAL FEES:

They are mostly included in Notary fees.

For a new property, and for a purchase with a mortgage loan, it will be the closest to 4% for an old one; for a purchase with a mortgage loan, it will be the closest to 8%.

REAL ESTATE AGENT:

International clients usually find a property with a real estate agent.

The commission is 5% of the purchase price, but it can be negotiated on expensive properties.

PURCHASING EUROS:

Usually costs 1% of total, depending on the amount to change. It's best to change all at once because of fixed charges.

THE COST OF TRIPS:

Depending on the company.

With **Air France**, approximately 762 euros
with **Easyjet**, approximately 205 euros

Properties for sale in the south of France are rare and expensive and it's often necessary to make a quick decision in order to secure a purchase

especially, a management company that services the entire building or complex. There are numerous holiday lettings companies to choose from, based in a wide range of countries. Some publicise properties solely on the internet, while others also display them in free brochures. Tourist offices also market holiday properties. For details of your local or regional tourist office, contact Maison de la France in France or overseas (see Useful Contacts).

MANAGING LETS

Overseeing the cleaning and changeover days of properties let for short periods can be difficult to manage from a distance, though not impossible. Some holiday home owners find they can rely on their clients to leave the property in a good state and simply send a key to them, though help can usually be hired in most of France's towns and villages to ensure these are seamless operations. A local job centre, or *agence nationale pour l'emploi*, can be good source of help. When you let your property for short periods through estate agents in parts of Paris and ski resorts, for example, the agent will often take on the responsibility of managing the tenancies and changeovers.

Any intermediary who lets a property for commercial or residential use must, by law, be licensed to do so, and anyone engaging a letting agent, or *agent locataire*, should ensure that both their own rights and obligations, and those of the agent, are clearly defined in a written agreement.

A letting agent will probably have standard tenancy agreements, but these can contain clauses that are disadvantageous to the landlord. If you are presented with such an agreement, consider asking an independent legal advisor to review it, even if it has been translated into your own language. If you are letting directly to tenants, you should have an agreement drawn up by an experienced lawyer. This should contain the necessary clauses to protect you as the landlord (the landlord should, for example, be able to ensure that the contract can be terminated if the tenant defaults on their rent) and a schedule of the condition of the property (*état de lieux*), and it should be signed by the parties concerned before the tenant moves in. This agreement must comply with French laws. The rights and obligations of landlords (*bailleurs*), and their tenants (*locataires*) will in most cases be governed by French law. Note that the obligations of a landlord are more formidable in the case of unfurnished property, for instance, the landlord must give the tenant at least six months notice to quit the property.

Before any contract becomes binding, make sure you communicate your terms and conditions clearly to your tenant. If you do not do so, you could face not only a claim for a refund, but also for damages for additional expenses incurred. Your terms and conditions should cover subjects such as your payment terms (including the amount of your deposit, when this and the balance will be payable, and details of what happens if they are not paid); booking cancellations in the case of holiday rentals; circumstances for which you will not be liable, such as the disruption of a holiday as a result of local water shortages or electricity cuts, and the correct complaints procedure. These terms and conditions must, of course, comply with the law governing the letting of a property of the relevant country.

Great care should be taken when advertising your property. If you are letting to British clients, for example, the UK Trade Descriptions Act 1968 makes it a criminal offence to knowingly or 'recklessly' misrepresent a property to clients. Under the Consumer Protection Act 1987 it is also a criminal offence for a business to mislead clients about prices, as well as accommodation, facilities and services.

Despite the potential pitfalls, it is common practice to let a property on an

FINANCE

informal basis, with only a verbal or a loosely worded written agreement. This is often the case when homes are rented out for short periods to holidaymakers. When a property is let without a formal contract, the tenancy will, however be governed by the French Civil Code, which offers landlords limited protection in the event of a dispute with the tenant. It is important to note that, whatever form the agreement has taken, if a tenant who has been renting on a short-term basis does decide to stay beyond the end of the letting period, it may be difficult to force their eviction if they do not have a permanent home elsewhere, if the property is unfurnished, or if the letting period exceeds three months.

In some cases the property must be registered with the local authorities and comply with standards and regulations set by them. When renting out a property that you use for holidays or that is your main residence, you should also ensure that your insurance policy covers damage caused by tenants, and injuries caused to tenants on the premises.

LETTING AS A BUSINESS

According to the French Commercial Code, a landlord is considered a tradesman, or *commerçant,* if the property is owned in the name of a commercial company, or if it is classed as commercial rather than residential. The latter is the case if, for example, the lease (*bail*) is taken on by a company which, or an individual who, operates a business on the premises, or if the property contains more than five furnished self-contained rooms or units available for let throughout the holiday season or for longer periods. In this case, the landlord must register with the local chamber of commerce within two months of starting to trade.

To run a property as a hotel you must register the business at the local chamber of commerce and obtain a licence to run it. The property must first be inspected by a number of administrative bodies to ensure that the establishment complies with safety and hygiene standards.

One disadvantage of being classified as a tradesman is that when any of your properties are sold, the sale can attract a transfer registration duty of 4.8 percent. There are ways of structuring the ownership of the property to avoid this, however, by buying through a civil company that does not engage in commercial activities itself, for example. If you buy a commercial property, or *fonds de commerce,* this rate of registration tax is payable if the property is up to 23,000 euros in value, or 15 euros and a rate of 4.8 percent if the value exceeds 23,000 euros.

To run a business in France, a number of documents must be filled in annually. Your local tax office, or *chambre des métiers,* and chamber of commerce should be able to help talk you through these.

FINANCE

If the letting of a property does not constitute a business in the eyes of the local authorities, both profits and losses from lettings must be reported on the normal French income tax return, Cerfa 2042. The tax applicable to French rental income is not the standard income tax. Residents should submit the form to the local tax office, and non-residents to the Centre des impôts des non-résidents in Paris (see Useful Contacts) before April 30 each year following the French tax year, which runs from January 1 to December 31. French rental income must be declared in France, even if disclosed to the tax authorities in the country of tax residency. A double tax treaty with countries such as Britain means France still has the principal right to tax - the French tax paid is simply set aside against any UK tax liability arising from the same source. ■

FINANCE TIPS

■ If you declare the income you receive from letting a property in France to the tax authorities in the country where you are resident, France still retains principle taxation rights on French sourced income.

■ This is the case no matter where both landlord and tenant reside, or where and in which currency the rent is paid.

■ French tax authorities may tax up to three years in arrears, and usually add interest and penalty charges on late tax returns.

■ When lettings qualify as a business for the purposes of French taxation, the method used to determine the taxable income depends on the level of annual turnover from the preceding year.

■ One, the 'simplified regime' (*régime simplifié*), is relatively straightforward, while the other, the 'normal regime' (*regime normal*), requires the preparation of detailed accounts and involves compliance formalities similar to those of a company liable to French corporation tax.

■ Some rentals may be subject to TVA and exempt TVA, and there are also local taxes that can be levied on leases.

■ Although the supply of food, telephone and other services to self-catering accommodation is subject to TVA at the standard rate, when an establishment provides accommodation on a full-board or half-board basis, TVA can be reduced. Other financial incentives to landlords come in the form of grants. In some French *départements*, owners can obtain grants from local authorities for the conversion of homes into rental accommodation. Contact the administrative offices of the local state representative, or *préfecture,* for information.

FINANCE

Buying Case Study

ALL PICS BY JEAN PAUL CASTAN

Names: Sheila and Guy Danhieux

Jobs: Both retired, they let out the private *gîte* part of their house

Where: Moved from Somerset to the Charente village of Grand Madieu, in Poitou Charente 10 years ago

Sixteen years ago, Guy and Sheila Danhieux decided that what they needed was a bolthole to escape to whenever they wanted to relax and enjoy country living. During a gîte holiday in Vendée, they had visited Charente, which has countryside similar to what they were used to in their home county of Somerset. After reading in a Sunday supplement that this was still relatively unknown territory for the British, they chose the area to start their search.

'There were two things that really interested us about Charente,' says Sheila. 'One was the wonderful weather you get here – as you travel across the Loire Valley, the sun comes out, even in the winter months. The other attraction was that, because we were not going to be surrounded by other foreigners, we would be able to immerse ourselves in a French community.' Charente has the added advantage of not being too far away from the ports in western France.

The couple chose their property above all for its location. 'We bought this house for its 270 degree views overlooking a valley. There was no sanitation and, although we did have electricity in the form of one switch and a bulb, an electrician came round and told us not to touch it.'

One thing Guy and Sheila have learned about buying a house in France is that, while the house itself is usually not overly expensive, renovation works can take an unexpected amount of money, effort and time, particularly if you want to get the detail exactly right. 'You can never calculate the true cost,' states Sheila. 'You can put a drain in and then have to lay another one down because the water seeps through it.' She adds that the cost can be kept down, but that if you want your renovation to be perfect, you have to pay for it, and recalls: 'In our gîte, as well as in our house, we had our electric cables buried in the walls. It cost more running the cables this way, but it is well worth doing, because it means that they will not be visible.'

When the couple had a chance to retire, they moved to their Charentais home permanently. Sheila notes that they were in a fortunate position to do this: 'We were lucky, because, depending on your priorities, the cost of living is about the same as in Britain. Some things, like wine for instance, can be cheaper, but taxes on commodities, for example, are expensive. And if you move to France before you reach the recognised retirement age, the French medical system, though wonderful, is not cheap. When you join the healthcare system, your contributions will be expensive.'

Guy and Sheila feel they have a fine quality of life in France. This they attribute not only to the good weather and peaceful country setting, but also to the fact that they have now successfully integrated into the local community. 'Luckily we had six years of visiting the area before we finally moved to it, and all but two of our friends here are French,' notes Sheila. 'The essential thing in all of this has been learning to speak French, as we

The couple's traditional *gîte* with an added mezzanine helps support their income.

had only studied French to 'O' level before moving here. It is imperative to speak the language, because you will never integrate properly unless you speak it. You will also find it extremely difficult to renovate a house unless you brush up on your vocabulary, because words like "architrave" are not taught at school.'

Changing their Charente bolthole into a full–time address inspired the couple's gîte business.

What also helped them be accepted into the local community was, Sheila notes, the fact that they only employed local tradesmen. This also, she says, meant the standard of work was higher. 'Good craftsmanship doesn't come cheap in France, but you do get what you pay for,' she adds.

The one thing that Guy and Sheila have found rather tiring about life in France is the bureaucracy that they have encountered. 'The bureaucracy you can come up against when applying for permission for building work or changing rights of way across your land, for instance, can be like a brick wall,' comments Sheila. 'You can find yourself filling in duplicate or even triplicate forms, and waiting an age for an official stamp for a document. And when a *notaire* gets involved, it can add a few noughts on to your bill, and lots more paperwork.'

Over the years that Guy and Sheila have owned their home in Charente, they have been letting out a gîte, which is a very private section of their large farmhouse. While they have been grateful that this has helped top up their income, they have learned that it is not a revenue stream to be relied upon, as many property seekers in this area believe is the case. 'People are often misguided into thinking that a property can be rented out for 20 weeks in France, but the season is usually no longer than 10. We managed to top 20 weeks last year, but it was the first time in 10 years. Competition is greater now than it has ever been, with many British buyers especially, buying in the region and opening up rental gîtes.'

The qualities that draw holidaying families to the area are exactly those that keep the couple enchanted with their home in France. 'Charente is still lovely,' enthuses Sheila. 'The way of life is relaxed; people take time over things – to enjoy their food, for example – and children play quite safely by themselves. It is a complete contrast to life back in Britain.' ■

'Good craftsmanship doesn't come cheap in France, but you do get what you pay for.'

Business Case Study

OLIVIER PICQUE

Names: David and Lynne Hammond

Jobs: David and Lynne run a select wine tour business

Where: Moved from Hertfordshire to a village between Autun and the wine centre of Beaune

David and Lynne During 20 years of holidaying in France, David and Lynne Hammond developed a passion for the country and its lifestyle that made them decide to move there a couple of years ago from Hertfordshire. Yet, unlike many British people who move to France, they were not quite ready to give up their business lives and knew that they needed to work on a plan that had every chance of succeeding in this new environment.

The corner of France in which they chose to settle down was southern Burgundy, near Beaune, their decision prompted by a trip to the South of France the previous year. The couple had stopped in Dijon, the capital of Burgundy, on their way back, and they discovered that 'it had everything: attractive countryside, an interesting heritage, and great food and wine'. David and Lynne were also impressed with its reasonable access back to the UK – a TGV station nearby has a high-speed train connection to the Eurostar at Lille, and by road Burgundy is approximately only 400 miles from Calais.

They chose to settle in a village between the Roman town of Autun and the wine centre of Beaune. About 45 minutes from the Morvan Regional Park, close to a choice of activities in Beaune and just an hour from Dijon, their new home offered the perfect combination of countryside and town life that they sought. 'As we used to live in Hertfordshire, with London on our doorstep, we knew that we enjoyed the countryside, but we also wanted to be near a town.' Another attraction was that they realised this was the perfect setting for a business idea they had, which would offer them the chance to immerse themselves in one of their great passions and make a living from it.

'We sold a business in the UK that we had run for about 20 years,' recounts David. 'We looked at my skills – in marketing, and developing and managing businesses – and those of my wife, who was an organiser and creative. We both have a love of wine, and saw a gap in the market for select wine tours, so we decided to grow our business around this and went for it.'

Although David had a strong business background, the first steps in establishing this new venture represented a challenge simply because it was new territory for the couple. 'Our first port of call was to see the mayor, tell him what we wanted to do and ask how we should go about it. The mayor went through our plan with us and pointed out the documents we should fill in. One of the challenges we experienced at the outset was in organising the setting-up of the business and our *cartes de séjour* at the same time; the process involved a lot of cross-referencing of documentation, and we needed to prove we had obtained one set in order to set up the other.'

'There are three documents that you must have when you want to live in France and start a business there,' adds David. 'They are a *carte d'immatriculation* to prove you are in business, a *carte de séjour* or resident's

The couple organise wine tours and tastings in the delightful villages of southern Burgundy.

permit, and a *carte vitale*, which gains you access to the benefits of the health service. When we got these, we were told we were half-French!'

The area near the wine centre of Beaune was the inspiration for the Hammonds' business idea

As well as a helping hand from the local mayor, the Hammonds found obtaining local accounting help a vital step to getting their business going. 'From a business point of view it is essential to find a local French accountant. They know their way around the system, are in regular contact with the local social services and tax office, and can advise on the format, be it *entreprise individuelle* (sole trader) or *SARL* (limited company) status, for instance.'

The Hammonds' accountant also helped them register with their nearest chamber of commerce, which is mandatory in France. The chamber of commerce issues the *certificat d'immatriculation*, something that Lynne and David thought would be a mere formality for registering their business. They were, however, pleasantly surprised by their interaction. 'When we approached our chamber of commerce and asked them to explain the documentation we had been handed, the chamber expressed a lot of interest in our business.'

That initial interest shown by the chamber of commerce soon developed into a plan of action. 'The chamber has been very helpful in plugging us into the networks that will help us develop our business,' notes David. 'They said that they would like to help us organise a tour in Châlons, and set up a meeting for us with winemakers there.'

David and Lynne feel they have been fully supported by their local chamber of commerce along the way. 'The French chambers of commerce are dedicated to helping business develop,' says David. 'They are closely linked to local government and have a much bigger budget than their equivalents do in the UK. The network is much more than a business club, which is the model more often found in the UK. They can achieve a great deal, and are a force for economic development.'

The couple currently organise one-day wine tours on which groups of up to six people are taken in a Land Rover Discovery through wine villages offering tours of wine merchants and tastings. They plan to build on the core business, and also to provide help to other British people planning to buy in this area, which offers 'elegant town houses, village homes with land and orchards, properties to renovate, and all manner of homes to fire the imagination'. ∎

'It was the perfect setting for a business idea that would immerse them in one of their great passions.'

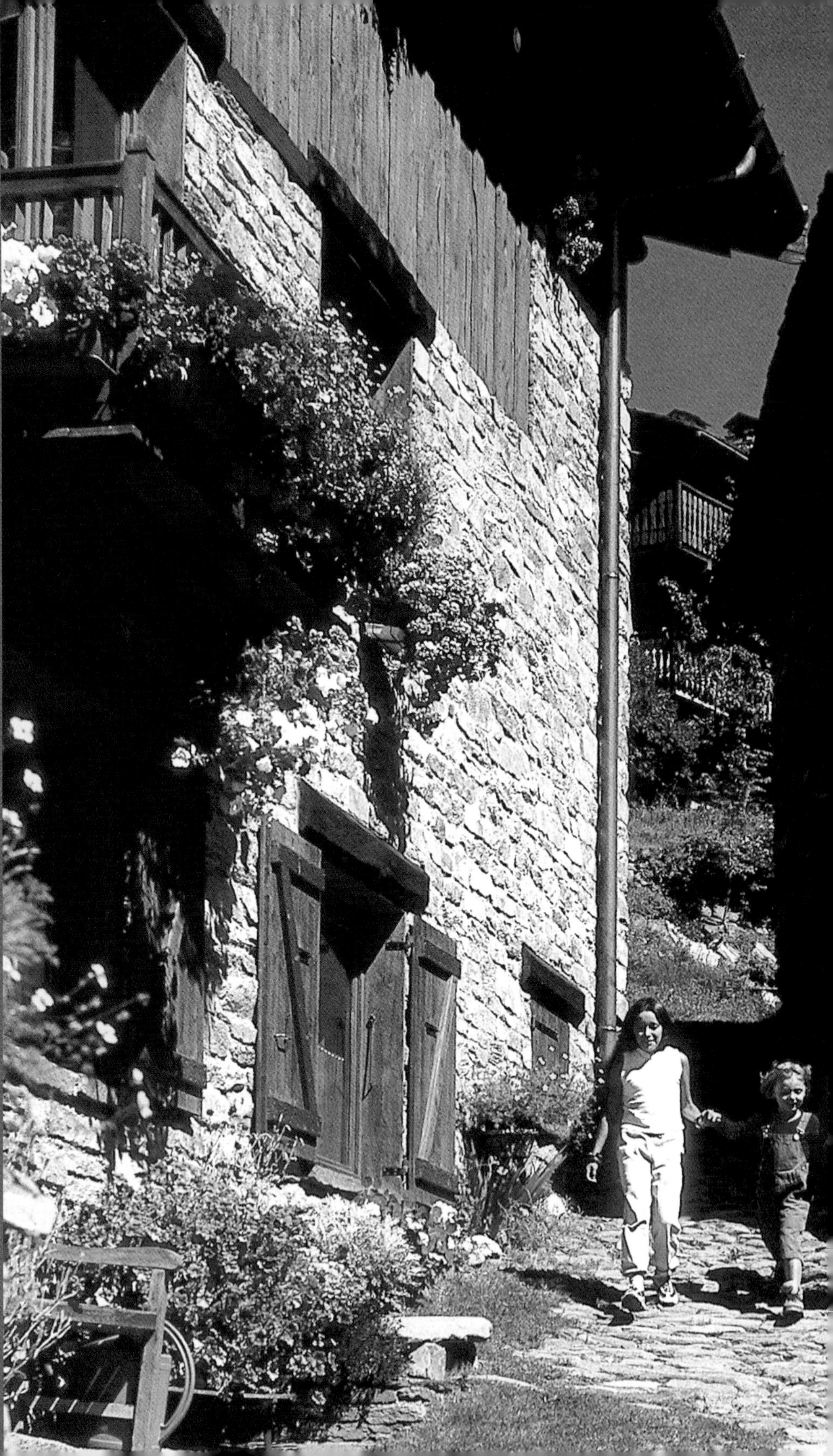

BENOIST

Regional Introductions
Market Information
Property Prices

Property Guide

BUYING GUIDE

PRICE GUIDE

How to use this Guide 58

Brittany 61

Normandy 81

Nord pas-de-Calais & Picardy 101

Ile de France 117

Champagne-Ardenne 137

Alsace, Lorriane & France-Comte 153

The Loire 169

Burgundy 187

Poitou-Charentes 203

Limousin & Auvergne 219

The Rhône-Alps 235

Aquitaine 257

The Midi-Pyrénées 273

Languedoc-Roussillon 289

Provence, Cote d'Azur & Corsica 309

The Rhône is one region that offers excellent investment potential for buyers

How to use this Guide

The 94 hotspots, property price matrices, and regional price guides all give purchasers a framework to calculate their possible investment.

This section of the guide is divided into 15 regions, with some neighbouring *départements* grouped together. These 15 are subdivided in turn into a total of 94 'hotspots', or towns and areas that share a common economic status for property. An introduction to each region includes an analysis of its property market, with details of the areas that offer best and worst value for money, as well as a profile of its highlights and information on new developments or transport plans.

MAPS

For each region a map of the area is provided. A number on the map marks the location of each hotspot mentioned in the chapter, which corresponds to the number next to that hotspot's profile. Major ports, airports, roads and rivers are also marked on this map.

PROPERTY PRICE MATRIX

To give you an impression at a glance of property values in your preferred hotspots, a property price matrix at the beginning of each region provides

average prices for two, three, four, five, six, seven and eight-bedroom properties in each hotspot, wherever available. These prices are averaged from sale prices – that is from marked, rather than achieved prices – supplied by a panel of French property market specialists.

At the back of the book you should find three matrices: one showing average 'for- sale' prices for houses, another showing average sales prices for flats and the other flats, in each of the 94 hotspots, and a further lettings matrix depicting average weekly revenues. Compiled from extensive research they are a true reflection of current market conditions. Use them to calculate the potential return you can expect from your investment.

HOTSPOT ESSENTIALS

The 'Essentials' bar for each hotspot provides information on the *Taxe d'habitation* – levied on the occupier only, and derived from the *valeur locative cadastrale*, multiplied by a communal tax rate – and the *Taxe foncière* – 50 per cent of the assessed *valeur locative cadastrale,* which is charged to the property owner. The nearest airport and the official population figures from the 1990 and 1999 censuses, show an area's growth.

HOTSPOT KEY FACTS BOXES

Under the title 'Key Facts' you will find details of each hotspot's rental market, its pros and cons, and the nearest medical centres and schools. In some cases we have been rigorously selective, for reasons of space.

YOUR GUIDE TO THE HOTSPOTS

A key to the Regional maps

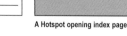

A Hotspot opening index page

A Regional Profile

For each hotspot's rental market there is an indication of whether it has long or short-term letting potential, and where this is short-term, details are provided of which months of the year you can expect to be able to let out your property. The 'Pros' and 'Cons' of each hotspot have been compiled in association with our panel of market experts, and include information on employment prospects, potential tenants and price trends.

For each hotspot, the nearest international or main hospital/medical centre where British people would be treated has been chosen. In some more cosmopolitan areas, such as Paris, where major international hospitals outnumber those of quieter areas, such as Normandy, we have selected the bigger medical centres, or those with a greater international flavour. Where possible we have attempted to give details for the nearest international school.

REGIONAL PRICE GUIDES

Go to the Price Guides to gain a clear impression of the type of property you can expect to find for your money within your chosen region. The properties are divided into the following price bands: under 100,000 euros (- £66,000); 100,000 - 200,000 euros (£66,000 - £133,000); 200,000 - 500,000 euros (£133,000 - £333,000); and 500,000 euros (£333,000) plus. Every effort has been made to include properties from all the hotspots within each price band. These properties have been collated from 56 agents and a wide range is included of each region's property styles, including flats, villas, cottages, town houses, manoirs and châteaux.

The price is in euros and the agent's three letter code, eg; LAT, for Latitudes is listed in the top line of the box, and these can be cross-referenced to the list of agent names and contact details, listed alphabetically with the codes in the Index to Agents (page 358).

The next line details the town/area and its *département* number, followed by a brief description of the property and underneath the price in £ Sterling.

Symbols indicate information on the number of bedrooms, garden, village/town location, proximity to a main road and whether there is parking, followed by a brief description or number.

These symbols are:

Bedrooms: ⬜ and the following number.

Garden: ❀ with the size in m², or a description, eg 'large garden'

Near a village: ⬜ followed by a brief description of the distance from the property, or with the assumption of within 5 miles of the property.

Near a road: ⬜ followed by a brief description of the location.

Parking: ⬜ followed by a brief description of what is available, either a carport, room for parking, or a garage. ■

A Regional price matrix

A sample Price Guide page

Rolling fields and moors
Long jagged coastlines
Magnificent beaches

Brittany

Profile 62

Hotspots 64

PRICE GUIDE

€20,000-€100,000 70

€100,000-€200,000 72

€200,000-€500,000 74

€500,000+ 78

Brittany Profile

Getting there

AIR Brittany can be reached easily by air and its main airports are Brest, Nantes and Rennes. **Ryanair** (0871 246 0000; www.ryanair.com) flies directly to Dinard and Brest from London Stansted, while **Aurigny Air** (01481 822886; www.aurignyair.com) offers direct flights to Dinard from Guernsey and Jersey, and via Guernsey from Manchester, East Midlands, Bristol, Stansted, Gatwick and Southampton. **Air France** (0845 366 5533; www.airfrance.co.uk) flies directly to Nantes, from where you can travel into Brittany, but there are no other direct flights.

SEA Ferries travel frequently into Saint-Malo and Roscoff. **Brittany Ferries** (0870 536 0360; www.brittany-ferries.com) sails between Portsmouth and Saint-Malo, and between Plymouth and Roscoff. **Condor ferries** (0845 345 2000; www.condorferries.com) sails from Poole and Weymouth to Saint-Malo.

ROAD In general, the best way of getting around Brittany is by road. The *autoroute* N12/N165 offers easy access into Brittany, running along the coast and on to Rennes. Travelling across Brittany's more isolated areas can prove to be much slower. There are *autoroutes* from Normandy and the Loire that run into Brittany, as well as the A11 from Paris.

COACH Brittany has an extensive local bus network, but services are infrequent. An express coach service operates from outside the terminal building to the central rail station in Saint-Malo. **Eurolines** (0870 514 3219; www.eurolines.com) operates a number of services from the UK to Brest, Lorient, Quimper, Rennes, Roscoff, Saint-Malo and Vannes.

RAIL Brittany has a good rail network that follows the coast, although the interior has only a limited number of stations. The high-speed **TGV** runs direct from Paris and Lille into Rennes, and across to Brest and Quimper, and there is a good local train service. The Eurostar runs from London Waterloo to Paris, and from there it is possible to get a connection to Dinan, which takes three hours. For all information contact **Rail Europe** (0870 584 8848; www.raileurope.co.uk).

ECONOMY

Brittany is France's main agricultural producer and has a strong agricultural and livestock industry. At a local level, the government has tried to encourage the development of new industries, and Rennes has now developed its motor trade, while Brest has a thriving engineering and electronics industry. Tourism is still a vital business in Brittany, with the fishing industry remaining active in the various ports along the western coast.

BEST/WORST VALUE FOR MONEY

Property is most expensive along the Gulf of Morbihan, where £150,000 will buy you a fairly modern property. However, it is difficult to recoup money through rental income as, although the French will always buy and rent here, the British are less keen and often plump for the cheaper, inland areas. Affordable family property tends to be located on the border between the Côtes d'Armor and Morbihan *départements*, which are experiencing more demand, especially as there are plenty of properties to choose from.

With most points in Brittany only one hour from the coast, the beach is still accessible, but property is generally cheaper inland, and there are many more renovation properties on the market. Most British people seeking property on

Many foreign buyers are attracted to Brittany through a desire to live by the Morbihan coast

the south coast are buying around the Baud area, just inland of Lorient and the band of expensive properties situated on the south coast, while Finistère's west coast offers some undiscovered areas and bargain properties.

WHERE TO GO FOR WHAT
Brittany has been given the nickname 'Little Britain' by the French because of the popularity of the region with the British who are looking for a holiday home or permanent residence. The Morbihan *département* offers warm winds washing up the Gulf of Morbihan, creating mild winters and a Mediterranean climate along Brittany's southernmost point. This is an ideal location for those seeking a certain Côte d'Azur decadence and glamour.

The triangle of Dinard, Dinan and Saint-Malo is convenient for those who desire easy and regular access to Britain. Finistère is frequently chosen by those who love nature, and seek more than just sea and sand. Traditionally, Brittany is the home of the British family holiday and it has an abundance of small villages within easy reach of the coast, ideal for a family holiday home.

PROPERTY PRICE TRENDS
Brittany remains one the most popular destinations in France, with the average property costing between 60,000 and 100,000 euros. The market remains buoyant and busy, and has always attracted buyers who are seeking cheap properties to renovate, a trend which is inevitably leading to a dearth of renovation projects.

This, combined with an increase in the average budget of British buyers who are seeking properties in Brittany has served to increase prices in the areas of demand. With the French dominating the market in the Gulf of Morbihan and recently inundating the Saint-Malo area, prices have also risen. Nevertheless, despite these increases, Brittany is still cheaper than most areas in France, and few foreign buyers apply for a mortgage when buying in the region.

NEW BUILD/TRANSPORT PLANS
Brittany does not experience a great demand for new developments and newly-built properties, although the demand for modern properties is increasing in the South, and some developments have sprung up. In recent years, the transport network has improved with the introduction of new rail and road links, and this has led to the development of previously isolated areas and of industrial projects within Brittany.

Few foreign buyers apply for a mortgage when buying in Brittany, and it remains one of the cheapest areas in France

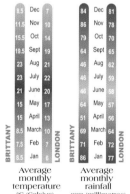

Average monthly temperature °C (Celsius)

Average monthly rainfall mm (millimetres)

Average House Sale Prices

HOTSPOT	2-BED	3-BED	4-BED	5-BED	6/7-BED	8-BED
Brest	€105K (£70K)	€120K (£80K)	€150K (£100K)	€225K (£150K)	€255K (£170K)	€375K (£250K)
Dinan	-	€150K (£100K)	€208K (£139K)	-	€300K (£200K)	-
Dinard	€128K (£85K)	€150K (£100K)	€315K (£120K)	€240K (£160K)	€315K (£210K)	€375K (£250K)
Golfe de Morbihan	€113K (£75K)	€128K (£85K)	€165K (£110K)	€203K (£135K)	€300K (£200K)	€450K (£300K)
Guingamp	€113K (£75K)	€135K (£90K)	€120K (£80K)	€150K (£100K)	€180K (£120K)	€225K (£150K)
Lorient	€105K (£70K)	€120K (£80K)	€150K (£100K)	€225K (£150K)	€255K (£170K)	€375K (£250K)
Quimper	€120K (£80K)	€150K (£100K)	-	-	€300K (£200K)	-
Rennes	€120K (£80K)	€143K (£95K)	€180K (£120K)	€225K (150K)	€300K (£200K)	€375K (£250K)
Saint Malo	€50K (£75K)	€98K (£65K)	€128K (£85K)	€165K (£110K)	€210K (£140K)	€300K (£200K)

Brittany Hotspots

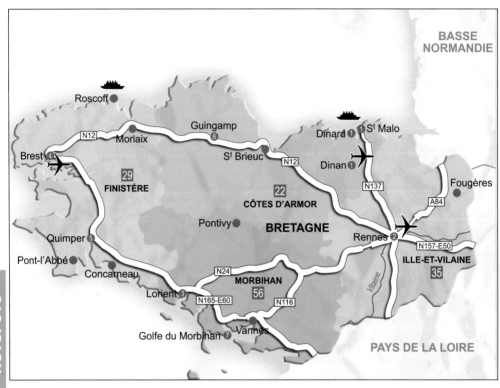

1. Dinard/ Dinan/ Saint-Malo

ESSENTIALS ■ **POP** 1990: -, 1999: 75,821 ■ **TAXES** Taxe d'habitation: 25.82%, Taxe foncière: 34.96% ■ **AIRPORT** Dinard/Pleurtuit/Saint-Malo Airport, L'Aérodrome, 35730 Pleurtuit, Tel: +33 2 99 46 18 46, Fax: +33 2 99 88 17 85.

KEY FACTS

SCHOOLS Contact the Rectorat de l'Académie de Rennes, 96 rue d'Antrain, 35044 Rennes Cedex, Tel: +33 2 99 28 78 78, Fax: +33 2 99 28 77 72, for advice on education.

MEDICAL Hospitalier de Saint-Malo, 1 rue Marne, 35400 Saint-Malo, Tel: +33 2 99 21 21 21.

RENTALS The rental season lasts from April to September, with winter seeing long-term rents ■ Properties in the area make for a good rental investment ■ Proximity to the coast and good access keeps this rental market healthy ■ Rental prices vary between 300 and 600 euros per week.

PROS Many Britons are choosing to buy their second home here and it is a very popular area ■ Exceptionally easy to get to, the area is good for commuters and second home buyers.

CONS Easy access for the UK market also results in high property prices ■ Owners of properties on Brittany's northern coast experience a climate that is colder and damper than that of southern Brittany ■ International schools are in short supply and many families send their children to a French-speaking school.

All located on Brittany's northern coastline, the seaside towns of Saint-Malo, Dinard and Dinan are becoming increasingly popular with both British and French property buyers, especially as the triangle has traditionally had a ready supply of older style properties. The large city of Saint-Malo and its old walled Intra Muros has a lively feel, with a citadel, marinas, restaurants and nightlife. Dinard boasts a casino, sea water therapy centre, antique shops, art galleries and a superb sandy beach with beautiful panoramic views over the Rance estuary. Dinan has been dubbed Brittany's most evocative town, its timbered houses (some on wooden pillars) making it a striking example of medieval architecture. The central region vigorously upholds its local culture and traditions, with several schools still teaching the Breton language and holding folk festivals, not just for the benefit of tourists. Sea views are breathtaking, with high cliffs, islands and rockpools named after their shapes and colours.

The best value homes are found in inland Brittany, throughout the Argoat, where the woods and heathland dotted alongside picturesque villages are graced with traditional granite and slate-roofed cottages, although many properties are in need of renovation. This is a popular area where many Britons choose to buy their second homes, but increased Parisian interest has raised property prices, as has the ease of access between Brittany and Britain. A traditional Breton, stone-built house costs approximately 280,000 euros. ■

2. Rennes

ESSENTIALS ■ **POP** 1990: 203,533, 1999: 212,494 ■ **TAXES** Taxe d'habitation: 27.44%, Taxe foncière: 33.28%
■ **AIRPORT** Rennes Saint-Jacques Airport, Avenue Joseph Le Brix, 35136 Saint-Jacques-de-la-Lande, Tel: +33 2 99 29 60 00.

The capital of Brittany, university city and cultural centre of Rennes. Students make up a quarter of its population and it has a distinctly cosmopolitan air compared to other cities in Brittany. Although you will find stylish squares and perfect medieval houses with pointed façades overlooking the streets, this is the business centre and market hub for the Breton region. Gutted by a fire in 1720, Rennes was then redesigned by Parisian architects, giving the impression in some parts that you are in Paris and not in Brittany. Nonetheless, the Place des Lices, just one of the four squares which dominate the city architecturally, provides useful navigational references for the visitor. The square itself is lined by some fine, late medieval houses, their crooked beams and oriel windows stretching high over the market stalls. The architectural interest of the Place des Lices is enhanced by the two *halles* in the middle of the square, and the thriving market and crêperies provide a focal point.

As the road network in the area is good, purchasing a cheaper property in the countryside surrounding the city is recommended. Property prices within Rennes itself can be very steep, as local agents deal primarily with the local French market. A student apartment in a modern block near the university will cost around 100,000 euros. A modern three-bedroom apartment can cost almost double this at around 180,000 euros, while a classic six-bedroom stone-built house can be bought for about 250,000 euros. ■

KEY FACTS
SCHOOLS Contact the Rectorat de l'Académie de Rennes, 96 rue d'Antrain, 35044 Rennes Cedex, Tel: +33 2 99 28 78 78, Fax: +33 2 99 28 77 72, for advice on education.
MEDICAL Centre Hospitalier Guillaume Régnier, 108 avenue Gén Leclerc, 35000 Rennes, Tel: +33 2 99 33 39 00.
RENTALS Long-term lets can be the best rental option ■ Rennes is too far inland and too industrialised to appeal to the holiday market ■ Rennes is primarily a French dominated city.
PROS Voted among the top 12 best places to live in France ■ Rennes is easily accessible by ferry and by air, and is well served by the *autoroute* ■ There are many services and amenities in the area and it is particularly geared for those relocating to work in France. ■ The biggest city in Brittany.
CONS As Brittany's capital, Rennes commands some of the highest prices in the region ■ This area is not popular with international holiday or second home buyers, and is mainly a local market.

3. Lorient

ESSENTIALS ■ **POP** 1990: -, 1999: 61,844 ■ **TAXES** Taxe d'habitation: 24.42%, Taxe foncière: 44.40% ■ **AIRPORT** Aéroport de Lann Bihoue, Lorient, 56270, Tel: + 33 3 14 90 44 44, Fax: + 33 3 14 90 63 28.

Situated in the region of Morbihan (which means 'Little Sea' in Breton, referring to the large tidal lagoon that cuts into the area's coastline) and located on an immense natural harbour, Lorient is the second largest fishing port in France. During the 18th century, the Compagnies des Indes (French East India Companies) were founded here, importing spices and salt into Lorient. Badly damaged during World War II, the town is functional rather than pretty, yet it has a delightful market, a very good beach at Larmor Plage and a great deal of restaurants serving the excellent local country fare. Lorient hosts the Inter-Celtic Festival, held for 10 days from the first Friday to the second Sunday in August. The biggest Celtic event in Brittany, it attracts participants from all seven Celtic-speaking countries. In a popular celebration of cultural solidarity, well over a quarter of a million people attend more than 150 different shows.

Property in Lorient itself can cost up to three times more than in areas just 20 minutes from town. As most people buy slightly further inland from Lorient, where property is cheaper, demand and quick turnover in this area can make it difficult to secure a property. Dominated by the local French market the area is consequently very expensive, and a two-bedroom apartment overlooking the marina can cost around 250,000 euros. Some estate agents can tend to try and close ranks, dealing only with French buyers, and over the last couple of years prices have increased significantly, as has demand. The Baud area, behind the southern coast experiences more demand due to cheaper prices and more property availability. ■

KEY FACTS
SCHOOLS Contact the Rectorat de l'Académie de Rennes, 96 rue d'Antrain, 35044 Rennes Cedex, Tel: +33 2 99 28 7 878, Fax: +33 2 99 28 77 72 for advice on education.
MEDICAL Centre Hospitalier de Bretagne Sud, 27 rue Doct Lettry, 56100 Lorient, Tel: +33 2 97 64 90 00.
RENTALS If you can afford to pay the high prices, you are guaranteed excellent rental income, especially from the French market ■ Property is expensive and there are few bargains on the south coast, with the majority of properties being modern and habitable. ■ Parisians have flooded the rental market on the Breton coast.
PROS Property in Lorient can cost up to three times more than in the areas only 20 minutes from town ■ The port is home to one of Brittany's most renowned festivals, the Inter-Celtic festival ■ Ideally located for those who want to be on the seafront ■ Foreign interest, particularly British, is high in this area.
CONS Lorient itself is not the most dynamic town on the south coast ■ Most people buy inland from Lorient where property is cheaper ■ Property is in very short supply in Lorient.

Brittany Hotspots

4. Brest

ESSENTIALS ■ **POP** 1990: 147,956, 1999: 156,210 ■ **TAXES** Taxe d'habitation: 33.43%, Taxe foncière: 35.55%
■ **AIRPORT** Brest Airport, 29490 Guipavas, Tel: +33 2 98 32 01 00.

KEY FACTS

SCHOOLS The only international school in the region is located in Rennes, which is 249 km from Brest ■ Rectorat de l'Académie de Rennes, 96 rue d'Antrain, 35044 Rennes Cedex, Tel: +33 2 99 28 78 78, Fax: +33 2 99 28 77 72.

MEDICAL Centre Hospitalier Universitaire, 5 avenue Foch, 29200 Brest, Tel: +33 2 98 22 33.33.

RENTALS Inclement weather prevents Brest from being a popular tourist and rental area ■ Foreigners generally are not interested in Brest and the Finistère département. ■ More of a tourist and lettings market.

PROS Located on a natural harbour, it is one of France's most important ports, with a very rich maritime history ■ The rugged landscape of the area is excellent for nature lovers and activities. ■ A strong employment area, excellent for relocation.

CONS This is not an area with a strong foreign property market ■ Brest's post-war architecture gives the city a rather bleak appearance ■ Brest lacks greenery, a result of the high winds that plague the city ■ Despite being located on the coast, Brest has no beaches ■ Rainfall is much higher here than in other parts of France.

Brest is a university town and seaport, located in the far northwest of Brittany where the Penfeld River meets the Bay of Brest in the *département* of Finistère. Being the main gateway into Brittany, Brest also boasts a rich maritime history and is France's premier naval facility, with a sheltered harbour and dry dock accommodation for ships of up to 500,000 tonnes. The river divides the city by flowing between the two hills upon which the city perches. Brest dates from Roman times when a settlement was established around 50 BC. During World War II, Brest was continuously bombed to prevent the Germans from using it as a submarine base. When liberated by the Americans in 1944 after a six-week siege, they found the town devastated beyond recognition and to this day, the architecture of the post-war town is in places raw and bleak. There have been attempts to make the centre more verdant, but as Brest experiences the heaviest rainfall in France, it has proved too windswept to respond. One remaining treasure is the 12th-century château, which is now a naval museum. Another major attraction is the futuristic Océanopolis, renowned for being the biggest open-air aquarium of its kind in Europe. Consisting of three immense tanks and a 3-D cinema, it focuses on the fishing industry of Brittany and Finistère.

Brest also offers a wide assortment of restaurants along rue Jean-Jaurès, while to the north, Place Guérin is the centre of the student *quartier,* Saint-Martin. There is no strong foreign property market here. The closer you buy to a city such as Brest, the more expensive the property. For a luxury six-bedroom house with sea views, expect to pay approximately 300,000 euros. ■

5. Quimper

ESSENTIALS ■ **POP** 1990: 59,437, 1999: 63,238 ■ **TAXES** Taxe d'habitation: 24.89%, Taxe foncière: 28.89%
■ **AIRPORT** Quimper Cornouaille Airport, Kermaduit, 29700 Pluguffan, Tel: +33 2 98 94 30 30.

KEY FACTS

SCHOOLS Contact the Rectorat de l'Académie de Rennes, 96 rue d'Antrain, 35044 Rennes Cedex, Tel: +33 2 99 28 78 78, Fax: +33 2 99 28 77 72 for advice on education.

MEDICAL Cornouaille Centre Hospitalier, 14 avenue Yves Thépot, 29000 Quimper, Tel: +33 2 98 52 60 60.

RENTALS Popular with the French, rental prices are higher than elsewhere in Brittany ■ Up-and-coming Pays Bigouden and Pont l'Abbé generate good rental income ■ It is difficult to attract the foreign market to such an expensive area.

PROS Quimper is Brittany's oldest city and was once the capital, maintaining a traditional Breton character ■ Quimper is easily accessible, with its own airport, and is located on the motorway and rail network ■ The town is within easy reach of the sea.

CONS Property is extremely expensive around Quimper and the surrounding coastline ■ More of a holiday and rentals market than a permanent home- buyers market

Split in two by the Odet river and surrounded by seven hills, Quimper is the ancient capital of the Cornouaille coast and head of the *département* of Finistere, where Breton traditions are still very much alive. Featuring decorative footbridges, and lined by rows of trees, lights and colourful hanging flower baskets, Quimper is well placed for exploring inland towns and villages, and offers quick access to the area's spectacular beaches.

A must-see is the Gothic 12th-century Cathédrale Saint-Corentin, named after Quimper's first bishop. Dominating the skyline, the cathedral was constructed between the 13th and 16th centuries and is the oldest Gothic structure in Lower Brittany. Walk directly to the old town from the cathedral's front to see cobbled squares, the Musée Départemental Breton and the charming narrow streets, teeming with half-timbered houses and the celebrated *crêperies*. In the Middle Ages, each street of the *vieux quartier* was devoted to a single trade and each still bears the names of its original trade. Shop for the local pottery called *faïence*, a type of provincial-style earthenware which has been crafted in this area for the last 400 years.

Property is very expensive around Quimper and the surrounding coastline, and this is primarily a French market, with foreign buyers reluctant to meet the prices. In the countryside within 20 minutes of Quimper, you could buy a stone and slate property to renovate for approximately 70,000 euros. ■

6. Guingamp

ESSENTIALS ■ **POP** 1990: 7,903, 1999: 8,830 ■ **TAXES** Taxe d'habitation: 24.67%, Taxe foncière: 40.01% ■ **AIRPORT** Dinard-Saint-Malo Airport, L'Aérodrome, 35730 Pleurtuit, Tel: +33 2 99 46 18 46.

Not far from the Côtes-d'Armor, on Brittany's rugged north coast, Guingamp - whose name is thought to be the source of the striped or checked fabric, gingham - is an attractive historic town of alleyways and cobbled streets. The town's university ensures a youthful atmosphere with plenty of nightlife and bars, while the Place du Centre is traffic-free with a Renaissance fountain. La Plomée is surrounded by fine old houses and hotels with wood and slate façades.

The three-turreted Basilica of Notre-Dame-de-Bon-Secours dates back to the 13th century, and each year on the first Saturday in July, it finds itself encircled by the annual Celtic festival, known as a *pardon*. This *fête* is one of Brittany's grandest, with a candle-lit night procession and bonfires, followed on the Sunday by a traditional dance festival performed by children. In August, the Fête de la Saint Loup continues for a week, during which there is folk-dancing in the streets. On the outskirts of town, the Warenghem Breton whisky distillery is interesting to visit: try one of the apple-based specialities, such as *pomig* (an apple liqueur).

Central Brittany offers some of the best bargains in the region, and is also the ideal place to look for properties suitable for renovation. Although there is demand for properties in this area, they remain cheaper than they would be on the coast, or in a slightly more upmarket area such as the Golfe du Morbihan. For instance, a two-bedroom semi-detached stone property located just five minutes from Guingamp can be found for approximately 60,000 euros. ■

KEY FACTS

SCHOOLS Contact the Rectorat de l'Académie de Rennes, 96 rue d'Antrain, 35044 Rennes Cedex, Tel: +33 2 99 28 78 78, Fax: +33 2 99 28 77 72 for advice on education.

MEDICAL Hôpital de Guingamp, 17 rue Armor, 22200 Pabu, Tel: +33 2 96 44 56 56.

RENTALS The Saint-Brieuc area, Côte de Granit Rose and Ile de Bréhat are more popular for rentals and generate a fair amount of interest from tourists ■ There is a guaranteed rental season from April to September ■ Weekly rental income for a two-bedroom property averages from 293 euros in low season to 450 euros in peak season.

PROS Guingamp is near the stunningly attractive Côtes d'Armor coast ■ Modern Guingamp has a football team in France's first division ■ There is a good demand for property, which is slightly cheaper here than coastal properties.

CONS Guingamp is not an easily accessible area ■ This is not a coastal area, making it less attractive for those seeking to rent property.

7. Golfe du Morbihan

ESSENTIALS ■ **POP** 1999: 32,988, 1990: 27,081 ■ **TAXES** Taxe d'habitation: 18.19%, Taxe foncière: 28.34% ■ **AIRPORT** Rennes Saint-Jacques Airport, avenue Joseph Le Brix, 35136 Saint-Jacques-de-la-Lande, Tel: +33 2 99 29 60 00.

The Gulf of Morbihan in southern Brittany enjoys its own balmy microclimate and is an ideal place for nautical activities, beachcombing or walking along the many kilometres of coastal paths. It is dotted with hundreds of small islands, the largest being Ile aux Moines, which has sub-tropical vegetation and a pretty fishing village. Although many islands are privately owned retreats, you can visit most of the bay by boat. Surrounded by the Gulf's inlets and islands, the historic town of Vannes enjoys a superb location, and has a wealth of exquisitely preserved buildings, particularly its classic half-timbered houses and medieval market square. Sample the main market, held every Wednesday and Saturday, and the Oceonography and Tropical Fish Aquarium, which contains thousands of species from all over the world.

Carnac, an elegant summer resort on the bay of Quiberon, offers low-rise villas and apartments, not unlike the Côte d'Azur. Famed for its megalithic monuments, the town also has a prehistoric museum and delightful pine-fringed beaches. The whole of the Golfe du Morbihan is extremely expensive, especially if you are intending to let your property. This area is dominated by the French market and consequently extremely expensive. A four-bedroom house in the centre of Vannes can be found for 250,000 euros. If you prefer the seclusion of a Golfe du Morbihan village, a one-bedroom country cottage close to the sea can be bought for under 70,000 euros. ■

KEY FACTS

SCHOOLS Contact the Rectorat de l'Académie de Rennes, 96 rue d'Antrain, 35044 Rennes Cedex, Tel: +33 2 99 28 78 78, Fax: +33 2 99 28 77 72 for advice on education.

MEDICAL Centre Hospitalier Bretagne Atlantique, 20 boulevard Gén Maurice Guillaudot, 56000 Vannes, Tel: +33 2 97 01 41 41.

RENTALS This is the most popular area in Brittany with British buyers ■ The warm climate of the Gulf of Morbihan guarantees the buyer the longest rental season in Brittany ■ The region's stunning coastline ensures a strong interest from holidaymakers.

PROS Areas such as Vannes and Carnac are extremely popular ■ This stretch of coastline offers a Mediterranean climate together with a healthy standard of living.

CONS The whole of the Gulf of Morbihan is extremely expensive ■ This is primarily a French market, with the foreign buyers purchasing further inland ■ The coast can become overcrowded in the busy summer months ■ Prices are creeping up almost to Mediterranean levels.

HOTSPOTS

Useful contacts

HOTSPOTS

Brittany is a region dominated by ports, with fishing still a major industry

PREFECTURE
Préfecture de la Région de Bretagne
3 rue Martenot, CS 26517
35065 Rennes Cedex
Tel: +33 2 99 02 10 35
Fax: +33 2 99 02 10 15

LEGAL
Chambre des Notaires d'Ille-et-Vilaine

2 mail Anne-Catherine
CS 54337
35043 Rennes Cedex
Tel: +33 2 99 65 23 24
Fax: +33 2 99 65 23 20

FINANCE
Direction Régionale des Impôts de l'Ouest
6 rue Jean Guéhenno
CS 14208

35042 Rennes Cedex
Tel: +33 2 99 87 18 30
Fax: +33 2 99 63 28 90

BUILDING AND PLANNING
Chambre Régionale des Métiers de Bretagne
2 cours des Alliés
35029 Rennes Cedex
Tel: +33 2 99 65 32 00
Fax: +33 2 99 65 32 59

CAUE du Morbihan
13 bis rue Olivier de Clisson
56000 Vannes
Tel: +33 2 97 54 17 35
Fax: +33 2 97 47 89 52

EDUCATION
Rectorat de l'Académie de Rennes
96 rue d'Antrain
35044 Rennes Cedex

Tel: +33 2 99 28 78 78
Fax: +33 2 99 28 77 72

HEALTH
Caisse Primaire d'Assurance Maladie d'Ille-et-Vilaine
7 cours des Alliés
35000 Rennes
Tel: +33 2 99 29 44 44
Fax: +33 2 99 29 45 74

International Estate Agency

ɒu were looking for a home in Wales, would you look for an estate agency in Brittany ?
No, of course not !

GO DIRECT TO *www.bretonhomes.com*

currently have four agencies in Brittany covering the whole of the Côtes d'Armor and
rdering on Ille et villaine, Finistere and Morbihan. We have around 1,000 properties available
ᵳging from 8,000€ to 1,000,000€. You will not find all of our properties on our web site.
 encourage you to make a reservation directly with any of the agencies shown or simply
ephone : 0033 2 96 50 1800 or e-mail *rendezvous@bretonhomes.com*

What can Breton Homes offer you ?

- Multi-lingual sales negotiators
- Global prices including notaire, agency fees and taxes
- Hand holding service without extra cost
- contacts for French company formations, inheritance advise etc...
- Introduction to management companies, builders, architects etc...

ᵉace du Général de Gaulle	44, rue du Val	1, avenue de la boule d'Or	17bis rue du Lac
ᵼo Plemet	22400 Lamballe	22100 Lanvallay (Dinan)	29690 Huelgoat
ᵱhone:	Telephone:	Telephone:	Telephone:
ᵌ.(0)2.96.66.32.32	00.33.(0)2.96.50.18.00	00.33.(0)2.96.85.98.98	00.33.(0)2.98.99.83.30
ᵃil:	e-mail:	e-mail:	e-mail:
ᵉet@bretonhomes.com	lamballe@bretonhomes.com	dinan@bretonhomes.com	huelgoat@bretonhomes.com

€20-100,000
(£13-66,000)

Brittany has always been a stronghold for bargain hunters, and although restoration projects are becoming increasingly rare, there are still cheap properties available within this price bracket. These properties range from basic shells, to requiring some work ready for habitation.

€13,000   CODE JBF

COSQUER, DÉPARTEMENT 56

A very basic property needing modernisation, and ideal for a holiday home

£8,665

🛏 1   ⬛ 70m^2 🖼 within 5 mins of village   🚫 not located on a main road
🏠 no private parking

€34,300   CODE JBF

COSQUER, DÉPARTEMENT 56

In a rustic setting, a character cottage to renovate in a popular location

£22,855

🛏 2   ⬛ 8,094m^2 🖼 within 10 mins of village   🚫 not located on a main road
🏠 no private parking

€34,440   CODE JBF

BEFFOU, DÉPARTEMENT 22

Requiring renovation, both on the interior and exterior, set in stunning forests

£22,960

🛏 1   ⬛ 500m^2 🖼 within 10 mins of village   🚫 not located on a main road
🏠 room for parking

€45,483   CODE AHB

CÔTES D'ARMOUR, DEPARTMENT 22

A 17th century farmhouse, comprising several buildings, for conversion

£30,322

🛏 n/a   ⬛ with a garden   🖼 very isolated   🚫 not located on a main road
🏠 room for parking

€62,431   CODE LAT

LANMODEZ, DÉPARTEMENT 22

A stone-built house requiring renovation, with an outbuilding to convert

£41,620

🛏2 🏡with a small garden 🖼within 5 mins of amenities 🚫not located on a main road 🚗no private parking

€62,797   CODE AHB

CORLAY, DÉPARTEMENT 22

An attractively situated cottage, ready to renovate, close to countryside

£41,865

🛏3 🏡with a large garden 🖼close to amenities 🚫located on a main road 🚗room for parking, with a garage

€64,630   CODE FRA

LIZIO, DÉPARTEMENT 56

A small stone gîte situated in a small hamlet. Ideal for a holiday home

£43,085

🛏1 🏡with a small front garden 🖼close to town and amenities 🚫not located on a main road 🚗no private parking

€72,032   CODE LAT

LANNION, DÉPARTEMENT 22

A traditional stone cottage, offering stunning views, requiring some renovation

£48,020

🛏1 🏡$3,196m^2$ 🖼close to town and amenities 🚫not located on a main road 🚗room for parking

€93,435   CODE AHB

PORDIC, DÉPARTEMENT 22

A small, secluded fisherman's cottage, located on the coast with great views

£62,290

🛏1 🏡no garden 🖼within 5 mins of village 🚫located by a road 🚗roadside parking

€98,865   CODE JBF

BOTHOA, DÉPARTEMENT 22

An attractive, established property, ideal for a permanent or holiday home

£65,910

🛏3 🏡$6,070m^2$ 🖼within 10 mins of village 🚫not located on a main road 🚗room for parking

PRICE GUIDE

€100-200,000
(£66-133,000)

Demand has increased over the last year and there is a distinct lack of old wrecks to modernise. Within this price bracket expect traditional Breton cottages and farmhouses, mostly requiring work, although some can be found fully habitable.

€106,000 **CODE** GEO

DINARD, DÉPARTEMENT 35

Apartments, with balconies or a terrace, located close to the beach

£70,665

🛏2/5 🌳*with private gardens* 🏙*within 5 mins of town centre* 🚫*not located on a main road* 🅿*room for parking*

€111,440+ **CODE** GEO

SAINT CAST, DÉPARTEMENT 22

A development of 20 apartments, all with views over town and the coast

£74,295

🛏2/5 🌳*no garden* 🏙*300m from town centre* 🚫*not located on a main road* 🅿*room for parking*

€125,400 **CODE** FWY

VILDE LA MARINE, DÉPARTEMENT 35

A small fisherman's house, located close to the bay of Mont-St-Michel

£83,600

🛏2 🏠$600m^2$ 🏙*within 5 mins of village* 🚫*not located on a main road* 🅿*room for parking*

€131,400 **CODE** LAT

DINAN, DÉPARTEMENT 22

This cottage requires some work to make it fully habitable. Ideal for holidays

£87,600

🛏4 🏠$400m^2$ 🏙*within 5 mins of town centre* 🚫*not located on a main road* 🅿*room for parking, with a garage*

€135,000
CODE AHB

MERDRIGNAC, DÉPARTEMENT 22

Located in the central Brittany countryside, a traditional Breton cottage

£90,000

🛏1 🏠1,500m² 🚌15 mins from village 🛣not located on a main road

🅿room for parking

€144,250
CODE FWY

CÔTE DE GRANIT ROSE, DÉPARTEMENT 22

A stone country house dating from the late 19th century, recently renovated

£96,165

🛏3 🏠1,000m² 🚌800m from town 🛣not located on a main road

🅿room for parking

€151,245
CODE FWY

CARHAIX–PLOUGUER, DÉPARTEMENT 29

A stone house with exposed wood-beam interior and an open fireplace

£100,830

🛏3 🏠2,370m² 🚌close to amenities 🛣not located on a main road

🅿room for parking

€190,803
CODE AHB

LAMBALLE, DÉPARTEMENT 22

A traditional Breton farmhouse, with an adjoining gîte and buildings to convert

£127,200

🛏5 🏠1,700m² 🚌within 5 mins of town 🛣not located on a main road

🅿room for parking

€192,048
CODE AHB

JUGON-LES-LACS, DÉPARTEMENT 22

Recently renovated to a high standard, this property is perfect for a family

£128,030

🛏3 🏠with a small garden 🚌within 5 mins of village 🛣located down a quiet rural lane 🅿with nearby parking

€197,510
CODE FWY

ROZ SUR COUESNON, DÉPARTEMENT 35

A cottage with views over the Bay St-Michel, and surrounded by countryside

£131,675

🛏5 🏠8,975m² 🚌within 5 mins of village 🛣not located on a main road

🅿room for parking

PRICE GUIDE

€200-500,000
(£133-333,000)

Those whose budget stretches to 200,000 plus euros can expect to purchase a property with a number of bedrooms and extensive gardens. Expect many old Breton manors and restored farmhouses, and characterful homes, with thatched roofs and landscaped gardens.

€200,000	CODE LAT

LOUANNEC, DÉPARTEMENT 22

A charming stone cottage, in habitable condition, with 116m^2 of living space

£133,335

🛏4 🌳1,012m^2 🏙situated in the centre of town 🚫not located on a main road 🅿room for parking

€200,800	CODE LAT

DINAN, DÉPARTEMENT 22

An 18th century stone farmhouse, with two outbuildings, close to the coast

£133,865

🛏n/a 🌳5,059m^2 🏙close to town and amenities 🚫not located on a main road 🅿room for parking, with a garage

€209,800	CODE LAT

PORDIC, DÉPARTEMENT 22

A restored stone house, full of character, 500 metres from the coast

£139,865

🛏4 🌳with a garden 🏙close to amenities 🚫not located on a main road 🅿room for parking

€213,984	CODE FWY

LE-VIVIER-SUR-MER, DÉPARTEMENT 35

A large property with sea views, offering a 60m^2 living space and outbuilding

£142,655

🛏5 🌳1,600m^2 🏙within 5 mins of village 🚫not located on a main road 🅿room for parking, with a garage

€215,800 CODE LAT

PLERIN-SUR-MER, DÉPARTEMENT 22

A south facing, traditional Breton style house, with a tree-lined garden

£143,865

⊟5 🏠4,047m² 🏫close to amenities 🚫not located on a main road
🚗room for parking

€218,917 CODE JBF

BEFFOU, DÉPARTEMENT 22

This property comprises of two gîtes and three outbuildings, in a rural area

£145,945

⊟4 🏠12,220m² 🏫only 10 mins from village 🚫not located on a main road
🚗room for parking, no garage

€224,967 CODE LAT

DINAN, DÉPARTMENT 22

A stone built, traditional farmhouse, with an attic and outbuildings to convert

£149,980

⊟4 🏠with small garden 🏫close to town's amenities 🚫not located on a main
road 🚗room for parking, with a garage

€224,970 CODE LAT

JUGON-LES-LACS, DÉPARTEMENT 22

A restored, detached stone property, with outbuildings to convert

£149,980

⊟6 🏠9,500m² 🏫in a rural location 🚫not located on a main road
🚗room for parking

€255,240 CODE FWY

SAINT-MELIOR, DÉPARTEMENT 22

A large, habitable property with a veranda and wine cellar, close to beach

£170,160

⊟5 🏠600m² 🏫located in the town centre 🚫not located on a main road
🚗room for parking

€268,700 CODE LAT

DINAN, DÉPARTEMENT 22

A tastefully renovated 19th century country house, with original features

£179,135

⊟4 🏠1,012m² 🏫close to town and amenities 🚫not located on a main road
🚗room for parking, with a double garage

PRICE GUIDE

€288,128   CODE LAT

RENNES, DÉPARTEMENT 35

A unique thatched cottage, in excellent condition, plus a separate house

£192,085

🛏5 🏠10,120m² 🚶within easy distance of town 🚫not located on a main road 🅿room for parking, with a garage

€313,200   CODE AHB

CONCARNEAU, DÉPARTEMENT 29

A thatched cottage, with a newly fitted kitchen, and glorious sea views

£208,800

🛏3 🏠1,500m² 🚶within walking distance of village 🚫not located on a main road 🅿room for parking

€319,000   CODE LAT

LE FOEIL, DÉPARTEMENT 22

An 18th century stone property, with a stone outbuilding, ideal for a gîte

£212,665

🛏3 🏠6,070m² 🚶close to amenities 🚫not located on a main road 🅿room for parking, with a garage

€320,145   CODE LAT

ROCHEFORT-EN-TERRE, DÉPARTEMENT 56

An 18th century village house, stone built, located in the centre of town

£213,430

🛏7 🏠4,047m² 🚶located in town centre, close to amenities 🚫not located on a main road 🅿room for parking

€350,600   CODE LAT

SAINT BRIEUC, DÉPARTEMENT 22

This manor, close to the coast, maintains all its original features. To restore

£233,733

🛏6 🏠5,059m² 🚶within 5 mins of village 🚫not located on a main road 🅿room for parking

€358,600   CODE FRA

PLUMELEC, DÉPARTEMENT 56

A beautiful house with mature, landscaped gardens, close to the coast

£239,065

🛏5 🏠5,690m² 🚶near town and amenities 🚫not located on a main road 🅿room for parking

€358,676   CODE FRA

LE GUILDO, DÉPARTEMENT 22

This property comprises of two dwellings and is surrounded by woodland

£239,115

🛏4   📐845m²   🏘within 20 mins of village   🚫not located on a main road

🅿room for parking

€396,367   CODE DEE

LANNION, DÉPARTEMENT 22

A 16th century Breton manor, close to the coast, and ready for habitation

£264,245

🛏3   📐35,000m²   🏘located 9.5kms from town   🚫not located on a main road

🅿room for parking

€399,000   CODE LAT

PLESTIN-LES-GREVES, DÉPARTEMENT 22

A tastefully renovated house dating from 1663, within easy reach of the sea

£266,000

🛏4   📐5,500m²   🏘within easy reach of town   🚫not located on a main road

🅿with a double garage

€428,077   CODE LAT

VANNES, DÉPARTEMENT 56

A 17th century mill house, habitable, with a heated pool and a guest house

£285,385

🛏3   📐24,280m²   🏘within easy reach of town   🚫not located on a main road

🅿room for parking

€440,840   CODE LAT

SAINT BRIEUC, DÉPARTEMENT 22

This manor, close to the coast, maintains all its original features. To restore

£233,733

🛏6   📐5,059m²   🏘within 5 mins of village   🚫not located on a main road

🅿room for parking

€493,935   CODE LAT

RENNES, DÉPARTEMENT 56

A modern house, with a pond and landscaped gardens, in a peaceful location

£329,290

🛏6   📐12,140m²   🏘close to amenities   🚫not located on a main road

🅿room for parking, with a double garage

PRICE GUIDE

€500,000+
(£333,000+)

Ample coastal properties and traditional style Breton mansions are not cheap, especially on the Gulf of Morbihan, so expect to pay 500,000 euros for such a property. Luxuriously restored châteaux and manors built from Breton stone, are readily available within this price bracket.

€510,399　　　　　　　　　　　　　**CODE** LAT

LANNION, DÉPARTEMENT 22

A stone farmhouse, 10kms from the coast with sea views, residing in parkland

£340,265

🛏5 　📐30,350m² 　🖼close to amenities 　🛣not located on a main road
🏠room for parking, with a garage

€527,159　　　　　　　　　　　　　**CODE** LAT

JOSSELIN, DÉPARTEMENT 56

This 17th century stone manor, situated in rural, wooded surroundings

£351,440

🛏5 　📐4,047m² 　🖼in a rural location 　🛣not located on a main road
🏠room for parking

€540,112　　　　　　　　　　　　　**CODE** AAA

TREVIGNON, DÉPARTEMENT 29

This property is only 100 metres from the beach, situated in a protected area

£360,075

🛏6 　📐800m² 　🖼close to amenities 　🛣not located on a main road
🏠room for parking, with a garage for four cars

€576,257　　　　　　　　　　　　　**CODE** LAT

SAINT BRIEUC, DÉPARTEMENT 22

A restored 16th century manor, with extensive outbuildings to convert

£384,170

🛏5 　📐30,350m² 　🖼within easy reach of town 　🛣not located on a main road
🏠room for parking, with a two-car garage

€579,306
CODE LAT

MORLAIX, DÉPARTEMENT 29

A delightful 19th century château with many original features, and sea views

£252,870

🛏8 ⬜10,120m^2 ⬜near town and amenities ⬜not located on a main road ⬜room for parking

€652,000
CODE LAT

LORIENT, DÉPARTEMENT 56

Two beautiful stone houses in excellent condition, and outbuildings to convert

£434,665

🛏4 ⬜141,600m^2 ⬜close to amenities ⬜not located on a main road ⬜room for parking

€686,000
CODE LAT

RENNES, DÉPARTEMENT 35

A 19th century manor house, featuring outbuildings and a heated pool

£457,335

🛏5 ⬜10,120m^2 ⬜close to the amenities of town ⬜not located on a main road ⬜room for parking

€721,722
CODE BUY

LANNION, DÉPARTEMENT 22

A traditional 16th century French property, with 900m^2 of living space

£481,150

🛏- ⬜70,000m^2 ⬜4 kms from amenities ⬜not located on a main road ⬜room for parking

€733,000
CODE LAT

GUINGAMP, DÉPARTEMENT 22

A 17th century manor, with a guest cottage, only five minutes from the coast

£488,665

🛏5 ⬜20,230m^2 ⬜close to amenities ⬜not located on a main road ⬜room for parking, with a garage

€807,980
CODE LAT

CÔTE D'ÉMERAUDE, DÉPARTEMENT 35

A renovated water mill, with a lake, offering a second house and apartments

£538,655

🛏11 ⬜101,200m^2 ⬜close to amenities ⬜not located on a main road ⬜room for parking

PRICE GUIDE

Peaceful and pastoral
Clean sandy beaches
Endless countryside

Normandy

Profile 82
Hotspots 84

PRICE GUIDE

€50,000-€100,000 90
€100,000-€200,000 92
€200,000-€500,000 94
€500,000+ 96

Normandy Profile

Getting there

AIR There is only one airline that flies directly from the UK into Normandy, and if you are planning on flying you have to go via Paris or into neighbouring Brittany. **Air France** (0845 359 1000; www.airfrance.co.uk) flies directly from Heathrow into Caen airport, while Caen's **Carpiquet** airport (Tel: +33 2 31 71 20 10) and Cherbourg's **Maupertus** (Tel: +33 233 88 57 60) handle domestic and some international flights. The closest airport outside of Normandy is **Dinard** (Tel: +33 2 99 46 18 46) which receives numerous flights from the UK.

SEA Normandy has four ferry ports: Cherbourg, Dieppe, Le Havre and Caen. **Brittany Ferries** (0870 366 5333; www.brittanyferries.co.uk) sails to Caen-Ouistreham from Portsmouth and from Poole to Cherbourg. **Transmanche Ferries** (0800 917 1201; www.transmancheferries.com) operates from Newhaven to Dieppe, while **Hoverspeed** (0870 240 8070; www.hoverspeed.co.uk) sails from Newhaven to Dieppe, and from Portsmouth to Le Havre. Services from Portsmouth to Le Havre and Cherbourg are operated by **P&O** (0870 520 2020; www.poportsmouth.com).

ROAD The A28/29 offers quick and direct access from Calais to the whole of Normandy, joining up to the A13 motorway, which runs west through Caen, and ends in Paris. The A16 runs from Calais to Rouen, while the D100 runs down the Manche peninsula to Avranches. Main roads link the ports of Dieppe, Le Havre, Caen and Cherbourg, but beyond this, the road networks are limited and travelling around Normandy can be difficult.

COACH Eurolines (0870 514 3219; www.eurolines.com) operates coaches from the UK to Caen, Cherbourg, Dieppe and Rouen.

RAIL The **TGV** rail network runs throughout Normandy linking Cherbourg, Bayeux, Caen, Evreux, Le Havre and Rouen, then continuing to Paris. The **Eurostar** (0870 518 6186; www.eurostar.com) arrives at Lille Europe train station, and from there **TGV** services operate to Rouen. **Rail Europe** (0870 584 8848; www.raileurope.co.uk) offers details on all services throughout Normandy. From Gare Saint-Lazare in Paris there are trains to Le Havre, Dieppe, Caen, Rouen, Cherbourg and Bayeux.

ECONOMY

Normandy is the land of the *bocage*, of farmlands, hedgerows and enclosed fields that are often compared to the countryside of southern England. Normandy prospers from its production of meat, milk, butter, cheese and cider apples, with 45 percent of Upper Normandy and 30 percent of Lower Normandy given over to arable land. The coastline boasts more than 50 ports, and the region is renowned for its cuisine, producing many speciality seafood dishes. The dairy industry has suffered of late at the hands of EU regulations, with many small dairy farms being forced to close, impacting on much of inland Normandy. Recent years have seen diversification into light industry and agri-foodstuffs, while Upper Normandy specialises in petro-chemicals and car manufacturing.

BEST/WORST VALUE FOR MONEY

Deauville and Trouville are both expensive, with wealthy Parisians driving prices up, which keeps British interest low. The best bargains can be found in the Orne department, where towns and cities, relatively undiscovered by the foreign market, offer cheap property. The areas near Rouen and Caen experience high prices, trading primarily to the French market, and high rates of turnover make property a good investment. The Manche peninsula yields a glut of affordable properties, with attractive countryside, proximity to the sea and a buoyant rental market. The area around Dieppe makes for a good rental investment, offering affordable property and excellent access routes.

With visually striking architecture, Rouen merges tradition with modernity

Normandy has long been a favourite with the British buyer, offering something for everyone

The coastline of Mont-St-Michel has long been popular with the foreign buyer

WHERE TO GO FOR WHAT

Normandy has long been a favourite destination of the British buyer, and it continues to offer something for everyone. Glamorous and glitzy resorts can be found in Deauville, Trouville and Honfleur, while the Manche peninsula offers traditionally French family resorts. Normandy is popular with commuters who live in France and work in the UK or own weekend homes here, aided by the convenience and ease of the transport system centred around Cherbourg, Dieppe and Caen. Avranches in the Manche peninsula is the ideal location for a family home, being close to the sea, affordable and surrounded by countryside.

PROPERTY PRICE TRENDS

In recent years, Normandy has mopped up the overflow of property seekers from neighbouring Brittany and has begun experiencing some market saturation. Overseas buyers who previously sought to buy in Brittany have been targeting Normandy because of its easy access and abundance of cheap property.

Two-thirds of foreign buyers are British, with concentrations previously centred around the expensive port resorts, though higher prices have driven many property seekers inland. The closer you get to Paris, the steeper the prices, and cheaper areas such as Orne have seen a resultant explosion of interest and prices.

The Seine-Maritime attracts high demand from London buyers, as commuters seek easy access to the UK. Although property prices are more expensive than in Brittany and have risen by 9.9 percent since last year, they are significantly lower than in London. Expected to rise by 20 percent over the next few years as demand continues, this should make cheap properties increasingly rare.

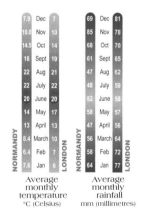

NORMANDY		LONDON	
7.9	Dec	7	
10.8	Nov	10	
14.5	Oct	14	
18	Sept	19	
22	Aug	21	
22	July	22	
20	June	20	
14	May	17	
13	April	13	
8.4	March	10	
6.4	Feb	7	
7.6	Jan	6	

Average monthly temperature
°C (Celsius)

NORMANDY		LONDON	
69	Dec	81	
85	Nov	78	
68	Oct	70	
61	Sept	65	
47	Aug	62	
48	July	59	
52	June	58	
58	May	57	
47	April	56	
56	March	64	
58	Feb	72	
64	Jan	77	

Average monthly rainfall
mm (millimetres)

Average House Sale Prices

HOTSPOT	2-BED	3-BED	4-BED	5-BED	6/7-BED	8-BED
Avranches	€75K (£50K)	€98K (£65K)	€113K (£75K)	€215K (£143K)	€225K (£149K)	€240K (£160K)
Caen	€113K (75K)	€128K (£85K)	€165K (£110K)	€210K (£140K)	€300K (£200K)	€375K (£250K)
Dieppe	-	-	-	-	-	-
Deauville/Trouville	€120K (£80K)	€135K (£90K)	€189K (£125K)	€233K (£155K)	€315K (£210K)	€450K (£300K)
Honfleur	-	-	-	-	-	-
Inland Calvados	€95K (£63K)	€257K (£171K)	€253K (£168K)	€450K (£300K)	€450K (£300K)	€543K (£362K)
Rouen	€113K (75K)	€128K (£85K)	€165K (£110K)	€210K (£140K)	€300K (£200K)	€375K (£250K)

Normandy Hotspots

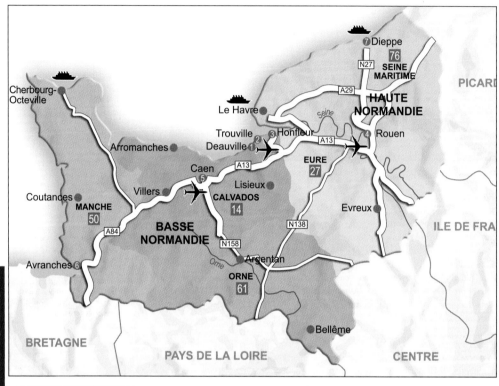

1. Deauville

ESSENTIALS ■ **POP** 1990: -, 1999: 4,300 ■ **TAXES** Taxe d'habitation: 11.99%, Taxe foncière: 32.90% ■ **AIRPORT** Aéroport de Deauville Saint Gatien, 14130 Saint-Gatien-des-Bois, Tel: +33 2 31 65 65 65, Fax: +33 2 31 65 46 46.

KEY FACTS

SCHOOLS Contact the Rectorat de l'Académie de Caen, 168 rue Caponière, BP 6184, 14061 Caen Cedex, Tel: +33 2 31 30 15 00, Fax: +33 23 10 15 92, for advice on education in the region.

MEDICAL Hôpital de Trouville, 20 rue Soeurs Hôpital, 14360 Trouville-sur-Mer, +33 2 31 81 84 84

RENTALS In such an expensive area it is difficult to make your money back through rentals ■ The British are reluctant to pay the high prices charged for apartments and villas, but the French market is more willing to pay a premium ■ Some two-bedroom properties can command prices from 675 up to 1425 euros in peak season ■ Châteaux in the resort can cost up to 3,300 euros per week.

PROS Located on the Côte Fleurie, Deauville is known as the 'Cannes of the North' and the 'Riviera of Normandy' ■ Deauville's own airport makes it easily accessible and the port of Caen is nearby.

CONS A slightly pretentious resort which is extortionately expensive, commanding prices on a level with the Cote d'Azur ■ This is primarily a market flooded by the French ■ There is an immensely rapid turnover of property.

Close to Paris and known as the '21st arrondissement', fashionable Deauville attracts the affluent weekend crowd and Parisian purchasing power has caused prices to soar. Frequented by film stars, millionaires and royals alike, this resort is full of glamour and glitz. With a picturesque port, wide sandy beaches and historic wooden walkways like the Promenade des Planches, Deauville is an authentically preserved village of Norman half-timbered architecture. Each year Deauville plays host to the International Festival of American Cinema, and the seafront is lined with Victorian-style beach huts named after Hollywood movie stars, past and present. There is also a casino and golf course, and the race track is one of the town's social hubs. Another must-see is the Wednesday to Saturday market, selling a wide range of regional specialities including seafood, cheeses, cider and calvados. A 10-minute drive inland from Deauville will take you into the Calvados region, where some of the most beautiful countryside in this part of Normandy is to be found.

Deauville's coastal situation pushes property prices up, because of the sea views. If you seek a sea view, expect to pay at least 170,000 euros for a one-bedroom apartment with waterfront aspect compared to prices of around 73,000 euros for an attractive property of similar size in the town's backstreets. A family-sized home, such as a thatched cottage just two minutes from the centre, will cost around 390,000 euros. ■

2. Trouville

ESSENTIALS ■ **POP** 1990: -, 1999: 5,600 ■ **TAXES** Taxe d'habitation: 15.28%, Taxe foncière: 41.61% ■ **AIRPORT**
Aéroport de Deauville Saint Gatien, 14130 Saint-Gatien-Des-Bois, Tel: +33 231 65 65 65, Fax: +33 2 31 65 46 46.

Separated from its 'twin' resort Deauville by the estuary of the river Touques, the fishing port of Trouville can be reached in five minutes by ferryboat. A smart, but more modest relation in terms of the glamour and social calander of the season, Trouville is arguably more authentic and family-friendly, and has a native population that makes it livelier out of season. It has an excellent beach, sports facilities, fish market and Planche promenade. Other interesting places to visit include its Napoleon III extravagant casino, Aquarium Vivarium de Trouville and Villa Montebello, Napoleon's old summer residence which holds regular art exhibitions.

British and Norman history have long been interwoven, and it was the British in the 19th century, along with painters such as Turner who first made the Normandy coast fashionable. These were followed by great French painters from Delacroix to the Impressionists and the Fauves, whose love of the clear light of the coast inspired many wonderful seascapes.

The love affair continues, but these days the British are reluctant to pay the average price tag of £150,000 to gain a foothold in Trouville – this includes the area's premium. As property here is sold essentially to the French market – the area is popular with people who commute to Caen, Paris and Rennes - it carries a premium. But you can still find a newly-built, three-bedroom home in the Trouville environs starting at 138,000 euros, or a two-bedroom *maison de pêcheur* (fisherman's cottage) for renovation at around 80,000 euros. ■

KEY FACTS

SCHOOLS Contact the Rectorat de l'Académie de Caen, 168 rue Caponière, BP 6184, 14061 Caen Cedex; Tel: +33 231 30 15 00, Fax: +33 231 30 15 92, for advice on education in the region.
MEDICAL Hôpital de Trouville, 20 rue Soeurs Hôpital, 14360 Trouville-sur-Mer, +33 2 31 81 84 84
RENTALS Trouville, as Deauville, is servicing the French rental market ■ Rental demand comes from Parisians and the cities of Caen and Rennes ■ The British are unwilling to pay the high rental prices the area commands.
PROS Selling property to the native market should be easy in this popular resort ■ A typical French resort, Trouville has a lovely beach and down-to-earth diversions ■ Located next to the glamorous Deauville, Trouville is considered much less pretentious than Deauville.
CONS Trouville property is expensive and carries a premium ■ The area is frequented by people commuting to Caen, Paris and Rennes ■ Despite the exclusive nature of the area, some describe this area as unmemorable and pretentious.

3. Honfleur

ESSENTIALS ■ **POP** 1990: -, 1999: 8,400 ■ **TAXES** Taxe d'habitation 14.17%, Taxe foncière 35.64% ■ **AIRPORT**
Caen Airport, Aéroport de Caen, Carpiquet, 14000 Caen, Tel: +33 2 31 71 20 10.

Honfleur's charms are hard to resist, as it remains picturesque with an unspoilt ambiance, while continuing to be a busy, working port. The Vieux Bassin or inner harbour is the hub, frequented these days by fishermen, yacht owners, painters and tourists rather than the explorers and corsairs of yesteryear. The tall, irregular houses flanking the harbour, house bars, eateries, antique shops and galleries which become crowded in season. Nearby is a museum charting Honfleur's seafaring history and way of life.

Miraculously still standing in the market square is the Eglise Sainte-Catherine, the 'temporary' Gothic church built of oak by shipwrights, too impatient to wait for the stonemasons busy with post-war reconstruction, to celebrate the departure of the English at the end of their occupation of Honfleur during the Hundred Years' War. The original farm (Ferme Saint-Siméon) where local artist Boudin and friends met to drink cider, and later formed the Impressionist movement, is now a very expensive hotel, and the Boudin museum displays some of the fine paintings and pastels from the period. The Pont de Normandie makes Honfleur easy to access from the ferryport of Le Havre. Many consider Honfleur the most attractive port in Normandy and one of the most popular spots in northern France. Along with other old ports like Étretat and Fécamp, Honfleur has long been a favourite with Parisians looking for properties to buy for their weekend breaks on the coast. Commuters from Caen and Rennes have also driven prices up. ■

KEY FACTS

SCHOOLS Contact the Rectorat de l'Académie de Caen, 168 rue Caponière, BP 6184, 14061 Caen Cedex, Tel: +33 2 31 30 15 00, Fax: +33 2 31 30 15 92, for advice on education in the region.
MEDICAL Centre Hospitalier de La Plane-Equemauville, 14600 Honfleur, Tel: +33 2 31 89 89 89, Fax: +33 2 31 89 88 81.
RENTALS One of the most popular resorts on the Calvados coastline ■ Honfleur and surrounding area are excellent for property lets ■ Particularly popular with Parisian daytrippers, Honfleur has huge local rental potential ■ The average price for a three-bedroom rental property is 300-700 euros ■ The rental season is active year round, particularly from April to September.
PROS Honfleur has become increasingly upmarket in recent years ■ Located close to Le Havre, the area is easily accessible ■ Although it is very popular with tourists, Honfleur retains its quaint and tranquil air.
CONS Honfleur is an attractive coastal resort but lacks a beach ■ There is relatively little economic prosperity ■ Commuters from Paris, Caen and Rennes have flooded the market and driven up prices.

Normandy Hotspots

4. Rouen

ESSENTIALS ▥ **POP** 1990: - 1999: 102,000 ▥ **TAXES** Taxe d'habitation 25.59%, Taxe foncière 37.21% ▥ **AIRPORT**
Aéroport Rouen, Vallée de Seine, 76520 Boos, Tel: +33 2 35 79 41 00.

KEY FACTS

SCHOOLS Contact the Rectorat de l'Académie de Rouen, 25 rue de Fontenelle, 76037 Rouen, Cedex, Tel: +33 2 35 14 75 00, Fax: +33 2 35 71 56 38 for advice on education.

MEDICAL Rouen University Hospital, 1 rue Germont, 76000 Rouen, Tel: +33 2 32 88 89 90.

RENTALS Rouen is not a major holiday rentals centre, tending to concentrate more on industry than tourism, however there is a market for long-term lets. ▥ In Rouen's old town, rental property can cost from 341 to 639 euros between September and January.

PROS A diverse and cultured city, Rouen combines industry and trade with a rich historical tradition. ▥ Offering a number of museums and churches, the tour-de-force is beyond doubt Notre-Dame cathedral. ▥ The majority of Rouen's streets are modern and sophisticated. ▥ As Rouen is a large city, there is an abundance of services and attractions.

CONS Once in the city, away from the countryside, property prices increase ▥ Once you leave the charming inner *quartier*, you come upon the sprawling industrial and dockyard areas ▥ Rouen is an area covered only by French estate agents, who often have scant experience of dealing with foreign buyers.

Capital of the Seine-Maritime *département* and France's fifth largest port, Rouen has a vivid cultural and architectural heritage and yet is expensive and densely populated, serving as a catchment area for Parisians who commute 30-40 kilometres to work. It is located at the crossroads of autoroutes A15, A28, A13 and Route Nationales 31 and 14. Like Paris, the city is laid out along the Seine, with a Rive Droite and a Rive Gauche. The old city, on the Right Bank, has been called the 'museum town' as it numbers 700 beamed, timber-framed medieval houses along its narrow pedestrian streets, many made of brick and wood, and decorated with statues. Other attractions include the Gothic cathedral, Archbishop's Palace and the tower where Joan of Arc was kept prisoner. Art lovers can savour the Flaubert Museum, and the Museum of Fine Arts and Ceramics which holds a collection of 17th to 18th-century French-European paintings by Caravaggio and Monet, along with porcelain and *faïence* from the 16th to 18th century. The city is excellent for shopping, with plenty of cafés, although the climate can be rainy.

Central Rouen is very expensive, but once you move out of town into the countryside, property prices decrease. Dominated by the French market, local estate agents are reluctant to deal with foreign buyers. Types of properties include the traditional Norman beamed houses' with velux windows and exposed beams, and the *maison de maitre* built in the classical colonial style by skilled artisans for a wealthy owner. A standard four-bedroom home with a garden can cost from 195,000 euros. ■

5. Caen

ESSENTIALS ▥ **POP** 1990: -, 1999: 200,000 ▥ **TAXES** Taxe d'habitation 21.52%, Taxe foncière 44.73% ▥ **AIRPORT**
Caen Airport, Aéroport de Caen Carpiquet, 14000 Caen, Tel: +33 2 31 71 20 10.

KEY FACTS

SCHOOLS Contact the Rectorat de l'Académie de Caen, 168 rue Caponière, BP 6184, 14061 Caen Cedex, Tel: +33 231 30 15 00, Fax: +33 231 30 15 92 for advice on education.

MEDICAL Central Hospital Caen, av Côte de Nacre, 14000 Caen, Tel: +33 2 31 06 31 06.

RENTALS Rental prices in the city are much higher than in the surrounding countryside ▥ Large cities such as Caen tend to attract long-term rentals rather than short-term ones ▥ Demand for rentals in the city comes from the local market.

PROS Caen is a dynamic and pleasant city ▥ Easily accessible from the UK, Caen has its own port and airport ▥ A bustling university city with many amenities and attractions, there is plenty to do ▥ Ideal for a buyer who seeks a vibrant metropolis.

CONS You may have to learn French to live and work here, as this is not a predominantly international town ▥ As ever, proximity to, or location in a city, drives property prices up.

Caen is a history lover's dream, with its roots dating back to the relic of William the Conqueror, whose femur is held in the Abbaye aux Hommes. Caen was heavily bombed during World War II, hence concrete buildings mingle with the 16th-century architecture. Learn more about the D-Day landings at the Caen Memorial, a museum dedicated to World War II, with a number of documentaries to view. Rekindle the spirit of the Norman conquest at the ramparts of Caen castle - built by William in his early days as Duke of Normandy and one of Europe's biggest - which also houses a fine art museum. William's consort, Mathilde, lies in the church of the Abbaye-aux-Dames, to the town's east, a building with an ornate deep blue and purple stained-glass window.

The surrounding lush landscape produces celebrated cheeses like Livarot, Pont L'Evêque and Camembert, and Caen's proximity to the coastline ensures a ready supply of top-class seafood. This is also the place to live if you prefer the quiet life. Caen's beaches may not possess the glitz of the Côte d'Azur, but they offer instead an unhurried lifestyle, with scenic charm. Turn north up Rue Froide and into Rue Saint-Sauveur, where a huge market is held on Fridays. The Rue Froide and Caen's centre offers many Parisian department stores.

Property in Caen has a quick turnover and is primarily dominated by the local French market. A large three-bedroom house just 10 minutes from Caen with swimming pool commands 470,000 euros. ■

6. Avranches

ESSENTIALS ■ **POP** 1990: -, 1999: 10,000 ■ **TAXES** Taxe d'habitation: 30.76%, Taxe foncière: 44.51% ■ **AIRPORT** Aéroport de Caen Carpiquet, 14000 Caen, Tel: +33 2 31 71 20 10.

Avranches is a small, rural town with tourist appeal, situated on a wooded hill in the La Manche *département* of Normandy, close to Mont-Saint-Michel and near the border with Brittany. A historically important, busy town, it serves as a convenient base for visits to the D-Day beaches, and the city of Bayeux is just one hour away. There are regular traditional *fêtes*, a Saturday market and daily local markets in the surrounding area, even on Sundays. The town commands fine views westward of the bay and rock of Mont-Saint-Michel, which has the highest tides in Europe, and is renowned as a World Heritage site. It is also France's second most popular tourist attraction after the Eiffel Tower. Avranches itself is surrounded by avenues which trace the ancient ramparts and secreted within is a secluded botanical garden.

There is a highly active British property market and presence in and around Avranches, and the prices are relatively cheap compared to the Calvados area and more industrial region of Upper Normandy. A four-bedroom, three-storey house with kitchen and bathroom, located in central Avranches starts at 127,000 euros. If you are looking for a property to restore, a small farmhouse built in traditional style from stone, and with a slate roof and an old well begins at around 102,500 euros. The market has remained constantly busy for the past decade and most British prefer to buy than rent as prices are so affordable. Many purchasers set out to buy-to-let, but fail to realise the full extent of renovating an outbuilding to convert to a gîte, and fall in love with their property, preferring not to share it. ■

KEY FACTS

SCHOOLS Contact the Rectorat de l'Académie de Rennes, 96 rue d'Antrain, 35044 Rennes, Cedex, Tel: +33 2 99 28 78 78, Fax: +33 2 99 28 77 72 for advice on education.

MEDICAL Centre Hospitalier Avranches-Granville, 59 rue Liberté, 50300 Avranches, Tel: +33 2 33 89 40 20, Fax: +33 2 33 89 41 25.

RENTALS Avranches is located in an extremely active tourist area, with a buoyant holiday rental market ■ Many holidaymakers are drawn to this area due to its proximity to Mont-Saint-Michel ■ The long-term rental market is cheap but properties tend to be shabby and not geared towards the foreign holiday market ■ The short-term holiday rentals market is booming between April and September.

PROS Well located - the port of Cherbourg is at the top of the Manche peninsula and close to the sea ■ This is an excellent location for purchasing a property ■ There is a highly active foreign community ■ An excellent, sunny climate.

CONS Most people buy between 10 and 20 miles away from Avranches where prices match the average £60,000 that the British are prepared to pay ■ Avranches itself is very expensive.

7. Dieppe

ESSENTIALS ■ **POP** 1990: -, 1999: 36,000 ■ **TAXES** Taxe d'habitation 24.13%, Taxe foncière 57.08% ■ **AIRPORT** Aéroport de Caen Carpiquet, 14000 Caen, Tel: +33 2 31 71 20 10.

Dieppe, France's first seaside resort, has undergone a transformation in recent years. The port has shaken off its reputation as a visual eyesore, the ugly terminal buildings having been replaced by a breezy promenade. The sea front is now set back from the shore, creating space for an expanse of lawns, waterside restaurants and family play areas nearly two kilometres long. Dieppe has long enjoyed its status as a destination for writers, musicians and painters. Visit the Café des Tribunaux, the favourite haunt of Renoir, Monet, Guy de Maupassant and Oscar Wilde. While in exile from England, Wilde came here to write his *Ballad of Reading Gaol*.

High on a cliff, the castle museum contains a collection of exhibits reflecting Dieppe's maritime history, including ivory sculptures carved by local sailors, dating from the 16th century, and it also displays paintings by Picasso. There are plenty of *fêtes* throughout the year, including a kite festival and the Festival of the Flowers. Out of town, you can see the birthplace of Guy de Maupassant at the Château de Miromesnil.

There is fair British interest in Dieppe due to the ease of access to it from the UK. The average property price is 60,000 euros for this area, which is the average budget of the British buyer. In recent years interest has waned in the Dieppe area as the Normandy Riviera in Calvados and the Manche peninsula have developed. A traditional Louis XIII Norman manor house within 30 minutes of Dieppe can be found for approximately 500,000 euros. ■

KEY FACTS

SCHOOLS Rectorat de l'Académie de Rouen, 25 rue de Fontenelle, 76037 Rouen, Cedex; Tel: +33 2 35 14 75 00, Fax: +33 2 35 71 56 38.

MEDICAL Hospitalier de Dieppe, av Pasteur, 76200 Dieppe, Tel:+33 2 32 14 76 76.

RENTALS This is less of a holiday centre than it used to be ■ Prices are expensive compared to the Lower Normandy area ■ Foreign holidaymakers do not desire to rent a property in Dieppe.

PROS Dieppe used to be a thriving seaside resort for the French and English in the 19th century, and it retains much of its authentic charm today ■ Dieppe is still an interesting and attractive place to visit, and is highly accessible ■ Dieppe offers many attractions both modern and historical ■ It is more welcoming than many of the neighbouring towns along the Seine-Maritime coast.

CONS Dieppe is very expensive, and most people buy cheaper property 20 minutes out of town ■ This town is less of a tourist resort than a thriving industrial and commercial port.

Useful contacts

The port of Honfleur has become a haunt for the upwardly mobile and Parisian second home buyer

PREFECTURE
Préfecture de la Région
Basse-Normandie
rue Saint-Laurent
14038 Caen Cedex
Tel: +33 2 31 30 64 00
Fax: +33 2 31 30 64 90

Préfecture de la Région
Haute-Normandie
7 place de la Madeleine
76036 Rouen Cedex
Tel: +33 2 32 76 50 00
Fax: +33 2 35 98 10 50

LEGAL
Chambre des Notaires
du Calvados
6 place Louis Guillouard
14000 Caen
Tel: +33 2 31 85 42 21

Fax: +33 2 31 85 82 62

Chambre des Notaires
de la Seine-Maritime
39 rue du Champ des Oiseaux
BP 248
76000 Rouen
Tel: +33 2 35 88 63 88
Fax: +33 2 35 98 70 61

FINANCE
Direction des Impôts du Nord
13–15 boulevard de la Liberté
59800 Lille
Tel: +33 3 20 17 64 90
Fax: +33 3 20 17 64 99

Direction des Impôts de
l'Ouest
6 rue Jean Guéhenno,
CS 14208

35042 Rennes Cedex
Tel: +33 2 99 87 18 30
Fax: +33 2 99 63 28 90

BUILDING & PLANNING
Chambre Régionale de
Métiers de Basse-Normandie
BP 5205
14074 Caen 5 Cedex
Tel: +33 2 31 95 42 00
Fax: +33 2 31 95 99 30

Chambre Régionale de
Métiers de Haute-Normandie
5–9 avenue de Caen
BP 1154
76176 Rouen Cedex
Tel: +33 2 32 18 06 40
Fax: +33 2 32 18 06 49

CAUE du Calvados

28 rue Jean Eudes
14000 Caen
Tel: +33 2 31 15 59 60
Fax: +33 2 31 15 59 65

CAUE de Seine-Maritime
5 rue Louis Blanc
BP 1283
76178 Rouen
Tel: +33 2 35 72 94 50
Fax: +33 2 35 72 09 72

EDUCATION
Rectorat de l'Académie
de Caen
168 rue Caponière
BP 6184
14061 Caen Cedex
Tel: +33 2 31 30 15 00
Fax: +33 2 31 30 15 92

Rectorat de l'Académie
de Rouen
25 rue de Fontenelle
76037 Rouen Cedex
Tel: +33 2 35 14 75 00
Fax: +33 2 35 71 56 38

HEALTH
Caisse Primaire d'Assurance
Maladie du Calvados, BP6048
boulevard Général Weygand
14031 Caen Cedex 4
Tel: +33 2 31 45 79 00
Fax: +33 2 31 45 79 80

Caisse Primaire d'Assurance
Maladie de Rouen
50 avenue Bretagne
76039 Rouen
Tel: +33 2 35 03 63 63
Fax: +33 2 35 03 63 03

€50–100,000
(£33–66,000)

Normandy has always been regarded as one of France's cheapest property markets, and there is an array of real estate available for under 100,000 euros. However, as the market becomes increasingly saturated, the once abundant renovation properties are becoming scarce, having been snapped up. Consequently, now is the time to invest.

€58,900 **CODE** IMO

TROUVILLE, DÉPARTEMENT 14

A studio apartment, overlooking the harbour, with 19.8m^2 of living space

£39,265

🛏1 🌳*no garden* 📷*within 5 mins of village* 🛣*located on a main road* 🅿*room for parking*

€63,878 **CODE** GEO

PORT AUDEMER, DÉPARTEMENT 27

A luxury block of flats, with a balcony and well-manicured private gardens

£42,585

🛏2/3 🌳*private gardens* 📷*within 5 mins of town centre* 🛣*not located on a main road* 🅿*room for parking*

€70,787 **CODE** GEO

ELBEUF, DÉPARTEMENT 76

A modern, newly-built development of flats overlooking the Seine river

£47,190

🛏2/5 🌳*no garden, with balcony* 📷*within a short walk of the town centre* 🛣*located on a main road* 🅿*room for parking*

€77,553 **CODE** JBF

VILLEDIEU, DÉPARTEMENT 61

A detached stone and slate property to renovate, set in rural surroundings

£51,700

🛏3 🌳8,660m^2 📷*10 mins from village* 🛣*not located on a main road* 🅿*room for parking, no garage*

€86,200 CODE FWY

DOMFRONT, DÉPARTEMENT 60

A large, traditional-style chalet, located close to many attractions and village

£57,465

🛏5/6 📐2,000m² within 5 mins of village not located on a main road
room for parking, with a garage for 3 cars

€89,000 CODE FWY

LE-MONT-ST-MICHEL, DÉPARTEMENT 50

A small farm to restore with lovely landscape views, close to a village

£59,335

🛏5/6 📐3,000m² within 5 mins of village not located on a main road
room for parking and to construct a garage

€95,060 CODE GEO

LE HAVRE, DÉPARTEMENT 76

Luxury flats with between two and five rooms, offering splendid harbour views

£63,375

🛏2/5 📐2,000m² near the town centre not located on a main road
with underground parking

€95,280 CODE FWY

CAROLLES, DÉPARTEMENT 50

Two stone houses with panoramic views requiring renovation

£63,520

🛏n/a with garden within 10 mins of village not located on a main road
room for parking

€95,280 CODE FWY

ST JAMES, DÉPARTEMENT 50

A large stone property divided into three apartments, with a garden

£63,520

🛏n/a 📐2,000m² close to a small town not located on a main road
no private parking

€99,200 CODE FWY

BLANGY-SUR-BRESLE, DÉPARTEMENT 76

A traditional Normandy *longére*, with potential for an attic conversion

£66,135

🛏2 📐685m² located close to all facilities not located on a main road
room for private parking

€100–200,000
(£66–133,000)

Normandy offers a real variety of property and this particular price bracket can offer the buyer anything from a luxury apartment to a semi-detached, fully restored stone cottage. The majority of these properties are not in coastal locations, given that such real estate retails at a premium.

€102.735	CODE GEO

HONFLEUR, DÉPARTEMENT 14

A small block of luxury flats, each with a cellar and a shared private garden

£68,490

🛏2/6 🌳*private garden* 🚉*close to town centre* 🛣*not located on a main road* 🏠*with underground parking and garages*

€110,525	CODE FWY

MORTAIN, DÉPARTEMENT 50

A charming stone house with elegant architecture, and a large barn to convert

£73,685

🛏5/6 🌳$20,230m^2$ 🚉*close to town* 🛣*not located on a main road* 🏠*room for parking*

€119,909	CODE LAT

VIRE, DÉPARTEMENT 14

A traditional farmhouse to renovate, with outbuildings ideal for conversion

£79,940

🛏1 🌳$15,000m^2$ 🚉*close to town* 🛣*not located on a main road* 🏠*room for parking, and space to build a garage*

€126,500	CODE HAM

SAINT-FRAIMBAULT, DÉPARTEMENT 61

A charming stone property with a veranda overlooking a barbeque area

£84,335

🛏3 🌳$1,101m^2$ 🚉*located in the village* 🛣*not located on a main road* 🏠*room for parking, with a garage*

€137,204   **CODE** LAT

BLANGY-SUR-BRESLE, DÉPARTEMENT 76

A character brick-built property in the process of being restored

£91,470

3   4,500m²   *close to town*   *not located on a main road*

room for parking

€142,000   **CODE** ISM

OUISTRÉHAM, DÉPARTEMENT 14

An old renovated house, south facing, surrounded by Norman *bocage*

£94,665

3   1,300m²   *40 mins from town*   *not located on a main road*

room for parking

€142,071   **CODE** HAM

LA-CHAPELLE-D'ANDAINE, DÉPARTEMENT 61

A detached, stone-built country property, located in a forested surroundings

£94,715

2   2,400m²   *located in the village*   *not located on a main road*

room for parking, with two garages

€175,000   **CODE** FWY

VIRE, DÉPARTEMENT 14

An attractive small farm in excellent condition, requiring some modification

£116,665

n/a   40,470m²   *close to town and amenities*   *not located on a main road*

room for parking

€177,700   **CODE** LAT

SAINT-MARS-D'EGRENNES, DÉPARTEMENT 61

A semi-detached, restored stone property, featuring exposed wood beams

£118,465

3   1,700m²   *within 5 mins of village*   *not located on a main road*

room for parking, with a garage

€180,183   **CODE** ISM

OUISTRÉHAM, DÉPARTEMENT 14

A traditional cottage with all mod-cons, close to Caen and Bayeux

£120,120

3   1,800m²   *20 mins from town*   *not located on a main road*

room for parking

PRICE GUIDE

€200–500,000
(£133–333,000)

Traditional farmhouses and timbered longère, all fully renovated and offering substantial grounds can be purchased for between 200,000 and 300,000 euros. More euros will secure you a little piece of luxury in the form of a character millhouse or an elegant mansion.

€204,277   **CODE** LAT

SOURDEVAL, DÉPARTEMENT 50

A detached stone property with outbuildings, ideal for a chambres d'hotes

£136,185

🛏4   1,482m^2 *situated in the centre of town*   *located on a main road*   *room for parking, with a garage*

€218,000   **CODE** LAT

BUCHY, DÉPARTEMENT 76

A fully restored, traditional Norman *longére* property, situated close to Rouen

£145,335

🛏3   2,173m^2 *close to village amenities*   *not located on a main road*   *room for parking, with a garage*

€232,800   **CODE** IMO

TROUVILLE, DÉPARTEMENT 76

A large, traditional-style chalet, located close to the ski slopes and village

£155,200

🛏2   *no garden*   *located in town*   *located on a main road*   *room for parking*

€238,000   **CODE** LAT

CHERBOURG, DÉPARTEMENT 50

A large farmhouse, featuring a two-bedroom gîte, a lake and a well

£158,665

🛏3   4,047m^2 *within 10 mins of village*   *not located on a main road*   *room for parking*

€245,000 **CODE** DEE

ALENÇON, DÉPARTEMENT 61

A 19th century mansion, within easy reach of Paris, perfect for a business

£163,335

⊞ 3 ▦ 1,500m² ▣ located in a small town ▣ not located on a main road

▣ room for parking and to build a garage

€246,963 **CODE** LAT

VIRE, DÉPARTEMENT 50

A traditionally-built stone house, with grounds bordered by a river

£164,640

⊞ 4 ▦ 1,300m² ▣ close to the centre of town ▣ not located on a main road

▣ room for parking, with a two-car garage

€248,200 **CODE** HAM

CHAMPSECRET, DÉPARTEMENT 61

Built at the end of the 19th century, this is an exceptional stone mansion

£165,465

⊞ 4 ▦ 3,100m² ▣ located in the village ▣ not located on a main road

▣ room for parking, with a garage

€275,000 **CODE** ISM

OUISTRÉHAM, DÉPARTEMENT 14

A manor in a peaceful location, surrounded by Norman *bocage* countryside

£183,335

⊞ 8 ▦ 10,000m² ▣ 30 mins from town ▣ not located on a main road

▣ room for parking

€343,010 **CODE** HAM

LE-MONT-ST-MICHEL, DÉPARTEMENT 50

A beautiful hotel in a profitable location, with seating for approximately 50

£228,675

⊞ 5 ▣ with a large terrace ▣ 70 kms from Mont-st-Michel ▣ not located on a main road ▣ with a large parking area

€440,000 **CODE** LAT

SAINT EMILION, DÉPARTEMENT 76

A millhouse with a second property included and stables, set on the river

£293,335

⊞ 4 ▦ 24,280m² ▣ close to amenities ▣ not located on a main road

▣ room for parking

€500,000+
(£333,000+)

Expect elegant châteaux, authentic colombages or magnificent mansions with acres of land and a scattering of outbuildings. The location of the property, maybe in the heart of the Norman bocage or on the coast, helps to explain why the home may fall into this premium price bracket.

PRICE GUIDE

€510,000   CODE LAT

LISIEUX, DÉPARTEMENT 14

A beautiful 17th century *colombage* with panoramic views over the grounds

£340,000

⌂5   10,120m²   3 kms from the market town and shops   not located on a main road   room for parking

€545,038   CODE FRA

DEAUVILLE, DÉPARTEMENT 14

An attractive 17th century manor, with stunning views of the countryside

£363,360

⌂5   with gardens   in an isolated location   not located on a main road   room for parking

€550,000   CODE LAT

PERCHE, DÉPARTEMENT 61

A property, comprising of a two-bedroom guest cottage and heated pool

£366,665

⌂5   32,370m²   close to amenities   not located on a main road   room for parking, with a garage

€581,745   CODE ISM

OUISTRÉHAM, DÉPARTEMENT 14

Located in a quiet rural area, this property is surrounded by Norman *bocage*

£387,830

⌂8   with extensive grounds   30 mins from town   not located on a main road   room for parking

€630,000   CODE FRA

PONTORSON, DÉPARTEMENT 35

An attractive farmhouse near the beach, comprising three holiday apartments

£420,000

🛏 4/5   ▦ 10,000m²   *5 mins from village and shops*   *not located on a main road*   *outdoor parking for 8/9 cars*

€686,020   CODE BUY

VALOGNES, DÉPARTEMENT 50

A magnificent mansion, built in the 18th century, ideal for a holiday complex

£457,345

🛏 7   ▦ 33,0000m²   *close to town and amenities*   *not located on a main road*   *room for parking*

€694,000   CODE LAT

VALOGNES, DÉPARTEMENT 50

A character, stone manor house, with grounds, a lake and stables

£462,665

🛏 4/5   ▦ 32,000m²   *within 5 mins of town*   *not located on a main road*   *room for parking, with a garage*

€750,000   CODE LAT

NEAR VIRE, DÉPARTEMENT 14

A 17th century manor with a gîte and outbuildings, offering huge potential

£500,000

🛏 10   ▦ 161900m²   *close to amenities*   *not located on a main road*   *room for parking*

€823,000   CODE LAT

EVREUX AREA, DÉPARTEMENT 27

An elegant château, with a guest house, stiuated in wooded grounds

£548,665

🛏 8   ▦ 40,470m²   *close to amenities*   *not located on a main road*   *room for parking*

€825,000   CODE LAT

GISORS, DÉPARTEMENT 27

A small château with a living area of 480m², featuring a luxurious interior

£550,000

🛏 8   ▦ 13,000m²   *3 kms from town*   *not located on a main road*   *room for parking, with a garage for five cars*

PRICE GUIDE

€840,000 CODE LAT

DEAUVILLE, DÉPARTEMENT 76

A delightful manor, enjoying a seperate guest house and apartment

£560,000

🛏4 📐242,800m² 🏙close to amenities 🚫not located on a main road
🅿room for parking

€840,000 CODE LAT

DEAUVILLE, DÉPARTEMENT 76

A superb 17th century manor situated in wooded grounds, with two ponds

£560,000

🛏5 📐8,000m² 🏙20 mins drive from town 🚫not located on a main road
🅿room for parking

€905,000 CODE LAT

PAYS D'AUGE, DÉPARTEMENT 61

An authentic 16th century *colombage* manor, surrounded by a moat

£605,335

🛏6 📐48,000m² 🏙30 kms from town 🚫not located on a main road
🅿garages with room for 35 cars

€1,100,000 CODE DEE

PERCHE, DÉPARTEMENT 61

A 16th century château, modified in the 18th century, in habitable condition.

£733,335

🛏7 📐109,300m² 🏙5 kms from shops and amenities 🚫located on a private
road 🅿room for parking

€1,700,000 CODE LAT

PAYS-DE-CAUX, DÉPARTEMENT 76

A listed building, this 19th century manor is partly restored and near the sea

£1,133,335

🛏12 📐80,940m² 🏙close to town's amenities 🚫not located on a main road
🅿room for parking

€1,940,000 CODE LAT

FALAISE, DÉPARTEMENT 14

A unique 18th century château, recently restored, with outbuildings to convert

£1,293,335

🛏9 📐372,300m² 🏙within easy reach of amenities 🚫not located on a main
road 🅿room for parking, with garages

avel to your property in France with your car

fast

From just £180 for car + 2 return*

There's no better or faster way to Brittany and Western France than with Condor Ferries. Our daily sailings from Weymouth to St. Malo† with your car can get you there in as little as $4\frac{1}{2}$ hours. On board you'll find spacious air-conditioned lounges, a café & bar, children's play area and our optional exclusive Club Class lounge. And what's more, you can pick up a bargain in our on-board Duty-Free shop.

And if you want to save money on all your journeys why not join our *Frequent Traveller Club*? Membership entitles you to 20% ongoing discount on all Condor Ferries routes.

For information and booking call
0845 641 0228

Condor*ferries*

www.condorferries.com

SeaFrance Carnet

5 Day Returns from only £90*

Cruise Ferry 2003 Cf awards
MOST SIGNIFICANT NEW BUILD FERRY
SEAFRANCE RODIN

The SeaFrance Carnet saves you money.

Choose a combination of any 5 crossings from:

5 Day Return from £90* each offer code FBSD

Standard Return from £129* each offer code FBSD

- Valid for a car and up to 9 people
- Allocation of one ticket to friends/family
- Flexible tickets valid for a year
- Travel anytime on any of our 18 daily departures**

To book these fares call us quoting the offer code on

0870 443 1685

or for further information
seafrance.com

A little bit of France no one else can offer!

SEAFRANCE
DOVER-CALAIS FERRIES

Memorials and battlefields
Busy, bustling coastline
Gothic cathedrals

Nord-pas-de-Calais & Picardy

Profile 102
Hotspots 104

PRICE GUIDE
€50,000-€100,000 108
€100,000-€200,000 110
€200,000-€500,000 112
€500,000+ 114

Nord-Pas-de-Calais & Picardy Profile

Getting there

AIR Ryan Air (0871 246 0000; www.ryanair.com) flies into Beauvais from Dublin and Glasgow. **Air France** (0845 359 1000; www.airfrance.co.uk) flies from Heathrow into Lille-Lequin airport, while **Lyddair** (01797 320000; www.lyddair.co.uk) flies into Le Touquet from Lydd.

SEA P&O (0870 520 2020; www.posl.com) sail from Dover to Calais, as do **SeaFrance** (0870 571 1711; www.seafrance.com). **Norfolkline** (0870 870 1020; www.norfolkline.com) sails between Dover and Dunkirk, while **Hoverspeed** (0870 240 8070; www.hoverspeed.co.uk) operates services between Dover and Calais.

ROAD From Calais port the A26 runs through Pas-de-Calais and Picardy. The A1 runs from Arras through to Picardy, while the A16 runs along the coast, linking up all the coastal resorts. The A16 and A25 also run from Calais to Lille, and if you are flying into Paris the A16 runs through to Amiens and on into Nord pas-de-Calais. **Eurolines** (0870 514 3219; www.eurolines.com) operates services to Amiens, Boulogne, Calais and Lille.

RAIL The Eurotunnel runs from Dover to Calais, and the **Eurostar** (08705 186186; www.eurostar.co.uk) runs from London through to Lille or Paris. The TGV network serves Lille, Calais and Dunkirk, call **Rail Europe** (0870 584 8848; www.raileurope.co.uk) for all details of local services.

THE ECONOMY

Industry and commerce form the mainstays of the Nord-Pas-de-Calais economy, being the European centre for mass retailing with companies including Lyreco and La Redoute. Lille is France's second largest print and publishing centre, third largest centre for mechanical and electrical industry and fourth largest food processing site. Amiens too, is a commerce rich city and pharmaceutical production takes place in both Calais and Lille. A prime export area, Nikko exports toys to Japan from Calais.

BEST/WORST VALUE FOR MONEY

Canny purchasers looking for good resale potential buy in Calais because of its vibrancy and popularity with French purchasers looking to live and work there. Although stable, market prices do look set to increase, and there is little available for less than 47,000 euros. Despite this prices are still competitive compared with Britain.

Calais is an area fuelled by trade and industry. Consequently the area is not as cheap as many think.

The commerical centre of Lille

Although Calais is extremely industrial and expensive, renowned for its hypermarkets and a popular booze cruise destination, once you leave its environs, cheap property can be secured. An isolated property and rental market exists in the chic seaside resort Le Touquet, where apartment prices start from 120,000 euros and houses from 300,000 euros. Popular with Parisian weekend visitors, foreign purchasers looking for pricetags cheaper than in the UK will not find them here. Le Touquet does not experience a lot of foreign interest, and constant French purchaser interest has sparked expensive prices in Amiens and Lille, making these cities unpopular with foreign buyers.

The idea that Calais is overrun by British commuters is a myth; there is also a strong local interest

WHERE TO GO FOR WHAT

There is no real difference between the foreign and local property market, thus proving the idea of swathes of British buyers commuting to south east England from Nord-Pas-de-Calais is a myth. Primarily chosen by UK buyers for holiday homes, or by businessmen desiring easy access of Britain, the region is dominated by Dutch and Germans, especially civil servants working in Brussels, who find it more cost effective to commute from the region as Belgium's lack of space and lack of new builds has made for an expensive market. Amiens and Lille are working cities, dominated by French purchasers.

PROPERTY PRICE TRENDS

Over the past 15 years Calais price rises were triggered by investment from the French Government into its once ailing industry, thus reversing the trend of locals migrating from Nord-Pas-de-Calais to seek employment. New residents are also flocking to the region, seeking employment, and have helped increase property prices. The attraction of new businesses to the area has also put added pressure on the property market. Foreign purchaser interest has centred around the Seven Valleys area, including the Opal coast, Montreuil, Hesdin and St Pol.

Only one in 10 British buyers choose to buy on the coast, as most foreign interest is centred around inland locations, primarily within easy reach of the ports. A case of location, the region's transport links to Britain have allowed Londoners to purchase and enjoy weekend homes, and has also created an expensive property market. Throughout the region property prices have risen annually by 18 percent, as demand has outstripped supply; this has been fuelled by the lack of new builds. Renovation properties priced under 50,000 euros are limited, although a few bargain properties can be purchased from 30,000 euros plus. This is a fast-moving market, where last minute decisions to pull out by purchasers are commonplace.

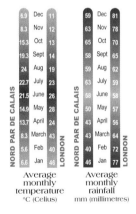

NORD PAR DE CALAIS	Month	LONDON
6.9	Dec	11
8.3	Nov	12
15.3	Oct	13
19.3	Sept	14
24	Aug	19
22.7	July	23
21.5	June	26
14.9	May	28
13.7	April	24
8.3	March	43
5.6	Feb	40
6.6	Jan	46

Average monthly temperature °C (Celius)

NORD PAR DE CALAIS	Month	LONDON
59	Dec	81
63	Nov	78
65	Oct	70
58	Sept	65
59	Aug	62
63	July	59
58	June	58
50	May	57
43	April	56
43	March	64
40	Feb	72
46	Jan	77

Average monthly rainfall mm (millimetres)

Average House Sale Prices

HOTSPOT	2-BED	3-BED	4 BED	5 BED	6/7 BED	8-BED
Amiens	-	€142K (£95K)	-	-	-	-
Hesdin	€148K (£99K)	€334K (£220K))	€355K (£237K)	€355K (£237K)	€500K (£330K)	€600K (£400K)
Le Touquet	€180K (£120K)	€225K (£150K)	€300K (£200K)	€525K (£350K)	€600K (£400K)	€900K (£600K)
Lille	-	-	-	-	-	-
Montreuil	€148K (£99K)	€334K (£220K)	€355K (£237K)	€355K (£237K)	€500K (£330K)	€600K (£400K)
The Somme Valley	€95K (£63K)	-	€400K (£260K)	-	-	-

Nord-Pas-de-Calais & Picardy Hotspots

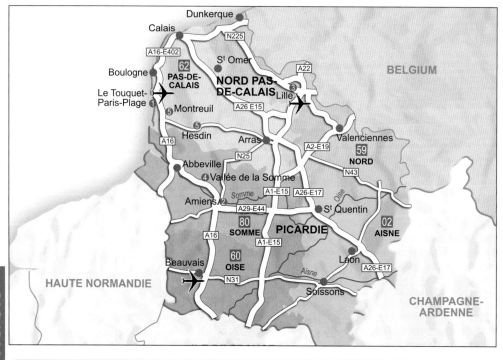

1. Le Touquet Paris Plage

ESSENTIALS ■ **POP** 1990: -, 1999: 6,000 ■ **TAXES** Taxe d'habitation 24.34%, Taxe foncière 40.97% ■ **AIRPORT** Aéroport du Touquet, Côte d'Opale, 62520 Le Touquet-Paris-Plage, Tel: +33 3 21 050399, Fax: +33 3 21 055934.

KEY FACTS

SCHOOLS Ecole Active Bilingue Jeannine Manuel-Ecole Internationale de Lille Métropole, 418 bis rue Albert Bailly, 59700, Marcq-en-Baroeul, Lille, Tel: +33 320 65 90 50.

MEDICAL Centre Hospitalier Docteur Duchenne, all Jacques Monod, 62200 Boulogne sur Mer, Tel: +33 321 993333.

RENTALS There are numerous tourist properties in Le Touquet-Paris-Plage ■ Le Touquet is unique in that there is a guaranteed summer rental season and a vibrant out of season rental market ■ Rental properties can cost from 710 to 1,200 euros per week during peak season.

PROS This is an affluent area with a sophisticated atmosphere ■ Offering wide beaches, sand dunes and unique architecture ■ Within two hours drive of London ■ This is an annually active resort.

CONS Can get very crowded in summer ■ This is a very expensive area in which to live and buy ■ Most foreign buyers buy in the Stella-Plage on the edge of Le Touquet.

Reflecting its creation by the British a century ago, this sophisticated seaside resort features houses called Wimbledon and Peppermint and was a magnet for wealthy celebrities who flocked here in the 1920s and 30s to play cricket and polo by day, then gamble at night in the casino. It is marketed by the local tourist board as a "Four Seasons" resort, as weekends are crammed throughout the year with all manner of activities from wine festivals to sporting events. The town is flourishing thanks to the Channel Tunnel and Lydd Air's direct flights from Lydd in Kent.

The beach stretches for seven miles, providing an ideal setting for sunbathing, jogging, horseriding or even sand yachting. Visitors can be revived with a treatment at the thalassotherapy centre, while nature lovers can savour The Park of the Estuary, a sign-posted reserve composed of 42 hectares, situated to the north of Le Touquet which marks out the sand dunes up to the river Canche. A grandiose 1930s covered market draws shoppers every Thursday and Saturday, while the rue de Metz and rue St Louis are lined with excellent speciality charcuteries, traiteurs and bakeries.

Further inland from Le Touquet are the cheaper towns of Hesdin and Montreuil which attract many who want to live in the Le Touquet area. This resort is highly popular with Parisians escaping the city at weekends, and consequently the British do not buy in this area as it is too expensive and not good value for money. A four-bedroom apartment located between the rue St Jean, with panoramic sea views, can cost from 485,000 euros. ■

2. Amiens

KEY FACTS ■ **POP** 1990: -, 1999: 132,000 ■ **TAXES** Taxe d'habitation 27.48%, Taxe foncière 44.92% ■ **AIRPORT** Aeroport de Beauvais, Service Chamco 60000, Beauvais, France, Tel: +33 3 44 114666, Fax: +33 3 44 114660.

Picardy's largest city, Amiens, is a university town in the Somme département renowned for its great gothic architecture, notably the Cathédrale Notre Dame, France's biggest Gothic building in France, which can be viewed from anywhere in the city. Its construction first started in 1218, when the citizens wanted a worthy monument to house what they believed was John the Baptist's head, brought back from the fourth crusade. The medieval quarter of St Leu, once the city's centre for its textile industry, lies to the north of the cathedral with its network of canals, renovated into neat brick cottages with cobbled streets, while the waterfront sparkles with restaurants and clubs. Each canal still functions as a waterway for the *hortillonnages*, a series of fertile market gardens reclaimed from the marshes created by the slow-flowing Somme river. Farmers travel about the canals in black punts and a few still take their produce into the city by boat for the Saturday morning *marché sur l'eau*. Jules Verne, science-fiction writer and Amiens' most prominent former citizen, lived in the city from 1856 until his death in 1905. The Maison Jules Verne at 2 Rue Charles Dubois has a model of a flying machine and the Nautilus.

Amiens caters for the local french market and is not popular with the foreign buyer. A three-bedroom house in north east Amiens starts at 142,900 euros. In Amiens centre a two-bedroom apartment costs around 110,000 euros. ■

KEY FACTS

SCHOOLS Ecole Active Bilingue Jeannine Manuel-Ecole Internationale de Lille Métropole, 418 bis rue Albert Bailly, 59700, Marcq-en-Baroeul, Lille, Tel: +33 320 65 90 50.

MEDICAL Centre Hospitalier Universitaire, 2 pl Victor Pauchet, 80080 Amiens, Tel: +33 3 22 66 80 00.

RENTALS Amiens is an area more designed for long term rentals ■ There are many business-connected rentals in this area, primarily from the French market.

PROS Boasts a vibrant atmosphere due to the presence of 25,000 students ■ A vibrant, cosmopolitan city excellent for those who desire a metropolitan lifestyle.

CONS Property turnover is very rapid in Amiens and it is primarily a French market ■ British buyers don't tend to buy in Amiens unless it is for work purposes ■ Many French estate agents prefer not to deal with the foreign market, but with the local French market.

3. Lille

ESSENTIALS ■ **POP** 1990: -, 1999: 1,100,000 ■ **TAXES** Taxe d'habitation 41.79%, Taxe foncière 34.90% ■ **AIRPORT** Lille airport, BP 227, 59812 Lesquin Cedex, France, Tel: +33 3 20 496868, Fax: +33 3 20 496810.

European Capital of Culture in 2004, Lille is France's fourth largest city with plenty of outstanding architecture, delectable food and drink and sophisticated shopping. It lies in the Nord département, bordering Belgium, combining a typically French atmosphere with a distinctive Flemish flavour.

Make your way to the city centre from the Lille-Flandres railway station, formerly the actual Paris Gare du Nord before being moved north brick-by-brick. The old quarter, Vieux Lille, has been tastefully revived in Flemish style, in particular the Vielle Bourse. Follow the thoroughfare into rue des Chats-Bossus, and branch left along rue de la Grande-Chaussée . This deposits you on the immense Place du Général de Gaulle, called simply Grand Place by locals. Don't miss the Musée des Beaux-Arts, a classical and modern architectural gem, with its priceless collection of paintings from Goya to Rubens. There are plenty of good cafes and brasseries serving local fare like carbonnades (beef braised in beer) and mussels and chips. The city's student population ensures that the streets are buzzing into the early hours. Cinemas and bars are found in the Halles district and old quarter, while the jazz scene is also popular. Events in Lille include the September beer festival and the December Christmas markets.

Lille only attracts foreign buyers who seek to move to the area for employment purposes. Otherwise, the area is dominated by the locals. A one-bedroom apartment overlooking the central park starts at 81,000 euros, while a three-bedroom apartment starts at 144,400 euros. ■

KEY FACTS

SCHOOLS Ecole Active Bilingue Jeannine Manuel-Ecole Internationale de Lille Métropole, 418 bis rue Albert Bailly, 59700, Marcq-en-Baroeul, Lille, Tel: +33 3 20 65 90 50.

MEDICAL Centre Hospitalier Régional Universitaire de Lille, av Oscar Lambret, 59037 Lille Cedex, Tel: +33 3 20 44 59 62.

RENTALS This is not a tourist area and therefore long term rentals are the norm in Lille ■ Lille is an area dominated by the business market and by the local French rental market.

PROS Lille is renowned for its dynamic shopping centres and abundance of retail outlets ■ Lille has an extremely buoyant property market, albeit primarily a local French market.

CONS Lille is essentially a French market dominated by the French buyer, and is a city where the French live and work ■ This is an expensive city in which to live and property prices are high due to the demand and rapid turnaround of property.

HOTSPOTS

Nord-Pas-de-Calais & Picardy Hotspots

4. The Fishing Lakes of the Somme Valley

ESSENTIALS ■ **POP** 1990: -, 1999: 553,100 ■ **TAXES** Taxe d'habitation 27.48%, Taxe foncière 44.92% ■ **AIRPORT** Aéroport du Touquet, Côte d'Opale, 62520 Le Touquet-Paris-Plage, Tel: +33 3 21 05 03 99, Fax: +33 3 21 05 59 34.

KEY FACTS

SCHOOLS Ecole Active Bilingue Jeannine Manuel-Ecole Internationale de Lille Métropole, 418 bis rue Albert Bailly, 59700, Marcq-en-Baroeul, Lille, Tel: +33 3 20 65 90 50.

MEDICAL Centre Hospitalier Universitaire, 2 pl Victor Pauchet, 80080 Amiens, Tel: +33 3 22 66 80 00.

RENTALS There is huge rental potential throughout the year for lakeside properties ■ This is a hugely popular area with anglers and those who desire to pursue an activities holiday.

PROS It is an excellent and profitable business to buy a fishing lake in Picardy ■ Easy access due to the proximity to the coast ■ The Avesnois regional park is a stunning natural park and there is great demand for property in this area ■ This is a must for those who love nature and outdoor or adventure sports ■ A great area for those who desire to be close to the south-east of England.

CONS Prices are increasing all the time due to the rising demand from the British market ■ Costs for lake properties are constantly altering and are not consistent ■ This is not a huge international buying area and parts of Picardy are undiscovered.

Picardy is a haven for anglers, especially the lakes of the Somme and the Oise, with their rich flora and fauna. You can catch many different types of fish including trout, carp and gudgeon in this peaceful, relatively undiscovered area of France. For the invigorating country life, choose the Avesnois, close to the Ardennes. Situated in the south-east of the Nord département, at the very tip of Nord-Pas-de-Calais against the Belgian border this area is fondly referred to as "little Switzerland", with its extensive network of rivers, canals and lakes making fishing, canoeing and other water sports very popular. Designated a départemental Nature Park, the Avesnois valleys and pine forests are interspersed with lush pastures and ancient walled towns. Val Joly at Eppe Sauvage is the largest lake north of Paris, with facilities including sailing, mini-golf and tennis. Many of the traditional arts and crafts of Nord are still practised in this area. Le Quesnoy is a noteworthy hotspot, with its three and a half kilometres of perfectly preserved 17th century fortifications bearing witness to centuries of invasion. Gateway to the Avesnois Regional Nature Park and its traditional *bocage* landscapes, Le Quesnoy is situated in close proximity to 10,000 hectares of the Mormal forest, which numbers an incredible seventy different tree varieties.

An increasingly popular activity, there is huge demand from the foreign market, particularly the British, for angling businesses. A house in Le Quesnoy costs around 110,000 euros, while a fishing business close to Calais costs from 375,000 euros. ■

5. Montreuil and Hesdin

ESSENTIALS ■ **POP** 1990: -, 1999: 5,431 ■ **TAXES** Taxe d'habitation 25.60%, Taxe foncière 34.57% ■ **AIRPORT** Aéroport du Touquet, Côte d'Opale, 62520 Le Touquet-Paris-Plage, Tel: +33 3 21 05 03 99, Fax: +33 3 21 05 59 34.

KEY FACTS

SCHOOLS Ecole Active Bilingue Jeannine Manuel-Ecole Internationale de Lille Métropole, 418 bis rue Albert Bailly, 59700, Marcq-en-Baroeul, Lille, Tel: +33 320 65 90 50.

MEDICAL Hôpital Rural, 13 bd Richelieu, 62140 Hesdin, Tel: +33 3 21 86 86 54, Fax: +33 3 21 81 71 82.

RENTALS A short term lets area, there is good demand for property to let, and many people buy with the intention of letting ■ Easy access means people come for short breaks, especially golfers ■ There is a lot of demand for hotels rather than cottages and gites.

PROS A major focal point in Pas-de-Calais for the British buyer ■ Located within 45 minutes to an hour of Calais, there is easy access to the UK ■ Exactly the attractive and affordable rural area the British buyer loves ■ Many international buyers are investing in the area such as civil servants from Brussels, plus many Dutch and Germans.

CONS This area has experienced a huge incline in prices in recent years ■ It is almost impossible to secure a habitable property for less than 100,000 euros.

At the heart of the historic Seven Valleys region, the town of Hesdin with its bridges, red brick and white stone *maisons de maitre*, is famed as a former outpost of the Austro-Hungarian Empire. Crossed by the rivers Canche and Ternoise, the focal points are the Town Hall, formerly the residence of Emperor Charles V's sister, Marie of Hungary, and The Wine Society, directly across from the square. This is a good base for exploring the battle site and museum at Agincourt. Other attractions include the flower-decked village of Boubers-sur-Canche and the Opal Coast, named after its white sandy beaches. The state-owned forestland in Hesdin stretches for more than 1,020 acres and lies over a limestone plateau, soaring above the Ternoise, Canche and Planquette valleys. Once a medieval port, Montreuil-sur-Mer commands a hilltop setting over its cobbled Vauban ramparts. A son et lumiere is acted biannually in the town in memory of Victor Hugo, who wrote the local mayor into the plot of Les Miserables.

Houses are excellent value compared to English equivalents, while buyers from the Netherlands, Belgium and Germany will find property is comparably cheap. Nevertheless, compared with last year's prices, there has been a sharp increase as demand has risen. A Montreuil-sur-Mer manor house with front courtyard starts at 640,000 euros. In Hesdin you can acquire a three-bedroom country house and large garden for 122,475 euros. ■

USEFUL CONTACTS

JUSTIN POSTLETHWAITE

HOTSPOTS

The vibrant city of Lille has been voted European Capital of Culture 2004, yet remains an area dominated by the French buyer

PREFECTURE
Préfecture de la Région
Nord-Pas-de-Calais
Place de la République
2 rue Jacquemars-Giélée
59039 Lille Cedex
Tel: +33 3 20 30 59 59
Fax: +33 3 20 30 52 58

Préfecture de la Région
Picardie
51 rue de la République
80026 Amiens Cedex 1
Tel: +33 3 22 97 80 80
Fax: +33 3 22 92 13 98

LEGAL
Chambre des Notaires
du Pas-de-Calais
1 rue du Collège

62000 Arras
Tel: +33 3 21 51 81 91
Fax: +33 3 21 71 42 20

Chambre des Notaires
de la Somme
11 place d'Aguesseau
BP 331
80003 Amiens Cedex 1
Tel: +33 3 22 82 08 92
Fax: +33 3 22 82 08 97

FINANCE
Direction des Impôts du
Nord
13–15 boulevard de la Liberté
59800 Lille
Tel: +33 3 20 17 64 90
Fax: +33 3 20 17 64 99

BUILDING & PLANNING
Chambre Régionale de
Métiers du Nord-Pas-de-
Calais
9 rue Léon Trulin, BP 114
59001 Lille Cedex
Tel: +33 3 20 14 96 14
Fax: +33 3 20 55 51 92

Chambre Régionale de
Métiers de Picardie
Cité des Métiers
80440 Boves
Tel: +33 3 22 50 40 55
Fax: +33 3 22 50 40 59

CAUE du Nord
148 rue Nationale
59800 Lille
Tel: +33 3 20 57 67 67

Fax: +33 3 20 30 93 40

CAUE de la Somme
5 rue Vincent Auriol
80000 Amiens
Tel: +33 3 22 91 11 65
Fax: +33 3 22 92 29 11

EDUCATION
Rectorat de l'Académie
d'Amiens
(Aisne, Oise, Somme)
20 boulevard d'Alsace-Lorraine
BP 2609
80026 Amiens Cedex 1
Tel: +33 3 22 82 38 23
Fax: +33 3 22 92 82 12

Rectorat de l'Académie
de Lille

(Nord, Pas-de-Calais)
20 rue Saint-Jacques
BP 709
59033 Lille Cedex
Tel: +33 3 20 15 60 00
Fax: +33 3 20 15 65 90

HEALTH
Caisse Primaire d'Assurance
Maladie du Nord
2 rue d'Iéna, BP 01
59895 Lille Cedex 9
Tel: +33 3 20 42 34 00
Fax: +33 3 20 54 33 64

Caisse Primaire d'Assurance
Maladie de la Somme
8 place Louis Sellier
80021 Amiens Cedex 1
Tel: +33 3 22 97 50 00

€50–100,000
(£33–66,000)

If your budget encompasses this price bracket, expect to be looking at renovation properties and properties requiring some work to make them habitable. However the number of renovation properties up for sale has fallen dramatically in recent years, and only the most modest remain.

€64,500   CODE LAT

HARDELOT, DÉPARTEMENT 62

A new development of apartments, located close to the beach and amenities

£43,000

studio/1/2   *no garden, with a balcony*   *close to all amenities*   *not located on a main road*   *room for parking*

€67,080   CODE LAT

FORMERIE, DÉPARTEMENT 60

A detached brick property, with outbuildings, requiring some modernisation

£44,720

3   *4,054m^2*   *Situated close to amenities*   *not located on a main road*   *room for parking*

€90,500   CODE LAT

HESDIN, DÉPARTEMENT 62

An attractive chalet-style house, featuring a pond, well and a terrace

£60,335

3   *4,886m^2*   *close to town and amenities*   *not located on a main road*   *room for parking*

€99,000   CODE LAT

HESDIN, DÉPARTEMENT 62

A bungalow property, in habitable condition, with a wood-beam interior

£66,000

2   *1,300m^2*   *close to town and amenities*   *not located on a main road*   *room for parking, with a double garage*

€100–200,000
(£66–133,000)

*Within Nord-Pas-de-Calais the average property price
ranges from between 100,000 and 200,000 euros. This
should procure a buyer a comfortable property requiring
a limited amount of renovation. Although a fairly cheap
area, recent interest in the region has driven prices up.*

€100,000   CODE LAT

HESDIN, DÉPARTEMENT 62

A detached, modern property, requiring some redecoration, with outbuildings

£66,665

2   2,000m²   *close to town and amenities*   *not located on a main road*   *room for parking*

€100,000   CODE LAT

WIMEREUX, DÉPARTEMENT 62

A new golfing development offering apartments and houses, with sea views

£66,665

1/3   *with small gardens/terraces*   *within 5 mins of amenities*   *not located on a main road*   *room for parking*

€115,907   CODE HEX

MONTREUIL, DÉPARTEMENT 62

A large village house located by the river and lakes, set in a rural hamlet

£77,270

5   530m²   *20 mins from town and amenities*   *not located on a main road*   *room for parking, with a garage*

€120,000   CODE FPP

HESDIN, DÉPARTEMENT 62

An old presbytery located in the centre of town, offering a small courtyard

£80,000

6   *no garden, with courtyard*   *close to all amenities*   *not located on a main road*   *room for parking*

€131,514
CODE GEO

LE CROTOY, DÉPARTEMENT 80

New luxury flats opposite the port, and close to the town centre and beach

£87,675

⌂2/4 ⌂no garden ⌂located close to amenities ⌂not located on a main road ⌂room for parking

€139,324
CODE HEX

SAINT-POL-SUR-TERNOISE, DÉPARTEMENT 62

An attractive bungalow ideal for a retirement property or second home.

£92,880

⌂2 ⌂2,000m^2 ⌂close to amenities ⌂not located on a main road ⌂room for parking, with a three car garage

€149,000
CODE FRA

HESDIN, DÉPARTEMENT 62

An attractive farmhouse, fully renovated and set in a quiet village

£99,335

⌂2 ⌂1,500m^2 ⌂close to all amenities ⌂not located on a main road ⌂room for parking

€164,650
CODE LAT

BLAGNY-SUR-BRESLES, DÉPARTEMENT 80

A *colombage* style property, with outbuildings, bordered by a river

£109,765

⌂4 ⌂916m^2 ⌂close to town and amenities ⌂not located on a main road ⌂room for parking

€178,626
CODE FRA

CRECY-EN-PONTHIEU, DÉPARTEMENT 62

A renovated farmhouse, situated in a small rural village, with a pond

£119,085

⌂4 ⌂3,000m^2 ⌂close to town and amenities ⌂not located on a main road ⌂room for parking

€182,940
CODE FPP

FRÉVENT, DÉPARTEMENT 62

An impressive character property, with spacious rooms and mature gardens

£121,960

⌂4 ⌂with a garden ⌂close to town and amenities ⌂not located on a main road ⌂room for parking, with garage

PRICE GUIDE

€200–500,000
(£133–333,000)

Sprawling farmhouses, traditional manor houses and thatched cottages are all available within this price bracket. The closer to the coast, the more expensive the property, and proximity to Calais is something that will boost the price to 200,000 euros or more.

€236,300 CODE LAT

HORNOY-LE-BOURG, DÉPARTEMENT 80

A traditional style house with numerous outbuildings ideal for a gîte complex

£157,335

4 10,000m^2 close to town and amenities not located on a main road room for parking, with a garage for two cars

€250,000 CODE FRA

HESDIN, DÉPARTEMENT 62

An attractive farmhouse, fully habitable, offering lovely views over the valley

£166,665

3 10,000m^2 close to town and amenities not located on a main road room for parking, with a garage

€251,000 CODE FRA

HESDIN, DÉPARTEMENT 62

A large farmhouse, completely renovated and situated in a small hamlet

£167,335

2 3,100m^2 near town and amenities not located on a main road room for parking, with a double garage

€257,639 CODE LAT

VALLEE-DE-LA-COURSE, DÉPARTEMENT 62

A delightful cottage with a guest annexe, in a rural area, bordered by the river

£171,760

4 7,500m^2 close to town and amenities not located on a main road room for parking, with a garage

€274,000 CODE FRA

HESDIN, DÉPARTEMENT 62

A large farmhouse, fully renovated, and well-located in a popular area

£182,665

🛏4 🗌4,800m² 🖼close to town and amenities 🖼not located on a main road
🏠room for parking, with three garages

€277,625 CODE HEX

ARDRES, DÉPARTEMENT 62

Dating from the 15th century, an old manor house, with a loft to convert

£185,085

🛏6 🗌38,730m² 🖼close to amenities 🖼not located on a main road
🏠room for parking

€337,500 CODE LAT

HUCQUELIERS, DÉPARTEMENT 62

A spacious country house with mature gardens and fruit trees, with views

£225,000

🛏2 🗌4,160m² 🖼situated close to town 🖼not located on a main road
🏠room for parking, with a garge for two cars

€359,100 CODE LAT

HARDELOT PLAGE, DÉPARTEMENT 62

A delightful thatched cottage, in a habitable condition, with spacious rooms

£239,400

🛏3 🗌1,120m² 🖼situated close to town 🖼not located on a main road
🏠room for parking

€436,613 CODE LAT

SONGEONS, DÉPARTEMENT 60

A large house with a number of outbuildings, beautifully located in Picardy

£291,075

🛏3 🗌18,400m² 🖼close to amenities 🖼not located on a main road
🏠room for parking

€475,000 CODE LAT

DESVRES, DÉPARTEMENT 62

A traditional millhouse, with gîtes and outbuildings, set alongside the river

£316,665

🛏9 🗌10,000m² 🖼close to town and amenities 🖼not located on a main road
🏠room for parking

PRICE GUIDE

€500,000+
(£333,000+)

Luxurious colombages houses, mansions and châteaux all fall into this price bracket. Sizeable grounds, outbuildings and landscaped gardens all come as standard with homes of this magnitude. For those with the budget to afford such a home, they will certainly be living in luxury.

€535,000   CODE LAT

MONTREUIL, DÉPARTEMENT 62

A fully renovated 19th century *Maison de Maitre*, with two houses to renovate

£356,665

🛏7   📐4,285m²   🚗30 mins from town   🛣not located on a main road 🏠room for parking, with a garage for three cars

€558,000   CODE LAT

HARDELOT PLAGE, DÉPARTEMENT 62

A traditionally-styled detached house with stunning landscaped gardens

£372,000

🛏4   📐3,000m²   🚗close to all amenities   🛣not located on a main road 🏠room for parking, with a garage

€593,000   CODE LAT

HESDIN, DÉPARTEMENT 62

A spacious 18th century property, with a studio apartment and outbuildings

£395,335

🛏7   📐5,990m²   🚗close to town and amenities   🛣not located on a main road 🏠room for parking, with a double garage

€615,000   CODE LAT

LE TOUQUET, DÉPARTEMENT 62

A character house, with stunning grounds and an orchard, fully renovated

£410,000

🛏7   📐5,240m²   🚗only 10 kms from town and amenities   🛣not located on a main road 🏠room for parking, with a garage

€865,000 CODE LAT

GOURNAY-EN-BRAY, DÉPARTEMENT 60

A large *colombage* property with a separate house, lake and stable block

£576,665

🛏7 🗺230,000m² *close to all amenities* *not located on a main road* *room for parking, with a garage*

€900,000 CODE SIF

GISORS, DÉPARTEMENT 60

Built in a mock medieval style, and set in beautifully landscaped grounds

£600,000

🛏9 🗺45,000m² *close to all amenities* *not located on a main road* *room for parking, with garages*

€915,000 CODE LAT

WIMEREUX, DÉPARTEMENT 62

A superb three storey character house, situated in a charming rural area

£610,000

🛏4 🗺1,800m² *situated in the heart of town by amenities* *not located on a main road* *room for parking, with a large garage*

€1,300,000 CODE LAT

DUNKERQUE, DÉPARTEMENT 59

An outstanding Renaissance château, with a courtyard and bridged moat

£866,665

🛏6 🗺50,590m² *10 kms from amenities* *not located on a main road* *room for parking*

€1,840,000 CODE LAT

CHANTILLY, DÉPARTEMENT 60

A luxurious house, with a separate staff apartment and guest cottage

£1,226,665

🛏6 🗺4,700m² *situated close to all amenities* *not located on a main road* *room for parking, with garages*

€6,100,000 CODE SIF

COMPIÈGNE, DÉPARTEMENT 60

A magnificent 18th century château, set within magnificent parkland

£4,066,665

🛏10 🗺3,000,000m² *close to amenities* *not located on a main road* *room for parking, garage space for seven cars*

PRICE GUIDE

Destination France?

Choose a familiar face for your finances

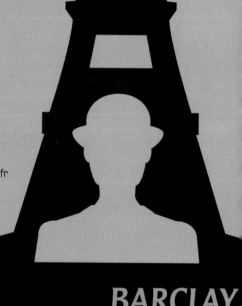

If you're thinking of buying a French property, talk to Barclays France. We can offer you competitive property finance, banking and investment services as well as an English speaking relationship manager For more information on our Destination France service, call 0800 917 0157 or visit www.barclays.fr

BARCLAY

FLUENT IN FINANC

Bustling arrondissements
Comfortable banlieu
Elegant apartments

Ile-de-France

Profile 118
Hotspots 120

PRICE GUIDE
€50,000-€200,000 127
€200,000-€500,000 128
€500,000+ 130

Ile-de-France Profile

Getting there

AIR Air France; (08453 591000; www.airfrance.co.uk), **easyJet;** (0871 750 0100; www.easyjet.com), **flybe;** (0870 889 0908; www.flybe.com), **British Airways;** (0870 850 9850; www.britishairways.com), **bmibaby;** (0870 607 0555; www.flybmi.co.uk) all fly to Charles de Gaulle airport in Paris. Orly Airport is visited by domestic and intra-European flights, with **Air France** and **flybe** services to Orly from London. London Gatwick; **British Airways, British Midland, Air France, British European**. **Air Littoral;** (+33 8 25 83 48 34; www.air-littoral.com) and **Astraeus** (01293 819800; www.flyastraeus.com) offer charter flights, bookable via various agents.

SEA SeaFrance; (0870 571 1711; www.seafrance.com) provides ferries to Calais, as does **Hoverspeed Fast Ferries;** (0870 240 8070; www.hoverspeed.co.uk) and **P&O Portsmouth;** (0870 520 2020; www.poportsmouth.com), **P&O Ferries, P&O Stena Line;** (0870 600 0600; www.posl.com) operate ferries to Le Havre, and from all ports access to Paris is very straightforward.

ROAD From Calais and the Channel Tunnel, take the A16 south to Amiens, and from there the A16 continues to the Parisian environs. From Le Havre the A15 runs to Rouen and then the A14 runs on into Paris, and the A4 runs into Paris from Reims.

COACH An express coach service operates from London Victoria Coach Station to Gare Routière **Eurolines Coach Station;** (+33 5 40 29 81 39; www.eurolines.com).

RAIL Eurostar; (0870 518 6186; www.eurostar.co.uk) operates services from London, Waterloo to the Gare de Nord station, Paris. **SNCF** offers services to Versailles and Fontainebleu; (www.sncf.com) or **Rail Europe;** (0870 584 8848; www.raileurope.co.uk).

PARIS METRO Paris has an extremely comprehensive public transport system that is easy to navigate. The 14-line metro system is part of the **RATP**, which incorporates bus, metro RER trains and tramways to the city's outskirts.

THE ECONOMY

A quarter of France's manufacturing industry is situated in Paris, and chemicals, pharmaceuticals, computer software, and electrical equipment are all produced here. An established centre of luxury, art, publishing, high fashion clothes and jewellery, more than 8,000 foreign companies, including Esso, IBM, Kodak, Honda, and Proctor and Gamble have headquarters in Paris. Even the city's most obvious symbol of tourism, the Eiffel Tower, has a working telecommunications' antennae which mirrors the importance of telecommunications in the city. Galleries, bookshops, antique dealers and restaurants all dominate the 6ème arrondissement, while La Défense business centre houses ELF, Esso and IBM. East of Paris, Disneyland Paris offers major employment to many in the area.

BEST/WORST VALUE FOR MONEY

Le Marais or the Jewish quarter, the 4ème, is a rising star for cheap prices, offering the picket fence unavailable elsewhere in Paris, for around 10 million euros. Regaining its old status as an artists quarter, Montmartre, in the 18ème, has some of the cheapest prices in the city and is very up-and-coming. The thriving 9ème and Montparnasse, in the not-so-glitzy 14ème, also feature affordable properties. Classic Haussmann-style buildings with high price tags, left in their original state and not divided into apartments dominate the 16ème.

The illustrious Champs-Elysées is a hugely popular area for foreign property buyers

But the most expensive properties are found around Saint Germain in the 7ème, where 6,500 euros per square metre is asked. Apartments in the 6ème and east 7ème cost on average 5,500 euros per square metre. The west 7ème offers better value for money with 4,500 to 5,000 euros per square metre, as does the area by the Trocadéro in the 16ème. The best value prices are elsewhere in the 16ème, where a square metre costs 3,500 euros.

WHERE TO GO FOR WHAT

Neuilly, Boulogne, Saint-Cloud and Levallois to the west of Paris represent peaceful *banlieu,* popular with families and central Parisian workers, as does Versailles. Cheaper properties have helped Versailles develop from being purely the site of King Louis XIV's château, into a self-contained community with its own identity. Houses offer more space and a garden for the same price as some Parisian apartments, hence Parisians often rent homes here. Avenue de la Reine or Queen's Avenue offers a fabulous, central location, overlooked by the château. The Champs Elysées, Avenue Montaigne and Avenue George V in the 1ème and 2ème, are popular with Middle Eastern purchasers. Smart and exclusive the 16ème offers a quiet life (middle-aged couples and families are the major buyers). The 6ème's lively nightlife suits students at upmarket universities and foreign buyers seeking a central pied-à-terre, while the 8ème's recent overhaul is attracting younger residents. The 19ème and 20ème are problem crime areas which are best avoided.

PROPERTY PRICE TRENDS

Recently christened fashionable, with new art galleries and squares emerging towards Clichy, where the 17ème meets the 8ème, the *Avenue de Clichy* and *Batignolles* areas in the 17ème have seen major price hikes. The 9ème is another new player, reflected by recent price rises, and the 7ème where prices levelled last year is equally so. Parisian Haussmann apartments in the 8ème, 16ème and 17ème are at a premium, selling at 15,380 euros a square metre. Non-French purchasers form about seven percent of the 1ème and 2ème's purchasing power making these areas the second most expensive to live in after the 7ème. This figure is doubled in the more desirable 5ème, 6ème, 7ème, 16ème and parts of the 17ème, perhaps as Parisians cannot, or will not, pay the high prices.

The Parisian pied-à-terre is hugely popular with the foreign buyer, and can cost more than a house in Versailles

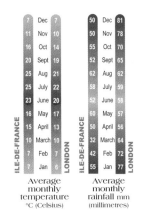

Average monthly temperature °C (Celsius)

Average monthly rainfall mm (millimetres)

Average House Sale Prices

HOTSPOT	2-BED	3-BED	4-BED	5-BED	6/7-BED	8-BED
1ere arrondissement	€500K (£330K)	€750K (£500K)	€1.5M (£1M)	-	-	-
2eme arrondissement	€500K (£330K)	€750K (£500K)	€1.5M (£1M)	-	-	-
3eme arrondissement	€500K (£330K)	€750K (£500K)	€1.5M (£1M)	-	-	-
4eme arrondissement	-	-	-	-	-	-
5eme arrondissement	-	-	-	-	-	-
6eme arrondissement	-	-	-	-	-	-
7eme arrondissement	-	-	-	-	-	-
8eme arrondissement	-	-	-	-	-	-
16eme arrondissement	€600K (£400K)	-	-	-	-	-
17eme arrondissement	€600K (£400K)	-	-	-	-	-
Versailles	-	-	-	-	-	-

Ile-de-France Hotspots

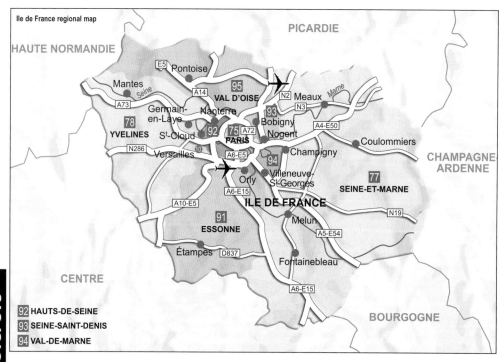

Ile de France regional map

PICARDIE

HAUTE NORMANDIE

E5 Pontoise

Mantes
Seine
A14
95
VAL D'OISE
N2 Meaux
Marne
A73
Germain-
en-Laye
Nanterre
93
N3
Bobigny
A4-E50
78
92
75
A72
Nogent
Coulommiers
YVELINES
St-Cloud
PARIS
N286
40
Versailles
A6-E5
94
Champigny
CHAMPAGNE
ARDENNE
Orly
Villeneuve-
St-Georges
77
A6-E15
SEINE-ET-MARNE
A10-E5
ILE DE FRANCE
N19
91
Melun
ESSONNE
A5-E54
Étampes
D837
Fontainebleau
CENTRE
A6-E15
BOURGOGNE

HOTSPOTS

92 HAUTS-DE-SEINE
93 SEINE-SAINT-DENIS
94 VAL-DE-MARNE

1. Arrondissement 1

ESSENTIALS ■ **POP** 1990: 18,365, 1999: 16,895 ■ **TAXES** Taxe d'habitation: 10.99%, Taxe foncière: 7.98% ■ **AIRPORT** Nearest airport: Aéroport de Paris Orly, Orly Sud, Orly Aérogare Cedex; Tel +33 1 49 75 15 15, www.adp.fr

KEY FACTS

SCHOOLS Nearest: 8ème and 7ème.

MEDICAL Clinique du Louvre, 17 rue des Prêtes, Saint-Germain l'Auxerrois, 75001 Paris; (+33 1 53 40 60 60; www.cliniquedulouvre.com) ■ Clinique Mont-Louis, 8, 10 rue de la Foile, Régnaut, 75011 Paris; Tel: +33 1 43 56 56 56; www.clinique-mont-louis.fr.

RENTAL Excellent. Arguably the most popular *arrondissement* with tourists, there is no real end of tourist season here ■ Average prices per night in m²: under 50 - 130 euros, starting at around 100 euros (specifying three nights minimum is wise, due to management costs); 51 to 100 - 220 euros; 100 to 150 - 478 euros ■ Prices are dependent upon the size and not the number of bedrooms.

PROS A sense of community exists. ■ A car is not necessary, because of the proximity to other arrondissements and the metro. ■ Many roads are pedestrianised and it is a lively locale. ■ It borders La Seinne and Le Marais' nightlife and clubs.

CONS It becomes packed with tourists ■ Property prices are high as the locale is exclusive.

The actual centre of Paris and geographical and historical heart, located on the Right Bank, the 1er *arrondissement* is the main tourist area, as it is the setting for the Louvre, Les Halles and the Palais Royal. Property for sale is scarce, the Louvre is much commercialised and there is little real sense of community in the area, although there are magnificent apartments for sale on the Rue de Rivoli, overlooking the Tuileries or Palais Royal gardens. You can also find unusual, little-known residences, one being the US Consulate, located in the one-time palace of the famous Talleyrand, although they can be difficult to locate. Renovated apartments are available near Les Halles. Place Vendôme is another elegant area. Ile de la Cité was the first city settlement and it is home to some of the greatest city sights - the Gothic Notre-Dame Cathedral, Sainte-Chapelle with its spectacular stained glass windows and the Conciergerie, where Marie Antoinette was held prisoner. Some spacious, quiet apartments with high ceilings and thick walls are hidden behind the courtyards of a few select commercial façades.

Starting price for a two-bedroom apartment in a Directoire building, is about 450,000 euros. Home to the second most expensive property market in Paris, property can cost from 5,344 to 12,213 euros per square metre. The 18th and 19th century listed buildings here cannot be altered in any way. But the majority of buyers remain between 25 and 45 and foreign purchasing demand which has pushed the market up over 2002 has now stablised. ■

Paris city map

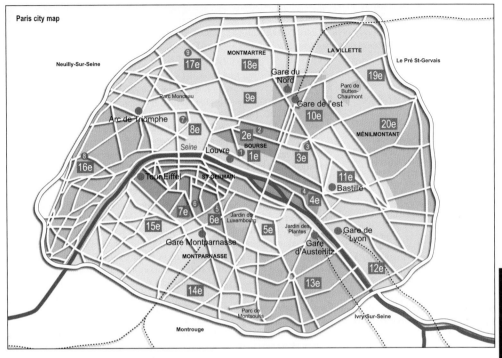

2. Arrondissement 2

ESSENTIALS ▪ **POP**: 1990: -, 1999: 90,697 ▪ **TAXES** Taxe d'habitation: 10.99%, Taxe foncière: 7.98% ▪ **AIRPORT**
Nearest airport: Aéroport de Paris Orly, Orly Sud, Orly Aérogare Cedex; Tel +33 1 49 75 15 15, www.adp.fr

Primarily a business district and home to the Paris stock market (Bourse) and the Bibliothèque Nationale, the 2ème *arrondissement* is located between the Palais Royal and the grand boulevards. Of late, prices in this area have increased more than in any other and, along with the 1ème, they are the second more expensive in Paris. Although most Parisians tend to rent here, buyers can occasionally find a bargain apartment near the Bourse.

Once the workers have left the area for the weekend, the district acquires a much more laid-back feel. Here you will find bargains and old-style shops among the maze of small alleys. Cinema buffs can delight in exploring a circuit of cinemas, along the Boulevard des Capucines for instance, and the Rex, an art deco building famous for its star-studded vault is located at 1 Boulevard Poissonnière. Gourmets may wish to visit Legrand, a family-run épicerie and wine merchant which has delighted Parisians since 1880, or you could dine at Vaudeville, which is a classic 1930s brasserie very popular with finance workers. Property is not as expensive as in the 1ème, 4ème, 6ème and 7ème.

In this *arrondissement* you could acquire a south-facing two or three-bedroom apartment of 86 square metres in a 17th-century building with exposed beams, fireplace, living room, equipped kitchen, bedroom overlooking a courtyard and basement parking from around 500,000 euros. ▪

KEY FACTS

SCHOOLS Nearest: 8ème, as listed.
MEDICAL Centre de Santé, Réaumur, 75008 Paris; Tel: +33 1 55 80 56 18.
RENTAL The letting potential is excellent ▪ There is no real end of season here; perhaps three months in the winter ▪ Average prices in m²: under 50 to 130 euros (a night); 51 to 100 - 220 euros (a night); 100 to 150m² - 478 euros (a night) ▪ Location, decor and size are the key deciding factors for cost ▪ Larger studios can raise more than 250 euros per night and there is no firm end of season ▪ The months from November to January are cheaper ▪ Factors such as an apartment's decor can attract higher fees; from 700 euros a week. ▪ It is a business district first, but tourist favourites are included in the mix, so it offers a good mix of potential tenants
PROS ▪ A fabulous place to live, there is no need for a car here and it is easy to walk to the opera district in the nearby 9ème *arrondissement* ▪
CONS 18th and 19th century buildings that are listed in this locale cannot be changed in any way.

Ile-de-France Hotspots

3. Arrondissement 3 Le Marais quartier

ESSENTIALS ■ **POP** 1990: 35,102, 1999: 34,248 ■ **TAXES** Taxe d'habitation: 10.99%, Taxe foncière: 7.98%
■ **AIRPORT** Nearest airport: Aéroport de Paris Orly, Orly Sud, Orly Aérogare Cedex; Tel +33 1 49 75 15 15, www.adp.fr

KEY FACTS
SCHOOLS Nearest: 15ème, 8ème.
MEDICAL Centre Médicio Social OSE, 106 rue
Vieille du Tenyle, 75003 Paris;
Tel: +33 1 48 87 87 85
RENTAL Excellent, purchasing property in this
arrondissement is a surefire investment ■ Factors
such as an apartment's decor can attract higher fees
■ 700 + euros per week. ■ Average prices per night
in m²: under 50m²- 130 euros; 51 to 100m² - 220
euros; 100 to 150m² - 478 euros, depending upon
arrondissement and not number of bedrooms. ■
Larger studios cost from 250+ euros per night.
PROS A quiet, dignified area where many 17th-
century homes remain ■ The Museum of Picasso
and the Carnavalet Museum are located here,
making it a great area for buying to let ■ The
métro, comprehensive public transport system, and
proximity to central Paris make a car unnecessary
■ The 1er, 2ème, 4ème, 11ème and 10ème
arrondissements surround the 3ème, so there are
incredible amenities on the doorstep.
CONS A lively, buzzy, area, there is always a lot of
activity and buyers wanting a quiet life could find it
rather noisy here.

The Marais *quartiers* (3ème *arrondissement*) is a trendy area with a lively, cultural feel, situated north of the Marais arrondissement (4eme). It features the oldest buildings in Paris, some of which are even medieval, while many 17th-century mansions that once belonged to the noblest Parisian families are still to be seen in this quiet, impressively preserved neighbourhood. Once marshland, monks and knights settled in this *arrondissement* but it was only at the beginning of the 17th century that the Marais began its reputation as a centre of regal elegance. Its name dates back to the market gardens that existed there in the Middle Ages.

Generally high-priced with a few exceptions along the Right Bank, there are discreet cobbled lanes hiding courtyards, gardens, and grand timbered apartments. There are also a few renovated offices, offering tall ceilings and huge windows. Many lesser-known museums like the Jewish Art and History Museum, the Musée de la Chasse et de la Nature, depicting hunting from the Stone Age, and Musée Carnavalet, which portrays Parisian history, are within walking distance. Few green open spaces exist, except for the exclusive Place des Vosges. The oldest area of Paris, this arrondissement and its neighbour, the 4ème have the most historical sights. Properties in the 3ème have characteristically high ceilings and are generally smaller.

Prices start at around 740,000 euros for a two-bedroom apartment in a 19th-century classic Parisian building. The area is home to modern day French nobility in exclusive homes and it has a postcode with an exclusive cachet. ■

4. Arrondissement 4 Le Marais (The Jewish Quarter)

ESSENTIALS ■ **POP** 1990: 32,226, 1999: 30,675 ■ **TAXES** Taxe d'habitation: 10.99%, Taxe foncière: 7.98% ■ **AIRPORT**
Nearest airport: Aéroport de Paris Orly, Orly Sud, Orly Aérogare Cedex; Tel +33 1 49 75 15 15, www.adp.fr

KEY FACTS
SCHOOLS Nearest 15ème and 7ème, as listed
MEDICAL Hôpital Hôtel Dieu, 1, place Pacuis Notre
Dame - 75004 Paris; Tel: +33 1 42 34 82 34.
RENTAL Excellent, there is no shortage of tourists
renting here, so purchasing a property here is a
sensible investment ■ 700 euros plus for a week ■
under 50m²: 130 + euros (a night) ■ 51 to 100 m² -
220 euros (a night) ■ 100 to 50 m² -478 euros (a
night) dependent upon *arrondissement*, not number of
bedrooms ■ November to January is considered a
little quieter, but no firm rental end of season. ■ A two-
bedroom property in Ile de St Louis in Marais can
accrue almost 3,000 euros per week rental.
PROS The historic heart of the city, its oldest
landmarks, Ile Saint-Louis, Ile de la Cité, the Saint-
Chapelle and Notre-Dame churches are here ■
Offering trendy designer boutiques, bars and
restaurants and the Centre Pompidou ■ A strong
alternative scene, with plenty of theatres.
CONS A busy and noisy area, it is not to every buyer's
taste, as this is where many Parisians come to
be entertained.

The centre of the Marais is a fun, lively and mainly young neighbourhood with a strong Bohemian flavour and it houses many trendy bars, shops, and restaurants. The Rue des Rosiers is a centrepiece of Jewish lifestyle in Paris, while the Ile-Saint-Louis and the Ile-de-la-Cité are the oldest parts of Paris. Nestled between the Latin Quarter and the Marais, leafy Ile-Saint-Louis has a tranquil village atmosphere and is especially popular with well-heeled Parisians and international residents. In summer, the island's quay retains popularity as the city's favourite sunbathing spot. Past luminaries include Voltaire, Cézanne, Baudelaire, Helena Rubenstein, and the Rothschilds. In the north of the locality you can find landmark attractions such as the avant-garde Pompidou centre at the heart of the Beaubourg neighbourhood, with its thriving street entertainment. To savour fine 17th and 18th century architecture, explore the neighbourhood from Saint Gervais-Saint Paul (between the Rue Saint-Antoine and the Rue de Rivoli) stopping by at the Musée de la Curiosité et de la Magie, the Maison Européenne de la Photographie and the l'Hôtel de Sens, with its collection of decorative arts from the Middle Ages.

For around 400,000 euros, a renovated 65 square metre one-bedroom apartment situated near the Seine and Ile-Saint-Louis could be yours. Considered trendy, property can be expensive here. It has become increasingly popular and is growing in stature. ■

5. Arrondissement 6: Saint-Germain-des-Prés

ESSENTIALS ■ **POP** 1990: 47,942, 1999: 44,903 ■ **TAXES** Taxe d'habitation: 10.99%, Taxe foncière: 7.98% ■ **AIRPORT** Nearest airport: Aéroport de Paris Orly, Orly Sud, Orly Aérogare Cedex; Tel +33 1 49 75 15 15, www.adp.fr

Once the favourite haunt of bohemians and intellectuals, this Left Bank neighbourhood, known as Saint-Germain-des-Prés, has undergone renovation and is now fashionably chic. Designer boutiques, art galleries and bistros like Polidor, which has been serving basic hearty food since1845, can be found throughout this district. Stop for coffee at Les Deux Magots, named after the two Chinese statues inside and the symbol of Saint-Germain's literary era, where Jean-Paul Sartre and Simone de Beauvoir spent their days absorbed in their writing, or refresh your spirits in the picture postcard setting of the family-friendly Palais de Luxembourg gardens. But its reputation was built on a thriving nightlife around the St Germain area, which is still a draw to Parisians seeking some night-time excitement.

Buyers of traditional property will find some superb 19th-century properties here. A two-bedroom 19th-century house starts at around 120,000 euros, but be aware that its new-found popularity has done much to push prices up.

Alternatively there is the classic six or seven-storey classic Haussmannian apartment, complete with wrought-iron balcony, railings and ornamental stonework. Close to the Jardin de Luxembourg, you can find an apartment with wood panelling and high ceilings, or a separate studio apartment with parking. The majority of properties in the area are apartments and sell from 6,400 to 7,600 euros per square metre.

Chosen for sophisticated pieds-à-terre by foreign purchasers and students at well-heeled universities and écoles, elegant properties can be found here. ■

KEY FACTS
SCHOOLS Nearest: 15ème, as listed.
MEDICAL Institut Arther Vernes, 36 rue d'Assas, 75006 Paris; (+33 144 39 5300; www.institut-vernes.fr).
RENTAL Excellent potential as one of the top four tourist *arrondissements* guaranteeing year round rental income ■ From 700 euros for a week ■ Average prices in m²: under 50m² - 130 euros (a night); 51 to 100m² - 220 euros (a night); 100 to 150m² - 478 euros (a night), depending upon *arrondissement*, not number of bedrooms ■ Up to 750 euros for a week.
PROS On the Left Bank, it is part of the famous Latin Quarter and home to the Luxembourg Palace, art, antiques, bookshops and stylish boutiques ■ An up-and-coming chic part of Paris following a makeover from its bohemian roots, it is currently 'the' *arrondissement'* ■ Posh boutiques, art galleries, theatres, nightclubs and restaurants are in plentiful supply ■ Near to the Eiffel Tower - in the 7ème.
CONS Properties here can cost from 6,400 euros per square metre. ■ One of the most sought-after areas.

6. Arrondissement 7

ESSENTIALS ■ **POP** 1990: 62,998, 1999: 56,988 ■ **TAXES** Taxe d'habitation: 10.99%, Taxe foncière: 7.98% ■ **AIRPORT** Nearest airport: Aéroport de Paris Orly, Orly Sud, Orly Aérogare Cedex; Tel +33 1 49 75 15 15, www.adp.fr

The 7ème is one of the city's chic postcodes, with traditional, bourgeois character. Bounded to the north by the Seine, with the 6ème to the east and the 15ème lying south-west, it is a draw for tourists. Here you will find the Musée d'Orsay with its Impressionist art collections, les Invalides where you can stroll by flower beds along the impressive 500 metre-long Esplanade - at the end of which sits the Eglise St Louis, where Napoleon is buried - and the Eiffel Tower. It's also home to UNESCO, the Assemblée Nationale where you can drop in to listen to a debate, and the Paris sewers which feature in Victor Hugo's *Les Misérables*. This expensive, well-kept area with designer chic apartments has a reputation for being quiet and safe; indeed, the French Prime Minister and several of the ministries are housed around Faubourg and Saint Germain. For a property with grandeur and privacy, the Boulevard des Invalides affords some beautiful architecture. Most of the period buildings are handsome, solid and discreet, but there are modern exceptions. A penthouse with magical views overlooking the main monuments and Montmartre can be bought from around 1,300 000 to 2,300 000 euros.

On a par with the 6ème, this is an expensive part of town and prices are higher than in the Marais. Apartments with underground parking and security remind purchasers of the 7ème's bourgeois flavour. The west side, from Esplanade des Invalides up to the 15ème is much younger and cheaper and properties are priced from 4,500 euros, compared to 5,500 on the east side. ■

KEY FACTS
SCHOOLS Nearest: 7ème, 15ème, as listed.
MEDICAL Hôpital de Jour 39, rue Varennes - 75007 Paris; Tel: +33 1 45 48 96 31.
RENTAL Excellent. One of the top four tourist *arrondissements* ■ There is no real end of season here; perhaps three months in the winter (November to January) might be priced slightly lower, but there is no average fee ■ From 700 euros for a week plus ■ This is tourist central, so any property purchase here is a watertight investment.
PROS A sought-after, select residential *arrondissement*. The main highlights are the Eiffel Tower, the Musée d'Orsay and the Hôtel des Invalides, where Napoleon's tomb is located ■ A wealthy, Left Bank district ■ Filled with dwellings and offices, this central location affords good employment opportunities ■ A central location where a car is not necessary ■ Other attractions are Parc Georges Brassens, the swimming pool theme park Aquaboulevard and the Musée Rodin.
CONS Very busy at weekends in the west side of the *arrondissement*, it attracts lots of tourists ■ Fewer shops, restaurants and cinemas and less amenities, it has increasing desirability for purchasers.

Ile-de-France Hotspots

7. Arrondissement 8

ESSENTIALS ■ **POP** 1990: 48,816, 1999: 39,303 ■ **TAXES** Taxe d'habitation: 10.99%, Taxe foncière: 7.98% ■ **AIRPORT** Nearest airport: Aéroport de Paris Orly, Orly Sud, Orly Aérogare Cedex; Tel +33 1 49 75 15 15, www.adp.fr

KEY FACTS

SCHOOLS Nearest: 8ème, as listed
MEDICAL Hôpital Européen Georges Pompidou, 20 rue Leblanc, 75908 Paris Cedex 15; www.hbroussais.fr/HEGP/
RENTAL Good. The best sized property is a two-bedroom property and for higher rates it is best to offer rental on a short-term basis ■ From 700+ euros for a week for a studio apartment of 20m², one of the most expensive letting locales ■ There is less of a rental scene, but it is still a prime area ■ Management costs for rental properties can be high
PROS Encompasses the Champs-Elysées, the Arc de Triomphe, the Elysées Palace, the Madeleine Church and the Avenue Montaigne and Faubourge Saint-Honoré fashion houses ■ The traditional Paris, it features the more residential-style Haussman-style buildings ■ Property prices are slightly lower than in 1ème to 6ème ■ A car is unnecessary, as there is excellent public transport.
CONS A Touristy area.

This Right Bank *arrondissement* is where the lavish elegance of Paris is to be found, making the 8ème the city's most expensive neighbourhood. You can discover famous fashion houses, multinational company offices, elegant hotels and first-class restaurants such as the Buddha Bar in this vibrant and elite *arrondissement*, along with the presidential Elysée Palace, the Champs-Elysées, the haute couture boutiques of the Rue Saint-Honoré and hotel palaces like the George V and the Crillon.

The locale is quite diverse with lots of tourists in the Champs Elysées area, while the shopping includes delicatessen delight, the Fauchon. In the area to the east, between the Champs-Elysées and Place de la Madeleine, there is a mixture of 19th-century buildings interspersed with businesses. History buffs can visit Place de la Concorde, Obélisque de Luxor, and Eglise de la Madeleine for sculpture and architecture.

If you appreciate scenic views, you can buy a top-floor, four-room apartment from around 800,000 euros. A family might choose a third-floor apartment inside a well-maintained freestone building, from around 2,300,000 euros.

The traditional heart of Paris, it features the residential Haussmannian buildings and slightly lower prices than in the 1er and 6ème. One of the most sought-after locales, this is a family-orientated, beautiful part of Paris. It is also close to the fun 4ème, and it offers a tranquil retreat. Hugely sought after by the foreign buyer, the Eighth *arrondissement* is a quiet residential area enormously respected and an excellent investment for those who can afford it, remaining slightly cheaper then some of the other popular areas. ■

8. Arrondissement 16

ESSENTIALS ■ **POP** 1990: 169,983, 1999: 161,817 ■ **TAXES** Taxe d'habitation: 10.99%, Taxe foncière: 7.98% ■ **AIRPORT** Nearest airport: Aéroport de Paris Orly, Orly Sud, Orly Aérogare Cedex; Tel +33 1 49 75 15 15, www.adp.fr

KEY FACTS

SCHOOLS Nearest: 16ème, 8ème (as listed).
MEDICAL Hôpital Européen Georges Pompidou, 20 rue Leblanc, 75908 Paris Cedex 15; (www.hbboussais.fr/HEGP/') ■ Centre Médical Edouaurd Rist, 14, rue Boileau - 75016 Paris; Tel: +33 1 40 50 52 00.
RENTAL Good, but priced slightly lower than other areas ■ Short-term rentals are better value and two-bedroom properties are most popular ■ Higher rents for short lets. Two-bedroom properties give good value ■ From 700+ euros for a 20m² studio apartment for a week. One of the most expensive places to rent in Paris ■ Steep management costs for short-term lets ■ Bourgois and older residents make it not as lively as the 1er to 8ème.
PROS The locale of wealthy Parisians ■ The Bois de Boulogne and Trocadéro are here (home to government institutions) ■ A growing number of international buyers ■ Near the Trocadéro, the Musée de la Marine and the well-known, Musée de l'Homme, specialising in anthropology.
CONS This quiet locale would not suit every purchaser or tenant ■ Not much nightlife.

This residential area - formerly the village of Passy and one of the biggest *arrondissements* - runs west from the Arc de Triomphe out to Bois de Boulogne, the city's huge, rambling park at the edge where you can run and ride horses. It is another area of expensive property, with large apartments both old and modern. Particularly in the west of the *arrondissement*, there is little street life and it is a quiet area at night. Its close-lying suburb, further west, the district of Neuilly, is a continuation of the same and is ideal for buyers seeking tranquility. Property is frequently owned and let by insurance companies and a growing number of Middle-Eastern purchasers are buying here. Some property owners are related to the original 19th century owners. Literary lovers can visit the apartment of Balzac, who wrote the Comédie Humaine. Close to the Musée Marmottan, it boasts the largest number of Monet paintings in the world. A one to four-bedroom apartment near the Trocadéro costs from 350,000 euros. With more residential emphasis than in other *arrondissements*, classic Haussmannian buildings can sell for millions of euros. Geographically the largest *arrondissement*, the 16ème is very smart. The older areas with very quiet avenues, are located in the south and east near the Trocadéro, and apartments here sell from 5,330 to 7,600 euros per square metre on average. Recently there has been a small decline in interest in this area.■

9. Arrondissement 17

ESSENTIALS ■ **POP** 1990: 161,983, 1999: 161,138 ■ **TAXES** Taxe d'habitation 10.99%, taxe foncière: 7.98% ■ **AIRPORT** Nearest airport: Aéroport de Paris Orly, Orly Sud, Orly Aérogare Cedex; Tel +33 1 49 75 15 15, www.adp.fr

This diverse district contains several residential areas, with the western part, near the Arc de Triomphe, being very upmarket. It is generally a chic area, but more accessible than the 16ème and smaller, it shares the pleasant Monceau park with the 8ème. Many embassies are based here, as are more artists' ateliers than any other *arrondissement* in the city. Areas like the Place des Ternes have a lively feel to them, while the Marché des Moines is one of the cheapest markets in the capital, with a warm and lively atmosphere. Luxury boutiques such as Kenzo, Armani and Louis Vuitton can be found here too.

Culture is perhaps not the speciality of the 17ème as this is a quiet, deserted area after office hours, although you can visit the Palais des Congrès which hosts various exhibitions. Most buildings are 19th century and have bigger rooms than most other *arrondissements*. A mere five minute journey from the Champs Elysée, it also has the feel and atmosphere of a self-contained community.

One to three-bedroom apartments, with security and underground parking can be found for around 230,000 euros. Alternatively, the quiet residential area between Portes de Champerret and Maillot, close to the Arc de Triomphe is ideal for a brand new, two-bedroom apartment. The classic Haussmann-style apartments start from around 490,000 euros. Prices in the Arc de Triomphe and Parc Monceau area to the west are more expensive. Prices increase in neighbourhoods near to Neuilly in the north .■

KEY FACTS
SCHOOLS Nearest: 16ème, 8ème and 17ème.
MEDICAL Centre Médico-Physique, 174, rue Courcelles - 75017 Paris; Tel: +33 1 45 74 75 15.
RENTAL Lower rental available, but still a good location. Traditional Haussmann buildings are found in this residential part of the city. Short-term lets are better value ■ Two-bedroom properties are the best investment for buyers to let ■ There is no real end of season here; perhaps November to January might be slightly cheaper, but there is no average fee ■ High management costs for short-term lets ■ Parts of the area are considered as lacking in life and activity, which could deter tourist tenants.
PROS One of the more wealthy areas ■ A growing number of international foreign buyers ■ Pretty old *Hotel Particulars* from the 19th century are found here ■ Smaller than the 16ème, it has a sense of community ■ A lively outlook, it has great restaurants, bars and nightclubs.
CONS High management costs for short-term lets ■ Parts of the area are considered as lacking in life and activity, which could deter tourist tenants.

HOTSPOTS

10. Versailles

ESSENTIALS ■ **POP** 1990: 87,789, 1999: 85,726 ■ **TAXES** Taxe d'habitation: 15.18%, taxe foncière: 18.20% ■ **AIRPORT1** Nearest airport: Aéroport de Paris Orly, Orly Sud, Orly Aérogare Cedex; Tel +33 1 49 75 15 15, www.adp.fr

Situated in *département* 78, Versailles is undoubtedly best known for the sumptuous palace of the same name that was created by Louis XIV to glorify his reign as the Sun King. Yet Versailles is also a stylish suburb of Paris, where elegant homes are to be found and there is easy access to the city centre by means of the *métro*. This smart town is well-served by the Paris D10 and A13 autoroutes, but far enough out to feel a whole world away from the life of the city. Versailles will be especially attractive to those property buyers who are happy to commute in return for plenty of spacious parkland. King Louis XIV was a great patron of the arts, hence theatre, *fêtes* and *spectacles* dominate the cultural scene. Characterised by its 17th and 18th-century buildings, a market, shops and the Rive Gauche railway station with routes into central Paris, the Left Bank Saint Louis area of Versailles is the oldest quarter, and has been regenerated over the past decade. Filled with exclusive boutiques, it is a desirable purchasing locale. Buyers pay from 4,300 euros per square metre. Prices for a renovated four-bedroom apartment with traditional features and a balcony start from around 1,300,000 euros. A good choice for families is the peaceful, leafy area of Gatigny. Here, a two-bedroom apartment costs around 440,000 euros. Exclusive and expensive, prices are still less than in the 6ème and 1ème and foreign buyers, young professionals and families enjoy its lively ambience. ■

KEY FACTS
SCHOOLS British School of Paris, 38 quai de l'Ecluse, 78290 Croissy-sur-Seine; Tel: 33 1 34 80 45 90 ■ Lycée International of St Germain-en-Laye (American School) Rue du Fer à Cheval BP 230, 78104 Saint-Germain-en-Laye; Tel: +33 1 34 51 74 85.
MEDICAL Clinique Internationale du Parc Monceau, 21 rue de Chazelles, 75017 Paris; Tel: +33 1 48 88 25 25; www.cinique-monceau.com.
RENTAL Average; mostly long-term lets for people who work in the city ■ A small apartment on a long-term basis is cheaper tthan in central Paris, attracting young marrieds ■ Not a tourist area
PROS An oasis of history, a select and glamorous area ■ More peaceful than the centre ■ The Avenue de la Reine is a beautiful place to live ■ Good local amenities and new shopping centres ■ A community in itself.
CONS Taxis from the centre are expensive ■ Traffic jams between Paris and Versaille are common ■ The RER can take up to an hour to reach central Paris and residents can get complacent about Paris.

Useful contacts

Many potential buyers are drawn by the culture and sophistication of the capital

PREFECTURE
Préfecture de la Région d'Ile-de-France
29 rue Barbet de Jouy
75007 Paris
Tel: +33 1 44 42 62 87
Fax: +33 1 44 42 63 37

LEGAL
Chambre des Notaires de Paris
12 avenue Victoria
75001 Paris
Tel: +33 1 44 82 24 00
Fax: +33 1 44 82 24 20

Chambre Interdépartementale des Notaires de Versailles
40 avenue de Paris
78000 Versailles
Tel: +33 1 39 50 01 75
Fax: +33 1 39 02 38 44

FINANCE
Direction des Impôts d'Ile-de-France
33 avenue de l'Opéra
75002 Paris
Tel: +33 1 44 77 99 59

Fax: +33 1 44 77 99 79

Centre des Impôts des Non-Résidents
9 rue d'Uzès
75094 Paris Cedex 02
Tel: +33 1 44 76 18 00
Fax: +33 1 42 21 45 04

BUILDING AND PLANNING
Chambre Régionale de Métiers d'Ile-de-France
72 rue de Reuilly
75592 Paris Cedex 12
Tel: +33 1 53 33 53 07
Fax: +33 1 43 43 71 74

Union Régionale des CAUEs d'Ile-de-France
37 rue du Chemin Vert
93000 Bobigny
Tel: +33 1 48 32 25 93
Fax: +33 1 48 31 15 36

EDUCATION
Rectorat de l'Académie (Seine-et-Marne, Seine-Saint-Denis, Val-de-Marne)
4 rue Georges-Enesco
94010 Crétail

Tel: +33 1 49 81 60 60
Fax: +33 1 49 81 65 90

Rectorat de l'Académie de Paris
47 rue des Ecoles
75230 Paris Cedex 5
Tel: +33 1 40 46 22 11
Fax: +33 1 40 46 20 10

Rectorat de l'Académie de Versailles
(Essonne, Hauts-de-Seine, Val-d'Oise, Yvelines)
3 boulevard de Lesseps
78017 Versailles Cedex
Tel: +33 1 30 83 44 44
Fax: +33 1 39 50 02 47

HEALTH
Caisse Primaire d'Assurance Maladie de Paris
21 rue Georges Auric
75948 Paris Cedex 19
Tel: +33 1 53 38 70 00
Fax: +33 1 53 38 73 47

Caisse Primaire d'Assurance Maladie des Yvelines
92 avenue de Paris

78014 Versailles
Tel: +33 1 39 20 30 00
Fax: +33 1 39 49 58 31

Caisse Primaire d'Assurance Maladie du Val de Marne
9 avenue Général de Gaulle
94031 Crétail
Tel: +33 1 43 99 33 33
Fax: +33 1 43 99 11 07

INTERNATIONAL SCHOOLS
Leonardo da Vinci
rue Sedillot
75007 Paris
Tel: +33 1 45 55 25 74

Ecole Active Bilangue117
Boulevard Malesherbes
75008 Paris
Tel: +33 1 45 63 47 00

Ecole Active Bilingue Maternelle
6 avenue Van Dyck
75008 Paris
Tel: +33 1 46 82 14 24

Ecole Active Bilingue
Jeannine Manuel

70 rue du Théâtre
75015 Paris
Tel: +33 1 44 37 00 80

Ecole Active Bilingue
70 rue du Théâtre
75015 Paris
Tel: +33 01 44 37 00 80

Ecole Active Bilangue
123 rue de la Pompe
75016 Paris
Tel: +33 1 45 53 89 36

International School of Paris
6 rue Beethoven
75016 Paris
Tel: +33 1 42 24 09 54

Eurécole,
5 rue de Lübeck
75016 Paris
Tel: +33 1 40 70 12 81

Ecole Active Bilangue
16 rue Margueritte
75017 Paris
Tel: +33 1 4622 40 20

€50-200,000
(£33-66,000)

Paris and its environs are dominated by pieds-à-terre that can cost as much as a comfortable, three bedroom Breton cottage. Prices vary depending on the arrondissement, but for those with a budget within this price bracket, expect no more than a one-bedroom flat in Paris' environs.

€74,737 — IMO

IVRY SUR SEINE, DÉPARTEMENT 94

A studio apartment located in the centre of Paris, in a developing area

£49,825

🛏1 🚫*no garden* 🚇*within 800m of central Paris* 🛣*located on a main road* 🅿*room for parking*

€155,000 — GRM

7ÉME, DÉPARTEMENT 75

Set in a quiet street, a renovated studio, located in an 18th century building

£103,335

🛏1 🚫*no garden* 🚇*close to all amenities* 🛣*located on a main road* 🅿*no private parking*

€178,949 — IMO

19ÉME, DÉPARTEMENT 75

A studio apartment, sleeping three, situated in the 19th arrondissement

£119,300

🛏3 🚫*no garden* 🚇*within easy reach of the centre* 🛣*located on a main road* 🅿*room for parking*

€195,000 — FRE

8ÉME, DÉPARTEMENT 75

A furnished Haussmann apartment well-located in this popular area of Paris

£130,000

🛏1 🚫*no garden, with courtyard* 🚇*within 5 mins of amenities* 🛣*not located on a main road* 🅿*no private parking*

HOTSPOTS

127

€200-500,000
(£133-333,000)

Within Paris itself, especially the 16th and 17th arrondissements, apartments and pieds-à-terre can cost 200,000 euros plus. Country properties surrounding Paris offer a greater number of bedrooms and gardens, and are significantly cheaper and larger than Parisian property.

€205,000 — FRE

7ÉME, DÉPARTEMENT 75

In a residential area, a furnished studio apartment, close to the market

£136,665

🛏1 🌳no garden 🏙located in central Paris 🛣not located on a main road
🅿room for parking

€210,000 — IMO

7ÉME, DÉPARTEMENT 75

An apartment set in central Paris, with stunning views over the Eiffel Tower

£140,000

🛏1 🌳no garden 🏙located in central Paris 🛣located on a main road
🅿room for parking

€228,675 — FRE

7ÉME, DÉPARTEMENT 75

An apartment located on the fifth floor of this 19th century building, with views

£152,450

🛏1 🌳no garden 🏙in a central location 🛣located on a main road
🅿no private parking

€314,000 — FRE

MONTMARTRE, DÉPARTEMENT 75

A lovely apartment offering stunning views over the Sacré Coeur monument

£209,335

🛏1 🌳no garden 🏙within walking distance of central Paris 🛣located on a
main road 🅿room for parking

€330,000
GRM

3ÉME, DÉPARTEMENT 75

A superb apartment, located on the second floor of a 17th century building

£220,000

⊟1   no garden   close to all amenities   not located on a main road

no private parking

€330,000
IMO

16ÉME, DÉPARTEMENT 75

A flat, located in the prestigious 16th *arrondissement*, with 84m living space

£220,000

⊟2   private garden   located in central Paris   not located on a main road

with private parking

€388,500
FRE

8ÉME, DÉPARTEMENT 75

A beautiful apartment located on the third floor, with a luxurious interior

£259,000

⊟1   no garden   within walking distance of central Paris   located on a main road   no private parking

---

€396,500
DEE

NR BOBIGNY, DÉPARTEMENT 77

Close to the international airport and central Paris, this is a new property

£264,335

⊟3 $1,800m^2$ within 20 kms of Paris   not located on a main road

room for parking, with a three-car garage

€403,989
FRA

NR CHESSY, DÉPARTEMENT 77

A charming country house in a rural location, close to Euro Disney

£269,326

⊟4 $3,000m^2$ 30 mins from central paris   not located on a main road

room for parking, with a garage

€450,000
FRE

6ÉME, DÉPARTEMENT 75

An ideal second home, this property is set in Paris' Golden Triangle

£300,000

⊟2   no garden   located in central Paris   located on a main road

room for parking

€500,000+
(£333,000+)

There is a huge demand for properties in Paris, both from those seeking a permanent home and those who are buying to rent. This is particularly focused around the sixth, seventh and eightharrondissements. Consequently the majority of properties cost 500,000 euros plus. Those with the budget can choose from pieds-à-terre, mansions in Versailles, or private Haussmannian apartments.

PRICE GUIDE

€500,000 — CODE DEE

MORET-SUR-LOING, DÉPARTEMENT 75

A traditional farmhouse, in a peaceful rural location, near Fontainebleau forest

£333,335

🛏4 ▦4,856m^2 📷1.5 kms from the village amenities 🚫not located on a main road 🅿room for parking

€525,000 — CODE SIF

LES CHEROLLES, DÉPARTEMENT 77

An 18th century property, situated in attractive woodland, with outbuildings

£350,000

🛏6 ▦40,000m^2 📷4 kms from town 🚫not located on a main road 🅿room for parking

€593,000 — CODE GRM

7ÉME, DÉPARTEMENT 75

Located in an 18th century building, a charming apartment to renovate

£395,335

🛏2 ▦no garden 📷close to all amenities 🚫located on a main road 🅿no private parking

€599,000 — CODE FRE

17ÉME, DÉPARTEMENT 75

An exclusive apartment, tastefully designed, with a living space of 100m^2

£399,335

🛏2 ▦86m^2 📷located in central Paris 🚫not located on a main road 🅿room for parking

€625,000
CODE GRM

15ÉME, DÉPARTEMENT 75

A luxurious apartment, close to the Eiffel Tower offering views over Paris

£416,665

🛏2 🌼no garden 🏙close to all amenities 🛣located on a main road
🅿no room for parking

€681,000
CODE FRE

11ÉME, DÉPARTEMENT 75

Located in the centre of Paris, this magnificent apartment enjoys great views

£454,000

🛏3 🌼no garden 🏙close to all amenities 🛣located on a main road
🅿no private parking

€750,000
CODE FRE

4ÉME, DÉPARTEMENT 75

An apartment on the second floor of this traditional building, fully refurbished

£500,000

🛏2 🌼no garden 🏙located close to all amenities 🛣located on a main road
🅿no private parking

€801,000
CODE GRM

7ÉME, DÉPARTEMENT 75

A unique *pied-à-terre*, located on the ground floor of this luxurious building

£534,000

🛏2/3 🌼no garden 🏙close to all amenities 🛣not located on a main road
🅿no private parking

€802,000
CODE IMO

2ÉME, DÉPARTEMENT 75

4-star apartments, located on the edge of the artistic Marais district

£534,665

🛏1/4 🌼no garden 🏙located in central Paris 🛣located on a main road
🅿room for parking

€969,580
CODE CBR

16ÉME, DÉPARTEMENT 75

Located on the third floor of this high quality house, an apartment with a lift

£646,385

🛏2 🌼no garden 🏙in the centre of Paris 🛣located on a main road
🅿room for parking

PRICE GUIDE

€1,150,000 GRM

7ÉME, DÉPARTEMENT 75

An apartment on the third floor of this Haussmannian building, to renovate

£766,665

⊟3 🏠no garden 🖼located close to all amenities 🖼located on a main road 🅿no private parking

€1,163,000 FRE

SAINT-CLOUD, DÉPARTEMENT 92

A large, luxurious apartment, located in an exclusive suburb, with great views

£775,335

⊟4 🏠no garden, with balcony 🖼within 5 mins of the heart of town 🖼not located on a main road 🅿including a parking space

€1,219,600 FRA

PORTE D'ORLEANS, DÉPARTEMENT 92?

A *Maison Bourgeoise*, with oak flooring, surrounded by protected parkland

£813,065

⊟7 🏠3,200m² 🖼within easy reach of central Paris 🖼not located on a main road 🅿with a garage

€1,295,206 CBR

16ÉME, DÉPARTEMENT 75

A south facing apartment, with splendid views, benefitting from a balcony

£863,470

⊟2 🏠no garden 🖼close to all amenities 🖼not located on a main road 🅿room for parking

€1,312,500 CBR

RAMBOUILLET, DÉPARTEMENT 78

Dating from 1930 and with various outbuildings, grounds and a lake

£875,000

⊟n/a 🏠530,000m² 🖼60 kms from Paris 🖼not located on a main road 🅿room for parking

€1,450,000 GRM

8ÉME, DÉPARTEMENT 75

Set in a Haussmannian-style building, a stunning third floor apartment

£966,665

⊟3 🏠no garden 🖼close to all amenities 🖼located on a main road 🅿room for parking

€1,450,000 · CBR

16ÉME, DÉPARTEMENT 75

An excellent quality apartment, on the second floor of this traditional building

£966,665

✉3 ▨no garden ▣located in the centre of Paris ▣not located on a main road ▣no room for private parking

€1,472,000 · GRM

7ÉME, DÉPARTEMENT 75

A unique stone building, offering a family apartment, set in a quiet location

£981,335

✉4 ▨with a balcony ▣close to all amenities ▣not located on a main road ▣no private parking

€1,500,000 · DEE

16ÉME, DÉPARTEMENT 75

This apartment is located on the third floor of a mansion in a private street

£1,000,000

✉2 ▨with two terraces ▣located in the centre of Paris ▣located on a main road ▣no private parking

€1,550,000 · CBR

8ÉME, DÉPARTEMENT 75

Located close to the Parc Monceau, a luxurious third floor apartment

£1,033,335

✉2 ▨no garden ▣located close to the centre ▣located on a main road ▣no private parking

€1,677,000 · CBR

RAMBOUILLET, DÉPARTEMENT 78

A fine 18th century manor, arranged over four floors, featuring a trout river

£1,118,000

✉13 ▨30,000m^2 ▣located in a village with all amenities ▣not located on a main road ▣room for parking, with garages

€1,750,000 · FRE

SAINT GERMAIN, DÉPARTEMENT 75

A large traditional style chalet, located close to the ski slopes and village

£1,166,665

✉3 ▨2,000m^2 ▣within 5 mins of village ▣not located on a main road ▣room for parking, with a garage for 3 cars

PRICE GUIDE

€1,926,400   CODE CBR

FÉROLLES-ANTTILLY, DÉPARTEMENT 77

A modern property, enjoying wooded grounds, a tennis court and pool

£1,284,265

🛏 7   🏞 with vast grounds   🚗 25 kms from Paris   🚫 not located on a main road

🏠 room for parking

€2,100,000   CODE CBR

ANDILLY, DÉPARTEMENT 95

A beautiful property, fully renovated and newly decorated, in a rural location

£1,400,000

🛏 6/7   🏞 15,000m²   🏘 close to village amenities   🚫 not located on a main road

🏠 room for parking, with a garage

€2,160,000   CODE DEE

16ÉME, DÉPARTEMENT 75

An exclusive mansion located on a private street, dating from the 19th century

£1,440,000

🛏 4   🏞 no garden   🏙 located in the centre of Paris   🚗 located in a private road

🏠 room for parking

€2,200,000   CODE DEE

VERSAILLES, DÉPARTEMENT 78

A large period house, located at the edge of a forest with exceptional views

£1,466,665

🛏 -   🏞 16,000m²   🚗 30 kms from central Paris   🚫 not located on a main road

🏠 room for parking

€2,400,000   CODE DEE

SOUTH PARIS, DÉPARTEMENT 75

Comprising of a château and various outbuildings converted to guest quarters

£1,600,000

🛏 4   🏞 11000m²   🚗 within 17 kms of Paris   🚫 not located on a main road

🏠 room for parking

€3,210,000   CODE DEE

BOULOGNE, DÉPARTEMENT 92

Beautifully and originally designed, a unique property with spacious rooms

£2,140,000

🛏 6   🏞 with garden   🏘 close to amenities   🚫 not located on a main road

🏠 room for parking

PRICE GUIDE

Woods and water meadows
Magnificent architecture
Chic champagne

Champagne-Ardenne

Profile 138
Hotspots 140

PRICE GUIDE
€10,000-€50,000 143
€50,000-€100,000 144
€100,000-€120,000 145
€120,000-€500,000 146
€500,000+ 148

Champagne-Ardenne Profile

PROFILE

Getting there

AIR Ryanair (0871 246 0000; www.ryanair.com) flies to Reims from London Stansted. **Air France** (0845 359 1000; www.airfrance.co.uk), **British Airways** (0870 850 9850; www.britishairways.com), **bmibaby** (0870 264 2229; www.bmibaby.com), **British European** (0870 567 6676; www.flybe.com) and **British Midland** all operate flights from various UK airports to Paris, where connections are available via air, rail and road to Champagne-Ardenne. For northern Champagne-Ardenne, Brussels-South Charleroi may be more convenient than Paris, and **Ryanair** flies to Charleroi from Glasgow, Liverpool and London Stansted.

ROAD The A26 runs from the ferry port at Calais straight through to Reims. Change on to the N43 at Arras for Charleville-Mézières. From Paris the A4 runs straight to Reims, and the N51 runs from Reims to Epernay.

COACH Eurolines coaches Eurolines (0870 514 3219; www.eurolines.com) travel from the UK to Reims, Troyes and Chaumont.

RAIL TGV trains serve Reims, while SNCF services operate from Paris Gare de l'Est and Reims, Châlons-en-Champagne, Troyes and Charleville-Mézières. You could take the **Eurostar** (0870 518 6186; www.eurostar.co.uk) to Lille-Europe and from there SNCF services to Champagne-Ardenne. For all rail enquiries and more details about local services, contact **Rail Europe** (0870 584 8848; www.raileurope.co.uk).

THE ECONOMY

Wine and champagne (including Moët et Chandon) production have dominated this region, and specifically Epernay and Reims, since the 16th century. But high-tech industries are now developing in Reims and Charleville-Mézières on the industrial park, the *Centre régional d'innovation et de transfert de technologie*, though unemployment remains a large problem in Charleville. Tourism is increasing in Reims and Champagne, especially wine tours and holidays.

BEST/WORST VALUE FOR MONEY

Growing tourism and an established wine industry have made Reims one of the priciest locations; apartments and houses cost 1,320 euros per m² on average), yet demand for relocation still makes buying an investment. Demand far outstrips supply, and a lack of rental properties has created a landlords' market.

Increasing numbers of foreign visitors and city centre regeneration plans for a shopping centre and recreation facilities give Chalôns-en-Champagne similar long-term buy-to-let value, with a planned TGV link as icing on the cake.

Brussels civil servants have pushed prices up in Chalôns-en-Champagne and in Ardenne's Charleville-Mézières, where prices for four and six-bedroom

Champagne-Ardenne
offers an abundance of
traditional architecture

Champagne's association with luxury means that foreign buyers are willing to pay more than the norm for property

The wine and champagne industry dominates the region's economy

houses start at 196,000 euros and between 80,000-216,000 euros, respectively. Cheaper renovation properties can be hunted out.

Epernay is a key buy-to-let area, with about 300,000 visitors a year, many of them British and American. Property prices here start at 198,000 euros. If a bargain area exists, the Vallée de la Marne would be it, with three- to four-bedroom houses from 164,500 euros. Bear in mind, however, that Champagne's association with luxury can make buyers willing to pay more.

WHERE TO GO FOR WHAT
Thriving employment markets in Charleville-Mézières and Reims make them ideal for relocators planning to live and work the French way. Culturally rich too, Reims has free summer concerts to suit any family. For long-term letting, Reims, Charleville-Mézières and Epernay are the best locations, but short-term seasonal letting is growing in Reims, with French, British, Belgian and German visitors. Charleville and Bogny-sur-Meuse offer tourist letting markets with high rents, a long season, and a good number of *fermettes* to renovate.

PROPERTY PRICE TRENDS
Prices are increasing throughout the region. A family house in Epernay costs around 305,000 euros and the same amount in Reims would buy a property with no garden. One hour from Paris by TGV and supported by international visitors, the market has soared in Reims and Epernay in the past two years, increasing by six per cent in Reims.

In and around the heart of Champagne, prices are higher, and a four-bedroom house in the countryside around Verzy is about 430,000 euros. Parisian buying power has pushed up prices in this area, ranging from 194,000 to 227,000 euros in Chalôns-en-Champagne .

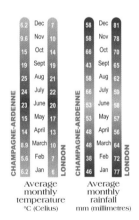

Average monthly temperature °C (Celius)

Average monthly rainfall mm (millimetres)

Average House Sale Prices

HOTSPOTS	2-BED	3-BED	4 BED	5 BED	6/7 BED	8-BED
Charleville-Mézières	-	€120K (£80K)	€275K (£185K)	-	-	-
Châlon-en-Champagne	-	€100K (£65K)	€175K (£115K)	-	€200K (£135K)	-
Epernay	-	-	€190K (£125K)	€230K (£155K)		-
Reims	-	€300K (£200K)	€430K (£285K)	-	-	-

Champagne-Ardenne Hotspots

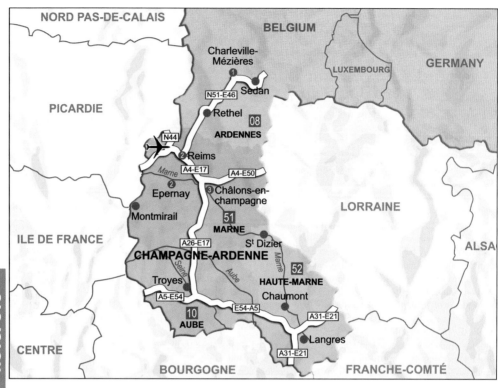

1. Charleville-Mézières and surrounds

ESSENTIALS ■ **POP** 1990: 59,439, 1999: 58,092 ■ **TAXES** Taxe d'habitation: 26.17%, Taxe foncière: 44.75%
■ **AIRPORT** Aéroport Reims Champagne, 51450 Betheny Aérogare, Tel: +33 3 26 07 15 15, Fax: +33 3 26 07 85 96.

KEY FACTS

SCHOOLS Contact the Rectorat de l'Académie de Reims, rue Navier 1, 51082 Reims Cedex, Tel: +33 3 26 05 69 69, Fax:+33 3 26 05 69 42, for advice.

MEDICAL Centre Hospitalier, av Manchester 45, 08000 Charleville-Mézières, Tel: +33 3 24 58 70 70.

RENTALS Tourism is the main growth industry in the Ardenne area, and rental property is expensive ■ Tourists are mainly French, Dutch and Belgian, with increasing numbers of Britons ■ The rental season lasts from May to September, with the average rental ranging from 200-360 euros a week in peak season.

PROS Foreign buyers are mainly from Luxembourg, Denmark and Brussels ■ More English buyers are being drawn here by the many *fermettes* to renovate, with parcels of land ■ Easy access from Paris into the region by the A4-E50, then the N51-E46 on from Reims ■ A destination, for families pursuing outdoor activity holidays .

CONS Overlooked by the British market and better known to the French and Germans ■ Proximity to Brussels makes this area more expensive, with many civil servants buying property.

The region of Champagne-Ardenne is formed by deep, thickly-wooded valleys which are magnificent in any season, and it is traversed by the winding Meuse and Semoy rivers. The capital is Charleville-Mézières, which was the birthplace of the poet Rimbaud, formed just 20 years ago from two competing communities, with Mézières the original main town, starting its life in 899AD as a fortress.

The town is now the world capital of puppetry, hosting a puppet festival for one week in September, every three years. In the 17th-century *vieux quartier*, christened the 'New Town', visit the Ardennes Museum, the Notre-Dame of Hope Basilica and the Musée Rimbaud, housed in a windmill near Place Ducale, with an entire room dedicated to the young poet. A few miles away lies Sedan, site of the largest fortified château in Europe. Enjoying a strategic position on the eastern border of France, it was constantly reinforced and modernised by the Dukes of Bouillon and sovereign princes of Sedan.

With more than 150,000 hectares of oak, beech and ash, the surrounding forests of the Ardennes provide plenty of hunting for wild boar and game. Local specialities reflect forest treasures such as game cooked in wild juniper and red turkey terrine, with bacon salad.

A popular area with foreign buyers due to its inexpensive and renovation property; prices range from 80,000 to 216,000 euros. A two-bedroom apartment in the centre of Charleville-Mézières starts from 190,000 euros. ■

2. Reims and Epernay

ESSENTIALS ■ POP 1990: 212,902, 1999: 218,358 ■ **TAXES** Taxe d'habitation: 38.64%, Taxe foncière: 29.69%
■ **AIRPORT** Aéroport Reims Champagne, 51450 Betheny Aérogare, Tel: +33 3 26 07 15 15, Fax: +33 3 26 07 85 96

In the heart of Champagne, home to the vineyards of the Pinot Noir and Pinot Meunier grape varieties, historic Reims owes its fame not only to champagne but to its numerous UNESCO treasures. The Cathedral of Our Lady is a masterpiece of Gothic architecture, housing a collection of renowned statues, and was on several occasions a coronation site for the kings of France. Even older is the Church of Saint-Rémi, half-Romanesque, half-Gothic in style, and comparable in size to the Notre-Dame-de-Paris.

Beneath the town and its suburbs are 150 miles of cellars cut into the chalk. During World War II bombing, the citizens of Reims sheltered there, but now they house more than a billion bottles of champagne! A visit to this capital city would not be complete without a wine tasting tour, perhaps visiting the houses of Mumm, Clicquot or Ruinart. Property buyers have the pick of the champagne trail from Reims to Epernay, which covers 45 miles of Champagne's villages and the vineyards between. On the left bank of the Marne Valley, Epernay rivals Reims as a champagne producer, boasting 200 miles of cellars. Unusual attractions include the Wedding Traditions Museum and the Snail Museum. If you prefer outdoor pursuits, boating on the Marne takes you past lush vineyards.

Buyers are prepared to pay high prices to live in the area, and interest from Paris has raised prices. The average cost of a four-bedroom property in Reims is 430,000 euros, while three-bedroom houses start from 178,000 euros. ■

KEY FACTS

SCHOOLS Rectorat de l'Académie de Reims, rue Navier 1, 51082 Reims Cedex, Tel: +33 3 26 05 69 69, Fax:+33 3 26 05 69 42 (for advice on education).
MEDICAL Centre Hospitalier Universitaire de Reims, rue Gén Koenig, 51100 Reims, Tel: +33 3 26 78 78 78.

RENTALS This area is very popular with tourists as the champagne route is centred on Reims and Epernay ■ Half the tourists are French, but there are also British, Belgians and Germans

PROS Just an hour from Paris, Reims is a popular destination and easily accessible ■ It is rich in culture and history ■ Epernay is less inspiring but is home to the champagne industry, with many cellars located in the Avenue de Champagne ■ Reims offers many smart townhouses and apartments ■ Most buyers are French, many moving here for work, not just to relocate or retire ■ The market for permanent relocation properties is larger than for holiday homes.

CONS Huge demand in the Reims market pushes up prices ■ Easy access from Paris to Reims makes property very expensive ■ The demand for property is much greater than the supply

HOTSPOTS

3. Châlons-en-Champagne

ESSENTIALS ■ POP 1990: -, 1999: 48,000 ■ **TAXES** Taxe d'habitation: 36.33%, Taxe foncière: 33.99%
■ **AIRPORT** Aéroport Reims Champagne, 51450 Betheny Aérogare, Tel: +33 3 26 07 15 15, Fax: +33 3 26 07 85 96.

Formerly known as Châlons-sur-Marne, the capital of the Marne *département* is historically linked to Attila the Hun, who was defeated here by Actius. Not just a champagne centre, it also produces beer, textiles and electrical equipment, and fortunately has retained its medieval architecture.

Running parallel to the Marne, the Châlons canals are spread through an area known as the Left Bank, with many stone bridges and old cafés. Close to Place Monseigneur Tissier is the town hall, one of the grandest buildings, and the church of Notre-Dame-en-Vaux is a UNESCO World Heritage Site. Place Notre-Dame is surrounded by charming little stone houses and the Gothic Cathedral of Saint-Étienne. Le Petit Jard, situated between two of the canals on the south side of town, is a peaceful riverside garden, a favourite place to stroll since the Middle Ages. Nearby, the little town of Saint-Ménéhould has contributed to the gastronomic world with its recipes for pigs' feet and carp, but is better known for the fact that in 1791 its postmaster spotted Louis XVI attempting to flee the Paris and the Revolution, and raised the alarm.
Just five miles from Châlons, champagne tastings take place at the Joseph Perrier estate.

In the countryside around Châlons, a renovated two-storey *maison en pierre* costs from 167,000 euros and in Châlons-sur-Vitry, a quiet canal suburb of the city, a seven-room house starts at 220,000 euros. ■

KEY FACTS

SCHOOLS Contact the Rectorat de l'Académie de Reims, rue Navier 1, 51082 Reims Cedex, Tel: +33 3 26 05 69 69, Fax:+33 3 26 05 69 42, for advice.
MEDICAL Hôpital de Châlons-en-Champagne, rue Commdt Derrien 51, 51000 Châlons-en-Champagne, Tel: +33 3 26 69 60 60, Fax: +33 3 26 21 38 20.

RENTALS Châlons-en-Champagne receives mainly French visitors, but many foreign tourists come between spring and autumn ■ Holiday rentals are very expensive, and rentals are mostly long-term ■ Little demand for seasonal rentals, but more people are buying to let.

PROS Foreign tourism is on the increase, and particularly from Britain ■ The area within a 3-mile radius of Châlons is very popular for buying property ■ There are excellent access routes.

CONS Houses are very expensive, with the lowest prices around 135,000 to 150,000 euros ■ A shortage of renovation properties here makes some people prefer to buy in the Ardenne and Argonne ■ Increasing demand for property is further pushing prices that are already high.

Useful contacts

The region offers characterful properties, ideal for those seeking a rural lifestyle

PREFECTURE
Préfecture de la Région
Champagne-Ardenne
rue Carnot 38
51036 Châlons-en-Champagne
Cedex
Tel: +33 3 26 26 10 10
Fax: +33 3 26 26 12 63

LEGAL
Chambre des Notaires

cours Jean-Baptiste Langlet 44
BP 1181
51100 Reims Cedex
Tel: +33 3 26 86 72 10
Fax: +33 3 26 86 72 11

FINANCE
Direction des Impôts de l'Est
rue du Cardinal Tisserant 2
BP 70307
54006 Nancy Cedex

Tel: +33 3 83 36 32 80
Fax: +33 3 83 36 32 89

BUILDING & PLANNING
Chambre Régionale de
Métiers de Champagne-
Ardenne
rue Titon 42
51000 Chalons-en-Champagne
Tel: +33 3 29 68 10 55
Fax: +33 3 26 66 88 06

CAUE de Haute-Marne
Maison de l'Habitat
BP 178
rue des Abbés Durand 16
52006
Chaumont Cedex
Tel: +33 3 25 32 52 62
Fax: +33 3 25 02 37 16

EDUCATION
Rectorat de l'Académie de

Reims
rue Navier 1
51082 Reims Cedex
Tel: +33 3 26 05 69 69

HEALTH
Caisse Primaire d'Assurance
Maladie de la Marne
rue Ruisselet 14
51100 Reims Cedex
Tel: +33 3 26 84 40 40

€10–50,000
(£6–33,000)

With property fetching high prices throughout this region it is difficult to secure a bargain even in the lowest price bracket. Most require extensive restoration or are situated in a quiet, unrecognised area of Champagne-Ardenne.

€12,300   **CODE** LUC

NR LANGRES, DÉPARTEMENT 52

This property requires restoration, and offers a spacious living area and cellar

£8,200

🛏 n/a 📐 215m² 🏘 close to town and amenities 🚫 not located on a main road 🚗 room for parking

€21,000   **CODE** LUC

NR LANGRES, DÉPARTEMENT 52

With splendid views over a lake, this newly-built house offers all amenities

£14,000

🛏 4 📐 386m² 🏘 close to town and services 🚫 not located on a main road 🚗 room for parking

€23,500   **CODE** DEV

VOUZIERS, DÉPARTEMENT 08

A 19th-century presbytery, located in a rural area, requiring full renovation

£15,500

🛏 n/a 🌳 with a small garden 🏘 close to amenities 🚫 not located on a main road 🚗 room for parking

€24,000   **CODE** DEV

ST DIZIER, DÉPARTEMENT 51

A small 19th-century farmhouse situated in a rural village, needing work

£16,000

🛏 n/a 🌳 with a garden 🏘 within 5 mins of village 🚫 not located on a main road 🚗 room for parking

€50–100,000
(£33–66,000)

Most properties within this price bracket require modernisation, and/or partial restoration. Some are fairly modern, but most are generally lacking in amenities or are fairly small. Some bargains are available, although few quality homes are on offer for less than 100,000 euros.

€73,900 CODE LUC

NR LANGRES, DÉPARTEMENT 52

With outbuildings and an attic to convert, perfect as a renovation project

£49,500

🛏2 🏠503m² 🖼close to amenities 🚫not located on a main road

🏠room for parking

€78,000 CODE DEV

RETHEL, DÉPARTEMENT 08

A period farmhouse, fully renovated and residing in extensive grounds

£52,000

🛏n/a 🏠with extensive grounds 🖼within 5 mins of amenities

🚫not located on a main road 🏠room for parking

€86,500 CODE LUC

NR LANGRES, DÉPARTEMENT 52

This modern property overlooks a lake and offers a fully-fitted kitchen

£57,500

🛏3 🏠303m² 🖼close to amenities 🚫not located on a main road

🏠room for parking, with a garage

€88,646 CODE FPP

FORET D'ORTHE, DÉPARTEMENT 10

A beautiful brick built *longere*, with an attached barn, set in wooded grounds

£59,095

🛏3 🏠6,070m² 🖼within 5 mins of village 🚫not located on a main road

🏠room for parking

€100–120,000
(£66–80,000)

Many of these properties are fully renovated, requiring very little work. Despite the increasing costs of the region, some potential bargains still exist, and a nice property can be secured in the 100,000-200,000 euro range.

€105,000   CODE LUC

NR LANGRES, DÉPARTEMENT 52

This house offers numerous outbuildings to convert, and a wood interior

£70,000

⊞ 3   ▣ 2,199m^2 ▨ close to all amenities   ▨ not located on a main road

▨ room for parking

€107,000   CODE LUC

NR LANGRES, DÉPARTEMENT 52

Requiring some work to make it fit for habitation, a modern property

£71,500

⊞ 3   ▣ 1,803m^2 ▨ close to town and amenities   ▨ not located on a main road

▨ room for parking

€117,300   CODE LUC

NR LANGRES, DÉPARTEMENT 52

A renovated property, with a spacious living area, ideal for a second home

£78,000

⊞ 3   ▣ 1,090m^2 ▨ close to amenities   ▨ not located on a main road

▨ room for parking

€120,000   CODE DEV

RETHEL, DÉPARTEMENT 08

A 65,000m^2 lake, with grounds suitable for a fishing development

£80,000

⊞ n/a   ▣ with grounds   ▨ within 5 mins of village   ▨ not located on a main road

▨ room for parking

€120–500,000
(£80–333,000)

Within this price range more unique and luxurious properties become available, such as the 4-berth barge and 19th-century manor house featured here. City centre houses can be found within this range, especially in the more affluent areas such as Reims.

€140,000 **CODE** DEV

CHARLEVILLE-MÉZIÈRES, DÉPARTEMENT 08

A small manor house, dating from the 13th century, requiring full renovation

£93,335

🛏 n/a 🏡 with a large garden 🖼 within 5 mins of village �road not located on a main road 🚗 room for parking

€183,000 **CODE** DEV

NR CHARLEVILLE-MÉZIÈRES, DÉPARTEMENT 08

An attractive detached property, with a library, workshop and a fishing river

£970,000

🛏 5 🏡 4,900m² 🖼 within 5 mins of village � not located on a main road 🚗 room for parking, with a double garage

€209,000 **CODE** LUC

NR LANGRES, DÉPARTEMENT 52

This farmhouse, located in a small village, offers outbuildings to convert

£139,500

🛏 3 🏡 4,200m² 🖼 close to town and amenities � not located on a main road 🚗 room for parking

€220,000 **CODE** DEV

SAINT MENEHOULD, DÉPARTEMENT 51

A hunting lodge, set in a forested area, ideal for a weekend retreat

£146,500

🛏 n/a 🏡 120,000m² 🖼 in a isolated area � not located on a main road 🚗 room for parking

€229,000   CODE DEV

NR REIMS, DÉPARTEMENT 51

A 19th-century manor house, in a *colombage* style, currently a restaurant

£152,500

🖼 *n/a* 🏠 *with a small garden* 🏘 *within 5 mins of village* 🛣 *located on a main road* 🅿 *room for parking*

€230,000   CODE DEV

SAINT MENEHOULD, DÉPARTEMENT 51

A large traditional-style chalet, located close to the ski slopes and village

£153,335

🖼 *n/a* 🏠 *with extensive grounds* 🏘 *within 5 mins of village* 🛣 *not located on a main road* 🅿 *room for parking*

€240,000   CODE LUC

NR LANGRES, DÉPARTEMENT 52

This period house offers a traditional interior, and a variety of outbuildings

£160,000

🖼 *6* 🏠 *1,715m²* 🏘 *close to amenities* 🛣 *not located on a main road* 🅿 *room for parking*

€308,000   CODE FRA

NR AUBETERRE, DÉPARTEMENT 10

A fully restored spacious country house with stunning views of the countryside

£205,335

🖼 *5* 🏠 *3,000m²* 🏘 *close to amenities* 🛣 *not located on a main road* 🅿 *room for parking*

€380,000   CODE DEE

NOGENT-SUR-SEINE, DÉPARTEMENT 10

A barge moored on the Seine, entirely renovated and serves as a hotel

£253,500

🖼 *4* 🏠 *n/a* 🏘 *moored close to all amenities* 🛣 *not located on a main road* 🅿 *Parking available by docking space*

€404,000   CODE FRA

NR EPERNAY, DÉPARTEMENT 51

A 19th century renovated farmhouse, with outbuildings ideal for a gite complex

£269,335

🖼 *4* 🏠 *5,000m²* 🏘 *close to town and amenities* 🛣 *not located on a main road* 🅿 *room for parking*

PRICE GUIDE

€500,000+
(£333,000+)

The countryside of Champagne offers an abundance of châteaux and elegant village properties, which command high prices and make for luxurious homes. Prices have risen in line with demand; as ever, luxury has to be paid for.

€520,000 **CODE** SIF

ÉPERNAY, DÉPARTEMENT 51

A lovely property dating from the 19th century, in a rustic style, with towers

£347,000

🛏 11 📐 7,000m^2 🚉 within 5 mins of village 🛣 not located on a main road

🅿 room for parking, with a garage for three cars

€750,000 **CODE** DEV

SEDAN, DÉPARTEMENT 08

A large 19th-century château in immaculate condition, with a lake

£500,000

🛏 n/a 📐 with extensive grounds 🚉 within 5 mins of village

🛣 not located on a main road 🅿 room for parking

€1,260,000 **CODE** LUC

CHARLEVILLE-MÉZIÈRES, DÉPARTEMENT 06

A listed 16th-century chateau, situated in landscaped gardens near the river

£840,000

🛏 8 📐 30,000m^2 🚉 4 kms from all shops and services

🛣 not located on a main road 🅿 room for parking

€1,284,000 **CODE** SIF

NR SEDAN, DÉPARTEMENT 08

With access to the Meuse, this 16th-century chateau is in a habitable state

£856,000

🛏 6 📐 30,000m^2 🚉 close to town and amenities 🛣 not located on a main road

🅿 room for parking

Medieval art and architecture
Mountains and forests
Fortified towns

Alsace, Lorraine and Franche-Comté

Profile 152

Hotspots 154

PRICE GUIDE

€**50,000**-€**100,000** 158

€**100,000**-€**200,000** 160

€**200,000**-€**500,000** 162

€**500,000+** 164

Alsace, Lorraine and Franche-Comté Profile

Getting there

AIR **Air France** (0845 084 5111; www.airfrance.co.uk) flies directly from Gatwick to Strasbourg. For the northern Lorraine area, it is easier to fly with **Ryanair** (0871 246 0000; www.ryanair.com) to Brussels-South Charleroi;

Ryan air flies from Glasgow, Liverpool and Stanstead to Charleroi.

ROAD The A26 runs from the Calais ferryport to Reims, and from there the A4 continues to Metz and Strasbourg. From Metz take the A31 south to Nancy and for Besançon follow the A26 from the Channel ports, or the A5 from Paris to Troyes, continuing on the A5 and the A31 for Dijon, changing to the A39 and then the A36. From Paris, the A4 runs through Reims to Metz and Strasbourg.

COACH **Eurolines** (0870 514 3219; www.euro-lines.com) runs services from the UK to Belfort, Besançon, Colmar, Metz, Mulhouse, Nancy and Strasbourg.

RAIL TGV services operate between Paris Gare de l'Est, and Nancy, Metz and Strasbourg. Paris Gare de Lyon operates services to Besançon, while the **Eurostar** (0870 518 6186; www.eurostar.co.uk) runs from the UK to Lille, where TGV services run on to Besançon. From Lille-Flandres there are direct train services to Metz. For all enquiries and more details on local services, contact **Rail Europe** (0870 584 8848; www.raileurope.co.uk).

THE ECONOMY

Service and tertiary industry are success stories in these regions, with food, chemicals, plastic, 55 percent of France's toys and 80 percent of the country's eyewear produced in Franche-Comté's Jura, where sawmills and metallurgy are also important industries. About 58 percent of workers are employed in service industry. Winter tourism is supported by French, Dutch, German and British visitors and telecommunications is bringing Metz up to date via its Technopole Metz 2000 base. Nancy and Strasbourg too are centres of commerce and industry.

BEST/WORST VALUE FOR MONEY

Strasbourg has great buy-to-let investment potential despite the relatively high, pricetag of 350,000 euros for a four to six-bedroom home in the centre. The constant flow of European workers ensures future profit from sales. Traditional buildings in the Orangerie district are the most expensive in Strasbourg, because of their historic links and a lack of available land. A 200,000 Euro price cut can be made for a four-bedroom home on the city's outskirts.

Prices are higher in Metz, which is popular with Luxemburgers looking for bargains across the border. A four-bedroom house starts at 400,000 euros, but renovation properties in surrounding villages can be purchased from as little as 50,000 euros.

Besançon's prices are increasing, but still offer good value regionally, with a four to six-bedroom home priced from 200,000 euros. Nancy, and the Jura's Clairvaux have four to six-bedroom homes starting at the 200,000 Euro mark, but the Jura is a rising star for purchasers wishing to buy to let. A renovation property can be found in Lons-le-Saunier from 70,000 euros, and with regular Swiss and German visitors, it would have very good investment potential.

Alsace offers some stunning traditional properties, but is not as cheap as the buyer may expect

The region has a thriving property market, with prices continually rising and demand exceeding supply

The region offers scenic surroundings and a peaceful lifestyle for relocaters

WHERE TO GO FOR WHAT

Constant European purchaser demand also guarantees Strasbourg investment potential and its cosmopolitan personality attracts foreigners wishing to relocate. If holiday gîtes/homes and short-term rentals are your aim, Metz and its villages offer low prices and long rental periods, and Metz and Strasbourg's Christmas markets attract winter rental.

Nancy and Besançon are ideal for relocation. Besançon has excellent investment and job opportunites, and emerging tourism and skiing seasons. The Jura offers established gîte country, as 48 percent of Franche-Comté's gîtes are to be found here. Third in France's competition for the best quality of life in 2003, its vast swathe of forest makes a relaxing relocation. For winter gîtes, Metabief and Les Rousses are developing ski resorts with populations doubling in winter. Haut-Doubs is still a big draw because of its winter sports potential.

PRICE TRENDS

From 2002 to 2003 prices in Strasbourg rose by four percent and the thriving market, fuelled by Europeans employed by the Human Rights Court, can only produce more demands for property. Metz and Nancy's prices have increased dramatically in the past five years, driven by a demand that supply is not meeting. A stable rental market exists in Metz and a central apartment is hard to find. Besançon's property prices are higher than the French average, and there is a spurt in demand. The Velotte district is very exclusive and in 2003 high specification properties were being constructed in Besançon.

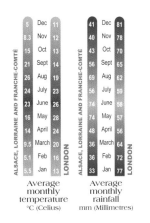

ALSACE, LORRAINE AND FRANCHE-COMTÉ	Month	LONDON
5	Dec	11
8.3	Nov	12
15	Oct	13
21	Sept	14
26	Aug	19
24	July	23
23	June	26
16	May	28
14	April	24
9.5	March	20
5.1	Feb	16
5.5	Jan	13

Average monthly temperature °C (Celius)

ALSACE, LORRAINE AND FRANCHE-COMTÉ	Month	LONDON
41	Dec	81
40	Nov	78
43	Oct	70
56	Sept	65
69	Aug	62
56	July	59
74	June	58
74	May	57
48	April	56
36	March	64
36	Feb	72
33	Jan	77

Average monthly rainfall mm (Millimetres)

Average House Sale Prices

HOTSPOT	2-BED	3-BED	4 BED	5 BED	6/7 BED	8-BED
Besançon	-	-	€225K (£150K)	€260K (£170K)	€280K (£185K)	-
Lons-le-Saunier	-	-	€150K (£100K)	-	€320K (£215K)	-
Metz	-	€215K (£145K)	€200K (£135K)	-	-	-
Nancy	-	€230K (£150K)	€260K (£175K)	-	-	-
Strasbourg	-	-	€250K (£165K)	€300K (£200K)	€350K (£235K)	-
Vosges	-	-	€195K (£130K)	€125K (£85K)	€200K (£130K)	-

Alsace, Lorraine and France-Comté Hotspots

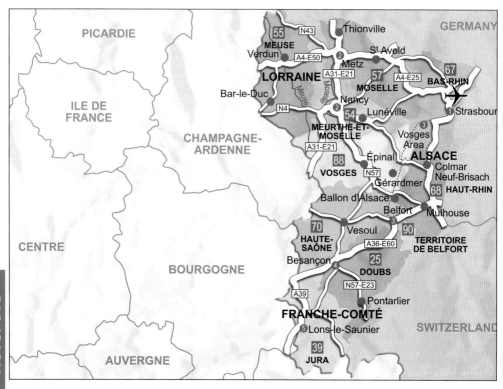

1. Strasbourg

ESSENTIALS ▪ **POP** 1990: 255,937, 1999: 267,051 ▪ **TAXES** Taxe d'habitation: 29.39%, Taxe foncière: 27.70%
▪ **AIRPORT** Strasbourg Airport, avenue de Strasbourg, 67960, Entzheim, Tel: +33 3 88 64 67 67, Fax: +33 3 88 64 67 64.

KEY FACTS

SCHOOLS Rectorat de l'Académie de Strasbourg, 6 rue de la Toussaint, 67081 Strasbourg Cedex 9, Tel: +33 3 88 23 37 23, Fax: +33 3 88 23 39 99.

MEDICAL Hôpitaux Universitaires de Strasbourg, 1 pl Hôpital, 67000 Strasbourg, Tel: +33 3 88 11 67 68.

RENTALS International students create a long term lets market, but there is a good demand for holidays ▪ Many tourists visit for the Christmas market ▪ Prices vary from 500 to 800 euros during peak season, and 400 to 550 euros in low season ▪ Strasbourg is a tourism magnet, especially for families **PROS** Mainly demand from the French and German market, but some international appeal ▪ Brussels encorages many eastern european buyers ▪ Strasbourg is a prominent and wealthy industrial city ▪ Accessible and well positioned for €urope **CONS** Demand makes property and land very expensive ▪ Proximity to the border increases demand and prices ▪ Huge demand for renovation property which is scarce due to a lack of migration ▪ L'Orangerie is a sought-after district.

Flanking the Franco-German border, Strasbourg is the base of the European Union, with a truly cosmopolitan air. Also a UNESCO World Heritage Site, Strasbourg has a medieval centre with a maze of cobbled squares, half-timbered houses and meandering canals. The pink sandstone Gothic Cathedral of Notre-Dame displays a rich tapestry of carved doorways, gargoyles and a rose window. Museums are clustered around this focal point, with the Musée des arts décoratifs housed in the 18th-century Palais Rohan.

The historic Grande Île is encircled by waterways. A guided walk from its western corner through Petite France shows the French and German influences that shaped the Old Town, where millers, tanners and fishermen lived. Narrow streets with half-timbered houses are criss-crossed by canals, with the watch-towers of the Ponts Couverts, part of the 14th-century fortifications, and the Vauban Dam, built to protect Strasbourg from river-bound attack, standing by.

Visit the striking European Court of Human Rights and the grandiose German Quarter, constructed during the Prussian occupation of 1870, dominating the Place de la République. For an insight into Alsace life do not miss the Musée alsacien and the famous Christmas market in December.

Despite the limited amount of foreign interest, this is a very expensive area. Property prices are well above the national average, with few renovation projects for sale. An Ile de France style mansion 10 kilometres west of Strasbourg costs from 1,300,000 euros. ▪

2. Metz and Nancy

ESSENTIALS ■ **POP** 1990: 247,840, 1999: 233,328 ■ **TAXES** Taxe d'habitation: 24.23%, Taxe foncière: 26.78% ■ **AIRPORT** Strasbourg Airport, avenue de Strasbourg, 67960, Entzheim, Tel: +33 3 88 64 67 67, Fax: +33 3 88 64 67 64.

Metz, just 40 miles from the German border, became part of France in 1552, but fell under German occupation from 1870 to 1918 and again during World War II. Not awash with tourists like Strasbourg, its ochre stone lends warmth to its Renaissance buildings. Leafy paths trace the Roman and medieval ramparts, and follow the Seille and Moselle rivers.

Late Gothic stained glass and additions by Marc Chagall adorn the Cathedral of Saint-Etienne, the third highest in France, with statues of the 'Graouly', the legendary dragon who haunted the ruins of the city's Roman amphitheatre. The Cour d'Or museum complex, with vestiges of Roman public baths uncovered during excavations, houses museums of history and architecture, a military collection and a fine arts museum. In Place de la Comédie is the oldest working theatre in France, built between 1738 and 1753. Another gem, the Arsenal, built aunder Napoleon III, is now a concert hall.

Upstream lies the university town of Nancy, the historical capital of Lorraine founded at a European crossroad. Its famed Place Stanislas, created by the Polish exiled King Stanislas Leszczinski, one of Europe's finest with many beautiful churches, including the 15th-century Franciscan and 18th-century Saint Sebastien churches and Notre-Dame-de-Bon-Secours. Nancy was the spiritual home of French Art Nouveau and the Flo Excelsior brasserie has a mouthwatering combination of classic regional cuisine and architecture.

The average cost of property is 200,000 euros, with a three-room apartment in a district of Metz costing from 130,000 euros. A newly-built, three to four-bedroom house Nancy's suburbs starts at 179,000 euros. ■

KEY FACTS

SCHOOLS Contact the Rectorat de l'Academie de Nancy-Metz, 2 rue Philippe-de-Gueldres, BP 13, Tel: +33 3 83 86 20 20, Fax: +33 3 83 86 23 01 for advice. **MEDICAL** Hôpital Clinique Claude Bernard, 97 rue Claude Bernard, 57072 Metz, Tel: +33 3 87 39 66 66. ■ C.H.U de Nancy, 29 av Mar De Lattre de Tassigny, 54000 Nancy, Tel: +33 3 83 85 85 85.

RENTALS Peak season is from July until August and there is rental activity until the end of September ■ Villages near Metz are extremely popular with the rentals market ■ Metz attracts many tourists, and both cities are popular rental areas ■ An in demand rentals market makes this a good area for investment **PROS** The rental market is very stable in Metz, if expensive. ■ Prices in both areas has increased dramatically during the last five years ■ Both cities are culturally and architecturally rich ■ High demand from Luxemburgers for property, as property across the border is cheaper ■ Apartments in both city centres are highly sought after.

CONS City centres are very expensive ■ Huge demand for renovation properties on the outskirts of the cities, but with limited property available ■ Prices have increased dramatically over the past five years.

3. The Vosges

ESSENTIALS ■ **POP** 1990: 100,320, 1999: 100,065 ■ **TAXES** Taxe d'habitation: 23.49%, Taxe foncière: 32.84% ■ **AIRPORT** Strasbourg Airport, avenue de Strasbourg, 67960 Entzheim, Tel: +33 3 88 64 67 67, Fax: +33 3 88 64 67 64.

The mountainous Vosges in western Alsace present an inviting panorama to buyers, with high forests, lakes, gorges and waterfalls. Two Regional Parks, one in the south, covering the Vosges massif from the valley of Sainte-Marie-aux-Mines to the edge of Belfort and Luxeuil-les-Bains and a northern one featuring a forest at its centre, are both excellent for outdoor pursuits like cross-country skiing, cycling and hiking.

In Haut Alsace, the Ballons des Vosges is dominated by a ridge characterised by rounded peaks or *ballons*. This land of the *marcaires* or mountain farmers tending their herds on moorland pastures in summer boasts geological splendours, with large quartz and feldspar crystals in its granite. Notable are the eroded volcanic hills of Petit Ballon and Grand Ballon.

Gérardmer is a popular southern Vosges resort, offering the surrounding winter skiing slopes of the Vosges Cristallines or its lake for activities in summer. A four-bedroom house in a sheltered wood with living room, *cheminée*, kitchen, workshop and 40-metre-square chalet costs about 185,000 euros.

Between the southern Vosges and the northern reaches of the Jura mountains, attractive Belfort has a restored old town with buildings displaying a harmonious range of colours. Dominated by a fortified castle and Bartholdi's red sandstone lion marking the city's resistance to siege during the Prussian War, Belfort is known for its antiques market held every weekend from March to December and Épicerie Perello, France's oldest grocery store. ■

KEY FACTS

SCHOOLS Rectorat de l'Académie de Besançon, 10 rue de la Convention, 25030 Besançon Cedex, Tel: +33 3 81 65 47 00, Fax:+33 3 81 65 47 60. **MEDICAL** Centre Hospitalier de Belfort-Montbéliard, 14 rue Mulhouse, 90000 Belfort, Tel:+33 3 84 57 40 00.

RENTALS A year-round rental season, mainly for outdoor holidaymakers ■ Growing tourist interest in the area, mostly from the French ■ Winter is the most popular season especially for skiing ■ An excellent rental/investment area ■ Short-term rental is the main trend ■ Gérardmer is the area's main draw. **PROS** Many outdoor activities, such as climbing and mountain biking ■ Forested mountains, lakes and wine routes stretch along the Rhine from Strasbourg ■ Belfort is popular with international buyers, particularly the Germans and Dutch ■ Some foreign, especially British, interest, but the French remain the main buyers ■ A central and accessible location **CONS** Prices are increasing as does demand ■ There is a short supply of sought-after renovation properties.

HOTSPOTS

Alsace, Lorraine and France-Comté Hotspots

4. Besançon and area

ESSENTIALS ■ **POP** 1990: -, 1999: 125,000 ■ **TAXES** Taxe d'habitation: 28.48%, Taxe foncière: 36.06% ■ **AIRPORT** Strasbourg Airport, Avenue de Strasbourg, hh 67960, Entzheim, France, Tel: +33 3 88 64 67 67, Fax: +33 3 88 64 67 64

KEY FACTS

SCHOOLS Contact the Rectorat de l'Académie de Besançon, 10 rue de la Convention, 25030 Besançon Cedex, Tel: +33 3 81 65 47 00, Fax:+33 3 81 65 47 60 for advice on education.

MEDICAL Centre Hospitalier Universitaire, 2 pl Saint-Jacques, 25030 Besançon Cedex, Tel: +33 3 81 66 81 66.

RENTALS This area is largely ignored by foreign tourists, making for a slow rentals market ■ It is difficult to rent out property out seasonally, but it can be done. The winter rentals market is particularly poor ■ The peak season here is between May and September, when foreign tourists visit primarily from Germany and America.

PROS There are good bargains to be found in this area, especially for those seeking winter rather than summer holiday homes ■ Prices are on the increase, but property is still currently good value for money. Now is the time to invest

CONS Property prices are higher than the French average ■ Growing demand is causing prices to rise and a shortage of available of property has also caused increases ■ There is a lack of renovated properties and of properties to renovate

The ancient, attractive grey-stone capital of Franche-Comté lies between Alsace and Burgundy on the northern edge of the Jura mountains, encircled by a bend in the River Doubs. Having first begun as a Gallo-Roman city, Besançon absorbed different identities as a Spanish settlement, then provincial town, becoming a famous clock-making centre, witnessed by its astronomical clock with 30,000 parts at Saint-Jean Cathedral and the Time Museum in the Granvelle Palace. The city was also the birthplace of artificial silk, or rayon, in 1890. It counts among its native sons the pioneering Lumière brothers and the epic novelist Victor Hugo.

Located on the banks of the Moulin Saint-Paul canal, in the heart of the town, Besançon Port enjoys a scenic setting, with facilities to accommodate pleasure boats, house boats and floating hotels. Sampling its waterside charms by barge is a must, passing through tunnels dug under the 19th century citadel via the lock of the Saint Paul windmill, classified as an historic monument, then past quays of outstanding architecture built by Vauban. There are plenty of lively and inexpensive restaurants, cafés and bars by the river near place Battant, particularly along those streets which run parallel to the river.

In central Besançon, an apartment approximately 60 metres square with one bedroom and living room costs 105,000 euros. A south-facing detached house with seven rooms and twelve acres of land in east Besançon will start at 270,000 euros. ■

5. Lons-le-Saunier, Haut-Jura and Vallee des Lacs

ESSENTIALS ■ **POP** 1990: 44,996, 1999: 43,601 ■ **TAXES** Taxe d'habitation: 20.91%, Taxe foncière:44,48%
■ **AIRPORT** Geneva International Airport, PO Box 100, 1215 Geneva 15, Switzerland, Tel: +41 2 27 17 71 05

KEY FACTS

SCHOOLS Rectorat de l'Académie de Besançon, 10 rue de la Convention, 25030 Besançon Cedex, Tel: +33 3 81 65 47 00, Fax: +33 3 81 65 47 60

MEDICAL Centre Hospitalier General, 55 rue Doct Jean-Michel, 39000 Lons-le-Saunier, Tel: +33 3 84 35 60 00

RENTALS Highly popular range of outdoor activities ■ Lons-le-Saunier, not an international tourist resort, attracting short term rentals ■ Rental potential comes from the popular Jura ski resort, Les Rousses ■ Main rental season from May to September ■ Prices very from 200 to 500 euros for a gîte in the Jura valley, and 700 euros for ski resorts.

PROS The mountains attract winter sports and nature lovers ■ The Jura region is increasingly popular ■ Prices are relatively low, and now is a good time to invest ■ Most demand is French, but increasingly Dutch, German and British ■ Most buyers seek relocation properties priced below 150,000 euros.

CONS Renovation properties are in high demand, but are expensive and rare. ■ Increasing local demand makes international buys difficult ■ Proximity to Geneva and Brussels makes prices relatively high.

Close to Switzerland, the Haut Jura and Doubs *départements* share an exceptional setting in a Regional Park full of opportunities for winter sports enthusiasts and nature lovers in summer. At altitudes ranging from 800 to 1,600 m and just an hour from Geneva, Haut Jura is the most authentic of French mountain ranges. With villages nestling at the foot of its valleys, Haut Jura sets the scene for the *Transjurassienne*, the cross-country ski race attracting thousands of participants from all over the world racing on 76 km (47.5 miles) between the villages of Lamoura and Mouthe. Saint-Claude, the largest city lies close to the ski resort of Les Rousses and has a history of pipe making and diamond cutting. Morbier is renowned for its rich creamy cheese characterised by a charcoal coloured layer in the middle.

At high altitude, Haut Doubs often experiences harsh winters, though summers are pleasant for swimming, fishing and sailing in the lakes and rivers. Locals maintain that its symbol, the gentian, can predict the severity of winters. From its bitter roots distilleries throughout this region produce excellent apéritifs and liqueurs. Pontarlier, the dynamic capital and second-highest town in France produced absinthe until 1915. It is a convenient base for Métabief's Mont d'Or, a dual-season leisure resort at the foot of the Mont d'Or mountain.

In Doubs a four-bedroom *maison individuelle* in 15 acres with living room, bathroom and garage is 254,000 euros. A Pontarlier farm costs from 196,000 euros and a seven-room townhouse in Saint-Claude from 107,000 euros. ■

Useful contacts

The Route du Vin is one of the regions most popular attractions, and covers an area of 180 kms

PREFECTURES
**Préfecture de la Région
Alsace**
Petit Broglie
67073 Strasbourg Cedex
Tel: +33 3 88 21 67 68
Fax: +33 3 88 21 60 56

**Préfecture de la Région
Lorraine**
place de la Préfecture
57034 Metz Cedex 1
Tel: +33 3 87 34 87 34
Fax: +33 3 87 32 57 39

**Préfecture de la Région
Franche-Comté**
8 bis rue Charles-Nodier
25035 Besançon Cedex
Tel: +33 3 81 25 10 00
Fax: +33 3 81 83 21 82

LEGAL
**Chambre des Notaires du
Doubs**
22a rue de Trey
25000 Besançon
Tel: +33 3 81 50 40 52

**Chambre des Notaires du
Bas-Rhin**
2 rue des Juifs
67000 Strasbourg
Tel: +33 3 88 32 10 55
Fax: +33 3 88 23 40 39

**Chambre des Notaires de la
Moselle**
1 rue de la Pierre Hardie
57000 Metz
Tel: +33 3 87 75 27 93
Fax: +33 3 87 74 08 20

FINANCE
Direction des Impôts de l'Est
2 rue du Cardinal Tisserant
BP 70307
54006 Nancy Cedex
Tel: +33 3 83 36 32 80
Fax: +33 3 83 36 32 89

BUILDING & PLANNING
**Chambre Régionale de
Métiers d'Alsace**
Espace Européen de
l'Entreprise
avenue de l'Europe

67300 Schiltigheim
Tel: +33 3 88 19 60 65
Fax: +33 3 88 19 79 79

**Chambre Régionale de
Métiers de Franche-Comté
Valparc**
Espace Valentin Est
25048 Besançon Cedex
Tel: +33 3 81 47 45 50
Fax: +33 3 81 53 45 31

**Chambre Régionale de
Métiers de Lorraine**
2 rue Augustin Fresnel
57082 Metz Cedex 3
Tel: +33 3 87 20 36 80
Fax: +33 3 87 75 41 79

CAUE du Bas-Rhin
5 rue Hannong
67000 Strasbourg
Tel: +33 3 88 15 02 30
Fax: +33 3 88 21 02 75

CAUE du Doubs
8 rue de la Vieille Monnaie
25000 Besançon

Tel: +33 3 81 82 19 22
Fax: +33 3 81 82 34 24

CAUE du Jura
9 avenue Jean Moulin, BP 48
39002 Lons le Saunier Cedex
Tel: +33 3 84 24 30 36
Fax: +33 3 84 24 63 89

EDUCATION
**Rectorat de l'Académie de
Nancy-Metz**
2 rue Philippe-de-Gueldres
BP 13
54035 Nancy Cedex
Tel: +33 3 83 86 20 20
Fax: +33 3 83 86 23 01

**Rectorat de l'Académiede
Strasbourg**
6 rue de la Toussaint
67081 Strasbourg
Cedex 9
Tel: +33 3 88 23 37 23
Fax: +33 3 88 23 39 99

**Rectorat de l'Académie de
Besançon**

10 rue de la Convention
25030 Besançon Cedex
Tel: +33 3 81 65 47 00
Fax: +33 3 81 65 47 60

HEALTH
**Caisse Primaire d'Assurance
Maladie du Doubs**
2 rue Denis Papin
25000 Besançon
Tel: +33 3 81 47 53 00
Fax: +33 3 81 47 53 40

**Caisse Primaire d'Assurance
Maladie de la Moselle**
18 rue Haute Seille
57000 Metz
Tel: +33 3 87 39 36 36
Fax: +33 3 87 76 15 71

**Caisse Primaire d'Assurance
Maladie du Bas-Rhin**
16 rue Lausanne
67000 Strasbourg
Tel: +33 8 20 90 41 50
Fax: +33 3 88 76 88 99

€50–150,000
(£33–100,000)

In this price bracket, most properties will need some renovation, which can range from minor work to improve habitability, to a full, ground-up restoration. Many of them are small village houses, though most have gardens and parking. For more space, expect to pay over 100,000 euros.

€33,000　　　　　　　　　　　　**CODE** DEV

MONTMEDY, DÉPARTEMENT 55

A small 18th century property, located in a quiet village, requiring some work

£22,000

🏠n/a 🏡with a small garden 🏘within 5 mins of village 🚫not located on a main road 🅿room for parking

€56,500　　　　　　　　　　　　**CODE** DEV

SAINT MIHIEL, DÉPARTEMENT 55

An 18th century village house with a barn to renovate, an ideal family home

£37,665

🏠n/a 🏡with a garden 🏘within 5 mins of village 🚫not located on a main road 🅿room for parking

€63,500　　　　　　　　　　　　**CODE** DEV

MONTMEDY, DÉPARTEMENT 55

An 18th century village house, with some modern additions, in a rural area

£42,335

🏠n/a 🏡with a garden 🏘within 5 mins of village 🚫not located on a main road 🅿no room for parking

€67,000　　　　　　　　　　　　**CODE** DEV

STENAY, DÉPARTEMENT 55

A small village house requiring full restoration, in an attractive Alsacien area

£44,665

🏠n/a 🏡with a small garden 🏘within 5 mins of village 🚫not located on a main road 🅿with on road parking

€76,500   CODE DEV

VERDUN, DÉPARTEMENT 55

A traditional style village house, with some renovations, requiring completion

£51,000

n/a   with a small garden   within 5 mins of village   not located on a main road   with on road parking

€85,000   CODE SIG

BASEL, DÉPARTEMENT 68

A traditional Alsatien house set within stunning grounds, requiring renovation

£56,665

n/a   24,280m2   within 5 mins of village   not located on a main road   room for parking

€121,715   CODE SIG

BASEL, DÉPARTEMENT 68

A typical Alsatien house requiring renovation, residing in charming surroundings

£81,145

n/a $28,330m^2$ within 5 mins of village   not located on a main road   room for parking

€135,000   CODE SIG

BASEL, DÉPARTEMENT 68

A spacious village house, newly renovated, enjoying views and mature gardens

£90,000

3   $38,850m^2$ within 5 mins of village   not located on a main road   room for parking

€145,500   CODE MOR

BELFORT, DÉPARTEMENT 90

This bungalow offers a south-facing terrace and enjoys a fully fitted kitchen

£97,000

3   $500m^2$ within 5 mins of village   not located on a main road   room for parking

€145,500   CODE MOR

BELFORT, DÉPARTEMENT 90

This Vosges style farmhouse to renovate, has a stone and wood beam interior

£97,000

6   $1,112m^2$ within 5 mins of village   not located on a main road   room for parking

PRICE GUIDE

€150-200,000
(£100–133,000)

Most properties within this price bracket are habitable and only require a limited amount of work. The majority are homes are built in a traditional French style with a rustic style interior and are comfortable and affordable.

PRICE GUIDE

€152,000　　　　　　　　　　　**CODE** SIG

BASEL, DÉPARTEMENT 68

A beautiful old house, ideal for a holiday home, with an attic and outbuildings

£101,335

🛏2　🗺643m²　📷within 5 mins of village　🚫not located on a main road

🅿room for parking

€153,500　　　　　　　　　　　**CODE** MOR

SEVENANS, DÉPARTEMENT 90

Located in a quiet area, this seven-roomed house requires some decoration

£102,335

🛏3　🗺2,732m²　📷located near all amenities　🚫not located on a main road

🅿room for parking

€159,000　　　　　　　　　　　**CODE** MOR

BELFORT, DÉPARTEMENT 90

This spacious house offers high ceilings and oak floors, requiring some work

£106,000

🛏3　🗺580m²　📷located on Belfort's southern outskirts　🚫not located on a main road　🅿room for parking

€178,000　　　　　　　　　　　**CODE** VOS

LE GRAND VALTIN, DÉPARTEMENT 88

Set in a tranquil mountain village, a newly built apartment near the ski slopes

£118,665

🛏1　🗺2,000m²　📷10 kms from amenities　🚫not located on a main road

🅿room for parking

€191,000

BELFORT, DÉPARTEMENT 90

This five-roomed flat is located in a traditional building in a rustic location

£127,335

🛏3 🌼1,062m² 🏠located on the outskirts of town 🚫not located on a main road 🏠room for parking, with a garage

€191,000

BELFORT, DÉPARTEMENT 90

A single storey house, with a terrace and a basement, enjoying large rooms

£127,335

🛏3 🌼9,000m² 🏠close to town and amenities 🚫not located on a main road 🏠room for parking, with a double garage

€194,000

BELFORT, DÉPARTEMENT 90

This bungalow offers tiled floors and a rustic style interior, and a terrace

£129,335

🛏3 🌼with a small garden and terrace 🏠located on the outskirts of town 🚫not located on a main road 🏠room for parking

€194,000

BELFORT, DÉPARTEMENT 90

This modern villa offers a spacious living area and a luxurious interior

£129,335

🛏4 🌼614m² 🏠close to town amenities 🚫not located on a main road 🏠room for parking

€194,000

DELLE, DÉPARTEMENT 90

Enjoying a rustic and pine interior, this property has an attic ideal to convert

£129,335

🛏3 🌼950m² 🏠close to amenities 🚫not located on a main road 🏠room for parking, with a double garage

€194,000

DELLE, DÉPARTEMENT 90

This property requires some decoration but enjoys a rustic style interior

£129,335

🛏3 🌼with small garden and terrace 🏠within 5 mins of village 🚫not located on a main road 🏠room for parking, with garage

PRICE GUIDE

€200–400,000
(£133–266,000)

With an abundance of period style buildings, this region offers everything from traditional farmhouse to modern french style chalets. This area is also renowned for offering the buyer a huge amount for their money and properties within this price bracket are truely luxurious.

€207,500	CODE MOR

ÉTUEFFONT, DÉPARTEMENT 90

Offering supurb views and located in stunning countryside, a modern property

£138,335

🛏5 🏠1,279m² 🚪*close to town and amenities* 🚫*not located on a main road* 🅿*room for parking*

€222,500	CODE MOR

FONTAINE, DÉPARTEMENT 90

A modern property, with french windows, tiled floors and an attic to convert

£148,335

🛏3 🏠614m² 🚪*close to amenities* 🚫*not located on a main road* 🅿*room for parking*

€255,000	CODE MOR

BELFORT, DÉPARTEMENT 90

A modern, fully habitable property designed and fitted to the highest standards

£170,000

🛏4 🏠2,382m² 🚪*10 kms from town and amenities* 🚫*not located on a main road* 🅿*room for parking*

€258,000	CODE MOR

BELFORT, DÉPARTEMENT 90

A meticulously maintained property in a quiet location, with oak floors

£172,000

🛏4 🏠*with a garden and terrace* 🚪*close to town and amenities* 🚫*not located on a main road* 🅿*room for parking*

€274,000 — CODE MOR

BELFORT, DÉPARTEMENT 90

A villa, offering 230m^2 of living space, with four french windows and a terrace

£182,665

🛏3 🗺1,000m^2 🏠close to town and amenities 🚫not located on a main road 🅿room for parking

€290,130 — CODE MOR

BELFORT, DÉPARTEMENT 90

A newly built property, with paved floors and enjoying a balcony and terrace

£193,420

🛏3 🗺with a small garden 🏠close to town and amenities 🚫not located on a main road 🅿room for parking, with a garage and car park

€296,000 — CODE MOR

BELFORT, DÉPARTEMENT 90

With views over the Vosges, this Franche-Comté farmhouse requires work

£197,335

🛏3 🗺10,000m^2 🏠close to town and amenities 🚫not located on a main road 🅿with car parking space

€299,500 — CODE SIG

BASEL, DÉPARTEMENT 68

A charming and very spacious Alsatien farmhouse, with outbuildings to convert

£199,665

🛏n/a 🗺with extensive grounds 🏠located on the outskirts of town 🚫not located on a main road 🅿room for parking

€320,000 — CODE MOR

BELFORT/MULHOUSE, DÉPARTEMENT 90

In a quiet location with excellent views over the Vosges, a traditional house

£213,335

🛏6 🗺3,314m^2 🏠located near to town 🚫not located on a main road 🅿room for parking, with a garage

€323,000 — CODE DEE

VITTEL, DÉPARTEMENT 88

A vast, unique 18th century property, offering three outbuildings to convert

£215,335

🛏n/a 🗺12,140m^2 🏠1 km from all amenities 🚫not located on a main road 🅿room for parking, with a garage

PRICE GUIDE

€400,000+
(£266,000+)

With Alsace remaining a relatively expensive region there are many properties that do cost upwards of 400,000 euros. Many of these properties come with an extensive amount of land and superb amenities, such as a swimming pool, and the buyer often pays a premiuim to be excellently located by riversides or mountains.

€400,000　　　　　　　　　　　　　**CODE** MOR

BELFORT, DÉPARTEMENT 90

In a rural location, ideal for a peaceful retreat, a rustic style house and flat

£266,665

🛏6 🖼2,460m² 🏠*located on the outskirts of town* 🚫*not located on a main road* 🏡*room for parking, with a double garage*

€400,000　　　　　　　　　　　　　**CODE** VOS

CORNIMONT, DÉPARTEMENT 88

On the outskirts of a mountain village, with a heated pool and stunning views

£266,665

🛏n/a 🖼10,000m² 🏠*within 5 mins of village* 🚫*not located on a main road* 🏡*room for parking, with two garages*

€400,000　　　　　　　　　　　　　**CODE** VOS

GERARDMER, DÉPARTEMENT 88

A fully renovated house and separate guest house, located close to the ski slopes

£263,335

🛏n/a 🖼28,330m² 🏠*1 km from town and amenities* 🚫*not located on a main road* 🏡*room for parking*

€400,200　　　　　　　　　　　　　**CODE** SIG

MULHOUSE, DÉPARTEMENT 68

Situated amidst a mature orchard, a newly built, original property

£266,800

🛏6 🖼2,000m² 🏠*within 5 mins of village* 🚫*not located on a main road* 🏡*room for parking, with a double garage*

€410,000   CODE SIG

MULHOUSE, DÉPARTEMENT 68

A modern property with a luxurious interior in a popular location

£273,335

⌂ n/a   ▦ 2,500m²   *within 5 mins of village*   *not located on a main road*   *room for parking*

€530,000   CODE SIG

BASEL, DÉPARTEMENT 74

A large property, with superb amenities, ideal for a family holiday home

£353,335

⌂ n/a   ▦ *with a large garden and terrace*   *within 5 mins of village*   *not located on a main road*   *room for parking*

€603,500   CODE DEV

BAR-LE-DUC, DÉPARTEMENT 55

A 20th century mansion in supurb condition with outbuildings, bordering lakes

£402,335

⌂ n/a   ▦ *with extensive grounds*   *within 5 mins of village*   *not located on a main road*   *room for parking*

€639,000   CODE DEV

ARDENNES FOREST, DÉPARTEMENT 08

A delightful, partially restored watermill, enjoying a stunning rural location

£426,000

⌂ n/a   ▦ *with a garden area*   *within 5 mins of village*   *not located on a main road*   *room for parking*

€680,000   CODE SIG

BASEL, DÉPARTEMENT 68

A beautiful water mill, partially renovated, enjoying a fantastic riverside location

£453,335

⌂ n/a   ▦ 10,000m²   *within 5 mins of village*   *not located on a main road*   *room for parking*

€720,000   CODE SIG

BASEL, DÉPARTEMENT 68

A luxurious home, fully furnished, with unimpeded views and mature gardens

£480,000

⌂ n/a   ▦ 2,500m²   *within 5 mins of village*   *not located on a main road*   *room for parking*

PRICE GUIDE

15365

A G E N C E
TRANSIMMO

28 Rue Victor-Hugo 49150 BAUGE

Tel: **+33 2 41 89 16 94**
Fax: +33 2 41 89 24 49
E: transimmo@aol.com

Looking for a house in our area, between Angers and Saumur, in the Loire Valley?
Do not hesitate to contact us.

www.transimmo.seloger.com

Lush and verdant valleys
Gastronomic delights
Elegant châteaux

The Loire

Profile 168

Hotspots 170

PRICE GUIDE

€10,000-€50,000 174

€50,000-€100,000 176

€100,000-€200,000 178

€200,000-€500,000 180

€500,000+ 182

The Loire Profile

Getting there

AIR Air France (0845 359 1000; www.airfrance.co.uk), **Flybe** (0870 889 0908; www.flybe.com) and **GB Airways** (0870 850 9850; www.gbairways.com) operate flights from Gatwick to Nantes; **Ryanair** (0871 246 0000; www.ryanair.com) serves Tours, La Rochelle and Poitiers from Stansted and **British Airways** (0870 850 9850; www.britishairways.co.uk) fly from Heathrow to Nantes.

ROAD Take the A26 from Calais and continue on to the A16-E40 and then the A16 and A26. From there follow the A16-E402 to Rouen, taking the A28 on to the A28-E402 at junction 23. From Le Havre the A13-E46 runs down to Rennes, and the N137 or the A81-E50 continues on into the Pays de la Loire. From Paris the A10-E6 runs into the centre and continues on to the south of the region, and the A11-E50 runs on into Pays de la Loire.

RAIL Rail Europe (0870 584 8848; www.raileurope.co.uk) operate TGV trains to Le Mans, Angers, Nantes, Poitiers, La Rochelle and Angoulême from Paris Gare Montparnasse.

COACH Eurolines, (0870 514 3219; www.eurolines.com) offer services to La Roche Sur Yonne, Le Mans, Les Sables d'Olonne, Nantes, Orléans and Tours.

Many of the Loire's agricultural lands are used for the purpose of market gardening

THE ECONOMY

A landscape of forests, small towns and villages dotted along the Loire's river lends itself particularly to gîte tourism. However, the celebrated wine industry, with 20 wine titles ranging from the Sauvignon grape in the east of the region to the Muscadet grape around Nantes, together with agricultural production still offer a stable support to the region's economy. Industry and commerce in the major towns of Le Mans and Nantes are strong supporters of the economy. Home to the famous Lu biscuit factory, there is also the ferry builder at St Nazaire, while finance and commerce are concentrated at San Sebastian and Carquefouon in the outskirts of Nantes.

BEST/WORST VALUE FOR MONEY

Baugé, Chandelais and Angers are the most popular destinations for buying followed by Saumur, Tours and Le Mans, for their tourist appeal, and despite rising prices, they mostly represent sound investments. Le Mans' property market has stagnated recently, and many properties have become very expensive in the commuter belt. Nevertheless the pretty tourist areas of the Touraine and Angers offer safe investments, with prices from 40,000 euros for a renovation project, to 900,000 euros for a prestigious property.

With property prices pushed up by Parisian second-home buyers, Le Mans properties do not give best value for money. Apart from its car rallies, visitors prefer the 30 degree summer heat available in the valley towns of Chinon, Baugé, Le Lude and Saumur, which remain key investment areas.

A UNESCO World Heritage Site, Tours represents one of the worst value purchases as French relocators have driven up prices. The coastal towns of the Vendée are top holiday home destinations for Parisians. Les Sables d'Olonne has long, clean beaches, a thriving market, and is just a two-hour train journey from the capital. Many French purchasers buy their holiday homes here, with a view to retiring. This makes the Loire an excellent area for purchasing because of the resale value and holiday market potential.

The popularity of the Loire's holiday market makes it a safe investment for those seeking rental income

WHERE TO GO FOR WHAT
Angers, Les Sables d'Olonne and slightly more inland, La Roche sur Yonne are excellent for families. Nantes' array of industry makes the city perfect for those looking for work. More for the relocator looking to run their own business, the Tourraine, Tours, and the river towns and villages are ideal for gîtes.

Tours, Ambilou and Saumur are key gîte areas with year-round rental and old properties are available from around 100,000 euros. With no particular foreign enclaves, Parcay les Pins stands out because of its almost 40 percent British home ownership.

PROPERTY PRICE TRENDS
Some gîte owners have introduced specialist holidays, including painting to counter disruption to the market caused by world events. Opinion is divided as to the stability of the holiday rental market. For châteaux, Tours and the Tourraine are key areas offering a secure investment for those buying to let, or buyers seeking holiday homes. Generally speaking, adding a swimming pool to a renovation property vastly increases the potential for rental income.

Prices have increased on average by 25 percent across Chinon, La Fleche, Baugé, Saumur, Tours, and the Loire in recent years, but continuously large visitor numbers maintain and boost the rental market and guarantee a return upon the investment made by those who buy in the area.

Generally speaking the Loire's property market is extremely healthy, but prices manage to remain competitive, making it an excellent time to invest. With the neighbouring region of Brittany becoming saturated and the increase of budget flights into the Loire region, prices will undoubtedly begin to rise over the next couple of years as demand inevitable overtakes supply.

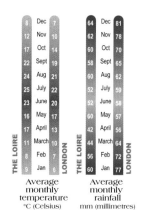

THE LOIRE		LONDON		THE LOIRE		LONDON	
	Dec 7		8		Dec 7		64 81
	Nov 10		12		Nov 10		62 78
	Oct 14		17		Oct 14		60 70
	Sept 19		22		Sept 19		58 65
	Aug 21		24		Aug 21		60 62
	July 22		25		July 22		52 59
	June 20		23		June 20		52 58
	May 17		16		May 17		60 57
	April 13		17		April 13		42 56
	March 10		11		March 10		44 64
	Feb 7		8		Feb 7		56 72
	Jan 6		9		Jan 6		60 77

Average monthly temperature
°C (Celsius)

Average monthly rainfall
mm (millimetres)

Average House Sale Prices

HOTSPOT	2-BED	3-BED	4 BED	5 BED	6/7 BED	8-BED
Angers/Saumur	-	€210K (£140K)	€300K (£200K)	-	€355K (£235K)	-
Le Mans	€125K (£85K)	-	€230K (£155K)	-	-	-
Nantes	€200K (£135K)	-	€350K (£235K)	-	-	-
Orléans	€200K (£135K)	-	€335K (£225K)	-	€425K (£285K)	-
Tourraine/Tours	€120K (£80K)	-	€365K (£245K)	-	-	-
Vendée	€135K (£90K)	€165K (£110K)	€200K (£135K)	€235K (£156K)	-	-

The Loire Hotspots

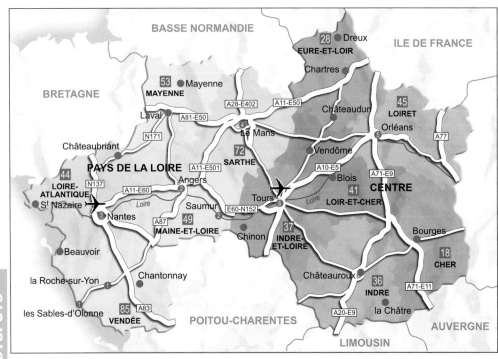

1. Vendée Coast

ESSENTIALS ■ **POP** 1990: 64,763, 1999: 68,992 ■ **TAXES** Taxe d'habitation: 26.45% , Taxe foncière: 32.19% ■ **AIRPORT** Nantes Atlantique International Airport, 44346 Bouguenais Cedex, Tel +33 2 40 84 80.

KEY FACTS

SCHOOLS The nearest school is the Cité scolaire internationale Grand Air, Lycée et Collège de Grand Air, 77 avenue du Bois d'Amour, 44 500 La Baule Escoublac; Tel: +33 2 40 11 58 00.

MEDICAL Centre Hospitalier Cote de Lumiere, 75, avenue Aquitaine, 5 100 les Sables d'Olonne; Tel: +33 2 51 21 85 85.

RENTALS The Loire offers good summer rental income ■ Good long-term in La Roche Sur Yon. ■ Average rental prices are 95 euros per week, low season in Les Sables d'Olonne for a two-bedroom property, and 450 euros in high season ■ The average annual rental in La Roche sur Yon is 204 euros per month for 2-bedrooms and 217 euros for three bedrooms.

PROS A famous Atlantic coast resort, there is no shortage of summer tourists to generate rental income ■ Easily accessible, it is well served by transport links via the N160 and nearby TGV links ■ Popular with permanent relocations ■ This resort offers good weather.

CONS There is little rental activity in winter ■ Very French, expect to learn the language.

Named after a river that runs through the south-east of the département, the Vendée features a variety of different landscapes, from coastal areas to the flat grasslands and lush *bocage* countryside. With near-white sand stretching for 250 kilometres and rocky escarpments tucked behind the Atlantic ocean's shores, safe bathing and gently sloping beaches offer a desirable location for families. Les Sables d'Olonne is a fishing port where cheerfully painted villas with sculpted décor lead onto a long promenade with sea-facing bistrots. The famous fish market on the quayside is extensive and it adjoins a large indoor food market. The town also has extensive shopping areas, ranging from designer clothes shops to the essential supermarkets.

Founded by Napoleon in 1804, the town of La Roche-sur-Yon used to be an isolated village. Since then it has become the principal town in the Vendée, with a programme of special events planned to mark its bicentenary. Locals are proud of their theatre - a temple-based design in a classic Italian-style - and the National Stud. Flanked by countryside, the Yon provides a natural North/South divide between La Roche-sur-Yon and Pays Yonnais. Easily accessible, the area is popular and experiences reasonable demand ensuring a healthy property market. A modern four-bedroom villa in La Sable d'Or with a fully fitted kitchen and a swimming pool starts at 465,000 euros, while a renovated house in La Roche costs from 140,800 euros. ■

2. Saumur and Angers

ESSENTIALS ■ **POP** 1990: 178,057, 1999: 188,027 ■ **TAXES** Taxe d'habitation: 22.24%, Taxe foncière: 38.58%
■ **AIRPORT** Nantes Atlantique International Airport, 44346 Bouguenais Cedex, Tel +33 2 40 84 80 00.

A historic town built into chalky white tufa stone, characteristic of the Loire Valley, Saumur is a wine-making town, specialising in sparkling wines. Its stunning clifftop château houses two magnificent museums, the decorative arts museum and the horse museum. There is the Musée Du Champignon, where you can watch the production of Saumur's famous button mushrooms plus more exotic varieties like shitake. Home to France's premier equestrian centre, horse lovers should visit the Cadre Noir, headquarters of the world famous National Horse and Riding School. At the western end of the Loire Valley, Angers occupies a site above the Maine river. During Roman times the town served as a crossroads for routes from Rennes, Nantes and Tours and is today known for its flowers, wines, liqueurs and umbrella production. It is home to an impressive castle and fine examples of Plantagenet Gothic architecture. In north east Angers, a seven-bedroom farmhouse with swimming pool costs from 355,000 euros, while a three-bedroom tuffeau house to renovate costs from 210,000 euros. In the town centre, a 19th century four-bedroom home starts at 300,000 euros. The area makes for a sound investment and there is a huge demand for rentals. The cheapest properties start from 70,000 euros and although it's cheaper than the neighbouring Dordogne, the area is hugely attractive. Angers also offers a buoyant property market and the excellent transport links ensure many people are drawn to the area. ■

KEY FACTS

SCHOOLS Nearest in the Vendée, as listed.
MEDICAL Centre Hospitalier de Saumur, Route de Fontevraud, 49400 Saumur, Tel: +33 2 41 53 30 30, www.ch-saumur.fr
RENTALS Good annual rentals with more long-term than short-term demand in Angers ■ Prices per month for a two-bedroom home start at 400 euros ■ There is huge demand for city rentals ■ Average price for Saumur in low season are 224 euros per week, for high season 287 euros per week ■ A two-bedroom property starts at 120 euros a week in peak season.
PROS A major tourism centre, there is great potential for those buying property to let ■ Excellent weather in both the valley and town ■ Angers has been voted best French city for three years running ■ The area houses a strong British community ■ Angers is extremely cosmopolitan, with a large foreign population ■ There is an excellent transport network.
CONS The market is extremely inconsistent ■ With little commercial industry, Angers relies on agriculture ■ The rental market experiences huge competition.

3. Nantes

ESSENTIALS ■ **POP** 1990: 107,965, 1999: 150,605 ■ **TAXES** Taxe d'habitation - 27.25% ■ Taxe foncière -32.24% ■
AIRPORT Nantes Atlantique International Airport, 44346 Bouguenais Cedex, Tel +33 2 40 84 80 00.

Situated in northwest France at the intersection of the Loire, Erdre, and Sèvre rivers, Nantes is officially part of the Loire region yet many regard themselves Brétons. The Château des Ducs de Bretagne where the edict was signed still occupies a central place in the city, and today houses a striking 14th century tapestry that stretches 100 yards.

Although France's seventh biggest city is geared towards innovation, encapsulated by Nantes resident Jules Verne in his novels, the old town features many historical gems, such as its fine cathedral, half-timbered mansions and art galleries, such as the Musée des Beaux Arts with collections by Kandinsky. Nantes' 850 acres of parks, such as the Japanese-style garden on the Ile de Versailles on the Erdre, are ideal starting points for touring the rivers, and pleasure steamers regularly leave from the quays to explore the Muscadet vineyards. For a meal with river views, head for seafood specialist L'Atlantide on the Place Gréslin.

A relatively new property hotspot to the international buyer, Nantes is a technological and research centre and is certainly not an area dominated by second home buyers; most tend to settle in the countryside surrounding Nantes. Consequently, those who desire to generate rental income from their property should not expect to secure a healthy income from Nantes. Property is much more expensive due to Nantes' status as a city, and prices start at around 350,000 euros and can rise to as much as 1,000,000 euros. Smaller town houses and terraced houses start at around 200,000 euros, while two to five-bedroom apartments in central Nantes cost from 2,667 euros to rent. ■

KEY FACTS

SCHOOLS Contact the Rectorat de l'Académie de Nantes, La Houssinière, BP 72616, 44326 Nantes Cedex 3, Tel: +33 2 40 37 37 37 for advice on education.
MEDICAL Hopitaux du C.H.U de Nantes, 1 pl Alexis Ricordeau 44000, Nantes, Tel: +33 2 40 08 33 33.
RENTALS There is a good long term rentals market, mainly for locals and long-terms visitors ■ Average rentals for Nantes, throughout the year are 226 euros per month for a 2-bedroom property and 280 euros per month for a 3-bedroom property.
PROS The area has excellent business and employment prospects ■ Nantes is a cosmopolitan city ■ There are excellent transport routes, with cheap flights from the UK ■ The old town centre is very attractive, as is the Château des Ducs de Bretagne ■ A big city, popular with relocators.
CONS The architecture can be ugly and modern ■ Not a typical tourist destination, the buying to let market is limited ■ The popular commuter belt including Sautron, Clisson, Haute Goulaine and Baine Goulaine offer very expensive properties.

The Loire Hotspots

4. Le Mans

ESSENTIALS ■ **POP** 1990: 148,465, 1999: 150,605 ■ **TAXES** Taxe d'habitation: 25.97%, Taxe foncière: 34.99%
■ **AIRPORT** Paris Orly, Aerogare Sud, 94310 Orly, Tel: +33 1 49 75 15 15.

KEY FACTS

SCHOOLS Contact the Rectorat de l'Académie d'Orleans-Tours, 21 rue Saint-Etienne, 45043 Orleans, Cedex 1, Tel: +33 2 38 79 38 79 for advice on education.

MEDICAL Centre Hospitalier du Mans,193, avenue Rublillard, 72000 Le Mans, Tel: +33 2 43 43 43.

RENTALS Primarily a local, long-term rental market, Le Mans has a busy short-term, tourist rental market from May to July ■ The average price per month for a 2-bedroom property is 233 euros, and 267 euros per month for three bedrooms.

PROS Popular with Parisians for second homes, property prices continue to rise ■ Perfect for commuting to Paris, wider employment possibilities are available here ■ The development of a popular commuter belt means property is guaranteed a price rise ■ With fantastic transport links to other main towns and cities in the Loire, the area remains popular and much in demand

CONS Very industrial, it is not traditionally popular with relocators to the Loire ■ The city has a limited tourist appeal ■ An industrial, working city not popular for holiday rentals ■ People tend to buy on the outskirts or in the surrounding countryside.

Located in the Sarthe département, a pageant of blossom in May, Le Mans is synonymous with motor racing but has a satisfying cultural scene. Visit the lovely old quarter enclosed within Gallo-Roman walls to view its medieval cobbled streets and half-timbered houses. The film Cyrano de Bergerac with Gerard Depardieu was filmed in the shadow of the glorious Cathedral Saint-Julien, a Gothic monument to the Plantagenet kings, while the car museum, part of the 24-hour race circuit complex, is a must for motor enthusiasts. There are two separate racing tracks at Le Mans, the Bugatti Circuit being the smaller, permanent circuit used throughout the year, and the Le Mans Circuit de la Sarthe. Visit the Musée de la Reine Bérengère to view various arts and crafts, while the Lude castle is a must see. Additionally, pay a trip to the Manoir of La Possonnière, beloved by the poet Pierre de Ronsard, or the war museum at Lavardin and the Benedictine abbey of Solesme. Gastronomically, Le Mans is renowned for its local delicacy of Rillettes, a pâté made from fine duck meat.

The property market here has become increasingly buoyant due to the influx of Parisian buyers. However to buy in Le Mans itself can be an expensive proposition. The city is also extremely industrialised and is not a popular location for the foreign buyer. Buying to rent also offers a limited market, because despite the cosmopolitan atmosphere induced by the Le Mans race, most of the year its rental and property market is dominated by the locals. A 19th-century farmhouse to renovate with four rooms and several outbuildings starts at 100,000 euros. ■

5. Orléans

ESSENTIALS ■ **POP** 1990: 107,965, 1999: 116,559 ■ **TAXES** Taxe d'habitation: 26.25%, Taxe foncière: 41.09%
■ **AIRPORT** Paris Orly, Aerogare Sud, 94310 Orly, Tel: +33 1 49 75 15 15.

KEY FACTS

SCHOOLS Contact the Rectorat de l'Académie d'Orléans-Tours, 21 rue Saint Etienne, 45043 Orleans, Cedex 1, Tel: +33 2 38 79 38 79 for advice on education.

MEDICAL Hôpital Régional Orléans, 1 rue Porte Madeleine, 45100 Orléans, Tel: +33 2 38 51 44 44.

RENTALS With a good annual rental market, Orléans is more of a tourist area ■ Average prices throughout the year in Orléans start at 258 euros per month for a 2-bedroom property, and 333 euros per month for a 3-bedroom property.

PROS Offering easy access to the capital, commuting is easy and prices are lower ■ Subject to the pleasant, Loire micro-climate, the weather is attractive ■ Plenty of historic tourist attractions, this is the city of Joan of Arc, with two impressive cathedrals ■ There are many job and educational opportunities.

CONS There are some concerns over the inconsistent nature of the rental market.

Capital of the Loire Valley, Orléans is famous for two reasons; firstly Joan of Arc, and secondly, its regional châteaux. Liberated by Joan of Arc in 1429, Orléans has expressed its gratitude to the Maid of Orléans each year via a Medieval Pageantry Festival on May 8th. As France's intellectual capital in the 13th century, Emperor Charlemagne attracted artists, poets and troubadours to seek his patronage at the royal court. Being close to Paris, many Orléanais go to the capital for evenings out as well as commuting there to work. Although many of the old buildings were destroyed during the Second World War, huge reconstruction efforts have been made since then in order to recover the city's former splendour. Worthy of attention are the Cathedral Saint Croix, the Musée des Beaux Arts where the main collections of 14th to 16th century Italian, Dutch and Flemish works, and canvases by Monet reside. There is also the Natural Sciences Museum and Maison de Jeanne d'Arc.

Orléans draws many tourists, providing a healthy rentals market and making it a safe investment for those buying to rent. Property is reasonably priced, but being a city prices rise considerably once you reach the environs. As with many areas, the best prices are to be found in the countryside surrounding the city. For example, a fully renovated farmhouse set in two acres of land can be purchased for 335,000 euros. ■

6. Tours and the Tourraine

ESSENTIALS ■ **POP** 1990: 168,132, 1999: 172,131 ■ **TAXES** Taxe d'habitation: 22.72%, Taxe foncière: 33.27%
■ **AIRPORT** Paris Orly, Aerogare Sud, 94310 Orly, Tel: +33 1 49 75 15 15.

Under Louis XI, Tours was the capital of France and became a centre for silk production. Today, the city attracts many tourists keen to maximise its location as gateway to the Tourraine département, with its remarkable châteaux and the Loire vineyards. Elegant Tours old town abounds with Renaissance and neo-classic architecture. A late Gothic creation, the Cathedral of Saint Gatien was the first in France to have cupolas topping the towers instead of spires. Not far from Tours is the fairy-tale Château de Chenonceau, also known as the 'ladies castle', because its history was shaped by a series of aristocratic women, including Catherine de Medici. Tourraine is known as the 'garden of France' due to its abundance of fruit, flowers and red wines. The region has a number of troglodyte dwellings carved from the local tuffeau rock, and Neolithic and Druid remains can be found throughout the region.

The property market is extremely healthy in this popular area of the Loire. There are many unique and luxurious châteaux properties; one example is a listed 19th century manor near Tours which costs 1,500,000 euros. Bear in mind that genuine restoration work should always be overseen by master craftsmen from the "Les Batiments de France" register.

Due to the healthy nature and demand in the market, property is more expensive than in other parts of the Loire, and much of this demand has come from the local French market. However there is international interest in the area and this is stimulated by Tours airport and the abundance of budget flights available from the UK. ■

KEY FACTS

SCHOOLS Contact the Rectorat de l'Académie d'Orléans-Tours, 21 rue Saint Etienne, 45043 Orléans, Cedex 1, Tel: +33 2 38 79 38 79 for advice on education.
MEDICAL Centre Hospitalier Régional Universitaire, 2 boulevard Tonnelé, 37000 Tours, Tel: +33 2 47 47 47 47, www.chu-tours.fr
RENTALS Tours has a good annual long term rentals market ■ Average rentals start at 224 euros per month for a 2-bedroom property, and 312 euros for a 3-bedroom property ■ The rental season lasts from March to October in the Tourraine towns of Chinon and Loches ■ The average rental for the Tourraine is 300 euros per week in high season.
PROS Often considered the most popular tourist area in the Loire, with UNESCO World Heritage status ■ A large university population and thriving boutique/cafe culture ■ Enjoys excellent transport links ■ Property is reasonably priced ■ There is a growing foreign (particularly British) community in Chinon and Loches.
CONS An expensive place to buy property ■ Azay le Rideau and Langeais in the Tourraine have few foreign buyers ■ Some French is essential ■ The Tourraine is fairly quiet.

HOTSPOTS

USEFUL CONTACTS

PREFECTURE
Préfecture de la Région Centre
181 rue de Bourgogne
45042 Orléans
Cedex 1
Tel: +33 821 80 30 45
Fax: +33 2 38 53 32 48

Préfecture de la Région Pays-de-la-Loire
6 quai Ceineray
BP 33515
44035 Nantes
Cedex 1
Tel: +33 2 40 41 20 20
Fax: +33 2 40 41 20 25

LEGAL
Chambre des Notaires de Loire-Atlantique
119 rue Coulmiers
44000 Nantes
Tel: +33 2 40 74 37 16
Fax: +33 2 40 29 21 29

Chambre des Notaires du Loiret
4 rue d'Escures

The Loire still offers an abundance of renovation properties

45000 Orléans
Tel: +33 2 38 24 04 24
Fax: +33 2 38 81 10 48

FINANCE
Direction des Impôts du Centre
70 rue de la Bretonnerie
BP 2457

45032 Orléans Cedex 1
Tel: +33 2 38 74 55 25
Fax: +33 2 38 74 55 62

Direction des Impôts de l'Ouest
6 rue Jean Guéhenno
CS 14208
35042 Rennes Cedex

Tel: +33 2 99 87 18 30
Fax: +33 2 99 63 28 90

BUILDING AND PLANNING
Chambre Régionale de Métiers du Centre
30 faubourg de Bourgogne
BP 24 45015
Orléans
Cedex 1
Tel: +33 2 38 68 03 32
Fax: +33 2 38 68 01 37

Chambre Régionale de Métiers des Pays de la Loire
6 boulevard des Pâtureaux
44980 Sainte-Luce-Sur-Loire
Tel: +33 2 51 13 31 31
Fax: +33 2 51 13 31 30

Union Régionale des CAUE des Pays de la Loire
Le Tertre au Jau
49100 Angers
Tel: +33 4 41 22 99 99
Fax: +33 4 41 22 99 00

EDUCATION
Rectorat de l'Académie

de Nantes
La Houssinière
BP 72616
44326 Nantes Cedex 3
Tel: +33 2 40 37 37 37
Fax: +33 2 40 37 37 00

Rectorat de l'Académie d'Orléans-Tours
21 rue Saint-Etienne
45043 Orléans
Cedex 1
Tel: +33 2 38 79 38 79
Fax: +33 2 38 62 41 79

HEALTH
Caisse Primaire d'Assurance Maladie de Loire-Atlantique
9 rue Gaëtan Rondeau
44200 Nantes
Tel: +33 2 51 88 88 88
Fax: +33 2 51 88 87 87

Caisse Primaire d'Assurance Maladie du Loiret
9 place Général de Gaulle
45000 Orléans
Tel: +33 2 38 79 47 00
Fax: +33 2 38 42 24 70

€10–50,000
(£6–33,000)

For around 20,000 euros you can buy a traditional stone-built village property requiring renovation. Otherwise, expect mainly unattractive townhouses. Availability of these properties is declining, given the amount of rental potential that can be reaped, and the popularity of this region.

€12,650   **CODE** SLP

CLAISE VALLEY, DÉPARTEMENT 37

A semi-detached cottage in a popular area, requiring complete renovation

£8,435

1   *no garden*   *within 5 mins of village*   *not located on a main road*   *no private parking*

€36,435   **CODE** HAM

AMBRIÈRES, DÉPARTEMENT 53

A townhouse, to modernise, offering outbuildings ideal for conversion

£24,290

3   *with garden*   *within 5 mins of amenities*   *located on a main road*   *no private parking*

€46,115   **CODE** HAM

LE PAS, DÉPARTEMENT 53

A large village property to renovate, with a second property ideal for a gîte

£30,745

3   *500m^2*   *close to amenities*   *located on a main road*   *room for parking*

€49,500   **CODE** SLP

CREUSE VALLEY, DÉPARTEMENT 37

A small townhouse, fully habitable, offering a small courtyard area

£33,000

3   *no garden, with courtyard*   *close to amenities*   *located on a main road*   *on road parking*

€50–100,000
(£33–66,000)

The Loire is still an area where property can be picked up cheaply. For around 50,000 euros, a habitable, modern property can be secured. Ideal for those seeking to buy to rent, there is huge variety, from a sprawling farmhouse requiring conversion to a comfortable modern bungalow.

PRICE GUIDE

€51,480   **CODE** FWY

ERNÉE, DÉPARTEMENT 53

A stone-built village house, requiring modernisation, with a wine cellar

£34,320

3 no garden within 5 mins of village not located on a main road on road parking

€52,000   **CODE** SLP

VIENNE, DÉPARTEMENT 45

A typical Charentaise farmhouse and outbuildings, requiring full restoration

£34,665

2/3 with grounds not far from amenities not located on a main road room for parking

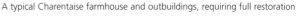

€55,000   **CODE** SLP

CREUSE VALLEY, DÉPARTEMENT 36

Situated in a small hamlet, comprising a house and various outbuildings

£36,665

1 $2,100m^2$ within 5 mins of village not located on a main road room for parking

€59,500   **CODE** SLP

TOURNON-ST-MARTIN, DÉPARTEMENT 36

A semi-detached property, recently used as a bar, for sale as a private home

£39,665

3 with a garden within 5 mins of amenities located on a main road with on road parking

€75,788   **CODE** FWY

ERNÉE, DÉPARTEMENT 53

A village house, fully restored and offering a courtyard and a small garden

£49,190

🛏4 🏠with a garden 🚶within 5 mins of village 🚗not located on a main road
🚗with on road parking

€83,390   **CODE** FWY

SION-LES-MINES, DÉPARTEMENT 44

Ideal as a holiday home, this house is fully habitable, with all mod cons

£55,590

🛏1 🏠285m² 🚶within 5 mins of village 🚗not located on a main road
🚗room for parking, with a garage

€84,456   **CODE** FWY

JUVIGNE, DÉPARTEMENT 53

A beautiful stone-built house, with wood and tile flooring and a cellar

£56,090

🛏2 🏠540m² 🚶in the centre of the village 🚗not located on a main road
🚗room for parking, with a garage

€86,000   **CODE** SLP

CREUSE VALLEY, DÉPARTEMENT 37

A modern property, habitable but requiring some renovation and decoration

£57,335

🛏2 🏠1,000m² 🚶within 5 mins of amenities 🚗not located on a main road
🚗room for parking

€89,450   **CODE** HAM

CEAUCÉ, DÉPARTEMENT 61

A fully licensed bar, built in a traditional style with exposed wood beams

£59,635

🛏5 🏠no garden 🚶located in the town centre 🚗not located on a main road
🚗room for parking

€99,500   **CODE** SLP

PAULNAY, DÉPARTEMENT 36

A modern bungalow in a popular area, well situated and fully habitable

£66,335

🛏3 🏠1,000m² 🚶within 5 mins of village 🚗not located on a main road
🚗room for parking, with a garage for 3 cars

€100–200,000
(£66–133,000)

This price bracket offers fully restored, habitable properties, many with outbuildings ideal for a gîte complex. Many farm properties are available throughout this region, and the average price rests within this price bracket. Despite demand, prices still remain relatively low.

€100,000   **CODE** SLP

BRENNE NATURAL PARK, DÉPARTEMENT 36

A modern bungalow, with plenty of storage space and a separate workshop

£66,665

🛏3 📐1,000m² *within 5 mins of village* *not located on a main road*
room for parking, with a garage

€106,000   **CODE** ALZ

FONTENAY-LE-COMTE, DÉPARTEMENT 85

A house, comprising of a separate property with two bedrooms and stables

£70,665

🛏2 *with land* *close to amenities* *not located on a main road*
room for parking, with a garage

€114,336   **CODE** HAM

SAINT-MARS, DÉPARTEMENT 53

A renovated property, offering a barn to convert, and grounds with a lake

£76,225

🛏2 📐20,000m² *within 5 mins of village* *not located on a main road*
room for parking, with a double garage

€114,800   **CODE** FWY

ERBRAY, DÉPARTEMENT 44

Set amidst traditional countryside, a renovated property, ideal for holidays

£76,535

🛏3 📐1,385m² *within 5 mins of amenities* *not located on a main road*
room for parking

€121,800   **CODE** FWY

LA-MEILLERAYE-DE-BRETAGNE, DÉPARTEMENT 44

Offering peaceful surroundings, this farm property is ideal for conversion

£81,200

⊟n/a ▦60,000m² ◻close to town and amenities ◻not located on a main road ◻room for parking

€139,500   **CODE** SLP

INDRE, DÉPARTEMENT 44

A restored property comprising of a cottage, gîte and various outbuildings

£93,000

⊟4 ▦4,047m² ◻close to all amenities ◻not located on a main road ◻room for parking

€141,488   **CODE** HAM

CEAUCE, DÉPARTEMENT 53

A very large property to modernise, with a traditional interior and large barn

£94,325

⊟3 ▦20,000m² ◻within 5 mins of village ◻not located on a main road ◻room for parking

PRICE GUIDE

€145,500   **CODE** ALZ

COULONGES-SUR-L'AUTIZE, DÉPARTEMENT 79

A character property, requiring some restoration, in a stunning rural setting

£97,000

⊟n/a ▦20,000m² ◻close to town and amenities ◻not located on a main road ◻room for parking

€169,000   **CODE** SLP

BRENNE NATURAL PARK, DÉPARTEMENT 36

Set in an isolated environment, this small property is traditionally built

£153,335

⊟1 ▦53,700m² ◻9kms from town ◻not located on a main road ◻room for parking

€193,706   **CODE** FWY

CHÂTEAUBRIANT DÉPARTEMENT 44

A beautiful stone house featuring all mod cons, offering a converted attic

£129,135

⊟n/a ▦8,140m² ◻close to all of town's amenities ◻not located on a main road ◻room for parking, with a large garage

€200–500,000
(£133–333,000)

Expect a wide variety of both modern and traditional properties to be available for this price. Most boast mature gardens and extensive grounds, and many are ideal for business purposes as well as perfect for those seeking to relocate permanently.

€210,000   **CODE** HIF

LUÇON, DÉPARTEMENT 85

A modern property located near the river, with splendid rural views

£140,000

📧 3 🏠 800m² 🖼 *located in a village with all amenities* 🚫 *not located on a main road* 🏠 *room for parking, with a double garage*

€236,296   **CODE** BUY

VIX, DÉPARTEMENT 85

Ideal for a *gîtes complax* or a *chambres d'Hotes*, a beautiful rural property

£157,530

📧 n/a 🏠 4,000m² 🖼 *within easy reach of town and amenities* 🚫 *not located on a main road* 🏠 *room for parking*

€241,500   **CODE** SLP

CLAISE VALLEY, DÉPARTEMENT 44

A lovely farm complex situated in a stunning valley, ideal for a holiday home

£161,000

📧 7 🏠 20,000m² 🖼 *within 5 mins of amenities* 🚫 *not located on a main road* 🏠 *room for parking*

€253,000   **CODE** SLP

CLAISE VALLEY, DÉPARTEMENT 37

A restored, detached property, situated in a verdant area, with a separate flat

£168,665

📧 3 🏠 1,900m² 🖼 *within 5 mins of amenities* 🚫 *not located on a main road* 🏠 *room for parking, with a double garage*

€281,000 **CODE** FWY

CHÂTEAUBRIANT, DÉPARTEMENT 44

A superb, luxurious property, with a fully equipped kitchen and airy rooms

£187,335

🛏4 ⬚5,000m² 🏙just south of town and amenities 🛣not located on a main road 🚗room for parking, with a garage for four cars

€315,000 **CODE** ALZ

FONTENAY-LE-COMTE, DÉPARTEMENT 85

A mansion house, with an annexe to restore, and a living space of 100m2

£210,000

🛏4 ⬚with a garden 🏙close to town and amenities 🛣not located on a main road 🚗room for parking

€330,000 **CODE** HIF

LUCON/LA ROCHELLE, DÉPARTEMENT 85

A stone house, ideal for a small business or B&B, with various outbuildings

£220,000

🛏4 ⬚3,000m² 🏙close to town and amenities 🛣not located on a main road 🚗room for parking

€350,000 **CODE** ALZ

MAILLEZAIS, DÉPARTEMENT 85

An old house, restored to a high standard, with an attractive interior and pool

£233,335

🛏3 ⬚5,300m² 🏙close to all amenities 🛣not located on a main road 🚗room for parking, with a two car garage

€355,000 **CODE** ALZ

FONTENAY-LE-COMTE, DÉPARTEMENT 85

A lovely 18th-century mansion, situated in private grounds, with a library

£236,665

🛏5 ⬚with extensive grounds 🏙close to town and amenities 🛣not located on a main road 🚗room for parking

€355,400 **CODE** ALZ

FONTENAY-LE-COMTE, DÉPARTEMENT 85

A lovely, spacious property, dating from the 18th century and fully renovated

£236,935

🛏4 ⬚3,700m² 🏙within 5 mins of village 🛣not located on a main road 🚗room for parking

PRICE GUIDE

€500,000+
(£330,000+)

Those able to stretch their budget to such lengths can find themselves the proud owner of an 18th century château, with extensive grounds and numerous outbuildings. Offering the height of luxury, the Loire boasts many idyllic, traditional properties that are excellent value for money.

€588,000   CODE SLP

LANGEAIS, DÉPARTEMENT 37

A stunning 18th-century château situated on the Loire, with a lake

£392,000

🛏8 🗺8,500m² 🚉within 5 mins of amenities 🚫not located on a main road

🅿parking for 10 cars

€610,000   CODE DEE

PORNIC, DÉPARTEMENT 44

Comprising of an 18th-century château with numerous outbuildings to convert

£406,665

🛏14 🗺133,500m² 🚉25kms from town 🚫not located on a main road

🅿room for parking

€1,140,000   CODE LAT

NANTES, DÉPARTEMENT 44

A 19th-century château offering a six-bedroom guest house and pool

£760,000

🛏8 🗺80,940m² 🚉within 5 mins of village 🚫not located on a main road

🅿room for parking

€1,525,000   CODE DEE

TOURS, DÉPARTEMENT 37

This unique 19th-century château is located in stunning surroundings

£1,016,665

🛏9 🗺110,000m² 🚉20kms from town 🚫not located on a main road

🅿room for parking

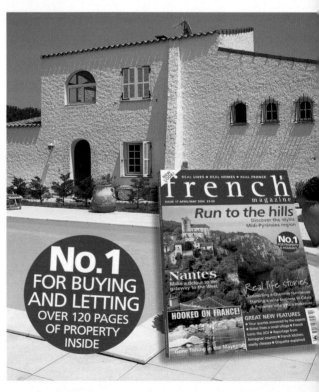

World-renowned vineyards
Gastronomic delights
Diverse landscapes

Burgundy

Profile 186
Hotspots 188

PRICE GUIDE

€20,000-€100,000 192
€100,000-€200,000 194
€200,000-€500,000 196
€500,000+ 198

Burgundy Profile

Getting there

AIR **Air France** (0845 359 1000; www.airfrance.co.uk) flies to Clermont-Ferrand and Lyon, while **British Airways** (0870 850 9850; www.britishairways.co.uk) and **Flybe** (0870 889 0908; www.flybe.com) operates flights from Heathrow to Lyon. In addition, Lyon receives **EasyJet** (0871 750 0100; www.easyjet.com) flights from London Stansted.

SEA The best ferry port destinations for access to Burgundy are Calais, Dieppe and Dunkirk. There are various operators for each of the ports, the main one being Calais. **P&O Ferries** (0870 520 2020; www.poportsmouth.com) operates from Dover to Calais, and Portsmouth to Le Havre, **Hoverspeed** (0870 240 8070; www.hoverspeed.co.uk) operates from Dover to Calais, as does **Sea France** (0870 571 1711; www.seafrance.com), and also between Newhaven to Dieppe. **Transmanche Ferries** (0800 917 1201; www.transmancheferries.com) sails between Newhaven and Dieppe, while **Norfolkline** (0130 421 8400; www.norfolkline.com) operates between Dover and Dunkirk.

ROAD The best route to take is from one of the the northern ferry ports such as Calais. From there the A26 leads you down to Reims and then on to Troyes, from where the A5 takes you into Burgundy. The A6 from Paris will take you straight to the heart of Burgundy, passing through Sens, Chablis, Beaune, Mâcon and finally in Dijon. The A43 also runs south from Lyon through Burgundy and on into the Rhône-Alps.

COACH **Eurolines** coaches (0870 514 3219; www.eurolines.com) operate services from destinations throughout the UK to Chalon-sur-Saône, Dijon and Mâcon.

RAIL A **TGV** service from London Waterloo reaches Dijon in six hours. From Paris there are numerous services to Dijon. The **Eurostar** (0870 518 6186; www.eurostar.com) runs through to Lille Europe, and from there a **TGV** operates between Lille and Dijon. Contact **Rail Europe** (0870 584 8848; www.raileurope.co.uk) for all details of train services in the region.

ECONOMY

Burgundy is renowned for its abundance of Michelin-starred restaurants and the production of fine wines, which are produced primarily in the Côte d'Or vineyard area. The regions vineyards, cultural and gastronomic treasures also generate a healthy income from the tourist industry. Given that Burgundy lacks a dominant sector in its economy, it is also responsible for various agricultural and industrial products.

BEST/WORST VALUE FOR MONEY

Despite being the area most in demand for property, the Côte d'Or is not the best value for money as properties are expensive and there is relatively little land to accompany them. Since this is a wine area, there is little room for property development and this, combined with such a high demand, continues to cause an upward trend in property prices. The northern areas are expensive due to the presence of Parisian holiday homes and the fact that the weather is

Burgundy is a region rich in architecture and history, with many traditional buildings available to buy

Agriculture remains a central industry in this quiet, rural region

slightly cooler than in southern Burgundy. The best value for money exists to the west of the Côte d'Or, towards the border with central France. Morvan is also very affordable, located away from the expensive wine areas. Dijon is an expensive, bustling French city where buyers are primarily French.

WHERE TO GO FOR WHAT

The area most in demand in Burgundy is the Côte d'Or. Recommended as the best place in which to buy a permanent home, it is also the most expensive. Within the Côte d'Or many foreign buyers purchase property outside of the wine area, in cheaper areas such as Autun and Auxois. Auxerre in the north of the region is also expensive due to the number of Parisian holiday homes which have raised its prices. Morvan is the most affordable area and is extremely busy during high season but can be quite isolated during winter.

Burgundy itself is a very peaceful region with a good standard of living, but is not recommended for families, as there is little for children to do. The region is situated at distance from the coast and its climate tends not to attract those who desire a warmer, Mediterranean feel.

PROPERTY PRICE TRENDS

Relatively isolated, Burgundy has never been popular with the foreign property market, which is surprising given the high standard of living and cheap property in the area.

The property market has increased by approximately seven to 10 percent in the last year, not solely because of British interest, but also due to Dutch and Belgian buyers. There aren't a great deal of British inhabitants here, given that most British buyers seek the Mediterranean climate and proximity to the coast, features that Burgundy does not offer. The market in the Côte d'Or is very fast-moving and renovation properties are rare to find.

A move to Burgundy should be motivated as much by its culture, history, cuisine and wine as for its cheap property. Not a family area, Burgundy is frequented more by couples seeking a sophisticated and peaceful retirement area.

The Burgundy property market is extremely fast moving, offering a limited amount of cheap property

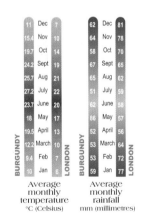

BURGUNDY		LONDON
11	Dec	7
15.4	Nov	10
19.7	Oct	14
24.2	Sept	19
25.7	Aug	21
27.2	July	22
23.7	June	20
18	May	17
19.5	April	13
12.2	March	10
9.4	Feb	7
10	Jan	6

Average monthly temperature
°C (Celsius)

BURGUNDY		LONDON
62	Dec	81
64	Nov	78
58	Oct	70
67	Sept	65
65	Aug	62
51	July	59
62	June	58
86	May	57
52	April	56
53	March	64
53	Feb	72
59	Jan	77

Average monthly rainfall
mm (millimetres)

Average House Sale Prices

HOTSPOT	2-BED	3-BED	4 BED	5 BED	6/7 BED	8-BED
Auxerre	-	€275K (£185K)	€325K (£215K)	-	-	-
Côte d'Or	€79K (£55K)	€100K (£65K)	€245K (£165K)	-	-	-
Dijon	-	-	€280K (£185K)	-	-	-
Morvan	€78K (£50K)	€240K (£160K)	€195K (£130K)	-	-	-

Burgundy Hotspots

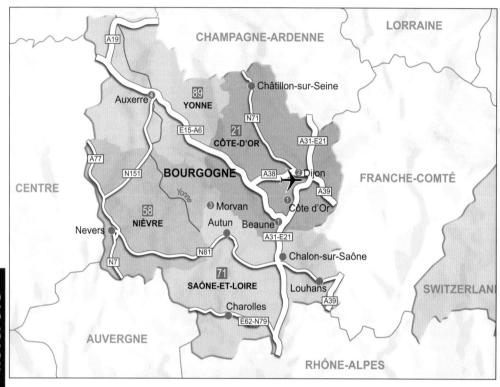

1. Côte d'Or vineyard areas

ESSENTIALS ■ **POP** 1990: -, 1999: 506,755 ■ **TAXES** Taxe d'habitation: 6.50%, Taxe foncière: 12.93%
■ **AIRPORT** Dijon Burgundy International Airport, 21600 Longvic, Tel: +33 3 80 67 67 67, Fax: +33 3 80 63 02 99.

KEY FACTS

SCHOOLS Contact the Rectorat de l'Académie de Dijon, 51 rue Monge, BP 1516, 21033 Dijon, Cedex, Tel: +33 3 80 44 84 00, Fax: +33 3 80 44 84 88.

MEDICAL The nearest major hospital is Beaune ■ Hôpital de Beaune, av Guigone de Salins, 21200 Beaune, Tel: +33 3 80 24 44 44.

RENTALS Côte d'Or is guaranteed at least a seven month rental season, as September and November are months for various wine festivals and auctions ■ This area, hugely in demand and popular with the foreign market, guarantees rental interest.

PROS It is the best permanent home location because of the sense of community it offers ■ A weathy area due to its association with the Dukes of Burgundy and its thriving wine trade ■ This is an ideal region for those seeking an authentic French environment ■ Côte d'Or is the commercial and cultural epicentre of Burgundy.

CONS There is no proximity to the coast and this is not a family area ■ The majority of British buyers purchase just outside of the Côte d'Or area to secure a cheaper property.

Côte d'Or is Burgundy's most famous winemaking region, and experiences huge demand for accommodation and sightseeing, as well as wine tasting. Its capital, Beaune, is well located for exploring the vineyards. A tourist draw in its own right, the old quarter is graced with a picturesque central square and the Hospice de Beaune, first created after the Hundred Years' War. In a region associated with the traditional *boeuf bourguignon*, which has long been famous outside of Burgundy, Charolais beef and top quality goat's cheese, there are many dishes prepared *en meurette*, in a red wine and bacon sauce. Beaune also has the finest French restaurants like *Ma Cuisine*, a bistro with a 12-page wine list.

The best known villages in the area include Meursault, Puligny-Montrachet and hillside hamlet Chassagne-Montrachet. The sleepy village of Meursault with its medieval church and Romanesque houses is home to Château Meursault, one of Burgundy's top wines.

The Côte d'Or is the most expensive and popular location in which to buy in the region and consequently prices in and around Beaune are above the national average, causing international buyers to seek renovation properties. In Beaune, a two-bedroom apartment starts from around 70,000 euros. Older houses are frequently stone built, with typically Burgundian multi-coloured tiled roofs, and there are occasionally rare finds such as a medieval limestone and clay watermill on the River Ouche, priced at 350 000 euros. ■

2. Dijon

KEY FACTS ■ **POP** 1990: -, 1999: 230,000 ■ **TAXES** Taxe d'habitation: 25.74%, Taxe Fonciere: 36.51% ■ **AIRPORT** Dijon Burgundy International Airport, 21600 Longvic, Tel: +33 380 67 67 67, Fax: +33 380 63 02 99

Dijon is a gourmet's dream, with snails, mustard and cheese galore. Here you'll find a mustard museum and the Dukes Palace, now the city hall incorporating the mayor's office. Take a climb up the Tour de Philippe le Bon for impressive city views. Other noteworthy examples of architecture are the colourfully tiled, preserved 17th-century town houses that formerly belonged to wealthy wine merchants and even more ancient ones from the 15th century with timber frames and overhanging upper storeys. Rue Sainte-Anne is the former monastery that now houses the Musée de la vie bourguignonne, a representation of regional heritage, including old, reconstructed shops and a series of exhibits on the process of winemaking.

Open air spaces are plentiful, the largest being the Botanical Garden, with its peaceful arboretum and park scattered with ponds, streams and children's play areas. October plays host to an annual gastronomy fair, an ideal opportunity to relish the local honey spice cake which was once used as military rations for the warriors of Genghis Khan. Cheese connoisseurs should sample Cîteaux, a white, young raw cheese produced throughout Burgundy.

More than two-thirds of jobs in the area are in the service sector, with industries settling around the city outskirts. Prices tend to be higher than average in Dijon, but you can still find inexpensive, habitable houses and farmhouses in need of restoration in most areas. It's not a huge international market and a three-bedroom apartment here starts at around 75,000 euros. ■

KEY FACTS

SCHOOLS Contact the Rectorat de l'Académie de Dijon, 51 rue Monge, BP 1516, 21033 Dijon, Cedex, Tel: +33 3 80 44 84 00, Fax: +33 3 80 44 84 88.
MEDICAL Hôpital Général, 3 rue du Faubourg Raines, 21000 Dijon, Tel: +33 3 80 29 30 31.
RENTALS Dijon is not regarded as a short-term rentals market, but rather as a long-term market ■ Dijon is not directed at the foreign buyers' market.
PROS Dijon is the very commercial and slick centre of Burgundy's wine trade ■ It has excellent transport connections.
CONS As this is a French market, prices can be very high and the turnover of property is rapid.

3. Morvan Regional park

ESSENTIALS ■ **POP** 1990: -, 1999: 34,405 ■ **TAXES** Taxe d'habitation: 15.01%, Taxe foncière: 33.75% ■ **AIRPORT** Dijon Burgundy International Airport, 21600 Longvic, Tel: +33 3 80 67 67 67, Fax: +33 3 80 63 02 99.

True to its Celtic name 'Morvan', meaning Black Mountain, this regional park is bursting with spectacular scenery. Created in 1970 to protect its cultural and natural heritage, Morvan is one of France's least densely populated areas, and yet is within easy reach of many tourist destinations, such as the tiny walled town of Vézelay. For centuries the park served as a backdrop for folk-tales of wolves and forest-bred legends filled with ghostly Gaelic tribes, Druids, strange human dialects and curious Celtic standing monoliths. Activities focus around the forests, hills and lakes, and include canoeing, rafting, mountain biking, potholing and horse riding.

To the northeast of the park lies Saulieu, an ancient market town which is well worth visiting for its 17th-century Basilica with animal motifs and the bible that once belonged to Emperor Charlemagne. The regional museum is also based here and has an entire floor dedicated to the animal sculptor François Pompon. Saulieu also has a reputation for fine dining, championed by late, world-renowned chef, Bernard Loiseau, whose refined cuisine made *The Côte d'Or* into one of France's most prestigious restaurants. His signature dish, sautéed frogs' legs in puréed garlic and parsley, is still on the menu, and the restaurant is now run by Loiseau's protégé, Patrick Bertron.

Properties here are less expensive than other Burgundy areas, owing to the park's distance from major wine areas and its seasonal nature. Renovation possibilities include a presbytery set in 3,000 square metres of grounds and priced at 122,000 euros. A detached *fermette* to renovate in the Nièvre *département* of the Parc starts at 102,000 euros. ■

KEY FACTS

SCHOOLS Contact the Rectorat de l'Académie de Dijon, 51 rue Monge, BP 1516, 21033 Dijon, Cedex, Tel: +33 3 80 44 84 00, Fax: +33 3 80 44 84 88.
MEDICAL The closest hospital in this area is in Saulieu, which is located on the edge of the Morvan National Park. ■ Hôpital Centre Hospitalier, 2 rue Courtepée, 21210 Saulieu, Tel: +33 3 80 90 55 05.
RENTALS This is a very busy holiday area and is exceptionally busy during the rental season from June to September ■ There are many diversions and activities, and nice surroundings to attract the rental market.
PROS This is an affordable area in which to live ■ Morvan is an excellent area for a second home.
CONS During the winter season the area becomes rather isolated and there is less of a community feel ■ This is not a recommended family area due to the lack of suitable activities and its isolation.

HOTSPOTS

Burgundy Hotspots

ESSENTIALS ■ **POP** 1990: 38,800, 1999: 37,800, 2003: 37,600 ■ **TAXES** Taxe d'habitation 25.15%, Taxe foncière 34.93%
■ **AIRPORT** Dijon Burgundy International Airport, 21600 Longvic, Tel: +33 3 80 67 67 67, Fax: +33 3 80 63 02 99.

KEY FACTS

SCHOOLS Contact the Rectorat de l'Académie de Dijon, 51 rue Monge, BP 1516, 21033 Dijon Cedex, Tel: +33 3 80 44 84 00, Fax: +33 3 80 44 84 88.

MEDICAL Centre Hospitalier, 2 bd Verdun, 89000 Auxerre, Tel: +33 3 86 48 48 48.

RENTALS A large number of Parisians own holiday homes in this northern area of Burgundy.

PROS The Yonne *département* is easily accessible from Paris and is considered to promote a much better lifestyle ■ Property is significantly cheaper here than it is in the *départements* situated closer to the capital.

CONS This is a cooler area than south Burgundy, with a much milder climate ■ The presence of many Parisian holiday homes here renders prices more expensive than further south.

Located southeast of Paris, the Yonne *département* is most widely known for Auxerre, which was originally the capital of Burgundy in medieval times, and for its river, the Yonne, the traditional waterway to Paris. This is the land where Chablis, the first of the great Burgundy whites is produced. The Auxerrois wine routes wind their way through medieval villages surrounded by their vines, with whole communities devoted to the production of wine.

Rising majestically above the river, Auxerre is celebrated for its Gallo-Roman remains, while its red-brown roofs covered with distinctive flat tiles - so characteristic of northern Burgundy - frame the Gothic spires of the Cathedral of Saint-Etienne. The Romanesque bell tower of the former abbey of Saint-Germain is another popular draw, its architecture decorated by the oldest recorded frescoes in France. At dusk when the city becomes illuminated, it is a wonderful treat to sample Burgundy truffles and cointreau-strawberry liqueur cocktails at the grand Restaurant Barnabet, a 17th-century centrally located post house.

Property is significantly cheaper in the area around Auxerre than it is in the expensive Côte d'Or wine region and in the capital, Dijon. However, many Parisians own holiday homes here and in recent years this has encouraged an increase in the cost of property. Just 30 minutes from Auxerre, you can buy a fully restored 200-year-old house with a detached cottage for roughly 330,000 euros. Another possibility is a half-timbered 18th-century mill from approximately 380,000 euros. ■

USEFUL CONTACTS

PREFECTURE
Préfecture de la Région Bourgogne
53 rue de la Préfecture
21041 Dijon Cedex
Tel: +33 3 80 44 64 00
Fax: +33 3 80 30 65 72

LEGAL
Chambre des Notaires de la Côte-d'Or
3 rue du Lycée
21000 Dijon
Tel: +33 3 80 67 12 21
Fax: +33 3 80 66 80 74

FINANCE
Direction Régionale des Impôts Rhône-Alpes Bourgogne
41 cours de la Liberté
69422 Lyon
Cedex 3
Tel: +33 4 78 63 54 10
Fax: +33 4 78 63 53 93

BUILDING & PLANNING
Chambre Régionale de Métiers de Bourgogne

The Canal du Nivernais is typical of the type of lush Burgundian countryside buyers can expect

46 boulevard de la Marne
BP 56721
21067 Dijon Cedex
Tel: +33 3 80 28 81 00
Fax: +33 3 80 28 81 01

CAUE de la Côte-d'Or
24 rue de la Préfecture

21000 Dijon
Tel: +33 3 80 30 02 38
Fax: +33 3 80 30 06 40

EDUCATION
Rectorat de l'Académie de Dijon
51 rue Monge

BP 1516
21033 Dijon
Cedex
Tel: +33 3 80 44 84 00
Fax: +33 3 80 44 84 88

HEALTH
Caisse Primaire d'Assurance

Maladie de la Côte-d'Or
8 rue du Docteur Maret
BP 1548
21045 Dijon
Cedex
Tel: +33 3 80 59 37 59
Fax: +33 3 80 59 37 77

HOTSPOTS

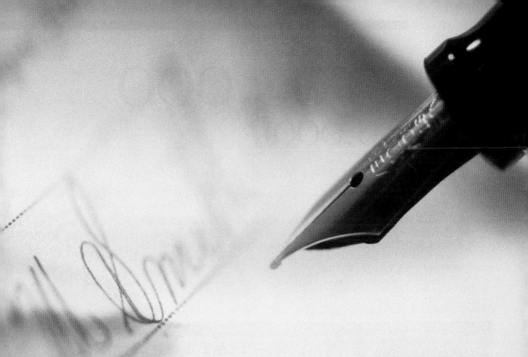

Writing out a big cheque?

When buying your place in France, Caxton FX can help you save money on your currency exchange. We offer excellent rates and free international transfers.

On top of that we understand that service matters – which is why we bend over backwards, sideways and forwards to make sure that your transaction happens quickly and smoothly.

To learn about our specialist foreign exchange service for property buyers, call James Hickman, our senior dealer, or one of his team today on 0845 658 2223. We will be pleased to hear from you.

Caxton FX Ltd. 2 Motcomb Street, London SW1X 8JU
Telephone 0845 658 2223 · www.caxtonfx.com

CAXTON *fx*

€20-100,000
(£13-66,000)

Burgundy has never been inundated with foreign buyers. Consequently, there is still an opportunity to pick up cheap renovation projects in the region. However these properties tend to be located away from the hub of the in-demand vineyard areas.

€26,680   SIP

MARCIGNY, DÉPARTEMENT 71

Set on the edge of this rural village, a stone barn ideal for conversion

£17,785

🛏 n/a   🏠 2,000m²   🚗 within 5 mins of village   🚫 not located on a main road 🅿 room for parking

€29,000   SIP

LOUHANS, DÉPARTEMENT 71

A traditional farmhouse requiring full renovation, and featuring two gîtes

£19,335

🛏 4   🏠 1,900m²   🚗 amenities are within easy reach   🚫 not located on a main road 🅿 room for parking

€30,000   BUR

SAULIEU, DÉPARTEMENT 21

A traditional property to renovate, with a separate barn, in a rural setting

£20,000

🛏 2   🏠 with a small garden   🚗 within 6 kms of town   🚫 not located on a main road 🅿 room for parking

€56,570   SIP

CORBIGNY, DÉPARTEMENT 58

A detached property to complete, comprising of a courtyard and outbuildings

£37,715

🛏 2   🏠 with a garden   🚗 close to small village   🚫 not located on a main road 🅿 room for parking, with a garage

€68,000 — BUR

MORVAN, DÉPARTEMENT 58

A newly built chalet located in a stunning woodland setting, ideal for holidays

£45,335

🛏 n/a 📐 20,000m² 🚲 close to amenities 🚫 not located on a main road
🅿 room for parking

€69,000 — BUD

BEAUNE, DÉPARTEMENT 21

A renovated property with a traditional interior, with a converted loft and cellar

£46,000

🛏 2 📐 with a small garden 🚲 within 5 mins of village 🚫 not located on a main
road 🅿 with on-road parking

€74,000 — BUR

COUCHOIS, DÉPARTEMENT 21

£49,300

A townhouse located in the medieval town of Couchois, with two cellars

🛏 4 📐 2,000m² 🚲 close to shops 🚫 not located on a main road
🅿 garage of 50m²

€77,700 — FPP

MORVAN NATURAL PARK, DÉPARTEMENT 58

A renovated village house with nice views from the spacious veranda

£51,800

🛏 2 📐 with a small garden 🚲 close to amenities 🚫 not located on a main road
🅿 room for parking

€89,000 — BUD

UCHON, DÉPARTEMENT 71

An attractive stone property, with a separate outbuilding, suitable for a gîte

£59,335

🛏 2 📐 with a small garden 🚲 close to town and amenities 🚫 not located on a
main road 🅿 with on-road parking

€99,000 — BUR

COUCHES, DÉPARTEMENT 71

A unique 18th-century house to be renovated. With a large barn

£66,000

🛏 5/6 📐 10,000² 🚲 within 5 mins of village 🚫 not located on a main road
🅿 room for parking

PRICE GUIDE

€100-200,000
(£60-130,000)

Anyone seeking a character property with a view and a garden should be expecting to pay at least 100,000 euros. Properties can range from a townhouse to a rural retreat requiring attention, thus giving the buyer a huge range of choice.

€101,805 CODE FPP

SEURRE, DÉPARTEMENT 71

A renovated period property, with outbuildings, enjoying landscaped gardens

£67,870

4 1,700m² close to town not located on a main road

room for parking

€106,000 CODE BUD

ARROUX VALLEY, DÉPARTEMENT 58

A village house with panoramic views over the Morvan Natural Park

£70,665

3 with a large garden within 5 mins of village not located on a main road room for parking

€125,000 CODE BUR

VOUVRES, DÉPARTEMENT 21

A detached property with a barn to be renovated, and a garden with orchard

£83,300

2 with a garden within 5 mins of village not located on a main road

room for parking

€134,154 CODE FWY

VÉZELAY, DÉPARTEMENT 89

Two unusual properties, one for renovation, very isolated, with fine views

£89,435

4 11,000m² requiring a car to reach amenities not located on a main road room for parking

€150,924
FWY

MORVAN, DÉPARTEMENT 58

A well renovated property, in a rural hamlet, within the Morvan Natural Park

£100,610

⊟4 ▦ *small garden* ▦ *within walking distance of a village* ▧ *not located on a main road* ⌂ *room for parking*

€168,000
FPP

SEURRE, DÉPARTEMENT 21

A large period house with a small lodging attached, located in a rural area

£112,000

⊟4 ▦ *3,035m^2* ▦ *located in the centre of the village* ▧ *not located on a main road* ⌂ *room for parking*

€170,000
BUR

AUTUN, DÉPARTEMENT 21

A newly built bungalow, with a fitted kitchen and open plan lounge area

£113,335

⊟3 ▦ *with a large garden* ▦ *within 5 mins of village* ▧ *not located on a main road* ⌂ *room for parking, with a double garage*

€174,000
FPP

MORVAN, DÉPARTEMENT 58

A village house with panoramic views located in protected natural park

£116,000

⊟4 ▦ *4,047m^2* ▦ *in a rural location, requiring a car to reach town* ▧ *not located on a main road* ⌂ *room for parking, with a large garage*

€189,700
BUR

COUCHES, DÉPARTEMENT 21

A shop, easy to transform into a holiday home, featuring a two-bedroom flat

£126,465

⊟2 ▦ *1,000m^2* ▦ *20 kms from town* ▧ *located on a main road* ⌂ *room for parking, with a garage*

€198,000
BUR

AUTUN, DÉPARTEMENT 21

A townhouse with a private courtyard, boasting a terrace and electric gates

£132,000

⊟4 ▦ *with a garden* ▦ *located in the town centre* ▧ *not located on a main road* ⌂ *with a garage*

PRICE GUIDE

€200-500,000
(£133-333,000)

Buying in the wine area is an expensive venture and it is here that costs begin to sky rocket. Once you begin to look at the price bracket of 200,000 euros plus, you can guarantee yourself a truly traditional French property, recently renovated and ready for habitation.

€210,000 — LAT

CHALON-SUR-SAÔNE, DÉPARTEMENT 71

A renovated farmhouse with stables and other outbuildings

£140,000

🛏4 🏠40,470m² within 5 mins of village not located on a main road room for parking

€220,000 — BUR

MORVAN, DÉPARTEMENT 21

A stone cottage requiring renovation, located in the stunning Morvan area

£146,665

🛏3 🏠35,000m² requiring a car to reach amenities not located on a main road room for parking

€220,000 — BUD

AUTUN, DÉPARTEMENT 71

A stone farmhouse, located in a small complex, with a variety of outbuildings

£145,000

🛏n/a 🏠35,000m² within 5 mins of village not located on a main road room for parking

€255,353 — FPP

SEURRE, DÉPARTEMENT 71

An impressively restored mansion, with numerous outbuildings to convert

£170,235

🛏4 🏠6,070m² set in a village location not located on a main road room for parking

€259,000 — SIP

ROANNE, DÉPARTEMENT 42

A superb mansion, situated in spacious grounds, with 300m^2 living space

£172,665

🛏7 🗺7,000m^2 *close to all amenities* *not located on a main road* *room for parking*

€260,000 — BUR

MORVAN, DÉPARTEMENT 58

A renovated house with several outbuildings, and the possibility to develop

£173,335

🛏3 🗺2,000m^2 *requiring a car to reach amenities* *not located on a main road* *room for parking, with a garage*

€260,000 — BUD

MORVAN, DÉPARTEMENT 58

With glorious views over the parklands, an superbly renovated farmhouse

£173,335

🛏4 🗺2,000m^2 *close to amenities* *not located on a main road* *room for parking, with a large garage*

€280,000 — SIP

CHABLIS, DÉPARTEMENT 21

A stone-built watermill requiring complete renovation, ideal for a holiday home

£186,665

🛏4 🗺1,0120m^2 *30 mins from town and amenities* *not located on a main road* *room for parking*

€280,000 — SIP

SAINT-CHRISTOPHE-EN-BRIONNAIS, DÉPARTEMENT 71

A superb, traditional farmhouse, enjoying glorious surroundings

£186,665

🛏4 🗺3,000m^2 *within 5 mins of village* *not located on a main road* *room for parking*

€290,800 — BUD

BEAUNE, DÉPARTEMENT 21

A modern pavillion-style property, with a heated pool and all mod cons

£193,865

🛏4 🗺with extensive grounds *within 5 mins of village* *not located on a main road* *room for parking*

€320,000 CODE SIP

GIVRY, DÉPARTEMENT 71

Situated in a small village, this traditional property is surrounded by vineyards

£213,335

🛏5 ⬚890m² *close to town and amenities* *not located on a main road* *room for parking*

€320,150 CODE SIP

MARCIGNY, DÉPARTEMENT 74

A traditional Burgundian farmhouse, comprising many original features

£213,435

🛏3 ⬚20,0000m² *8 kms from town and amenities* *not located on a main road* *room for parking*

€330,000 CODE SIP

CHALON-SUR-SAÔNE, DÉPARTEMENT 71

Set in a wine growing village, this is a timbered, Bressan-style farmhouse

£220,000

🛏4 ⬚13,000m² *within 5 mins of village* *not located on a main road* *room for parking*

€340,000 CODE SIP

CHALON-SUR-SAONE, DÉPARTEMENT 71

A secluded property, recently renovated, located in a wine growing region

£226,665

🛏5/6 ⬚1,400m² *within 5 mins of village amenities* *not located on a main road* *room for parking*

€348,700 CODE BUD

BEAUNE, DÉPARTEMENT 21

A traditional house, offering a wood beam interior and Jacobite windows

£232,465

🛏- ⬚with large gardens *within 5 mins of village* *not located on a main road* *room for parking*

€365,800 CODE FPP

VALLEE DE L'OUCHE, DÉPARTEMENT 21

A 19th century property, traditionally restored, with a separate gîte

£243,865

🛏3 ⬚809.4m² *close to amenities* *not located on a main road* *room for parking*

€500,000+
(£330,000+)

Burgundy's rich heritage means that the Burgundian countryside is littered with châteaux and character properties offering luxurious surroundings and interiors. Some require renovation, although most are renovated and offer the benefits of a swimming pool and outbuildings to convert.

€500,000   DEE

CHABLIS, DÉPARTEMENT 89

An 18th-century watermill requiring renovation, set in beautiful surroundings

£333,335

🛏7   ⬛25,000m²   *5 kms from amenities*   *not located on a main road*   *room for parking, with a garage*

€650,000   DEE

CHABLIS, DÉPARTEMENT 89

An estate 195kms from Paris, this château was built in the 17th century

£433,335

🛏10   ⬛90,000m²   *within 5 kms from amenities*   *not located on a main road*   *room for parking*

€750,000   BUR

CHABLIS, DÉPARTEMENT 89

A renovated house, with a swimming pool and a separate studio apartment

£500,000

🛏3   ⬛25,000m²   *close to amenities*   *not located on a main road*   *room for parking, with a garage*

€750,000   BUR

COUCHOIS, DÉPARTEMENT 21

A 17th-century wine grower's manor, with outbuildings and a swimming pool

£500,000

🛏7   ⬛24,000m²   *close to amenities*   *not located on a main road*   *room for parking*

Rolling plains and *bocage*
Traditional country towns
Historic Atlantic ports

Poitou-Charentes

Profile 202
Hotspots 204

PRICE GUIDE
€20,000-€100,000 208
€100,000-€200,000 210
€200,000-€500,000 212
€500,000+ 214

Poitou-Charentes Profile

PROFILE

Getting there

AIR Air France (0845 359 1000; www.airfrance.co.uk), **Flybe** (0870 567 6676; www.flybe.com) and **GB Airways** (0870 850 9850; www.gbairways.com) fly from Gatwick to Nantes; **Ryanair** (0871 246 0000; www.ryanair.com) operates flights to Tours, La Rochelle and Poitiers from Stansted; and Nantes receives **British Airways** (0870 850 9850; www.britishairways.com) flights from Heathrow.

ROAD From Paris, the A1 links with the A10 via the N10 to Pont de Sèvres and the A10-E5 junction with the A10. From the A10 take the Lyon junction with the N104 on to the A10-E5. This leads to the N147-E62 at Junction 29 for Poitiers and Limoges, after a right turn at the Saumur, Angers, Nantes signpost. Take the N147 at the junction for Migné-Auxances, which joins the N10 into Poitiers. To reach La Rochelle, take the N11 west from the A10 to La Rochelle, or the N10 south to Angoulême.

COACH Eurolines France (0870 514 3219, www.eurolines.com) operates coaches to Angoulême, La Rochelle and Poitiers.

RAIL An excellent **TGV** route links Le Mans, Angers, Nantes, Poitiers, La Rochelle and Angoulême to Paris Gare Montparnasse. For more information contact **Rail Europe**; (0870 584 8848; www.raileurope.co.uk).

ECONOMY

A series of town or inter-regional cottage industries supports this area, whose economy leans mainly towards agricultural production. Office blocks and commerce in Tours interrupt the array of crops in and around Poitiers, which includes the market town of Chauvigny. Cognac's heart and soul revolve around the production of its namesake brandy, both in field and factory, by the Henessy Cognac company. Angoulême in Charente continues its tradition of paper mills, although on a smaller scale than previously, while tourism is a developing strand of the economy. Unsurprisingly, mussel and oyster fishing form the mainstay of Ile de Ré, the island that is a tourist favourite, while fishing, tourism and commerce support La Rochelle.

BEST/WORST VALUE FOR MONEY

Properties in La Rochelle, a popular town with Parisians for second homes, make excellent investments which are sure to hold their value and make good resales.

Generally speaking, a property in the southeast of Charente (Châtellerault) represents excellent value, as they are cheaper than those in the west and central areas, including the towns of Angoulême and Saintes. The Charente-Maritime (Ile de Ré, and Ile d'Oloron) region is seen as a real alternative to Dordogne and it affords good value for buyers to let.

La Rochelle's traditional *colombage* architecture dominates the area's property

Property values have doubled in the last year, and are continuing to rise fast

Mussel and oyster fishing form the mainstay of this region's economy

Although Ile de Ré properties are expensive, pushed up by Parisian second home purchasers, they offer excellent rental potential. The island's 500,000 younger visitors are willing to pay 900 euros a week during the weather-dependent summer season, but these are not sustainable year-long and the island's north all but closes down in winter.

Slightly nearer to Dordogne, Angoulême's property price tags are higher than elsewhere in the region, but rental can be accrued year-long. Buyers get less value for money in Cognac and Saintes.

WHERE TO GO FOR WHAT
Gîtes are speckled throughout the Charente-Maritime, with no real pocket of British buyers, though La Rochelle, Ile de Ré, Angoulême and their environs are popular. Chadurie, near Angoulême, has a stream of visitors renting more or less throughout the year. Saintes, Angoulême and the Charente area are favourites with British relocators, and investment purchases here have excellent future sales potential. Especially popular with British tourists, towns to the west of Poitiers, including Chauvigny, Bellac, L'Isle Jordain, Saint- Savin, Montmorillon, and Bussière Poitevine are prime holiday home locales.

PROPERTY PRICE TRENDS
Renovation properties dominate the market throughout Charente and there tends to be fewer fully modernised, habitable properties available. The area has seen some dramatic price increases though, and the willingness of some British buyers to pay more for properties has encouraged some agents to charge twice their market value.

Property values at the lower end of the market have at least doubled in the last 18 months. A detached house and barn for renovation, for example, with a large garden in a hamlet setting, has increased from 18-27,000 to 52-75,000 euros. All other budget areas are maintaining a steady 25 to 35 per cent annual price rise, except for detached properties with land and outbuildings to convert, which are rising faster here. Urban properties generally stay at the cheaper end, but are less popular with many international buyers who also seek gardens.

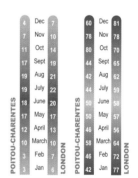

POITOU-CHARENTES		LONDON
4	Dec	7
7	Nov	10
11	Oct	14
17	Sept	19
19	Aug	21
19	July	22
18	June	20
17	May	17
12	April	13
10	March	10
3	Feb	7
3	Jan	6

Average monthly temperature °C (Celius)

POITOU-CHARENTES		LONDON
60	Dec	81
78	Nov	78
80	Oct	70
44	Sept	65
42	Aug	62
44	July	59
50	June	58
50	May	57
46	April	56
58	March	64
46	Feb	72
42	Jan	77

Average monthly rainfall mm (millimetres)

Average House Sale Prices

HOTSPOT	2-BED	3-BED	4 BED	5 BED	6/7 BED	8-BED
Charante département	€115K (£75K)	€150K (£100K)	-	€240K (£160K)	€650K (£435K)	-
Châtellerault	-	€225K (£150K)	-	-	-	-
Ile-de-Ré/ La Rochelle	€175K (£115K)	€185K (£125K)	€215K (£145K)	-	-	-
Poitiers	€100K (£65K)	E160K (£	€180K (£120K)	€395K (£265K)	-	-

Poitou-Charentes Profile

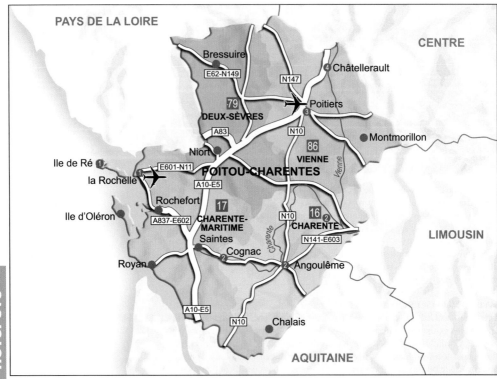

1. Ile de Ré and La Rochelle

ESSENTIALS ▪ **POP** 1990: 73,744, 1999: 96,555 ▪ **TAXES** Taxe d'habitation: 24.90%, Taxe foncière: 48.17% ▪ **AIRPORT** Airport La Rochelle-Ile de Ré, rue du Jura, 17 000 La Rochelle; Tel: +33 5 46 42 30 26.

KEY FACTS

SCHOOLS Cité scolaire internationale Grand Air, Lycée et collège de Grand Air, avenue du Bois d'Amour 17, 44 500 La Baule-Escoublac; Tel: +33 2 40 11 58 00, www.lycee-grand-air.net.

MEDICAL Hôpital Rural Saint Honoré, rue l'hôpital 53, 17410 Saint Martin de Ré; Tel: +33 5 46 09 20 01 ▪ Centre Hospitalier de La Rochelle, rue du Docteur Schweitzer, 17 000 La Rochelle; Tel: +33 5 46 45 50 50

RENTALS Ile de Ré: difficult to secure year-round rental ▪ La Rochelle University ensures regular tenants. ▪ Tourism brings good short-term summer rentals ▪ A house lets from 760 euros a month in low season and 915 a week in high.

PROS Coastal resorts are popular with foreign second-home buyers. ▪ Property in Saint-Martin-de-Ré is also popular and La Rochelle has a busy, stable market ▪ Ile-de-Ré enforces a two-storey height limit, plus white-washed walls, green shutters and tiled roofs on all buildings. ▪ Good transport links.

CONS Parisian second homes have raised prices, and both locations are expensive. ▪ Ile de Ré is quiet in winter, but very busy (500,000 visitors) in summer.

La Rochelle is an unspoilt French Atlantic seaside town in Charente-Maritime, with a historic centre and waterfront protected from redevelopment and traffic.There are four distinct neighbourhoods: the 17th to 18th-century centre; the innovative Les Minimes marina development, the residential and industrial inner suburbs, and to Ile de Ré Island.

Within the triangle of Place de Verdun, the Porte Royale and the Tour de la Lanterne is the historical centre where most of La Rochelle's architectural treasures lie, such as the military Tour Saint-Nicolas, providing a beautiful view of the Vieux Port. As well as the cathedral, you'll find le Musée du Nouveau Monde and le Musée des Beaux-Arts here.

Inspired by Scandinavian design, Les Minimes or'timber town' is one of Europe's biggest marinas. The university is here, along with Technoforum (a research centre for new technologies), and the Musée Maritime Neptunéa.

Two miles away, the Ile de Ré, reached by a 18-mile bridge, benefits from the Gulf Stream and year-round warmth. The north is a haven of oyster farms, salt marshes, wildlife sanctuaries and miles of unspoiled beaches. The east is more residential, with villages such as Saint-Martin or Sainte-Marie and their whitewashed cottages with brightly painted shutters. Here you can buy a *maison de village* to renovate, comprising five large rooms with walled garden and sea views for 323,000 euros. A five-bedroom town house starts from 484,000 euros. ▪

2. Charente Département

ESSENTIALS ■ **POP** 1990: 64,863, 1999: 68,552 ■ **TAXES** Taxe d'habitation: 17.48%, Taxe foncière: 40.12%
■ **AIRPORT** Bordeaux Airport, Cedex 40, 33700 Merignac; Tel: +33 5 56 34 50 00, www.bordeaux.aeroport.fr.

Very popular with British buyers looking for permanent rather than holiday homes, this western *département* between Bordeaux and the Loire Valley features miles of sandy Atlantic beaches. Inland you find the wooded valleys of several large rivers including the Charente, and vineyards producing Cognac brandy.

The capital of Charente is the walled city of Angoulême, with many amenities and an annual World Music Festival, despite the high unemployment of recent years caused by the closure of the local paper mills. Its most famous museum, the Centre national de la bande dessinée, celebrates cartoon characters from Astérix to Peanuts. The museum, in a former brewery, with contemporary high-rise and glass additions, houses some 4,000 original drawings and a family-friendly library with English editions.

Prosperous Cognac is the base of the main cognac houses. The oldest, Martell, was founded by a former smuggler. Although most attractions are connected with cognac, there are other interesting sites to visit such as the château ruins, the birthplace of King François I, and the town's museum which contains an exhibition on the history of the region's wine-making industry. Not only famous for its brandy, Cognac is also well-known for its annual detective thriller film festival.

House prices typically increase westwards in the region, although these remain cheaper than in Dordogne. The typical Charentaise house is made from stone, with an ochre-tiled roof. House prices in Cognac start at 70,000 euros rising to a 210,000 five-bedroom property with an orchard. ■

KEY FACTS
SCHOOLS Cité scolairé internationale Grand Air, Lycée et collège de Grand Air, avenue du Bois d'Amour 77, 44500 La Baule-Escoublac; Tel: +33 2 40 11 58 00, www.lycee-grand-air.net.
MEDICAL Centre Hospitalier, rue Montesquieu, 16100 Cognac; Tel: +33 5 45 36 75 75 ■ Centre Hospitalier Camille Claudel, rue Alphonse Aulard 37, 16 000 Angoulême; Tel: +33 5 45 62 14 85.
RENTALS Good to average market, rental period up to 4 months a year. ■ Market is intermittent from Easter to end of October, but winter lets are possible ■ Average high season weekly rents in euros for Cognac: 314 (two-bed), 375 (4-6 people), 525 (6-8 people); for Angoulême: 313 (4-6 people), 546 (6-8).
PROS Large foreign community, particularly British ■ Cheap renovation properties ■ Easy access TGV route links Poitiers and Angoulême to Bordeaux. ■ A wealthy area, and Angoulême is a lively town ■ Coined the second sunniest French region
CONS Fewer habitable properties and poorer employment prospects ■ Growing popularity means rising prices ■ Angoulême and south Angoulême, Blanzac and Montmoreau are very expensive ■ Some prices have doubled due to foreign interest.

3. Poitiers and area

ESSENTIALS ■ **POP:** 1990: 82,507, 1999: 87,012 ■ **TAXES** Taxe d'habitation: 30.28%, Taxe foncière: 37.53%
■ **AIRPORT** Airport, France, Biard, 86000 Poitiers; Tel: +33 5 49 30 04 40, Fax: +33 5 49 58 81 71.

Overlooking the Clain and Boivre rivers, Poitiers was seat to the dukes of Aquitaine and has tempted capture by many past conquerors from Joan of Arc to Richard the Lion Heart. It boasts a thriving University, stunning Romanesque Notre Dame Cathedral and lively nightlife. Open spaces are plentiful, the 18th-century Parc de Blossac with its elegant terraced limestone gardens is set on the town's ramparts. Unusual events take place throughout the year with a dog fair and the *CollaVoce*, a festival of music for organ and voice.

Six miles from the city is Futuroscope, the futuristic theme park set in more than 130 acres devoted to giant screens, 3D cinemas, circular cinemas and other state-of-the-art audio-visual spectacles. Space Station 3D recounts the daring in-orbit assembly of the International Space Station. At night the finale is a fantastic laser light show with fireworks.

A two-bedroomed semi-detached town house, close to the cathedral, on four levels starts at 42,500 euros. If you're looking for a home to renovate, try the Thenezay, a small market town just 30 minutes from Poitiers. For 146,000 euros you can acquire a large house with 300 square metres living area with a courtyard, exposed beams and private walled garden. In the quiet village of Vivonne, southwest of Poitiers, you can find a Basilique dating from 1880, in local hand-dressed stone with brick vaulted ceilings and stained glass windows and sculpted motifs selling for 162,000 euros. ■

KEY FACTS
SCHOOLS Cite scolairé internationale Grand Air, Lycée et collège de Grand Air, avenue du Bois d'Amour 77, 44500 La Baule Escoublac, Tel: +33 2 40 11 58 00, www.lycee-grand-air.net.
MEDICAL Centre Hospitalier Universitaire de Poitiers, rue de la Milétrie 2, 86021 Poitiers Cedex, BP 577; Tel: +33 5 49 44 44 44, www.chu-poitiers.fr.
RENTALS Average weekly rents for Poitiers and environs are 292 euros in high season (426 euros for 6-8 people).
PROS Poitiers is attracting more foreign buyers ■ Good rail links and cheap flights from London Stansted ■ Excellent climate ■ The Vendée coast is just 1.5 hours away and ski resorts two hours to the west ■ Bellac, Montmorillon, Saint-Savin, Chauvigny, L'Isle-Jordain and Bussière-Poitevine are increasingly popular with foreign buyers ■ Good potential returns on cheap renovation properties.
CONS Once one of the cheapest property markets, prices have at least doubled here during the past 18 months.

4. Châtellerault and area

ESSENTIALS ■ **POP** 1990: 35,646, 1999: 37,275 ■ **TAXES** Taxe d'habitation: 21.79%, Taxe foncière: 39.90% ■ **AIRPORT**
Airport Angers-Marcé, 49 190 Marcé; Tel: +33 2 41 33 50 00; www.angers.aeroport.fr

KEY FACTS

SCHOOLS Cité scolairé internationale Grand Air,
Lycée et collège de Grand Air, avenue du Bois
d'Amour 77, 44500 La Baule Escoublac; Tel: +33 2 40
11 58 00, www.lycee-grand-air.net
MEDICAL Centre Hospitalier Camille Guérin, rue
Aimé Souché 17, 86 100 Châtellerault.
RENTALS Not a tourist area, short-term rents are not
commonplace in Châtellerault ■ Long-term rents
average at 580 to 610 euros a month ■ Average
rents for a two-bedroom property is 200 euros per
month ■ A three-bedroom propertty costs 260 euros
per month, and 170 euros a month in La Roche
Posay ■ La Roche-Posay is a popular tourist
destination in summer, with a popular short-term
rental market.
PROS Cheap properties are available, and it is still
possible to pick up a barn plus a piece of land for
around 10,000 euros ■ Steeped in history, this area
played a crucial role in the 100-year war between
France and England ■ There is still demand for
farm complexes, and demand for all property still
outstrips supply ■ This is still a good property
investment area.
CONS Châtellerault is not really a tourist area ■ Few
foreign buyers, and the market is primarily French
■ There are limited employment opportunities.

Located 19 miles northeast of Poitiers, Châtellerault is situated on the right and eastern bank of the Vienne, en route to the Loire Valley. Founded in the 10th century, Châtellerault became a favoured stopover for travellers and pilgrims while the Henri IV bridge, constructed on order of Catherine de Médici, opened the way to development as a major river port. Visit the limestone underground caves at nearby Availles en Châtellerault – legend says these were inhabited by gnomes during the 12th century and there are carved stone benches and air holes cut into the rock. The Discovery Farm at Thuré provides an introduction to local farming methods and to gastronomy like honey and goats cheese.

A beautiful, busy spa town founded by the Romans in the 15th century, la Roche-Posay is frequently visited for its healing waters, and has an old town encircled by defence walls towering above the valley, with donjon and fortified church. There are nine- and 18-hole golf courses, a casino and horse racing, while the Tardes river is a favourite for kayaking. The nearby Regional Park of the Brenne is one of the largest wildlife sanctuaries in Europe, being especially popular with bird-watchers.

Cheap properties are available in the area, and although there is not a huge amount of foreign interest, demand still outstrips supply. French buyers are the biggest group, and this is a good location in which to invest in property. A typical country house built in limestone with clay roof tiles, a courtyard garden and outbuildings can cost from around 135,000 euros. ■

USEFUL CONTACTS

PREFECTURE
Préfecture de la Région
Poitou-Charentes
place Aristide-Briand
86021 Poitiers Cedex
Tel: +33 5 49 55 70 00
Fax: +33 5 49 88 25 34

LEGAL
Chambre des Notaires de la
Vienne
avenue Thomas Edison
86360 Chasseneuil-du-Poitou
Tel: +33 5 49 49 42 60
Fax: +33 5 49 49 42 63

FINANCE
Direction des Impôts du
Sud-Ouest
rue des Piliers de Tutelle
BP 45
33025 Bordeaux Cedex
Tel: +33 5 57 14 21 00
Fax: +33 5 57 14 21 09

BUILDING & PLANNING
Chambre Régionale de
Métiers de Poitou-Charentes
place Charles de Gaulle 13

86000 Poitiers Cedex
Tel: +33 5 49 88 70 52
Fax: +33 5 49 60 72 80

CAUE de Charente-Maritime
boulevard de la République 85
Les Minimes
17076 La Rochelle Cedex 9
Tel: +33 5 46 31 71 90
Fax: +33 5 46 31 71 91

EDUCATION
Rectorat de l'Académie de
Poitiers
cité de la Traverse 5
BP 625
86022 Poitiers
Cedex
Tel: +33 5 49 54 70 00
Fax: +33 5 49 54 70 01

HEALTH
Caisse Primaire d'Assurance
Maladie de la Vienne
rue Touffenet 41
86000 Poitiers
Cedex
Tel: +33 5 49 44 59 97
Fax: +33 5 49 44 54 20

Eels, mussels, oysters
and other fresh seafood
dominate the region's diet

€20–100,000
(£13–66,000)

Poitou-Charentes offers many renovation properties, with a village house requiring total renovation starting at 40,000 euros. Now is an excellent time to invest as the lack of renovation properties in the Loire and Dordogne has forced bargain buyers to seek cheap property elsewhere.

€17,250 CODE FWY

ST FORT, DÉPARTEMENT 17

A typical Charentaise house, partially restored, enjoying rural surroundings

£11,500

🛏 n/a 📐 208m² 🏘 close to all amenities 🚗 not located on a main road

🅿 no private parking

€28,660 CODE FWY

ST-GENIS-DE-SAINTONGE, DÉPARTEMENT 17

A house to renovate, in a small rural hamlet, with an outbuilding and a cellar

£19,105

🛏 3 📐 with an 45m² enclosed courtyard 🏘 within 5 mins of village

🚗 located on a main road 🅿 with on road parking

€39,100 CODE FPP

ROUSSINES, DÉPARTEMENT 16

An old village house with a barn and terrace, requiring total renovation

£26,000

🛏 2 📐 with a garden 🏘 within 5 mins of village 🚗 not located on a main road

🅿 room for parking, with two garages

€41,912 CODE FWY

ST-DIZANT-DU-GUA, DÉPARTEMENT 17

A house to renovate with a mature garden and a traditional interior

£27.940

🛏 2 📐 207m² 🏘 close to town and amenities 🚗 not located on a main road

🅿 room for parking

€48,400

CHALAIS, DÉPARTEMENT 16

A bungalow in excellent condition, with a large fishing lake and outbuildings

£32,500

3 120,000m^2 *within easy reach of amenities* *not located on a main road* *room for parking, with a garage*

€56,600

ROMAGNE, DÉPARTEMENT 86

A village house, located in a traditional hamlet, requiring full renovation

£37,500

1 *with a small garden* *close to amenities* *not located on a main road* *room for parking*

€65,553

NR COZES, DÉPARTEMENT 17

Located in a small village, a bar with a separate flat above the premises

£43,702

4 702m^2 *close to town and amenities* *located on a main road* *room for parking, with a garage*

€69,200

SAINT-STRONG, DÉPARTEMENT 17

A traditional style property, with a modern, open plan interior and a veranda

£46,135

2 *with a small garden* *close to town's amenities* *not located on a main road* *room for parking, with a garage*

€82,026

MATHA, DÉPARTEMENT 17

A typical Charentaise house, fully habitable, with a modern fitted kitchen

£54,684

2 *with a small garden and courtyard* *close to town and amenities* *not located on a main road* *room for parking, with a garage*

€98,100

MIRAMBEAU, DÉPARTEMENT 17

A traditional Charentaise house to be completed, with a separate laundry

£65,500

4 1,360m^2 *close to town and amenities* *not located on a main road* *room for parking, with a garage*

€100–200,000
(£66–133,000)

100,000 plus euros will secure you a large property with some outbuildings to convert, although the premises will require renovation. The majority of the properties are stone-built, constructed in a traditional style, and are ideal for a second home or a family holiday home.

€100,000 **CODE** SLP

CHATELLERAULT, DÉPARTEMENT 86

A converted farmhouse offering a variety of outbuildings ideal for conversion

£66,500

🛏3 🌐1,100m² 🏙close to town and amenities 🛣not located on a main road
🏠room for parking

€101,244 **CODE** FWY

COZES, DÉPARTEMENT 17

Requiring renovation, this traditional property makes for an ideal holiday home

£67,500

🛏3 🌐with a small garden and courtyard 🏙close to amenities
🛣not located on a main road 🏠room for parking, with a garage

€105,950 **CODE** FWY

PONS, DÉPARTEMENT 17

A modern bungalow, enjoying rural surroundings and panoramic views

£70,500

🛏3 🌐1,100m² 🏙close to town's amenities 🛣not located on a main road
🏠room for parking, with a garage

€122,000 **CODE** ALZ

COULONGES, DÉPARTEMENT 79

An old stone house to be fully renovated, comprising of two outbuildings

£81,500

🛏n/a 🌐2,000m² 🏙close to amenities 🛣not located on a main road
🏠room for parking

€152,000   CODE FDC

SAINT-JUNIEN, DÉPARTEMENT 16

A large stone property, built in a traditional style in fully habitable condition

£101,500

3 *with large mature gardens* *within 5 mins of village*
not located on a main road *room for parking*

€157,400   CODE FWY

COZES, DÉPARTEMENT 17

A traditional Charentaise house to finish renovating, with an attic to convert

£105,000

2 *$5,949m^2$* *close to town amenities* *not located on a main road*
room for parking, with a garage

€163,175   CODE ALZ

MELLE, DÉPARTEMENT 17

An attractive stone house, with two gîtes and a barn ideal for conversion

£109,000

3 *with a garden* *close to all amenities* *not located on a main road*
room for parking

€172,000   CODE LAT

NR BASSAC, DÉPARTEMENT 16

A stone property, comprising of a separate apartment and attic, to convert

£114,500

4 *$1,012m^2$* *close to town and amenities* *not located on a main road*
room for parking

€190,082   CODE FWY

COZES, DÉPARTEMENT 17

A traditional-style Charentaise house, ideal for a holiday home, to convert

£126,500

2 *$529m^2$* *close to town's amenities* *not located on a main road*
room for parking, with a garage

€197,640   CODE HIF

CHALAIS, DÉPARTEMENT 16

Suitable for a small gîte complex, a modern property with various outbuildings

132,000

3 *$10,000m^2$* *close to town and amenities* *not located on a main road*
room for parking, with a garage

PRICE GUIDE

€200–500,000
(£133–333,000)

As the price increases so does the luxury, although Poitou-Charentes as a region does not offer modern, newly-built properties or developments; most are traditional Charentaise homes, and fully renovated. Rustic farmhouses, elegant mansions and converted watermills flood the market within this price band.

€209,880　　　　　　　　　　　　　**CODE** ALZ

PARTHENAY, DÉPARTEMENT 79

A fully renovated farmhouse with a variety of outbuildings, ideal to convert

£140,000

▦ 4/5　▦ 6,000m² ▦ *close to town and amenities* ▦ *not located on a main road* ▦ *room for parking*

€225,357　　　　　　　　　　　　　**CODE** ALZ

CHIZE, DÉPARTEMENT 79

An excellent stone-built property, with an exposed, wood-beam interior

£150,000

▦ 4　▦ 1,150m² ▦ *close to all amenities* ▦ *not located on a main road* ▦ *room for parking*

€263,412　　　　　　　　　　　　　**CODE** HIF

DRONNE RIVER VALLEY, DÉPARTEMENT 79

A restored Charentaise house in good condition, with a pool and tennis courts

£175,500

▦ 3　▦ 13,000m² ▦ *requiring a car to reach amenities* ▦ *not located on a main road* ▦ *room for parking*

€275,600　　　　　　　　　　　　　**CODE** ALZ

MELLE, DÉPARTEMENT 79

A traditional farmhouse, comprising of outbuildings, ideal to convert to gîtes

£183,500

▦ 4　▦ 25,000m² ▦ *close to amenities* ▦ *not located on a main road* ▦ *room for parking*

€290,440 **CODE** ALZ

MELLE, DÉPARTEMENT 79

An old property requiring renovation, with spacious rooms and outbuildings

£193,500

5 *8,000m²* *close to amenities* *not located on a main road*
room for parking, with a garage

€381,123 **CODE** HIF

SAINT-MAIXENT, DÉPARTEMENT 79

To renovate, a luxurious mansion, with a pool, tennis courts and outbuildings

£254,000

3 *50,000m²* *close to town and amenities* *not located on a main road*
room for parking

€387,000 **CODE** MUR

SAINT-CLAUD, DÉPARTEMENT 16

Located in the heart of this pretty valley, a cosy country property with a pool

£258,000

n/a *3,000m²* *requiring a car to reach amenities* *not located on a main
road* *room for parking*

€444,400 **CODE** ALZ

PARTHENAY, DÉPARTEMENT 79

An old forge house, set in stunning grounds alongside the river, with views

£296,500

n/a *with spacious grounds* *within 5 mins of village amenities*
not located on a main road *room for parking*

€445,200 **CODE** ALZ

SEMOUSSAC, DÉPARTEMENT 17

A 19th-century Charentaise farmhouse, with a swimming pool and a gîte

£297,000

3 *with mature gardens* *close to amenities and town*
not located on a main road *room for parking*

€456,738 **CODE** HIF

MONTGUYON, DÉPARTEMENT 17

A tasteful property, with separate outbuildings and a gatehouse to convert

£304,500

6 *30,000m²* *close to town and amenities* *not located on a main road*
room for parking

PRICE GUIDE

€500,000+
(£333,000+)

If you can extend to a budget of 500,000 plus euros, the sky's the limit! Stunning mansions, luxurious riverside property or a traditionally renovated cottage, with a second property and a pool. Anything is possible and there is plenty of variety available. There is also huge potential for a rental income.

€502,100　　　　　　　　　　　　　　　　**CODE** PAP

LUSSERAY, DÉPARTEMENT 79

A detached property, located in a quiet village, enjoying airy, light rooms

£334,500

🛏8　🖼2,605m²　🖼*within 5 mins of village*　🖼*not located on a main road*　🏠*room for parking*

€518,200　　　　　　　　　　　　　　　　**CODE** FDC

RUFFEC, DÉPARTEMENT 16

A country house to refurbish, with large rooms, and two cottages to convert

£345,500

🛏4　🖼36,420m²　🖼*within 5 mins of village*　🖼*not located on a main road*　🏠*room for parking*

€520,000　　　　　　　　　　　　　　　　**CODE** ALZ

SAINT-MAIXENT, DÉPARTEMENT 79

A characterful mansion property, in established, mature parkland

£346,500

🛏7　🖼10,000m²　🖼*close to amenities*　🖼*not located on a main road*　🏠*room for parking*

€533,180　　　　　　　　　　　　　　　　**CODE** MUR

ANGOULÊME, DÉPARTEMENT 16

Ideal for farming and hunting, this property is peacefully located in woodland

£355,500

🛏n/a　🖼500,000m²　🖼*requiring a car to reach amenities*　🖼*not located on a main road*　🏠*room for parking*

€556,500

MATHA, DÉPARTEMENT 79

A stunning country property, offering two separate cottages and a pool

£371,000

🛏5 🌳with a garden 🏢close to amenities 🚫not located on a main road
🅿room for parking

€614,750 CODE FDC

MANSLE, DÉPARTEMENT 16

A stunning rural property, superbly restored offering a luxurious interior

£410,000

🛏5 🌳20,230m² 🏢within 5 mins of village 🚫not located on a main road
🅿room for parking

€630,000 CODE FPP

CHATEAUNEUF, DÉPARTEMENT 16

A luxurious riverside property, featuring a swimming pool and a gymnasium

£420,000

🛏6 🌳with a private garden 🏢located on the outskirts of town
🚫not located on a main road 🅿room for parking

€705,000 CODE FDC

CHASSENEUIL, DÉPARTEMENT 16

A marvellous country property, featuring two luxury apartments ideal for rental

£470,000

🛏5 🌳350,000m² 🏢within 5 mins of town 🚫not located on a main road
🅿room for parking

€947,200 CODE PAP

PIOUSSAY, DÉPARTEMENT 79

This 15th-century property enjoys numerous outbuildings and extended land

£631,500

🛏n/a 🌳220,000m² 🏢close to amenities 🚫not located on a main road
🅿room for parking

€983,296 CODE FPP

CHATELLERAULT, DÉPARTEMENT 86

A restored 17th-century property, with the possibility of further development

£655,500

🛏3 🌳10,120m² 🏢close to town and amenities 🚫not located on a main road
🅿room for parking, with a garage

PRICE GUIDE

Volcanic mountain ranges
Hot springs and spas
Untamed coutryside

Limousin & Auvergne

Profile 218
Hotspots 220

PRICE GUIDE
€50,000-€100,000 224
€100,000-€130,000 226
€200,000-€500,000 228
€500,000+ 230

Limousin and Auvergne Profile

Getting there

AIR Air France (08453 591000; www.airfrance.co.uk) flies from London City, Heathrow, Bristol, Glasgow, Manchester, Southampton, Newcastle, Edinburgh, Glasgow and Aberdeen to Clermont-Ferrand and Limoges via Paris' Orly airport, while **Ryanair** (08712 460000, www.ryanair.com) offers direct flights from London Stansted to Limoges and Clermont-Ferrand.

ROAD Take the A10 from Paris, continuing on the A10-E5 and then the A71-E9 at the junction with the A71 for Limoges. At the Junction for the A85 take-take the A20-E09 into Limousin and Limoges. For Clermont-Ferrand and the rest of Auvergne, follow the A10 from Paris to Orléans, taking the A71-E9 and then Junction 5 on to the A71-E11, then the N9 into Clermont-Ferrand.

RAIL A **TGV** service operates between Gare d'Austerlitz in Paris and Limoges. Gare de Lyon is linked with Clermont-Ferrand by an efficient, quick link. **Rail Europe** (08705 848848; www.raileurope.co.uk) has further details.

COACH Eurolines; (08705 808080; www.eurolines.com) operate services to Brive and Clermont-Ferrand.

For those seeking to buy a property in the heart of nature, Limousin is the ideal region for an outdoor lifestyle

THE ECONOMY

Tourism and the technological industry, including the production of electrical fittings, dominates Limoges' economy. Clermont-Ferrand is one of France's centre's of excellence, with the Michellin tyre factory and Limagrain, one of the world's largest seed providers. Auvergne has a thriving blend of industry and commerce. The relocation of part of the French civil service to Limoges, and the positive attitude given to new business development by the regional capital's chamber of commerce, illustrates the developing economy. Corrèze's economy is slowly changing from its tourism and agricultural roots, to the production of Airbus components, which has earnt the city the nickname 'Mechanic Valley'.

BEST/WORST VALUE FOR MONEY

This region's reputation for holding one of the cheapest property portfolio's in France is born out by renovation bargains in Reno, where prices range from

20,000-35,000 euros. Towns offering excellent value include Limoges where a two- to three-bedroom house is available from 45,000 euros and La Creuse, which although isolated, offers some of France's cheapest price tags. Prices are highest in Corrèze, but its proximity to Brive and planned transport links give this area long-term investment potential. The villages around the Puy de Sancy mountain provide buyers-to-let with a healthy rental season, with summer visitors being drawn to the lakes and various watersports, and winter visitors enjoying the snow. The property market remains buoyant despite a 30 per cent growth in property prices in the past three years.

Properties in Besse-en-Chandesse are more expensive, a well-renovated stone house is priced from 350,000 euros, and the only real source of income is generated by the tourist industry. Clermont-Ferrand matches competitive price tags with a quick-paced, long-term rental market giving a good return for purchasers planning to let. Parisians favour it for second homes and its strong winter rental market is being fuelled by the nearby Mont Dore ski station. French, Dutch and Belgian tourists create excellent rental potential, while the Massif de Centrale has growing tourist popularity and good investment potential. Vichy offers the worst value, with semi-retired visitors and expensive property making for a bad investment.

With excellent rental potential and a tourist driven economy, Limousin is a good place to invest

WHERE TO GO FOR WHAT
La Souterraine in La Creuse and Chalus to the southwest of Limoges offer excellent properties, and make for a good investment due to the western Corrèze's high rental demand which can generate a healthy rental income. Clermont-Ferrand (near Vichy) is sensible for relocation and short and long-term lets. New business is welcomed in Vichy, Limoges and the Corrèze and Brive and Tulle have good facilities for relocators to the area. Uzerche offers a 4-6 bed house to renovate from £35,000-£60,000, and around 80-90 per cent of French and foreign buyers relocate to Uzerche to start gîte businesses.

PROPERTY PRICE TRENDS
Property prices are increasing across this region and raised in Limoges by 9 percent between 2002 and 2003, as British and Dutch buyers vying with French purchasers have created a buoyant market. However renovation properties in the Corrèze are becoming harder to find and prices are rising, with a large house to renovate starting from 150,000 euros. Vichy's prices increased by 5 per cent between 2002 and 2003.

NEW DEVELOPMENT/TRANSPORT
Increased accessibility will undoubtedly bring in foreign buyers and raise prices in the region. An airport is planned for Brive in eight years time and a tram service is due for completion in Clermont-Ferrand in the next five to six years.

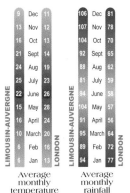

Average monthly temperature
°C (Celius)

Average monthly rainfall
mm (Millimetres)

Average House Sale Prices

HOTSPOT	2-BED	3-BED	4 BED	5 BED	6/7 BED	8-BED
Auvergne lakes/mountains	-	-	-	-	-	-
Clermont-Ferrand	-	€170K (£113K)	-	€350K (£235K)	-	-
Corrèze	€200k (£135K)	-	-	€300K (£200K)	-	-
Limoges	€75K (£50K)	€120K (£80K)	€150K (£100K)	€225K (£150K)	-	-
Vichy	-	-	-	€400K (£265K)	-	-

Limousin and Auvergne Hotspots

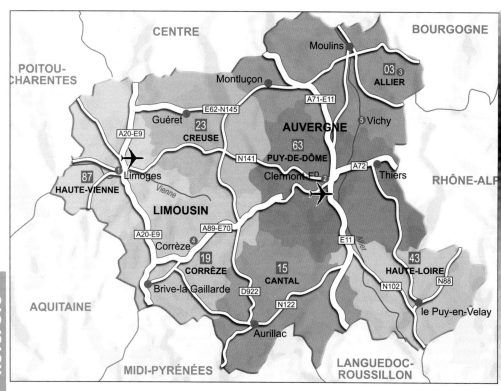

1. Limoges

ESSENTIALS ■ **POP** 1990: 136,407, 1999: 137,502, ■ **TAXES** Taxe d'habitation: 23.93%, Taxe foncière: 29.04%
■ **AIRPORT** Aeroport International de Limoges, 81 av Aeroport, 87100 Limoges; Tel: +33 5 55 43 30 30

KEY FACTS

SCHOOLS Bordeaux International School, 53 rue de Laseppe, Bordeaux; Tel: +33 5 57 87 02 11
MEDICAL Centre Hôpitalier Universitaire, 2 av Martin Luther King, 87000 Limoges; Tel: +33 5 55 06 61 23
RENTALS There is an average to good rental potential.■ Mainly a long-term, local rental market, and approximately 16-weeks summer rental for short-term visitors ■ Still relatively unknown, rental income may not be forthcoming than in more established areas ■ There are very few established agents ■ A 2- to 3-bedroom house can be let from 750 euros per month
PROS Limoges is ideal for purchasers seeking a traditional French lifestyle ■ Limoges is packed with amenities and culture ■ With good transport links.■ There are good employment opportunities.
CONS The climate is cooler than the southern regions ■ Prices are rapidly rising, and the relocation of part of the Parisian civil service has driven property prices up ■ More than 52 per cent of the population is under 40 ■ Not a big English-speaking community.

Located in northern Limousin, criss-crossed by rivers and lakes, Limoges offers good value for money and attractive surroundings. Initially built by the Romans, Limoges is not only France's Lake District and former home to Molière but provides all the shopping, gastronomic and cultural attractions of a historic regional capital. The city's situation between the Loire and Bordeaux regions has resulted in a fertile soil ideal for vineyards, with wines aged in the sought-after Limoges oak, deriving from the nearby forests. By the Middle Ages, Limoges was known for its high-quality enamel work, and in the 18th century, the porcelain industry took off, making the city the world capital for the ceramics and glass industries. There are 12 miles of underground tunnels to explore, that served as a giant food safe in the 13th century, when locals hid their provisions from the invading Black Prince. First created as a subterranean network during Roman Times, it was made up of galleries used to supply the city with water, expanding to carry supplies into town from springs 3-4 miles away. On December 28 each year, Limoges hosts the Saint Innocent Fair, a winter extravaganza of produits du terroir in a tradition dating back to the 16th century when the town was granted a market licence by Charles IX.

Limoges is not an area renowned for its foreign property market, and it is primarily a French property market. Prices are some of the cheapest in France, with a three-bedroom modern property from 210,000 euros. ■

2. Clermont Ferrand

ESSENTIALS ■ **POP** 1990: 140,167, 1999: 141,004 ■ **TAXES** Taxe d'habitation: 24.73%, Taxe foncière: 32.98% ■ **AIRPORT** Aeroport Internationale Clermont-Ferrand, BP 163510, Aulnut, Clermond Ferrand; Tel: +33 4 73 62 71 00

At the heart of Auvergne in the Massif Central, Clermont Ferrand is one of France's oldest and most culturally dynamic cities. Clermont and Montferrand originally formed as two rival cities, until being merged under Louis XIV. Today's Clermont thrives as both a university town and the capital of the Puy de Dome department. Sculpted by volcanic eruptions and glaciers, Clermont Ferrand city centre is just half an hour's drive from the Parc des Volcans, a natural open-air geological exhibition made up of 80 *dormant puys* (volcanic chains). Its volcano kept the city isolated from the rest of France, with the Auvergnats first adopting the French language from the 16th century. Many musuems and attractions are dotted around this historic city, and shopping centres on Place de Jaude, magically illuminated every Christmas with an open air ice rink. The yearly Court Métrage Film Festival has become an international affair, showing cinema shorts from around the world. To the south lies Mont-Dore massif, known for spa towns like La Bourbole, and the Super Besse ski resort.

Clermont-Ferrand is little known by the British and has been overlooked by buyers in favour of the Provence and Cote d'Azur cities, despite property costing half the price. The best value for money can be found in the suburbs surrounding the city, and as the city is undergoing a major redevelopment, property is likely to accrue value, with city centre property becoming very expensive. Prices are competitive compared to many areas, with a three-bedroom apartment costing from 110,000 euros. Fifteen minutes south of the centre, you can buy a renovated *maison de caractere* for 144,800 euros. ■

KEY FACTS
SCHOOLS L'Ecole Internationale Massillon, 5 rue Bansac, 63000 Clermont-Ferrand, Tel: +33 4 73 98 09 70
MEDICAL C.H.U Hôpital Gabriel Montpied, 58 rue Montalembert, 63000 Clermont-Ferrand, Tel: +33 4 73 75 07 50
RENTALS There is interest during summer and winter due to the town's proximity to the Mont Dore ski station ■ A 2- to 3-bedroom apartment in Clermont-Ferrand starts at around 700 euros per month ■ Lets are usually long term, and a one-bedroom apartment starts at 495 euros a month ■ With a long term, in demand, rental market
PROS There are excellent transport links to the area and new budget flights ■ A 3-bedroom property starts at 170,000 euros ■ The city is nearly 100% populated by foreigners, and has a well-established and well-resourced international school ■ A place of cultural importance and national interest ■ With good employment prospects
CONS Clermont-Ferrand is a university city and is lively and cosmopolitan, but may not suit those seeking a peaceful location ■ Buying to let short term may be difficult ■ It has heavily industrialised parts.

3. Volcanic Mountains and Lakes of Auvergne

ESSENTIALS ■ **POP** 1990: 8,541, 1999: 6,401 ■ **TAXES** Taxe d'habitation: 18.22%, Taxe foncière: 28.44% ■ **AIRPORT** Aeroport Internationale Clermont-Ferrand Auvergne, BP 163510, Aulnut, Clermond Ferrand; Tel: +33 4 73 62 71 00

One of the cheapest places to buy property, the Allier département in North Auvergne is the birthplace of the Bourbon dukes with 15th century manor houses and châteaux available to buy. Criss-crossed by lakes and home to the Forest of Tronçais, a national park covering 25,000 acres, this part of France is a true historic treasure. It is also referred to as 'the land of a thousand and one châteaux,' fifty being open to the public. Located on the Allier river north of Lyon, the agricultural town of Moulins is this region's capital, although tourism focuses on neo-classical Vichy, whose spas were first recognized by the Romans for their healing properties. Outdoor activities can be enjoyed on Lake Allier, a 300-acre expanse of water lined with open air cafés and aquatic leisure centres. To the centre of Allier lies the Bocage Bourbonnais, a cattle-rearing area known for its monuments, castles and Romanesque churches. Close to Vichy, the volcanic Montagne Bourbonnaise Mountain is a popular terrain favoured by hikers, mountain bikers, horse riders and skiers in winter.

This is a rural, undeveloped area that will not suit buyers looking for easy reach of city life. However the area is popular with those seeking an active holiday and is a good area in which to set up a tourist based business. Gradually, the foreign market are becoming more aware of the merits of the area, so now is a good time to invest. Property around Vichy costs from 156,000 euros for a renovated house, and the area is fairly cheap. ■

KEY FACTS
SCHOOLS L'Ecole Internationale Massillon, 5 rue Bansac, 63000 Clermont-Ferrand, Tel: +33 4 73 98 09 70
MEDICAL C.H.U Hôpital Gabriel Montpied, 58 rue Montalembert, 63000 Clermont-Ferrand, Tel: +33 4 73 75 07 50
RENTALS Tourists quadruple the population in peak season, creating very high demand for rental properties for 20 weeks of the year ■ A 6- to 7-bedroom property in the most popular ski areas of Besse en Chandesse and Le Mont Dorre costs from around 380 euros per week in peak season, and around 325 euros per week during low season
PROS The Massif de Sancy offers outdoor activities and watersports ■ Clermont-Ferrand is easily accessible, with a comprehensive transport network. ■ The Massif de Sancy is an established tourist destination, with many foreign buyers rapidly recognising the area's merits.
CONS A car is essential, otherwise it can be a very isolated place to live or stay ■ Apart from high season the area is quiet and under-populated.

Limousin and Auvergne Hotspots

4. Corrèze

ESSENTIALS ▦ **POP** 1990: 87,852, 1999: 84,927 ▦ **TAXES** Taxe d'habitation: 15.13%, Taxe foncière: 33.83%
▦ **AIRPORT** Aeroport International de Limoges, 81 av Aeroport, 87100 Limoges; Tel: +33 5 55 43 30 30

KEY FACTS

SCHOOLS L'Ecole Internationale Massillon, 5 rue Bansac, 63000 Clermont-Ferrand, Tel: +33 4 73 98 09 70

MEDICAL Centre Hospitalier, 3 pl Doct Machat, 19000 Tulle, Tel: +33 5 55 29 79 00

RENTALS Demand for properties to let is currently outstripping supply, but it is difficult to generate rental income ▦ High season is predominantly June-August ▦ Around 80-90 per cent of people relocating to this area wish to establish a tourist based business ▦ A good quality 4-6 bedroom house in a tourist area could fetch around 450 euros per week high season.

PROS Brive is easily accessible, with good transport links ▦ Brive and Tulle, the capital of Corrèze, both have good facilities and amenities ▦ The area is attracting an increasing number of English, Dutch and foreign buyers, so there is a growing international community.

CONS The weather is similar to the Dordogne but milder in the north ▦ The bus service is irregular ▦ Property is hard to find in the most popular areas of Corrèze, particularly Vallee de la Dordogne region and the south-west area of Turenne and Larche.

The Corrèze area has been popular for some time with holiday makers and buyers who want better value for money than the Dordogne region, without compromising on the quality of their destination. This means that there is already a short term lets market driven by the many tourists, who regularly visit the area. A good area to buy-to-let, it has a lot to offer tourists in terms of outstanding natural beauty, culture and gastronomy. The area also offers its visitors and residents a good quality of life away from the bustle and stress of the cities. Areas of interest in this region include Uzerche and Arnac-Pompadour with their beautiful romanesque churches and châteaux, plus the picturesque villages of Turenne and Collogne-la-Rouge with their spectacular views over ridges and valleys to the mountains of Cantal and Gimel-les-Cascades which although busy in summer has a stunning waterfall. The Vallee de la Dordogne with its rivers, gorges and pretty villages is also a very popular tourist destination. Well-developed cycle and walking tracks in breathtaking surroundings make it popular in the summer months and add to its short-term, holiday rental potential. Besse-en-Chandesse has seen a 30 per cent growth in property prices during the past three years and a six-bedroom well-renovated stone house in Besse-en-Chandesse can cost from 350 000 euros which may put people off buying as the price is rather steep in relation to the lack of facilities in the area. Houses can still be bought relatively cheaply in north-western Corrèze. A good quality 4/6-bedroom renovated stone house can be found for around 120,000 euros to 86,000 euros in the area around Uzerche. ■

5. Vichy

ESSENTIALS ▦ **POP** 1990: 1,158, 1999: 1,246 ▦ **TAXES** Taxe d'habitation: 25.09%, Taxe foncière: 34.08% ▦ **AIRPORT** Aeroport Internationale Clermont-Ferrand Auvergne, BP 163510, Aulnut, Clermond Ferrand; Tel: +33 4 73 62 71 00

KEY FACTS

SCHOOLS L'Ecole Internationale Massillon, 5 rue Bansac, 63000 Clermont-Ferrand, Tel: +33 4 73 98 09 70

MEDICAL Hôpital de Vichy bld Deniere, 03200 Vichy; Tel: +33 4 70 97 33 33

RENTALS A good rental season, lasting from May until September ▦ A 6-bedroom house costs from 572 euros per week in high season and 408 euros a week in low season ▦ A high quality house in the Plan d'eau area costs from 1,500 euros a week ▦ The main season for thermal spas is April to October.

PROS An established centre of tourism, Vichy has been relaunched as a major European centre for health, beauty and fitness ▦ An increasing amount of Dutch and French tourists have created a short-term rental market ▦ Near to Clermont-Ferrand, it is easily reachable ▦ There is an increasing number of foreign buyers, but 90 per cent of buyers are currently French retirees.

CONS The area's rising popularity with semi-retired and retired couples has created a buoyant property market and prices have increased by 30 percent ▦ Properties can be expensive.

Renowned for its cusine and thermal spas, Vichy is a spa town and the birthplace of the Bourbon dynasty, as well as Pétain's 'Vichy France'. Over the last ten years Vichy has been revamped in an attempt to give the town international appeal. The city has invested in a spa, health farms and business tourism, and has undergone architectural renovation and a redevelopment of the town centre. Offering a relaxed cosmopolitan atmosphere, Vichy has a certain *belle époque* charm, and there is an abundance of cultural diversions. Vichy is a remarkable cheap area in which to take a holiday, given that the area has only recently begun to shake off its economic problems. Tourism is the biggest industry in the area, especially given that Vichy is central, and easily accessible for Clermont-Ferrand and its airport. This town has begun to attract an increasing number of Dutch and French buyers, and demand for property is certainly on the increase. As the property market becomes increasingly buoyant property prices have risen by approximately 30-40per cent. The international market is split between those who are buying to retire and those who are permanently relocating to the area, and although there is an ever increasing number of British buyers, 90per cent of those who buy in Vichy are French; most British buy in the Ebreuil area, 28km from Vichy. A 3-bedroom renovated cottage would cost approximately 75,000 euros, while a 6-bedroom property on the outskirts of Vichy would cost just over 200,000 euros. ■

seful Contacts

potential buyer will be greeted by many quiet, traditional villages, where quality property can be uncovered at bargain prices

EFECTURES
fecture de la Région
ergne
boulevard Desaix
33 Clermont-Ferrand
ex
+33 4 73 98 63 63
: +33 4 73 98 61 00

fecture de la Région
ousin
e Stalingrad
31 Limoges Cedex
+33 5 55 44 18 00
: +33 5 55 44 17 54

GAL
mbre des Notaires du
-de-Dôme
rue du Maréchal Foch
00 Clermont-Ferrand

Tel: +33 4 73 29 16 66

Chambre des Notaires de la
Corrèze
3 place Winston-Churchill
87000 Limoges
Tel: +33 5 55 77 15 91
Fax: +33 5 55 79 28 33

FINANCE
Direction des Impôts du
Centre
70 rue de la Bretonnerie
BP 2457
45032 Orléans Cedex 1
Tel: +33 2 38 74 55 25
Fax: +33 2 38 74 66 62

Direction des Impôts du Sud-
Ouest
2 rue des Piliers de Tutelle

BP 45
33025 Bordeaux Cedex
Tel: +33 5 57 14 21 00

BUILDING & PLANNING
Chambre Régionale de
Métiers d'Auvergne
Centre Victoire
1 avenue de Cottages
BP 358
63010 Clermont-Ferrand
Cedex 1
Tel: +33 4 73 29 42 00
Fax: +33 4 73 29 42 09

Chambre Régionale de
Métiers du Limousin
14 rue de Belfort
87100 Limoges
Tel: +33 5 55 79 45 02
Fax: +33 5 55 79 30 29

CAUE de Haute-Vienne
1 rue des Allois
87000 Limoges
Tel: +33 5 55 32 32 40
Fax: +33 5 55 32 23 25

CAUE du Puy-de-Dôme
Hôtel du Département
30 rue Saint Esprit
63000 Clermont-Ferrand
Tel: +33 4 73 42 21 20
Fax: +33 4 73 93 27 64

EDUCATION
Rectorat de l'Académie de
Clermont-Ferrand
3 avenue Vercingétorix
63033 Clermont-Ferrand
Cedex 1
Tel: +33 4 73 99 30 00
Fax: +33 4 73 99 30 01

Rectorat de l'Académie de
Limoges
13 rue François-Chénieux
87031 Limoges Cedex
Tel: +33 5 55 11 40 40
Fax: +33 5 55 79 82 21

HEALTH
Caisse Primaire d'Assurance
Maladie de la Haute-Vienne
22 avenue Jean Gagnant
87037 Limoges
Tel: +33 820 90 41 31
Fax: +33 5 55 45 88 29

Caisse Primaire d'Assurance
Maladie du Puy-de-Dôme
rue Pélissier
63000 Clermont-Ferrand
Cedex 9
Tel: +33 4 73 42 81 00

€20-100,000
(£13-66,000)

With a reputation as one of the cheapest regions for property in France, many bargain renovation properties can be picked up in this area, which currently experiences limited demand. Consequently there should be a plethora of properties for those whose budget falls into this category.

€35,065   CODE HOM
LA CHAPELLE BALOUE, DÉPARTEMENT 23

A stone, terraced *fermette* requiring internal renovation, with an outbuilding

£23,375

🛏 n/a   🏠 800m²   📷 close to amenities   🚫 not located on a main road   🅿 room for parking

€47,260   CODE FWY
LIMOGES, DÉPARTEMENT 87

A stone house requiring extension, with stunning views over the Parc Naturel

£31,505

🛏 2   🏠 2,000m²   📷 30 mins from town   🚫 not located on a main road   🅿 room for parking, with a carport

€48,000   CODE HOM
AZERABLES, DÉPARTEMENT 23

A traditional style village house, stone built, with a small barn to convert

£32,000

🛏 1   🏠 with a small garden to the front and rear   📷 within 5 mins of village   🚫 not located on a main road   🅿 with on-road parking

€49,500   CODE HOM
GOUZON, DÉPARTEMENT 23

A stone *fermette*, requiring interior renovation, with a large barn and cellar

£33,000

🛏 2   🏠 5,000m²   📷 within 5 mins of village   🚫 not located on a main road   🅿 room for parking

CODE HOM

FLEURAT, DÉPARTEMENT 23

This lake enjoys vast grounds and is ideal for a gîte complex or fishery

£33,540

🛏*n/a* 🗺*50,000m²* 🏘*close to town and amenities* 🛣*not located on a main road* 🅿*no on-site parking*

€58,800   **CODE** HOM

SAINT-SRONIN-LEULAC, DÉPARTEMENT 87

An end of terrace, village stone property, with gas central heating and an attic

£39,200

🛏*2* 🗺*2,800m²* 🏘*within 5 mins of village* 🛣*not located on a main road* 🅿*room for parking*

€61,000   **CODE** HOM

ARNAC-LA-POSTE, DÉPARTEMENT 87

A stone built village house, with a wood-burning fire and small courtyard

£40,665

🛏*2* 🗺*with a courtyard* 🏘*within 5 mins of village* 🛣*not located on a main road* 🅿*room for parking, with a double garage*

€65,555   **CODE** HOM

BAZELAT, DÉPARTEMENT 23

A *fermette* in need of renovation, with a detached barn and workshop

£43,705

🛏*4* 🗺*2,000m²* 🏘*within 5 mins of village* 🛣*not located on a main road* 🅿*room for parking*

€70,125   **CODE** HOM

LA CELLE DUNOISE, DÉPARTEMENT 23

Two stone houses requiring renovation, with a separate barn and stables

£46,750

🛏*2* 🗺*500m²* 🏘*within 5 mins of village* 🛣*not located on a main road* 🅿*room for parking, with a garage*

€83,846   **CODE** FWY

LIMOGES, DÉPARTEMENT 87

Requiring modernisation, this is a traditional farming property

£55,897

🛏*5* 🗺*1,880m²* 🏘*close to town centre* 🛣*not located on a main road* 🅿*room for parking*

€100-200,000
(£66-133,000)

Those seeking a luxury property at a low price should be able to look to Limousin and this price bracket. Many of these properties are fully habitable and set in stunning rural locations. Those who desire a peaceful and comfortable life should look no further.

€104,940   CODE FPP

ORADOUR, DÉPARTEMENT 87

A village house, restored and fully habitable, with outbuildings and a well

£69,960

🛏2   ▣4,047m²   *close to amenities*   *not located on a main road*   *room for parking*

€111,288   CODE HOM

LA SOUTERRAINE, DÉPARTEMENT 23

A renovated village house, with an office, terrace and open plan lounge

£74,190

🛏2   *with a garden and terrace*   *close to amenities*   *located on a main road*   *room for parking*

€117,385   CODE FWY

LIMOGES, DÉPARTEMENT 87

A restored village post office, now a comfortable property, with pretty views

£78,255

🛏3   *with garden*   *located in the village centre*   *not located on a main road*   *room for parking*

€117,500   CODE FWY

LIMOGES, DÉPARTEMENT 87

A 17th-century farmhouse, with a barn, fully habitable with central heating

£78,335

🛏4   ▣2,500m²   *near to town and amenities*   *not located on a main road*   *room for parking*

€121,960

LA SOUTERRAINE, DÉPARTEMENT 23

A stone house with a cellar and two separate barns ideal for conversion

£81,065

🛏2 📐4,500m² 🏘within 5 mins of village 🛣not located on a main road
🅿room for parking

€122,000

LIMOGES, DÉPARTEMENT 87

With potential to convert into apartments, this property offers riverside views

£81,335

🛏2/4 🌳no garden 🏘in town centre 🛣not located on a main road
🅿room for parking

€129,581

CHÉRONNAC, DÉPARTEMENT 87

A well restored character cottage, with views and a small swimming pool

£86,385

🛏2 🌳with garden 🏘near to town and amenities 🛣not located on a main road
🅿room for parking

€139,150

ARS, DÉPARTEMENT 23

Two adjoining properties, one fully habitable, the other requiring some work

£92,765

🛏5/6 🌳with a large garden 🏘close to amenities 🛣not located on a main road
🅿room for parking, with a double garage

€157,850

MERINCHAL, DÉPARTEMENT 23

A unique country cottage, with many pretty features, set in a lush landscape

£105,235

🛏3 🌳with garden 🏘close to all amenities 🛣not located on a main road
🅿room for parking

€165,000

MALEMORT, DÉPARTEMENT 19

This property is set in a rural location, with country views and outbuildings

£110,000

🛏4 📐4,047m² 🏘near amenities 🛣not located on a main road
🅿room for parking, with a garage

€200-500,000
(£133-333,000)

Fully restored, unique and traditional is the best way to describe many of the characterful propeties that can be purchased for this amount of euros. With Limousin boasting the lowest prices, now is the time to be before the inevitable boom in costs.

€200,000   **CODE** FRA

LE-PUY-EN-VELAY, DÉPARTEMENT 43

A beautifully restored stone farmhouse, with views over the Ardeche valley

£133,335

4   2,500m²   *5 mins from town*   *not located on a main road*   *room for parking, with a garage*

€213,428   **CODE** HOM

DUN-LA-PALESTEL, DÉPARTEMENT 23

An isolated and peaceful property, stone built, with a separate barn to convert

£142,285

3   6,000m²   *in an isolated setting*   *not located on a main road*   *room for parking, with a garage and car port*

€213,428   **CODE** HOM

SAINT-SULPICE-LES-FEUILLES, DÉPARTEMENT 87

A renovated stone property, with a swimming pool and all mod-cons

£142,285

4   *with a large garden*   *close to amenities*   *not located on a main road*   *room for parking*

€221,000   **CODE** HOM

LA SOUTERRAINE, DÉPARTEMENT 23

A large three-storey town house, with a separate workshop ideal to convert

£147,335

3   2,500m² *of land*   *within 5 mins of village*   *not located on a main road*   *room for parking, with a garage*

€222,950   CODE VEF

VAUX, DÉPARTEMENT 03

A magnificent spacious property, enjoying a lake and grounds full of fruit trees

£148,635

- *with extensive grounds* *close to amenities* *not located on a main road* *room for parking*

€228,826   CODE FDC

LIMOGES, DÉPARTEMENT 87

A superb property, with scenic views and a separate barn ideal for conversion

£152,550

2 *with extensive grounds* *close to amenities* *located on a main road* *room for parking*

€239,840   CODE VEF

PEYRAT-LA-NONIÈRE, DÉPARTEMENT 23

A character house, retaining many of its original features, ready for habitation

£159,895

2 *with a garden and pool* *close to amenities* *not located on a main road* *room for parking*

€239,840   CODE VEF

AHUN, DÉPARTEMENT 23

A stunning property set in well mainucured grounds, with panoramic views

£159,895

3 *with extensive grounds* *close to amenities* *not located on a main road* *room for parking*

€242,395   CODE HOM

TOULX-SAINT-CROIX, DÉPARTEMENT 23

A large stone house, with mature grounds, offering total peace and seclusion

£161,965

3 *13,000m^2* *close to amenities* *not located on a main road* *room for parking, with a garage*

€258,555   CODE HOM

PEYRABOUT, DÉPARTEMENT 23

A large stone *fermette* with various outbuildings ideal for conversion

£172,370

6 *15,000m^2* *within 5 mins of village* *not located on a main road* *room for parking*

€272,600 CODE VEF

AHUN, DÉPARTEMENT 23

A beautiful, well-preserved stone property, with pretty views, in a rural location

£181,735

🛏n/a 🌳with a large garden 🏬close to amenities 🚫not located on a main road

🚗room for parking

€277,000 CODE FDC

ORADOUR, DÉPARTEMENT 87

A large, traditional style property, in an attractive setting, with a small lake

£184,665

🛏4 🌳with a large garden 🏬close to amenities 🚫not located on a main road

🚗room for parking, with a car port

€278,780 CODE HOM

DOMEYROT, DÉPARTEMENT 23

A stone *fermette*, with two detached barns and a bakery, ideal to convert

£185,855

🛏2 🌳290,000m^2 🏬within 5 mins of village 🚫located on a main road

🚗room for parking

€298,000 CODE FDC

ROCHECHOUART, DÉPARTEMENT 87

Set in a quiet hamlet, an impressive Bougeoise style property, fully habitable

£198,665

🛏4 🌳1,000m^2 🏬within 40 mins of town 🚫not located on a main road

🚗room for parking

€350,635 CODE HOM

AIXE-SUR-VIENNE, DÉPARTEMENT 87

A lake of seven metres depth, stocked with fish, ideal for a fishing business

£233,755

🛏- 🌳60,000m^2 of land, 45,000m^2 lake 🏬within 5 mins of village

🚫not located on a main road 🚗no room for parking

€488,000 CODE DEE

SAINT-ÉTIENNE, DÉPARTEMENT 43

A 19th-century castle, set in a stunning hamlet, near Auvergne's volcanoes

£325,335

🛏7 🌳30,000m^2 🏬close to town and amenities 🚫not located on a main road

🚗room for parking, with garages

€500,000+
(£333,000+)

*Properties asking 500,000+ euros tend to fall into
the category of either a listed building or chateau,
or a business premises. Given the rural nature of the
Limousin-Auvergne region, most tend to be luxurious
mansions or châteaux.*

€518,400   **CODE** VEF

FOURNEAUX, DÉPARTEMENT 23

A chambre d'hote complex and house, with a swimming pool and a resturant

£345,600

⊟*4* ⌂*with a large garden* ⌁*within 5 mins of town* ⊠*not located on a main road* ⌂*room for parking, with a garage*

€640,285   **CODE** HOM

LIMOGES, DÉPARTEMENT 23

A farmhouse, fully renovated, with two separate houses and outbuildings

£426,855

⊟*5* ⌂*752,700m^2* ⌁*within 5 mins of town* ⊠*not located on a main road* ⌂*room for parking, with a double garage*

€807,980   **CODE** HOM

GUÉRET, DÉPARTEMENT 23

A 17th-century château, requiring completion, ideal as a renovation project.

£538,655

⊟*6* ⌂*6,000m^2* ⌁*close to amenities* ⊠*not located on a main road* ⌂*room for parking*

€915,000   **CODE** DEE

NR LIMOGES, DÉPARTEMENT 23

A stunning 17th-century chateau, located in a small, rural hamlet, with views

£610,000

⊟*11* ⌂*250,000m^2* ⌁*10 kms from town and amenities* ⊠*not located on a main road* ⌂*room for parking*

Snow-capped mountains
Lush green valleys
Lakes and rivers

Rhône-Alps

Profile 234

Hotspots 236

PRICE GUIDE

€20,000-€100,000 244

€100,000-€200,000 246

€200,000-€500,000 248

€500,000+ 252

Rhône-Alps Profile

Getting there

AIR **British Airways** (08708 509850) flies to Lyon Airport from Birmingham, Gatwick and Manchester; **Ryanair** (08712 460000; www.ryanair.com) operates flights to Chambéry, Lyon and Geneva Airports from Stansted; **easyJet** (08717 500100; www.easyjet.com) flies to Geneva International Airport from Manchester, Gatwick and Liverpool; **Air France** (08453 591000; www.airfrance.co.uk) operates from Heathrow to Lyon Airport. (Buses operate from Lyon Airport to Les Gets; +33 4 72 35 94 96). In addition, **BMI Baby** (08702 64 2229; www.bmibaby.com). **Virgin Express** (08707 301134; virgin-express.com), **Aer Lingus** (08450 844444; www.aerlingus.com), **Air France**; (08453 460000; www.airfrance.co.uk) and **British Airways** (08708 509850) can all provide flights to Geneva International Airport.

ROAD From Paris take the A6 to Lyon, and then the A43 which takes a fairly direct route to Chambéry and Grenoble. For Lake Annecy and its environs, take the A6-E15 (with toll booths) from Lyon. This links to the A40-E21 at the junction with the A40, then take the N508 to Annecy. For Megève and the Trois Vallées break off the A40-E21 at the A401 'Genève-centre' junction. From here take the A40-E25 via its junction with the A411. This leads to the N205, then the N212.

COACH National Express **Eurolines** operates to Lyon (08705 143219; www.eurolines.com).

RAIL Fast **TGV** trains run from Gare de Lyon in Paris to Lyon and Grenoble, which provides convenient access to Annecy, Megève, Evian-les-Bains and all the town/ski-resort hotspots (www.voyages-sncf.com, www.sncf.fr or www.tgv.com). Taxis operate from Chambéry, Lyon, Annecy and Genève stations to the Courchevel, Val d'Isère, Les Menuires, Val Thorens and Tignes ski stations **Eurostar** (0870 518 6186; www.eurostar.co.uk) offers a direct route (twice a week in the skiing season, one overnight and one in daytime) to Bourg-Saint-Maurice or Moutiers in the centre of the ski resorts from London Waterloo or Ashford in Kent (08705 353535; www.eurotunnel.com).

THE ECONOMY

The Rhône-Alps resorts around Mont Blanc have a tourism-based economy, with international stars like Chamonix trading off restaurants and boutiques. This extends to the Lake Annecy villages and resorts of Annecy, Talloires and Thonon-les-Bains. Very much the ski locale's capital and historically an industrial town (cement, paper mills and mining), Grenoble is less glitz and more substance, with four universities as well as a thriving industrial sector. For business, Lyon is the main draw in the Beaujolais area. The third largest city in France, it relies on banking and commerce and is famous for its gastronomy. Wine production, tourism and, to the southwest of Villefranche, one of France's premier wine routes, are mainstays of the Beaujolais economy.

BEST/WORST VALUE FOR MONEY

Megève's lower position in the slopes and resulting poor snow record should make this international resort an insecure investment, but its golf course, hotels and restaurants make it a year-round rental proposition. Val d'Isère's lengthy ski season and good snow record make it a hit for buying to let.

A rising star for relocators, the western side of the Beaujolais, stretching

Tourism, coupled with a shortage of land has led to price hikes in the region

PROFILE

from La Clayette in the north of the region to Tarare in the south, is very different from the vineyard region between Lyon and Mâcon. Its remoteness from these big cities makes its properties cheaper to buy than the former wine-growers' homes around Mâcon overlooking the Saône valley and built of the characteristic *pierre dorée* stone.

Any renovation-ready village house (starting at around 60,000 euros) in Chamonix, Annecy, or Chambéry is a sound investment, as the long-term rental potential is good. Perhaps the 'Knightsbridge' of the Trois Vallées are Courchevel — a resort particularly favoured by Parisians — and Méribel where properties are expensive. These resorts are, however, empty in summer.

A shortage of available building land and increasing land prices in the winter ski resorts of Chamonix, Morzine, Val d'Isère and Chambéry, plus a ban on building permits in Les Gets for the next two years, point to demand outstripping supply, and increasing prices on the horizon. There are fewer new building initiatives, and many properties coming on to the market are bought 'off-plan' for completion in 2004/5. Few construction projects are being discussed for Chamonix and Flaine (apartments and chalets) and rumours abound that permission for building in parts of Morzine could be revoked, as the *loi de montagne* or mountain law, reinforced in 2003, is to reduce the land-for-build allowance by half in Les Gets. Individual plots are in short supply and many chalet builders are block-buying land to house their workers, which ties up land.

WHERE TO GO FOR WHAT
More of a town than a resort, Grenoble is a great family locale. Chambéry also has town status and both have British communities. Talloires and Annecy have excellent all-year amenities, and British buyers can use the pistes of La Clusaz and Grand Bornard. French purchasers buy here to retire.

TRANSPORT PLANS/NEW BUILDS
New routes due to open up access to the ski resorts include TGV extensions from Dijon to Milan in Italy, via Montmélian to Modena in Italy, and Besançon and Belfort to Mulhouse, which should be completed by 2020.

> *Foreign buyers are reminded that demand outstrips supply, rendering property expensive*

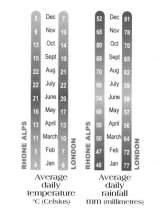

Average daily temperature °C (Celsius)

Average daily rainfall mm (millimetres)

Average House Sale Prices

HOTSPOTS	2-BED	3-BED	4-BED	5-BED	6/7-BED	8-BED
Beaujolais	€175K (£115K)	-	-	-	-	-
Chamonix	-	€510K (£340K)	-	-	€1M (£600K)	-
Courchevel	-	-	-	-	-	-
Grenoble	-	-	-	€190K (£125K)	-	-
Lake Annecy	-	€300K (£200K)	€360 (£240)	-	€1.5M (£1M)	-
Lake Geneva	-	-	-	-	-	-
Les Portes du Soleil	€220K (£140K)	-	€395K (£260K)	€1.5M (£1M)	-	-
Les Menuires	-	-	-	-	-	-
Lyon	-	-	-	-	-	€450K (£300K)
Megève	-	-	€2.2M (£1.5M)	-	-	-
Méribel	-	-	-	-	-	-
Val d'Isère-	-	€250K (£165K)	-	€3M (£1.5M)	-	-

Rhône-Alps Hotspots

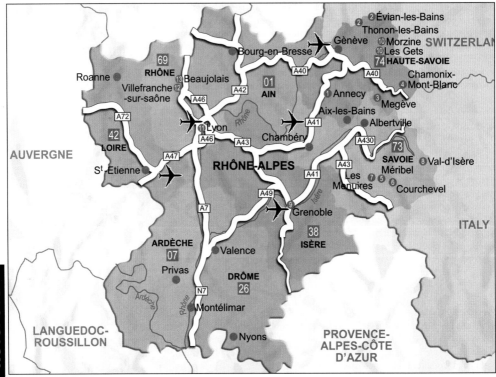

1. Lake Annecy (including Annecy and Talloires)

ESSENTIALS ■ **POP** 1990: 52,435, 1999: 53,571 ■ **TAXES** Taxe d'habitation: 18.70%, Taxe foncière: 22.64% ■ **AIRPORT**
Annecy Metz Airport, 8 route de Côte Merle, 74370 Metz-Tessy. France ; Tel +33 4 50 27 30 06; www.annecy.aeroport.fr

KEY FACTS

SCHOOLS Nearest: Albertville, Megève and Ferney
Voltaire, as listed.

MEDICAL Centre Hospitalier, av Trésum 1, 74000
Annecy, Tel +33 4 50 88 33 33.

RENTALS Good. Foreign buyers choose Talloires
for year-round stays ■ Average rental for a two-
bedroom house in Talloires is 920 euros a week
■ A popular tourist resort, winter is peak season ■
Annecy's average rental fees are from 600 to 1,800
euros per week for a two-bedroom villa ■ Talloires'
average rental for a two-bedroom house is 920
euros a week.

PROS Plenty of tourist amenities including shops
and art exhibitions ■ Excellent transport links ■ On
a par with the Côte d'Azur for French retirees ■
Annecy Old Town is very attractive ■ Golfing
facilities are nearby.

CONS Annecy's old town is very crowded in
summer. More of a summer resort – skiers do not
like to travel in winter.

Annecy is a charming Alpine town with a medieval quarter,
canals, flower-covered bridges and narrow streets. In the 19th
century, European nobility rediscovered it and built lavish
palaces on the lake, which at nine miles long and framed by
woodland, is reputedly Europe's cleanest. Outdoor pursuits
including swimming, sailing, and lakeside cycling give it
standing on a par with the Côte d'Azur,and there are many first-class ski resorts
within a 90-minute drive.

Villas with swimming pools, chalets and apartments in and around the
lakeside villages are much cheaper than in the mountain resorts. Some villages
can be reached by steamer and many have their own beaches.

Talloires lies eight miles south, on the east side of the Tournette, Annecy's
highest surrounding mountain. It houses the Michelin-starred Auberge du Père-
Bise restaurant and an 11th-century Benedictine abbey, now the luxurious Hôtel
de l'Abbaye (Cézanne and Churchill were famous residents). In August French
families come to hike and camp. With good property choice, a studio apartment
with private garden in Talloires is around 100,000 euros, with larger properties
priced from 300,000 euros. A renovated 17th-century stone house with lake
views starts from 3,800,000 euros. Properties with lake views are especially
pricey, a shortage of land to build on means properties are in demand and a
three-bedroom, renovated chalet with lake views is around 640,000 euros. ■

2. Lake Geneva (including Thonon-les-Bains and Evian-les-Bains)

ESSENTIALS ■ **POP** 1990: -, 1999: 37,480 ■ **TAXES** Taxe d'habitation: 16.44%, Taxe foncière: 25.45% ■ **AIRPORT** Nearest airport: Geneva Airport, PO BOX 100, CH-1215 Geneva 15, Switzerland Tel: + 41 22 717 71 11.

Popular with aristocrats during the *Belle Époque*, Thonon-les-Bains spa lies in the lower Chablais region, north of Haute-Savoie on Lake Geneva. Constructed on three levels between lake and mountains, in a naturally arched bay, the views of Lake Geneva are magnificent from the upper part of town, while the spa centre of Les Thermes overlooks the waterfront. The Versoie spring was first discovered by the Romans and opened to the public in the 19th century. Thonon-les-Bains is also the first stage on the Route des Alpes, covering the main Alpine passes and several nature reserves from Lake Geneva to the Mediterranean.

Attractions include the Eco Fishing Museum, the Chablais Museum and Gorges du Pont du Diable, a partly submerged network of jagged, grey marble eroded into spectacular shapes over time. Thonon's fishing port, tucked behind Rives castle, is active throughout the year and a large market sells produce every Monday and Thursday. The annual Foire de Crête takes place in early September and is one of the oldest fairs in France.

Property prices begin at 20,000 euros for a two-bedroom, central apartment of 83 square metres, rising to around 140,000 euros for a larger apartment. For a waterfront location, a four-bedroom house at Port Ripaille costs around 457,000 euros.This is a prime tourist rental locale, excellently positioned for tourists drawn to the French Alps and Annecy. ■

KEY FACTS

SCHOOLS Nearest: Albertville, Megève and Ferney Voltaire, as listed.

MEDICAL Annecy Centre Hospitalier, av Trésum 1, 74000 Annecy; Tel: +33 4 50 88 33 33 ■ Hôpitaux du Léman, avenue de la Dame 3, 74 200 Thonon-Les-Bains; Tel: +33 4 50 83 20 00; www.ch-leman.fr.

RENTALS Good for four to six months in Thonon les Bains ■ Average rental for a one-bedroom apartment is 560 euros a month long-term in Thonon-les-Bains ■ Short-term average rental for a studio apartment in high season is 380 euros per week.

PROS Amenities include a golf course and nearby skiing in La Clusaz and Grand Bornand (30 mins away) ■ Excellent transport links to the area ■ Evian's reputation as Lake Geneva's tourist trap attracts hordes of visitors in summer.

CONS Not really a winter spot, Thonon is a 40-minute journey from Morzine and Portes du Soleil, and cannot compete with the ski resorts.

3. Megève

ESSENTIALS ■ **POP** 1990: 4,976, 1999: 4,509 ■ **TAXES** Taxe d'habitation: 19.22%, Taxe foncière: 24.92% ■ **AIRPORT** Chambéry/Aix Les Bains Airport, Chambre de Commerce, 73420 Viviers du Lac; Tel +33 4 79 54 49 54.

West of Mont Blanc, the medieval Savoyard town of Megève is ultra-chic. 'Discovered' by the Baroness de Rothschild in 1921, it still attracts the rich out of season from the French Riviera and most of its visitors are French. More than 70 farms in alpine pastures make regional specialities like Tomme de Savoie cheese.

The 180 miles of ski-runs are ideal for intermediate skiers and there is a varied cross-country route. For snowboarders, Chamonix is less than 30 minutes away and is included in the Mont Blanc ski pass, which accesses 13 other resorts. This World Cup ski venue, so different from the purpose-built resorts, is a good choice for non-skiers too, who can easily access Michelin mountain restaurants and enjoy a first-class spa or lively, varied après-ski.

 Property is expensive but high-quality, with a choice of large luxury chalets rather than new apartments. The main hotspots of Mont d'Arbois (an area on the golf course, above the resort) and villages like Ormaret, with views of Mont Blanc, also attract a premium. Centrally located chalets start from one million euros and new chalets built in original materials to add old Savoyard cachet are priced from two to five million euros. Le Hameau des Ours may offer the best value, with two-bedroom apartments from 480,000 euros, three-bedroom from 595,000 euros and new chalets from 970,000 euros. Properties in the nearby villages of Combloux and Saint-Gervais are more reasonably priced.

Property prices per square metre have increased over the past two years, with a four-bedroom property rising from 2,432 to 5,165 euros per sq m. ■

KEY FACTS

SCHOOLS Nearest: Megève, as listed.

MEDICAL Centre Hospitalier, rte Pèlerins 509, 74400 Chamonix Mont Blanc; Tel: +33 4 50 53 84 00.

RENTALS Excellent ■ With plenty of demand, the rental season lasts more than 15 weeks ■ Peak is December through to April ■ The average rental price per week is 497 to 1,005 euros for a two-bedroom chalet ■ Average short-term rentals for high season are 500 euros per week for a studio, 660 euros per week for a one-bedroom apartment, 880 euros per week for a two-bedroom apartment.

PROS Coined the most beautiful of the French ski resorts, it combines the modern jet-set feel with an old-world charm ■ Top international resort with winter and summer appeal. ■ Good golf course, restaurants and hotels ■ Easy to access with excellent transport links.

CONS Roads are congested during the winter months; chains for your wheels are mandatory ■ The snow record is poor as Megeve lies at a low altitude, so is not for the most advanced skier ■ A huge tourist influx for the winter sports.

HOTSPOTS

Rhône-Alps Hotspots

4. Chamonix

ESSENTIALS ▨ **POP** 1990: 9,701, 1999: 9,830 ▨ **TAXES** Taxe d'habitation: 19.34%, Taxe foncière: 24.04% ▨ **AIRPORT** Chambéry/Aix Les Bains Airport, Chambre de Commerce, 73420 Viviers du Lac; Tel +33 4 79 54 49 54

KEY FACTS

SCHOOLS Nearest: Megève, as listed.
MEDICAL Centre Hospitalier, rte Pélerins 509, 74400 Chamonix Mont Blanc Tel: +33 4 50 53 84 00.
RENTALS Excellent, with a season lasting for more than 15 weeks (December to April) ▨ A fashionable, cosmopolitan resort with international rental appeal ▨ The average rental price per week is between 300 euros off-season to 1,000 euros in peak season for a two-bedroom property ▨ A two-bedroom standard property costs 420 to 842 euros per week
PROS Budget easyjet flights into Geneva Airport have made travelling to a second home here cheap ▨ An upmarket Italian development, Résidence Les Alpes, has sold well, and more buildings are due for completion in 2005 ▨ Best in the region for advanced skiers, despite its accessibility problems ▨ Low availability of land for build makes property purchase a sound investment ▨ Popular second and permanent homes. ▨ Dog sledding, mountain biking, paragliding, and helicopter trips, an ice-rink and climbing centre are available here.
CONS Much traffic and people ▨ Difficult access. Skiers rely on shuttle buses or cars to reach the slopes ▨ Dramatic price increases in recent years. ▨ An almost seven-hour car journey from Paris.

Situated at the foot of Mont Blanc and at the crossroads of France, Italy and Switzerland, with easy access to Italy via the Mont Blanc tunnel, Chamonix is much sought after for both its sporting and scenic qualities. Although developed as a summertime mountaineering centre, the resort is internationally renowned as a destination for expert skiers, and there are many who consider it the world's best, so there's a high demand for quality property.

Throughout the year the village is continuously busy, but it has retained its traditional charm, with narrow streets lining the car-free centre and a river tearing through the valley floor. While visitors here are cosmopolitan, they choose Chamonix primarily to ski at high altitude, taking in a circuit from the main village to the valley across Le Brévent, La Flégère, Les Grand Montets, and Le Tour, including seven glaciers and the world's biggest lift-served vertical drop of 2,807 metres. Non-ski activities, too, are plentiful by French standards.

New, traditionally constructed apartments are good-value buys and often have superior mountain views and a concierge. Three and four-bedroom apartments start at around 300,000 euros, rising to 1,000,000 euros for larger ones. Smaller one and two-bedroom apartments are from 150,000 euros, while a three-bedroom chalet costs around 510,000 euros.

Purchasers should be ready to act quickly; at the re-opening of the Mont Blanc Tunnel a queue of Italians were waiting to sign contracts for first-phase buildings. Little building land is available. ■

5. Méribel

ESSENTIALS ▨ **POP** 1990: 1,743, 1999: 1,850 ▨ **TAXES** Taxe d'habitation: 18.70%, Taxe foncière: 13.79% ▨ **AIRPORT** Chambéry/Aix Les Bains Airport, Chambre de Commerce, 73420 Viviers du Lac; (Tel +33 4 79 54 49 54).

KEY FACTS

SCHOOLS Nearest: Albertville, as listed.
MEDICAL Nearest: Hôpital de Moutiers, rue Ecole des Mines, 73 600 Moutiers Toulentaise; Tel: +33 4 79 09 60 60.
RENTALS Excellent rental season from December to April ▨ Popular international location with bags of potential for permanent and second homes ▨ Again, a low availability of land to build has made property a premium investment ▨ The average price for renting a property is between 671 euros a week off-season and 2,691 euros in peak season ▨ An example of the price of a basic standard two-bedroom apartment would be from 840 to 2,100 euros ▨ A more luxurious apartment can cost from 1,350 to 2,400 euros.
PROS Budget easyjet flights and excellent transport networks make for easy access ▨ Méribel is the most British-dominated of all the resorts in the Alps ▨ Plenty of apres-ski amenities.
CONS Busy tourist location and slightly less sophisticated than other resorts in the region ▨ Almost seven hours from Paris by road.

High up in the Alps at 1,450 metres, in the centre of the Trois Vallées, Méribel has access to 450 miles of pistes, both nursery slopes and off-piste for the more experienced skier. Snow cannons ensure that links to Courchevel remain open throughout the long season. Méribel's night life revolves largely around British-run bars with live music. Good restaurants specialise in Savoyard dishes like *raclette*, *tartiflette* and *pizza savoyarde* made with Beaufort, Comté and Emmental cheese over dried meats. Méribel-Les-Allues is 10 minutes from the main lift station at Chaudanne, and a quieter base from which to explore the Trois Vallées. La Chaudanne Olympic Park has a swimming pool, sauna, ice rink, parapenting, snowbiking, ice karting and dog sledding. Almost everything built since development started in 1931 has been traditional in style, using pinewood, slate-covered roofs and local stone, making Méribel one of the most tasteful French purpose-built resorts, but chalets are rarely available and can cost more than one and a half million euros, though some of the region's cheapest prices can be found here. Buyers prefer newer properties, particularly apartments, as they have larger rooms and are of better quality, but the dearth of such properties in Val d'Isère and Méribel sends buyers to cheaper areas like Sainte Foy, less than 30 minutes away, where high quality detached chalets are built to blend with 100-year-old chalets. Chamonix is still possibly number one for British wanting a good year-round holiday. ■

6. Courchevel

ESSENTIALS ▪ **POP** 1990: 1,743, 1999: 1,850 ▪ **TAXES** Taxe d'habitation: 4.78%, Taxe foncière: 8.92% ▪ **AIRPORT** Annecy Metz Airport, route de Côte Merle 8, 74370 Metz-Tessy. France ; Tel +33 04 50 27 30 06; Annecy.aeroport.fr

Courchevel is located in the Trois Vallées ski area, along with Méribel, Les Menuires and Val Thorens, and boasts an excellent snow record. With nearly 400 miles of piste and superb skiing, this area constitutes the largest interconnected ski resort in France and one of the two largest in Europe. Here, the world's largest cable car and the ski lifts carry 52,000 skiers per hour.

Four hours from Geneva, the resort is built on four levels, named according to their elevation in metres: 1300, 1550, 1650, and 1850. All have luxury private villas or chalets that are ski-in, ski-out, but Courchevel 1850 is the most upmarket, drawing royalty and international celebrities. Extensive and varied terrain suits everyone from beginners to experts, though some slopes get very crowded. Courchevel 1650 has an extra hour's sunlight per day. The two lower areas are Le Praz (1300m), a traditional Savoie hamlet, and family-friendly La Tania (also at 1300m), where it is still possible to find a village house or small chalet for under three million euros.

Chalets are built in the traditional Savoyard style of architecture, featuring exposed stone, large roof beams and handcrafted wooden doors. Prices range from 7,000 to 8,500 euros per square metre for apartments, and from 10,000 to 11,500 euros per square metre for chalets. A chalet measuring 200 square metres sells between one and half million and two million euros.

A decreasing amount of land to build on has meant a competitive market with ski companies chasing chalets to run as winter rentals. ▪

KEY FACTS
SCHOOLS Nearest: Albertville, as listed.
MEDICAL Hôpital de Moutier, rue Ecole des Mines, 73600 Tcoutiers Tarentaise; Tel: +33 4 79 09 60 60
RENTALS Excellent in the high-season winter months. ▪ A 15 week+ rental season. ▪ The average rental price per week varies from 2,100 to 2,550 euros during peak season ▪ Good winter rentals ▪ Average short-term, high-season rental prices: 630 euros per week for a studio and 1,200 euros per week for a two-bedroom apartment.
PROS Budget airline easyjet flies into Geneva Airport and has made travelling to a second home quick, easy and cheap. ▪ Courchevel exudes luxury and glamour both on and off the piste, so is a key tourist area with a tried and tested tourist market. ▪ Luxury shops, gourmet restaurants, an active après-ski life and illuminated sledge run.
CONS The town gets taken over by tourists in the winter months and can have a crowded feel; population increases 17-fold during the winter and the town is occupied by 30,000 people each week. ▪ Slightly off the beaten track, off the N 90 ▪ The top resort hotels only open in winter. ▪ Not offering easy access.

7. Les Menuires

ESSENTIALS ▪ **POP** 1990: 2,341, 1999: 2,532 ▪ **TAXES** Taxe d'habitation: 8.92%, Taxe foncière: 4.78% ▪ **AIRPORT** Annecy Metz Airport, route de Côte Merle 8, 74370 Metz-Tessy. France ; Tel +33 04 50 27 30 06

Many consider Les Menuires the least attractive resort in the Alps, with few woodland slopes. Located in the Belleville Valley at the head of the Trois Vallées ski area, it remains much in demand as a purpose-built resort, offering immediate access to the challenging pistes of La Masse, rarely used by visitors from the other valleys.

Popular with low-budget skiers, the main intermediate and beginner slopes also benefit from a lot of sun while Allemands, the red run twisting from the top of Roc des Trois Marches into Les Menuires, is one of the very finest. Split into three main levels, the resort is composed of Reberty (the highest section with most visual charm), the main resort of Croisette and low-lying Preyerand. While it is less renowned for its après-ski than other Alpine resorts, the first-class restaurant of La Mercée is rated as one of the best eateries by those in the know. You cannot ski directly to it, but the restaurant shuttle bus takes diners back to the ski lifts after lunching out. Reberty is made up of two parts — 1850 and 2000 — the latter slightly higher yet the best choice for buyers in search of a new residence. In 1850 you can acquire a north-facing, furnished studio for two people from a starting price of 180,000 euros. A family could choose a southwest-facing three-bedroom apartment, equipped for six with living room, corner kitchen, separate bathroom and lift access for 84,000 euros. Limited land for build has helped the rental market. ▪

KEY FACTS
SCHOOLS Nearest: Albertville, as listed.
MEDICAL Nearest: Hôpital de Moutiers, as listed.
RENTALS Excellent, year-round potential ▪ Being a base for second and permanent homes, and having a shortage of land to build new homes on, has fuelled the rental market ▪ The peak season during winter is from December to April ▪ Summer months offer activity holidays ▪ The average rent for this area per week is from 935 to 1,882 euros ▪ A timber chalet costs 326 to 709 euros per week ▪ Average, short-term rental costs for high season are 450 euros a week for a studio apartment and 630 euros per week for a one-bedroom apartment.
PROS Nearly 400 miles of pistes make up the 'Trois Vallées' area, plus a snow park for snowboarders and three snow-makers, which ensure snow ▪ A family orientated resort with some cheap hotels ▪ Convenient link to Val Thorens, the highest ski resort in Europe ▪ Many small apartments, good for low budget skiers.
CONS Many unattractive apartments ▪ An unsightly resort ▪ More than seven hours by road from Paris.

Rhône-Alps Hotspots

8. Val d' Isère

ESSENTIALS ■ **POP** 1990: 1,702, 1999: 1,660 ■ **TAXES** Taxe d'habitation: 15.97%, Taxe foncière: 34.93% ■ **AIRPORT** Annecy Metz Airport, route de Côte Merle 8, 74370 Metz-Tessy. France ; Tel +33 04 50 27 30 06; Annecy.aeroport.fr

KEY FACTS

SCHOOLS Nearest: Albertville, as listed.

MEDICAL Nearest is Hôpital, rue Nantet 139, 73700 Bourg Saint-Maurice Tel: +33 479 417979.

RENTALS Excellent winter resort. ■ Val d'Isère has international, year-round appeal with a five-month long winter season ■ The average rental price for a property is approximately 1,000 euros a week ■ Average rental prices for short-term rental are 730 euros a week for a studio apartment in high season and 1,350 euros per week for a two-bedroom apartment.

PROS One of the best resorts in the region and a favourite with skiers ■ Covers a massive area and has more than 100 lifts with numerous ski runs, (some reaching 3,200m) ■ A must for the sociable skier ■ Après-ski for serious partygoers, with lots of bars and more than 70 restaurants offering a huge range of food at all price levels. ■ Long ski season and good snow record ■ Masses of winter sports, and the shortage of building land contributes to its soundness for investment.

CONS Lack of available property ■ A demand for larger apartments and chalets.

Located at high altitude, with the peaks of La Grande Motte and La Grande Casse towering in the background, Val d'Isère enjoys frequent snowfalls and is one of the best resorts for experts and intermediate skiers attracted by the extent of lift-served off-piste runs and incredible vertical drops. It is not a picturesque resort, with unattractive high-rise apartment blocks at La Daille, but the town centre has a more upmarket feel and look. Over the years the resort has proved popular with the British.

Val D'Isère's slopes are divided into three main sectors: Bellevarde, which can be accessed from the centre; La Daille, Solaise, which is accessed directly from the centre; and Col de L'Iseran which is reached from Le Fornet. The Pissaillas glacier is open from late June to mid-August .

In summer, there are few facilities for the non-skier; so the Trois Vallées is a better choice for buyers sourcing a property for both summer and winter seasons, while still having access to a large ski area.

Apartments sell very quickly, especially those recently built. Prices start at around one million euros, but if you have a more modest budget, consider the nearby resort of Sainte-Foy. It has retained it original charm, yet is only 30 minutes by car from Val d'Isère. Here, new chalets are blended in with existing homes, some of which are more than a century old. Prices start at around £250,000 for a linked three-bedroom chalet.

Properties make a sound investment with an apparently guaranteed climbing value and have been seen as more secure investments than the stock market. ■

9. Grenoble

ESSENTIALS ■ **POP** 1990: 153,973, 1999: 156,203 ■ **TAXES** Taxe d'habitation - 26.18%, Taxe foncière - 46.09% ■ **AIRPORT** Grenoble Saint-Geois Airport, 38590 Saint-Etienne-de-Saint-Geois; Tel: +33 4 76 65 48 48

KEY FACTS

SCHOOLS Nearest: Grenoble.

MEDICAL Mutuelle Générale de l'Education Nationale, rue Félix Poulat 38000 3, Grenoble Tel: + 33 4 76 86 63 63.

RENTALS Excellent: a huge international appeal ■ A university town: more than 50,000 students a year need rental properties. ■ Purchases less common here, more common in the ski resorts ■ Average rental prices (long-term): 370 euros per month, 470 euros per month for a one-bedroom apartment, 650 euros for a two-bedroom apartment.

PROS Perfectly placed for Switzerland, Italy and the Mediterranean; hiking, mountain climbing, skiing, snowboarding, rafting, kayaking and canoeing are available ■ The city is surrounded by three French Alpine ranges.

CONS Approximately 10,000 visitors a month pour into Grenoble between December and January ■ 250 British, 7,000 French and other nationals stayed in Grenoble as visitors during January 2003, so it can get crowded.

Grenoble has the distinction of being the capital of the French Alps, with strong international appeal. It is a beautiful, highly advanced city with numerous industrial and technological sites — CERN (European Centre for Particle Physics) and many other research laboratories have been set up here. A university town with 50,000 students making up 10 per cent of its suburban population, Grenoble has some wonderful heritage sites, such as the Dauphinois museum and the Fort de la Bastille, accessible by cable car over the river. Helping to keep Italian heritage alive are the 200 pizzerias to be found in the Italian quarter.

Capital of the Dauphiné – a former province – Grenoble has an exceptional geographic setting, with the skiing season beginning from mid-November. Close to Switzerland, Italy, and the Mediterranean Sea, it offers a fast gateway to Les Deux Alpes and Alpes d'Huez, which are just half an hour away. It is not generally a hotspot area, but as the ski resorts are more popular, a lack of new developments makes property a premium investment and prices are climbing.

For superb rural views and a peaceful haven, try Saint-Pierre-de-Chartreuse, a medieval mountain village in the heart of the Chartreuse Regional Park, famous for the Chartreuse liqueur made in its monastery. A five-bedroom mountain chalet starts at 190,000 euros. Or here too, you could buy (for conversion into apartments) an old stone house of 300 square metres for 336,000 euros. ■

HOTSPOTS

10. Les Portes Du Soleil (Les Gets and Morzine)

ESSENTIALS ■ **POP** 1990: 1,293, 1999: 1,369 ■ **TAXES** Taxe d'habitation: 21.15%, Taxe foncière - 24.01% ■ **AIRPORT** Annecy Metz Airport, route de Côte Merle 8, 74370 Metz-Tessy, France ; Tel +33 4 50 27 30 06; Annecy.aeroport.fr

Set on a sunny mountain pass, just over the border from Switzerland in Haute-Savoie, family-friendly Les Gets is a traditional Alpine village that is also one of the most popular smaller ski resorts. Part of the Portes du Soleil network that links 12 resorts on either side of the French/Swiss border, Les Gets is not acclaimed for its nightlife, but appeals instead to the many families who want to sample the great outdoors rather than après-ski.

The skiing area spreads to both sides of Les Gets with the smaller, but less crowded Mont Chéry offering more challenging skiing, while Les Chavannes is a much more suitable area for families and beginners/intermediates.

Properties to suit families start at 180,000 euros, with spacious, renovated farmhouses especially popular, if there are excellent views. In Les Gets, brand new locations near the Chavannes ski slope, close to the village centre, are highly desirable.

There is a common trend of climbing prices and stringent property laws that have clamped down on the square metrage of land permitted to build. These have been reduced by half in Morzine, from 0.4 to 0.2 per cent, even on projects approved before July 2003, resulting in a lack of individual plots. Planning permission is now only given for 'filling in' existing hamlets, or if a property fronts a main road. Further building in Les Gets is banned for two years. Chalet builders are snapping up blocks of land to ensure their businesses keep running so recent builds have been snapped up 'off-plan'. ■

KEY FACTS

SCHOOLS Nearest: Megève and Ferney Voltaire, as listed.

MEDICAL Hôpitaux du Léman, avenue de la Dame 3, 74 200 Thonon-Les-Bains; Tel: +33 4 50 83 2000; www.ch-leman.fr

RENTALS Excellent winter rental season from December to April ■ A traditional three-bedroom property off-season costs between 568 to 1,413 euros. ■ A two-bedroom apartment costs from 142 to 994 euros per week.

PROS Budget flights into Geneva airport ■ Lots of family-friendly outdoor activities are available, including swimming in hill-top lakes, horse riding, canyoning and alpine boarding ■ A mecca for the sporty, there are 19 mountain walks (served by an efficient lift service) and cross-country cycle routes.

CONS Purchasers are competing with French, Swiss, Italian and Dutch buyers. ■ Les Gets is quite low (1,175 metres), the top reaching 2,350 metres with access to high-level skiing areas. ■ It is unknown to many British as a summer resort ■ Buyer demand is outstripping supply.

HOTSPOTS

11. Lyon

ESSENTIALS ■ **POP** 1990: 422,444, 1999: 453,187 ■ **TAXES** Taxe d'habitation: 25.86%, Taxe foncière: 23.18% ■ **AIRPORT** Nearest airport: Lyon-Exupéry Aeroport, BP113, 69125 Lyon; Tel: +33 7 72 22 72 21, www.lyon.aeroport.fr

Lyon is France's third largest city, located at the junction of the Rhône and Saône rivers in the Rhône Valley. With more restaurants per square metre than any other world city, it is justifiably the gastronomic capital with a lively night scene and cultural life. Top Michelin restaurants sit alongside *bouchons* (bistros owing their name to medieval times when the bill for wine was calculated by the number of wine corks on the table), serving Lyonnais specialities in a picturesque setting.

The city is graced with Roman amphitheatres, Renaissance architecture and a silk-weaving tradition, found in the district of Croix Rousse. The *traboules* or secret passageways linking streets and houses were used by the Resistance during World War II. The Basilique Notre-Dame de Fourvière is the old town's landmark, its interior adorned with ornate stone carvings and gilded mosaics, and its exterior affording panoramic views of the city. In 2000, four of Lyon's neighbourhoods were designated UNESCO World Heritage Sites, including the Croix Rousse, Fourvière, the Presqu'île peninsula and Vieux Lyon.

A double-glazed fully-furnished *art deco*-style apartment by the 260-acre Parc de la Tête d'Or starts at 450,000 euros, with concierge. Half an hour away, overlooking the Saône Valley, an eight-bedroom home with 16th/17th-century frontage, is around the same price. There are not many foreign buyers here and there is not a big tourist scene. ■

KEY FACTS

SCHOOLS Nearest: Cité scolaire internationale, place de Montréal 2, 69361 Lyon Cedex; Tel: +33 4 78 69 60 06.

MEDICAL Hôpital de l'Hôtel Dieu, place de l'Hôpital, 69288 Lyon Cedex; Tel: +33 4 72 41 30 24; www.chu-lyon.fr.

RENTALS Average rentals throughout the year: two bedrooms at 277 euros per month, 3 bedrooms at 362 euros a month ■ This is a working city with a long term rental market.

PROS A centre of commercial activity, with great employment opportunity ■ Well-served by TGV trains, it has a convenient link to Paris for commuters, and its own international airport ■ The 6ème is an expensive *arrondissement*, as is the Croix Rousse, but cheaper properties can be bought in the 8ème ■ The large population of university students provide an annual pool of tenants ■ A thriving array of amenities, including slick shopping centres.

CONS You may need to be willing to learn French as a language to relocate here.

Rhône-Alps Hotspots

12. Beaujolais

ESSENTIALS ■ **POP** 1990: 29,889, 1999: 31,213 ■ **TAXES** Taxe d'habitation 22.30%, Taxe foncière - 26.04%
■ **AIRPORT** Nearest Airport: Lyon-Exupéry Aeroport, BP113, 69125 Lyon; Tel: +33 7 72 22 72 21, www.lyon.aeroport.fr

KEY FACTS

SCHOOLS Nearest: Cité Scolaire Internationale, place de Montréal 2, 69361 Lyon Cedex 07; Tel: +33 4 78 69 60 06.

MEDICAL Nearest: Centre Hospitalier de Villefranche sur Saône, Quilly Gleizé BP 436, 69655 Villefranche sur Saône Cedex; Tel: +33 4 74 09 29 29; www.ch-villefranche.fr.

RENTALS A four-bedroom farmhouse in the Beaujolais region costs from 582 to 794 euros between September and November.

PROS Within an 18 miles of Lyon, it has cheaper properties than the region's capital ■ An area full of rivers, tributaries, granite peaks, farms and forests ■ Full of gastronomic delights, olive oil and fine wines ■ Villefranche has an excellent choice of restaurants and shops along its Rue Nationale ■ Amenities include the Nicéphore Niepce Museum, that includes the first colour photographs, holograms and audio-visual exhibits.

CONS Incredibly appealing, hence properties in the Lyon to Mâcon area are expensive ■ From La Clayette to Tarare (an area with mountains 500 to 1,000 metres high) properties are cheaper.

The Beaujolais in central France is a region of lush fertile hills, picturesque villages and rolling vineyards, on the southeastern side of France between Mâcon and Lyon.

Perched above the valley of the River Saône and surrounding the town of Villefranche-sur-Saône, with glorious countryside and numerous vineyards in which to sample the area's quality wines, the Beaujolais offers a glimpse of the traditional vineyard lifestyle and local life. This is the northern sector of the Beaujolais *appellation*, a cluster of villages like Fleurie, Chénas, Juliénas, Brouilly and others allowed to sell wines by their own name. The vineyard region stretches from Lyon in the south to Mâcon, and properties here are often former winegrowers' homes built of stone with the typical *pierre dorée* colour. There are nearly 60 square miles of vineyards.

The east of Beaujolais is the best known part and Villefranche-sur-Saône has become the economic hub of this area of the Rhône *département*, succeeding Beaujeu, the historic capital, over the years. Near to the core of Beaujolais' wine villages, its church dates back to the 12th century and there are fine Renaissance houses and a 17th-century hospital. A 17th-century house can be bought for around 425,000 euros, and a more modern, fully renovated property will start at around 175,000 euros.

This area is rich in history and architecture, with many of the tiny, wine-producing villages containing some architectural gems. Properties are cheaper from La Clayette to Tarare, an area with 500 to 1,000-metre high mountains. ■

USEFUL CONTACTS

PREFECTURE
Préfecture de la Région Rhône-Alps
106 rue Pierre-Corneille
69419 Lyon Cedex 03
Tel: +33 4 72 61 60 60
Fax: +33 4 78 60 49 38

LEGAL
Chambre des Notaires du Rhône
58 boulevard des Belges
BP 6079
69412 Lyon Cedex 06
Tel: +33 4 78 93 32 49
Fax: +33 4 72 44 05 47

FINANCE
Direction Régionale des Impôts Rhône-Alps Bourgogne
41 cours de la Liberté
69422 Lyon Cedex 3
Tel: +33 4 78 63 54 10
Fax: +33 4 78 63 53 93

BUILDING & PLANNING
Chambre Régionale de

Métiers de Rhône-Alps
Central Parc 1
boulevard Stalingrad 119
69100 Villeurbanne
Tel: +33 4 72 44 13 30
Fax: +33 4 78 89 93 73

CAUE du Rhône
bis quai Saint-Vincent 6
69283 Lyon Cedex 01
Tel: +33 4 72 07 44 55
Fax: +33 4 72 07 44 59

EDUCATION
Rectorat de l'Académie de Grenoble
(Ardèche, Drôme, Isère, Savoie, Haute-Savoie)
place Bir-Hakeim 7
BP 1065
38021 Grenoble Cedex
Tel: +33 4 76 74 70 00
Fax: +33 4 76 74 75 00

Rectorat de l'Académie de Lyon (Loire, Rhône, Ain)
rue de Marseille 92
BP 7227

Tourism helps to keep the property market buoyant

69365 Lyon Cedex 07
Tel: +33 4 72 73 54 54
Fax: +33 4 78 58 54 78

HEALTH
Caisse Primaire d'Assurance Maladie de Lyon
rue Masséna 102
69471 Lyon Cedex 6
Tel: +33 820 90 41 15
Fax: +33 4 72 75 82 30

SCHOOLS
Cité Scolaire Internationale,
place de Sfax 4,
BP 1570
38012 Grenoble
+33 4 38 12 25 47
(www.ac-grenoble.fr/cite. scolaire. internationale)

Groupe Scolaire Houille Blance

rue Houille Blance
38100 Grenoble
+33 4 76 96 51 75

Annecy: Language School Centre International de Formation Exchange Linguistique (CIFEL),
Ada Djumisic,
place Grenette 17,
73200 Albertville
+33 4 79 37 19 78

(CIFEL) Ada Djumisic,
place de l'Eglise 28,
74120 Megève
+33 4 50 91 91 33

Lycée/Collège International,
BP 159
01216 Ferney Voltaire Cedex
+33 4 50 40 00 00

Marseille: Directorat de l'Académie de Lyon
rue de Marseille
72765 Lyon Cedex 07;
+33 4 72 73 54 54

HOTSPOTS

€20–100,000
(£13–66,000)

The Rhone-Alps region is dominated by chalets and apartments located in the ski resorts of the area, and this is where demand is centred. A basic one-bedroom chalet located in some of the less popular resorts will fall into this price bracket.

€48,400 — CODE IMO

ALPE D'HUEZ, DÉPARTEMENT 74

A studio apartment, with a living area of $16.9m^2$, and excellent rental income

£32,265

🛏 2 *no garden* *close to resort amenities* *not located on a main road* *room for parking*

€76,220 — CODE CAC

MORZINE, DÉPARTEMENT 74

A ski-in/ski-out chalet, with a south-facing balcony and mountain views

£50,815

🛏 1 *no garden* *a few mins walk from the resort centre* *not located on a main road* *room for parking*

€79,832 — CODE IMO

MOÛTIERS, DÉPARTEMENT 73

A chalet located in the centre of the Belle Plagne resort, with a balcony

£53,220

🛏 1 *no garden* *in the centre of the resort* *located on a main road* *room for parking*

€99,555 — CODE IMO

BARCELONNETTE, DÉPARTEMENT 04

A chalet with $35m^2$ living space and a balcony, with high rental income

£66,370

🛏 2 *no garden* *close to resort amenities* *not located on a main road* *room for parking*

€75,937+
LAT

NR VALLOIRE, DÉPARTEMENT 73

A new development of ski apartments, with all modern convienences

£50,625+

🛏 1 🪴 no garden 🏔 situated close to amenities at the foot of the Alps

🛣 not located on a main road 🅿 with private parking

€98,114+
LAT

VALMEINIER, DÉPARTEMENT 73

A new development set at the foot of the ski slopes, with amenities on site

£65,409+

🛏 1/2/chalets 🪴 with no garden 🏔 close to all amenities 🛣 not located on a main road 🅿 with a separate garage for each apartment

€68,500
LAT

GIEZ, DÉPARTEMENT 74

A new development of apartments built in the traditional style of the area

£45,665

🛏 1 🪴 with private gardens 🏔 near the resort centre 🛣 not located on a main road 🅿 room for parking

€99,400
CAC

VALLOIRE, DÉPARTEMENT 73

Modern ski chalets with a high quality finish, with a pool, sauna and jacuzzi

£66,265

🛏 1/2/3 🪴 no garden 🏔 close to all resort amenities

🛣 not located on a main road 🅿 with private parking

€85,372
AAA

LES HOUCHES, DÉPARTEMENT 74

Ten fully furnished, new apartments located at the centre of this small town

£56,915

🛏 n/a 🪴 no garden 🏔 within 5 mins of resort amenities 🛣 not located on a main road 🅿 room for parking

€92,000+
AAA

LAKE ANNECY, DÉPARTEMENT 74

Newly built, a block of 12 apartments, with stunning lake and mountain views

£61,335+

🛏 1/4 🪴 with private gardens 🏔 10 mins from town 🛣 not located on a main road 🅿 with private parking

PRICE GUIDE

€100–200,000
(£66–133,000)

The intense and increasing demand for 'ski-in' chalets located close to the piste has meant that chalet prices have rocketed. Within the larger resorts between 100,000 and 200,000 euros will secure you a small chalet, apartment or a farmhouse located some way from the piste and ski areas.

€112,800+   AAA

LES ARCS, DÉPARTEMENT 73

Located in one of Europe's largest ski areas, a new apartment development

£75,200

⌧n/a ▨no garden, with a balcony or terrace ▨within 5 mins of resort amenities ▨not located on a main road ▨room for parking, with garages

€129,582   LAT

BELLEY, DÉPARTEMENT 01

A stone house, with stunning mountain views, located in a quiet rural area

£86,390

⌧3 ▨935m^2 ▨situated 24 kms from town ▨not located on a main road ▨room for parking, with a double garage

€132,000   CAC

MORZINE, DÉPARTEMENT 74

A stunning farmhouse to renovate, with beautiful mountain views

£88,000

⌧5/8 ▨300m^2 ▨only 10 mins drive from Morzine centre ▨not located on a main road ▨room for parking

€133,974   IMO

CHAMBÉRY, DÉPARTEMENT 74

Located in Valmorel ski resort, this property has a balcony and stunning views

£89,315

⌧1 ▨no garden ▨close to resort amenities ▨not located on a main road ▨room for parking

€137,000 CAC

LES HOUCHES, DÉPARTEMENT 74

A renovated farmhouse, this first-floor apartment is only 500m from the ski lifts

£91,335

🛏1 🌐2,000m² 🖼situated in the heart of the resort 🚫not located on a main road 🏠with a garage and private parking

€148,000 CAC

LES CARROZ, DÉPARTEMENT 74

A chalet with seven apartments, newly built and accessible for the ski slopes

£98,665

🛏1 🌐2,000m² 🖼800m from Les Carroz centre 🚫not located on a main road 🏠with a separate garage for each apartment

€149,400 CAC

VERCHAIX, DÉPARTEMENT 74

A newly built ski chalet, with stunning views over the Grand Massif

£99,600

🛏2 🌐no garden 🖼near the resort centre 🚫not located on a main road 🏠room for parking

€160,000 CAC

MORZINE, DÉPARTEMENT 74

A spacious chalet with easy access to amenities and the ski slopes

£106,665

🛏1 🌐no garden 🖼located in the centre of Morzine 🚫not located on a main road 🏠with private parking

€178,500+ AAA

SAMOËNS, DÉPARTEMENT 74

A new apartment development, each arranged over three floors, with views

£119,000

🛏1/2 🌐no garden, with a balcony or terrace 🖼within 5 mins of resort amenities 🚫not located on a main road 🏠room for parking, with a garage

€198,000 LAT

VILLEFRANCHE, DÉPARTEMENT 69

A 19th-century property, with 130m² of living space, with a traditional interior

£132,000

🛏3 🌐400m² 🖼10 kms from town 🚫not located on a main road 🏠room for parking, with a garage

PRICE GUIDE

€200–500,000
(£133–333,000)

Outside of the ski resorts there are some truly magnificent and extensive modern villas and traditional mansions availiable. Most require some renovation work, but overall are in fairly good condition. Within the ski resorts themselves, the more luxurious, well-located chalets are available.

€200,000
CODE FRA

LE PUY EN VELAY, DÉPARTEMENT 74

A large traditional-style chalet, located close to the ski slopes and village

£133,500

5/6 2,000m² within 5 mins of village not located on a main road room for parking, with a garage

€220,000
CODE PFI

MEGÈVE, DÉPARTEMENT 74

Two large apartments located at the foot of the ski slopes, with stunning views

£146,500

1/2 no garden within 5 mins of town not located on a main road with private parking

€223,800
CODE IMO

MORZINE, DÉPARTEMENT 74

A chalet, with balcony, enjoying splendid views, and capable of sleeping six

£149,000

2 no garden, with balcony close to resort amenities not located on a main road no private parking

€243,000
CODE LAT

VILLEFRANCHE, DÉPARTEMENT 69

A modern villa, with a swimming pool set in enclosed woodland

£162,000

4 with a garden within 5 mins of village not located on a main road room for parking, with a garage

€252,000 CODE LAT

MERCUROL, DÉPARTEMENT 26

A 19th-century renovated property with stunning views over the Rhone

£168,000

🛏2 🏠700m² 🏘situated in the village centre 🚫not located on a main road

🅿room for parking

€256,200 CODE LAT

ROANNE, DÉPARTEMENT 42

A character property, with an original interior, featuring a library and cellar

£171,000

🛏4 🏠5,791m² 🏘situated close to shops and amenities

🚫not located on a main road 🅿room for parking, with a double garage

€358,255 CODE AAA

LES PORTES DU SOLEIL, DÉPARTEMENT 74

A large hotel, an ideal business venture, arranged over five floors

£239,000

🛏n/a 🏠no garden 🏘near the town centre 🚫not located on a main road

🅿room for parking

€362,000 CODE LAT

BEAUREGARD, DÉPARTEMENT 26

A stone farmhouse, offering a separate apartment and various outbuildings

£241,500

🛏6 🏠51,000m² 🏘situated 2 kms from village 🚫not located on a main road

🅿room for parking, with a garage

€363,000 CODE AAA

ANNECY, DÉPARTEMENT 74

A luxurious duplex, capable of sleeping 12, offering excellent rental income

£242,000

🛏4 🏠no garden, with a terrace 🏘close to resort amenities 🚫not located on a
main road 🅿room for parking

€370,000+ CODE AAA

LES GETS, DÉPARTEMENT 74

New chalets, with eight deluxe apartments, and all modern conveniences

£246,500

🛏2/4 🏠no garden 🏘close to resort amenities 🚫not located on a main road

🅿with private parking

PRICE GUIDE

€396,400 CODE LAT

ANSE, DÉPARTEMENT 69

A modern house with a swimming pool, situated in a quiet residential area

£264,500

4   with a garden   6 kms from town   not located on a main road
room for parking, with a garage

€400,000+ CODE AAA

GRAND-BORNAND, DÉPARTEMENT 74

This traditional chalet has wonderful south facing views and a balcony

£266,500

4   no garden   within 5 mins of resort centre   not located on a main road
with a private garage

€415,000 CODE LAT

VILLEFRANCHE, DÉPARTEMENT 69

A charming mansion, with outbuildings ideal for conversion and a courtyard

£276,500

7   with a garden   within 15 mins of town   not located on a main road
room for parking

€420,000 CODE PFI

MORZINE, DÉPARTEMENT 74

A magnificent, semi-detached farmhouse, fully renovated and enjoying views

£280,000

4   460m^2 close to town centre   not located on a main road
room for parking

€449,725 CODE LAT

GRIGNAN, DÉPARTEMENT 26

A beautifully restored property, surrounded by lavender fields and woodland

£300,000

4   9,800m^2 close to town amenities   not located on a main road
room for parking, with a garage

€475,000 CODE LAT

VILLEFRANCHE-SUR-SAONE, DÉPARTEMENT 69

A renovated property, offering a second house, ideal for a tourist business

£316,500

5   1,800m^2 within easy reach of Lyon   not located on a main road
room for parking

Get more for your money when buying abroad with Currencies4less.

- Better rates than high street banks
- No commission
- Protection from unpredictable exchange rates
- A dedicated dealer to guide you every step of the way

Buying abroad is not without its worries. Currency fluctuations can significantly increase the final price of your property purchase.

Currencies4less can help you avoid this. We specialise in foreign property transactions, offer highly competitive rates, but most of all we assign a dedicated dealer to guide you through every stage of the transaction.

Call Currencies4less. We are part of The 4Less Group plc, a publicly quoted foreign exchange company offering a wide range of foreign exchange, overseas mortgage products, associated insurance and finance services.

+44 (0)20 7594 0594
www.currencies4less.com

Currencies4less

part of
The 4Less Group plc

PRICE GUIDE

€500,000+
(£333,000+)

With a starting budget of 500,000 euros, luxurious properties are readily avalaible. From beautiful wooden chalets located on the piste with mountain views, to renovated 17th-century farmhouses and elegant villas. Each property exudes character and offers all necessary amenities.

€598,000   CODE AAA

SAMOËNS, DÉPARTEMENT 74

Traditionally renovated farmhouse, a truly unique property, with views

£398,500

🛏 5/6   📐 5,200m²   🏙 close to village amenities   🛣 not located on a main road   🏠 room for parking, with a double garage

€655,600   CODE AAA

LES GETS, DÉPARTEMENT 74

A chalet comprising of three apartments, only 100 kms from the ski slopes

£437,000

🛏 n/a   📐 with a small garden   🏙 1 km from town centre   🛣 not located on a main road   🏠 room for parking, with four garages

€864,000   CODE DEE

SAINT-JALLE, DÉPARTEMENT 26

A stone farmhouse dating from the 17th century, requiring some renovation

£576,000

🛏 3   📐 1,400,000m²   🏙 within 5 mins of town   🛣 not located on a main road   🏠 room for parking, with a garage

€1,044,000   CODE FRA

CHAMONIX, DÉPARTEMENT 74

A beautiful wooden chalet with a swimming pool, and views of Mont Blanc

£696,000

🛏 6   📐 1,165m²   🏙 10 kms from town   🛣 not located on a main road   🏠 room for parking, with a garage for one car

€1,450,000 — AAA

LES GETS, DÉPARTEMENT 74

A deluxe chalet located close to the ski lifts, this property offers a sauna

£966,500

5/6 🖼 2,000m² 🖼 close to village amenities 🖼 not located on a main road
🏠 room for parking, with a garage for 3 cars

€1,525,000 — AAA

LAKE ANNECY, DÉPARTEMENT 74

A large, renovated villa, with stunning lake views and a large swimming pool

£1,016,500

7 🖼 with a garden 🖼 close to amenities 🖼 not located on a main road
🏠 room for parking, with a garage

€1,900,000 — DEE

MEGÈVE, DÉPARTEMENT 74

A renovated 19th-century chalet, overlooking the Mont Blanc mountains

£1,266,500

4 🖼 2,000m² 🖼 located close to village amenities
🖼 not located on a main road 🏠 room for parking, with a garage for four cars

€2,100,000 — AAA

LES GETS, DÉPARTEMENT 74

A luxurious chalet comprising of three apartments, enjoying panoramic views

£1,400,000

3 🖼 2,700m² 🖼 close to resort amenities 🖼 not located on a main road
🏠 room for parking, with a garage

€2,560,000 — AAA

MEGÈVE, DÉPARTEMENT 74

A chalet, located close to a golf course, with use of a pool and tennis courts

£1,706,500

4 🖼 1,600m² 🖼 close to amenities 🖼 not located on a main road
🏠 room for parking, with a garage

€3,100,000 — PFI

VAL D'ISÈRE, DÉPARTEMENT 73

A superb chalet located close to the ski lifts, offering two terraces and views

£2,066,500

5 🖼 no garden, with terrace 🖼 close to resort amenities
🖼 not located on a main road 🏠 no private parking

Imposing Atlantic coastline
Marshes and pine forests
Lush countryside

Aquitaine

Profile 256
Hotspots 258

PRICE GUIDE
€20,000-€100,000 262
€100,000-€200,000 264
€200,000-€500,000 266
€500,000+ 268

Aquitaine Profile

PROFILE

Getting there

AIR Bordeaux-Merignac receives **British Airways** flights (0870 850 9850; www.britishairways.co.uk) from major UK airports and **Ryanair** (0871 246 0000) flies direct from Stansted to Biarritz and Pau. **Flybe** (0870 889 0908; www.flybe.com) operates flights into Bergerac (from London and Bristol) and Bordeaux, and in addition **Air France** (0845 359 1000; www.airfrance.co.uk) flies direct to Bordeaux.

ROAD The region's main motorway is the A10 which connects Paris and Poitiers with Bordeaux and Toulouse, before continuing into Spain. For Biarritz, take the A63. As the A10 is often highly congested, you may prefer to travel on smaller roads. From Paris the A71/A20 leads to Limoges, from where the N20 takes you to Toulouse. For Pau, take the A64. The A20 for Limoges provides access to Dordogne and Quercy, while the Autoroute des Deux Mers (A62-A61) links Bordeaux, the Atlantic coast and the Mediterranean.

COACH Eurolines (0870 514 3219; www.eurolines.com) offers services to Agen, Arcachon. Bayonne, Bergerac, Biarritz, Bordeaux and Périgueux.

RAIL The **TGV** takes just 3.25 hours from Gare Montparnasse in Paris to Bordeaux, on the Paris-Poiters-Angoulême-Bordeaux line. The Toulouse, Biarritz and Bayonne areas are served by the **TGV** service from the Gare d'Austerlitz in Paris. There is a direct TGV service to Bordeaux from the **Eurostar** interchange at Lille. **Rail Europe** provides full details of services in France (0870 584 8848; www.raileurope.co.uk).

ECONOMY

Renowned for producing some of France's finest wines, the Aquitaine region owes its immense wealth to vineyards and pine forests. The area has recently diversified into the aerospace industry, agri-foodstuffs and the wood pulp industry, while the strikingly beautiful coastline has contributed to the development of the tourist industry. Lot-et-Garonne, one of France's largest fruit producers, is known as the 'granary of France' and is particularly famous for its truffles.

BEST/WORST VALUE FOR MONEY

Southwest Dordogne has become so popular, that it is in danger of being spoiled by tourism. Demand in southern Dordogne has caused prices to sky-rocket, and there few areas in the southwest of France represent really good value for money. Lot-et-Garonne has always been an expensive area, situated as it is midway between Bordeaux and Toulouse. Properties on the southwest coast, from Arcachon to Biarritz and Bayonne, are all extremely expensive, with demand from both the French and foreign markets. Only in the Pyrénées-Atlantiques are there cheaper properties available for renovation, and these are all to be found inland.

WHERE TO GO FOR WHAT

Aquitaine is a hugely popular area, with a foreign market and prices on the rise

The refuge of retirees and families alike, Dordogne is fast becoming the permanent home of an array of foreign and French buyers who are flooding the market. This is not an ideal area in which to seek a renovation property, as most of Aquitaine is expensive. Those who are drawn to the area enjoy easy access to both the coast and the Pyrenean ski resorts, while its attractive rolling landscape and the ever-increasing number of British ex-pats offer familiarity and comfort to many who seek to buy here. The western coastline features the exclusive and expensive resorts of Biarritz and Bayonne, which are frequently compared to Nice on the Côte d'Azur.

The Arcachon coastline is famous for its oysters, attracting many tourists and a healthy rental market

PROPERTY PRICE TRENDS

Known as 'the Alternative South', this southwest region of France is more expensive than most regions in the country, and yet its increasing ease of access has been attracting the foreign buyer. Except for Dordogne, most of Aquitaine is relatively unknown, in spite of a substantial increase in property purchases. Lot-et-Garonne has always been an expensive region, as is most of southwest France currently, while the coastal resorts of Biarritz and Arcachon are very popular, with many French and Britons buying there. The Pyrénées-Atlantiques area is already popular with the French and is forecast as the next up-and-coming foreign market, since property there is cheap. Now is considered to be the best time to invest.

NEW BUILD/TRANSPORT PLANS

Some holiday homes are centred in small developments around a swimming pool and have a particular appeal for those seeking a second home, although more people are now seeking permanent homes here. As access to the Aquitaine region has improved, areas other than Dordogne have become increasingly popular with, and recognised by, the foreign market. With Pau a new destination for Ryanair flights, the last six months have witnessed a real explosion of interest.

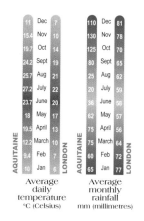

	AQUITAINE	LONDON
Dec	11	7
Nov	15.4	10
Oct	19.7	14
Sept	24.2	19
Aug	25.7	21
July	27.2	22
June	23.7	20
May	18	17
April	19.5	13
March	12.2	10
Feb	9.4	7
Jan	10	6

Average daily temperature °C (Celsius)

	AQUITAINE	LONDON
Dec	110	81
Nov	130	78
Oct	125	70
Sept	80	65
Aug	25	62
July	20	59
June	36	58
May	62	57
April	75	56
March	75	64
Feb	60	72
Jan	65	77

Average monthly rainfall mm (millimetres)

Average House Sale Prices

HOTPSOT	2-BED	3-BED	4 BED	5 BED	6/7 BED	8-BED
Agen	€100K (£66K)	€210K (£140K)	€350K (£233K)	€500K (£333K)	€680K (£453K)	€1M (£666K)
Arcachon/Cap Ferret	-	-	€265K (£176K)	-	€375K (£250K)	-
Bayonne/Biarritz	€120K (£80K)	-	-	-	€375K (£250K)	-
Bordeaux	-	-	€265K (£176K)	-	€375K (£250K)	-
Dordogne	€100K (£66K)	€210K (£140K)	€350K (£233K)	€500K (£333K)	€680K (£453K)	€1M (£666K

Aquitaine Hotspots

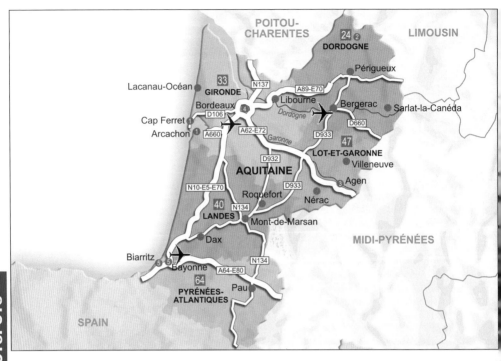

1. Cap Ferret/Bay of Arcachon

ESSENTIALS ▉ **POP** Arcachon: 1,800, Cap Ferret: 6,307 ▉ **TAXES** Taxe d'habitation: 14.08%, Taxe foncière: 22.60%
▉ **AIRPORT** Aéroport de Bordeaux, Cedex 40, 33700 Merignac, Tel: +33 5 56 34 50 50.

KEY FACTS

SCHOOLS The nearest international school is in Bordeaux, which is 70.5 km, 50 minutes, from Arcachon: Bordeaux International School, 53 rue de Laseppe, 33000 Bordeaux, Tel:+33 5 57 87 02 11, www.bordeaux-school.com.

MEDICAL Centre De Secteur, Villa Asphodèle, 68 bd Deganne, 33120 Arcachon, Tel: +33 5 57 52 55 90, Fax: +33 5 57 52 55 99.

RENTALS The area is very popular for rentals, particularly with the French market ▉ The location of Arcachon makes it very popular for holiday rentals and guarantees a good income ▉ The season lasts from June to September.

PROS The preserve of the wealthy and a highly exclusive resort ▉ Located on the northern headland of the Bassin d'Arcachon, this is a protected area with stunning beaches.

CONS During the high season, Arcachon tends to become extremely overcrowded ▉ Certain bay areas, particularly Lacanau-Océan, can be overpriced ▉ Outside of the tourist season, a lack of tourist attractions can give the area a relatively deserted feel.

Cap Ferret and the Bay of Arcachon are situated in southwest France on the Aquitaine peninsula, where sand dunes stretch west, scattered with breathtaking bays, 7,000 hectares of forest and many oyster-farming villages. Arcachon has a mild climate, with the Atlantic Ocean lapping the west coast. Built during the 19th-century, the town has long enjoyed a reputation as an exclusive holiday resort. It was visited by the Rothschilds, who came to here to take its mineral-rich marine curatives.

The town presents two varied styles. La Ville d'Hiver (winter town) is perched on a sand dune overlooking the community and is constructed like a labyrinth to avoid blustery sea weather. The whole neighbourhood reflects 19th-century architecture, with Swiss chalets and châteaux symbolising decadent bourgeois leisure. It is best to avoid bringing your car here at weekends in the high season, when one-way streets and scarce parking can make a driver's life far from easy.

Arcachon's most appealing attraction is its vivid and lively Saturday market, where you will find a good range of local cuisine, including fresh oysters and Bayonne ham. Visit the nearby heritage-listed, oyster-farming harbours of Gujan-Mestras and Biganos, or take a trip to the natural salt marshes of Arès. A popular area with French and international buyers alike, there is great demand for holiday homes in the area. A traditional four-bedroom villa close to Cap Ferret centre and located in 1,500 square metres of grounds starts at 528,000 euros. ▉

2. Dordogne

ESSENTIALS ■ **POP** 1990: 203,533, 1999: 212,494 ■ **TAXES** Taxe d'habitation: 27.44%, Taxe foncière: 33.28% ■ **AIRPORT** Aéroport de Rennes Saint-Jacques, avenue Joseph Le Brix, 35136 Saint-Jacques-de-la-Lande, Tel: +33 2 99 29 60 00.

Situated in the southwest of historic Dordogne, which boasts more than 1000 castles, Bergerac and Périgord are within easy reach of superb châteaux, fortified towns crowning precipitous hills and gentle countryside. As one of the oldest inhabited regions of France with some of the world's greatest prehistoric cave settlements, Dordogne is also often referred to by its historic name of Périgord.

Devastated during the Wars of Religion, Bergerac is the main market centre for the surrounding maize, vine and tobacco farms. The old quarter has lots of charm, with numerous late-medieval houses and in the square there's a statue of Cyrano de Bergerac, the town's literary hero, portrayed by Gérard Depardieu in the film of the same name. Try sampling the local sweet wine of Château Montbazillac or enjoy a coffee in the timeless Café des Tilleuls.

To the east is Sarlat, the capital of Périgord Noir, which has an alluring medieval *quartier* packed with houses of historical interest. Périgueux, the old capital city of Dordogne, boasts one of the largest clusters of ancient Roman ruins outside of Rome itself, and a colourful Wednesday market.

Popular with the international and French buyer, demand has soared as have prices. Owing to the vast numbers of British people who move to the area, prices are high for rural France. A village house 12 miles from Bergerac costs approximately 530,000 euros. A 19th-century château in Périgord, near the airport, can be purchased for around 1,300,000 euros. ■

KEY FACTS

SCHOOLS Bordeaux's international school is the only one in the area and is 94.5 km from Bergerac Bordeaux International School, 53 rue de Laseppe, 33000, Bordeaux, Tel:+33 5 57 87 02 11, www.bordeaux-school.com.

MEDICAL Centre Hospitalier de Périgueux, 80 av Georges Pompidou, 24000 Périgueux, Tel: +33 5.53 45.25.25.

RENTALS One of the most popular holiday areas in France ■ Southwest Dordogne, the most popular part, is scattered with holiday rental properties ■ The area generates a huge amount of rental income and guarantees a rental season from June to September ■ Rentals become long term in winter.

PROS The climate is warmer than in north Dordogne ■ Low-cost flights to the region have developed the foreign market.

CONS This area is becoming overcrowded, and risks becoming spoiled and overrun by tourists ■ Massive price rises have forced many buyers to seek property in damper north Dordogne ■ The area is heavily colonised by British buyers.

HOTSPOTS

3. Agen

ESSENTIALS ■ **POP** 1990:-, 1999: 32,180 ■ **TAXES** Taxe d'habitation: 26.69%, Taxe foncière: 50.83% ■ **AIRPORT** Bergerac Roumanières, aéroport de Roumanières, rue d'Agen, Bergerac, Tel : +33 5 53 22 25 25, Fax: +33 5 53 24 35 43.

The westerly region of Lot-et-Garonne is the agricultural heartland of Aquitaine, rich in orchards, vines and scenic villages. Its prosperous capital, Agen, lies on the powerful Garonne river, halfway between Bordeaux and Toulouse, and has earned culinary praise for its famous prunes and plums.

Rue Beauville with its heavily restored but beautiful medieval houses, leads through to Rue Voltaire, which has many ethnic restaurants. The Musée Municipal des Beaux-Arts, magnificently housed in four 16th and 17th-century mansions, displays collections of archaeological finds, medieval furniture and paintings which include five by Goya.

Despite the fact that river navigation is impossible for three months of the year due to flooding, the Garonne is nevertheless considered one of France's most attractive inland waterways. You can cross the river by footbridge close to the gardens at Le Gravier. This former island became the site of one of the area's most important medieval fairs, which is now protected by a flood-proof esplanade. Agen's canal bridge is the second longest in France, offering panoramic views of the town from a height of ten metres, or you may prefer to gaze upwards at it from a trip on one of the river boats.

The Lot-et-Garonne department has always been expensive, even in the days before Dordogne became popular. Its excellent location and rolling countryside have been attracting foreign buyers for a very long time and the French too continue to buy here. A spacious Lot-et-Garonne restored five-bedroom stone farmhouse with swimming pool will cost around 350,000 euros. In Agen, a two-bedroom apartment costs roughly 27,500 euros. ■

KEY FACTS

SCHOOLS The only International school in Aquitaine is in Bordeaux, 140.5 km from Agen. Bordeaux International School, 53 rue de Laseppe, 33000, Bordeaux, Tel:+33 557 87 02 11, www.bordeaux-school.com.

RENTALS Agen itself is not renowned for its rental market, but the areas surrounding it and throughout the Lot-et-Garonne countryside are guaranteed a June to September rental season.

PROS This is the capital of the Garonne, a 'rural unhurried town', located on the river Garonne ■ It is well located, half way between Bordeaux and Toulouse ■ Reliant upon agriculture, Agen is known for its production of prunes and plums ■ The Place Goya is the centre of Agen's most interesting district, featuring the Musée Municipal des Beaux-Arts and the 13th-century church of Notre-Dame.

CONS The Lot-et-Garonne *département* was always very expensive, even before Dordogne became popular ■ Very few renovation properties still exist, and property is not good value for money here.

Aquitaine Hotspots

4. Bordeaux

ESSENTIALS ■ **POP** 1990:-, 1999: 735,000 ■ **TAXES** Taxe d'habitation: 28.63%, Taxe foncière: 38.09% ■ **AIRPORT**
Aéroport de Bordeaux, Cedex 40, 33700 Merignac, Tel: +33 5 56 34 50 50.

KEY FACTS

SCHOOLS Bordeaux International School, 53 rue de Laseppe, 33000 Bordeaux, Tel:+33 5 57 87 02 11, www.bordeaux-school.com.

MEDICAL Hôpital Saint-André, 1 rue Jean Burguet, Tel: +33 5 56 79 56 79.

RENTALS Rentals are targeted at the long-term French market, rather than the foreign holiday market ■ Britons tend to focus on the areas outside of Bordeaux.

PROS As a city of wealth, Bordeaux is an expensive place in which to live and stay ■ Home to the Bordeaux wine trade and one of the oldest trading ports in France, Bordeaux produces more than 44 million cases of wine each year ■ Bordeaux is a dynamic city with a university that boasts 60,000 students ■ Easily accessible and the centre of transport for the region.

CONS Apart from its small 18th-century city centre, Bordeaux is a relatively shabby city with some less attractive areas ■ As Bordeaux is primarily a city in which the French live and work, it is not geared towards foreign buyers ■ Most activity in the foreign property market takes place in areas outside of the city.

Approached from the south along the Garonne river in Gironde, Bordeaux – France's largest *département* – has been a wealthy city since Roman times, and has recently received millions of euros for urban regeneration. Yet apart from its 18th-century centre, graced by buildings constructed from limestone and adorned by ornate cast-iron balconies, this urban sprawl of more than half a million people is, in parts, notably shabby. The city centre is easily explored on foot and its attractions include restaurants selling the region's world-renowned wines. The Palais de la Douane et de la Bourse, and the residences of well-to-do merchants display window arches adorned with bunches of grapes and sculptures of Bacchus. Just off the river bank, the opulent 18th-century Grand Théâtre is surrounded by Corinthian-style columns and is said to possess perfect acoustics to match a near-perfect interior.

This is primarily an area in which the French live and work. It has encouraged long-term property lets and generated interest from the local, rather than international property market. International interest is centred on Bordeaux's surrounding countryside which attracts many Britons, and property prices having soared in recent years as a result. The most seductive landscape is the vast pine-covered expanse of Les Landes, to the south, or the huge Atlantic beaches. A traditional Girondine house, set in eight hectares of vineyard and woodland and 15 minutes from the city centre, starts at 840,300 euros. A three-bedroom stone house situated in five and a half acres of land and forest, 30 minutes from the city centre, costs 760,580 euros. ■

5. Biarritz and Bayonne

ESSENTIALS ■ **POP** 1990: -, 1999: 72,000 ■ **TAXES** Taxe d'habitation: 29.02%, Taxe foncière: 26.45% ■ **AIRPORT**
Biarritz-Anglet-Bayonne Airport, 7 esplanade de l'Europe, 64600 Anglet, Tel: +33 5 59 43 83 83, Fax : +33 5 59 43 83 86.

KEY FACTS

SCHOOLS Bordeaux International School, 53 rue de Laseppe, 33000 Bordeaux, Tel:+33 5 57 87 02 11, www.bordeaux-school.com.

MEDICAL Centre Hospitalier Côte Basque, 13 av Interne Jacques Loëb, 64100 Bayonne, Tel: +33 5 59 44 35 35.

RENTALS Situated in a well-known resort area, these towns have always been popular with the international market ■ The area's exclusivity is guaranteed to produce rental income in a season lasting from June to September ■ More appealing to the French market, the two resorts are very expensive.

PROS Located very close to the Spanish border, an area popular for relocation ■ Enjoying a warm winter climate, this is an attractive, comfortable area ■ Close to the coast and also easily accessible.

CONS This popular area can become very busy and overrun ■ Almost exclusively a French resort; international buyers buy more in the surrounding area ■ Property is poor value for money and few renovation properties exist ■ Lying between Toulouse and Bordeaux, the area is expensive.

Once christened 'the Monte Carlo of the Atlantic coast' after being transformed by Napoleon III in the 19th century into a playground for the affluent, Biarritz was overshadowed by the rise of the Côte d'Azur. Now rediscovered by Parisians, surfers and celebrities, the town is a showcase of impressive Victorian buildings, alongside traditional Basque homes and modern apartments. Blessed with a long soft sandy beach, a casino serving as the town's main entertainment focus, a promenade and numerous restaurants, Biarritz also has a quieter side, with many sheltered and intimate beaches next to the Plage du Vieux Port. Place Clémenceau is the main shopping area and there is a good selection of museums, from the Musée du Chocolat (the city claims to be France's first chocolate producer from the 17th century onwards) to the historical museum. The Bonnat Museum displays works by Rubens, Titian and Raphaël.

A few miles inland from Biarritz at the Adour-Nives river junction, lies Bayonne, the region's capital. More commercial than Biarritz, its Basque essence is, however, reflected in the tall, half-timbered *colombage* houses with woodwork painted in the traditional Basque colours of green and red. The Basque people are proud of their distinct, lively culture, their language (one of Europe's oldest) and their sport of pelota. Bayonne is very popular with the affluent French market. A south-facing three-bedroom *maison de ville* starts at 320,000 euros, while a six-bedroom house is priced at 405,000 euros. ■

HOTSPOTS

Useful contacts

HOTSPOTS

Aquitaine's coastal resorts, such as Biarritz and Bayonne, are extremely exclusive and expensive areas in which to buy

PREFECTURE
Préfecture (Région Aquitaine),
bis Esplanade
Charles-de-Gaulle, 4
33077 Bordeaux Cedex
Tel: +33 5 56 90 60 60
Fax: +33 5 56 24 08 03

LEGAL
Chambre des Notaires de la Gironde

rue Mably, 6
33000 Bordeaux
Tel: +33 5 56 48 00 75
Fax: +33 5 56 81 34 75

FINANCE
Direction des Impôts du Sud-Ouest
rue des Piliers de Tutelle, 2
BP 45
33025 Bordeaux Cedex
Tel: +33 5 57 14 21 00

Fax: +33 5 57 14 21

BUILDING & PLANNING
Chambre Régionale de Métiers d'Aquitaine
boulevard du Président Wilson, 353
33200 Bordeaux
Tel: +33 5 57 22 57 22
Fax: +33 5 57 22 57 20

Union Régionale des

CAUE d'Aquitaine
Maison des Maires
rue Etienne Dolet
47000 Agen
Tel: +33 5 53 69 42 42
Fax: +33 5 53 69 42 41

EDUCATION
Rectorat de l'Académie de Bordeaux
rue Joseph de Carayon Latour, 5

BP 935
33060 Bordeaux Cedex
Tel: +33 5 57 57 38 00
Fax: +33 5 56 96 29 42

HEALTH
Caisse Primaire d'Assurance Maladie de la Gironde
cours Médoc, 148
33000 Bordeaux
Tel: +33 8 20 90 41 40
Fax: +33 5 56 11 54 55

€20-100,000
(£13-66,000)

Property is available in the region for less than 100,000 euros, although all the those featured here are renovation projects, requiring a lot of work to render them habitable. Most are located in small hamlets or villages, which are perfect for those seeking an idyllic rural retreat or who desire to create a small gîte complex.

€23,000   CODE VIA

SAINT-MAURIN, DÉPARTEMENT 47

A small village house, requiring restoration and located in a pretty area

£15,500

🛏 2   🌳 *no garden*   🏘 *situated within the village*   🛣 *located on a main road*

🅿 *no private parking*

€25,500   CODE CAC

SAINT-MARTIN-DE-GURSON, DÉPARTEMENT 24

Formerly a metal forge, this cottage requires complete restoration

£17,000

🛏 5/6   🌳 *small garden*   🏘 *located in a tiny hamlet*   🛣 *not located on a main road*

🅿 *room for parking*

€43,000   CODE CAC

SAINT-MARTIN-DE-GURSON, DÉPARTEMENT 24

A large rural property, with outbuildings, requiring complete restoration

£29,000

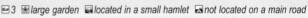

🛏 3   🌳 *large garden*   🏘 *located in a small hamlet*   🛣 *not located on a main road*

🅿 *room for parking*

€50,600   CODE VIA

BEAUVILLE, DÉPARTEMENT 47

An old stone watermill, completely renovated and with stunning views

£34,000

🛏 1   🌳 *large garden*   🏘 *within 5 mins of town*   🛣 *not located on a main road*

🅿 *room for parking*

€52,940
CODE VEF

ORTHEZ, DÉPARTEMENT 64

A charming barn to convert, requiring renovation, ideal as a holiday home

£35,500

1 *with a small garden* *located in town* *not located on a main road* *room for parking*

€56,975
CODE FRA

PERIGORD VERT, DÉPARTEMENT 24

A 15th-century village house requiring renovation and with outbuildings

£38,000

4 *large garden* *located in a small village* *not located on a main road* *room for parking*

€58,389
CODE EQU

CUSSAC, DÉPARTEMENT 87

A terraced property for renovation, with two outbuildings for conversion

£39,000

2 *30,000m^2* *within 5 mins of village* *located on a main road* *room for parking and to construct a garage*

€65,860
CODE EYM

MONFLANQUIN, DÉPARTEMENT 47

A large house and barn for complete restoration, in a pretty, rural area

£44,000

5/6 *10,000m^2* *within 5 mins of village* *located on a road* *room for parking*

€73,624
CODE LAF

BOUTEILLES-ST-SEBASTIEN, DÉPARTEMENT 24

This house is set in a rural location, within a complex with a shared pool

£49,000

2 *shared gardens* *within 5 mins of village* *not located on a main road* *room for parking*

€83,000
CODE VIA

CANCON, DÉPARTEMENT 47

A small stone cottage with an attached barn, requiring complete renovation

£55,500

1 *4,047m^2* *car required to access town* *not located on a main road* *room for parking*

€100-200,000
(£63-133,000)

Within this price bracket properties become increasingly habitable, and some true bargains can be found. Large estate or farmland properties requiring renovation can be purchased, while a budget nearer 200,000 euros will secure the buyer a traditional three-bedroom, character property.

€109,452   CODE EQU

SAINT-MATHIEU, DEPARTEMENT 87

A newly renovated property with outbuildings ideal for conversion

£72,970

🛏 n/a   🏠 2,200m²   🏞 located in the Périgord-Limousin nature reserve
🚫 not located on a main road   🚗 with a garage

€110,068   CODE EQU

BLACK PERIGORD, DÉPARTEMENT 24

Three old stone buildings requiring renovation, ideal for a holiday home

£73,500

🛏 n/a   🏠 1,000m²   🏞 2 kms from amenities   🚫 not located on a main road
🚗 room to construct a garage

€142,000   CODE LEB

PAU, DÉPARTEMENT 64

A restored house with a barn to convert and glorious views of the Pyrenees

£95,000

🛏 2   🏠 1,169m²   🏞 25 kms from town   🚫 not located on a main road
🚗 room for parking, no garage

€163,884   CODE LAF

RIBERAC, DÉPARTEMENT 24

A modern, habitable Périgordine house in impeccable condition

£109,500

🛏 3   🏠 3,300m²   🏞 located on the edge of town   🚫 not located on a main road
🚗 with a garage and room for parking

€164,000   CODE SOU

SOUILLAC, DÉPARTEMENT 24

A detached house with private pool, set within a golf course development

£109,500

🛏2   ▦2,000m²   *within easy reach of amenities*

not located on a main road   *with private parking*

€176,550   CODE EYM

NR BEAUMONT, DÉPARTEMENT 24

A modern detached property, built in the traditional Périgordine style

£118,000

🛏3   ▦3,000m²   *on the edge of the village*   *located on a road*

room for parking

€180,278   CODE LAF

VERTEILLAC, DÉPARTEMENT 24

A partially restored farmhouse, with various outbuildings

£120,185

🛏3   ▦7,000m²   *located in a small hamlet*   *not located on a main road*

room for parking

€190,000   CODE VIA

BEAUVILLE, DÉPARTEMENT 47

A contemporary home with a swimming pool and splendid valley views

£127,000

🛏3   ▦4,047m²   *within easy reach of amenities*   *not located on a main road*

with a garage

€190,350   CODE VEF

NR MAULEON, DÉPARTEMENT 64

A restored house with many original features, set at the foot of the Pyrénées

£127,000

🛏3   ▦a large garden with vineyard   *3 kms from the largest village*

not located on a main road   *with a large garage area*

€195,750   CODE EYM

LOUBES BERNAC, DÉPARTEMENT 47

A habitable property in a rural and elevated position, with panoramic views

£130,500

🛏4   ▦6,000m²   *7 kms from town*   *not located on a main road*

room to construct a garage

PRICE GUIDE

€200-500,000
(£133-333,000)

Those who wish to relocate permanently to Aquitaine should be looking for property within this price bracket. With this sort of budget, property within the popular Dordogne area, and along the southwest coast, is within reach, in areas such as Biarritz and Bayonne.

€203,000   **CODE** SOU

SOUILLAC, DÉPARTEMENT 24

A detached property located within a golfing development, with a shared pool

£135,500

🛏4   🏡 *with a small garden*   🏙 *close to on-site amenities and 10 mins from town*   🛣 *not located on a main road*   🅿 *private parking available*

€299,000   **CODE** SOU

SOUILLAC, DÉPARTEMENT 24

A luxury house with splendid views over the valley, set in a golfing complex

£199,500

🛏3   🏡 *with a small garden*   🏙 *within 5 mins of facilities*   🛣 *not located on a main road*   🅿 *with private parking*

€307,400   **CODE** FRA

LA TOUR BLANCHE, DÉPARTEMENT 24

A charming stone house, fully renovated, including a separate gîte and barn

£205,000

🛏4   🏡 $2,500m^2$ 🏙 *10 kms from town*   🛣 *not located on a main road*   🅿 *room for parking and to construct a garage*

€327,000   **CODE** LAT

TOMBEBOEUF, DÉPARTEMENT 47

A house with camping business and gîtes; completely restored

£218,000

🛏4   🏡 $9,712m^2$ 🏙 *within easy reach of town*   🛣 *not located on a main road*   🅿 *room for parking*

€355,000   **CODE** FRA

HAUTEFORT, DÉPARTEMENT 24

Beautifully restored Périgordine house with a courtyard and outbuildings

£237,000

🛏3 ▦3,500m^2 *close to town and amenities* *not located on a main road*

room for parking

€367,500   **CODE** EYM

NR MARMANDE, DÉPARTEMENT 47

An old restored stone cottage with a converted gîte, offering stunning views

£245,000

🛏3 ▦5,000m^2 *4 kms from town* *not located on a main road*

room for parking

€396,400   **CODE** DAV

NERAC, DÉPARTEMENT 47

A charming stone country property, offering various outbuildings to convert

£264,500

🛏2 ▦5,000m^2 *10 kms from Nérac* *situated in a quiet country lane*

with a garage

€417,000   **CODE** LAT

DAX, DÉPARTEMENT 40

A large traditional-style chalet, located close to the ski slopes and village

£278,000

🛏10 ▦12,140m^2 *within 5 mins of village* *not located on a main road*

room for parking

€456,875   **CODE** LAF

RIBERAC, DÉPARTEMENT 24

A country house with a swimming pool, large workshop and conservatory

£305,000

🛏2 ▦40,000m^2 *within 5 mins of village* *not located on a main road*

with a garage

€490,000   **CODE** LAT

NR PRAYSSAS, DÉPARTEMENT 47

A beautifully restored character house, with swimming pool and separate gîte

£327,000

🛏5 *large terraced gardens* *set in village, close to amenities*

not located on a main road *room for parking*

PRICE GUIDE

€500,000+
(£333,000+)

For those with the budget, there are some truly luxurious properties available in some of Aquitaine's most exclusive resorts. Most offer their own swimming pools and spacious grounds, and many are recently renovated manors or châteaux. There's also a good range of tourist businesses within this price range.

€533,572   **CODE** LEB

LEMBEYE, DÉPARTEMENT 64

A mill house with a swimming pool and tennis courts, in an idyllic setting

£356,000

🛏4   🌐17,000m²   *within easy reach of town*   *situated off a quiet lane*   *room for parking*

€534,000   **CODE** LAT

SAINT-EMILION, DÉPARTEMENT 33

A beautiful 18th-century mill house, with a guest apartment and heated pool

£356,000

🛏3   🌐65,000m²   *close to village and amenities*   *not located on a main road*   *with garages*

€535,000   **CODE** LAT

BEARN, DÉPARTEMENT 64

An 18th-century manor, with a swimming pool and various outbuildings

£357,000

🛏5   🌐13,000m²   *within 5 mins of village*   *not located on a main road*   *with a garage*

€535,000   **CODE** LAT

DAX, DÉPARTEMENT 40

A Landaise-style detached property, with a 300m² living area and a pool

£357,000

🛏4   🌐4,723m²   *2 kms from a village*   *not located on a main road*   *with a garage*

€561,800   CODE FRA

NR PERIGUEUX, DÉPARTEMENT 24

A manor house with swimming pool, in a location offering an excellent climate

£375,000

🛏 5   📐 3,000m²   *located in the centre of town*   *not situated on a main road*   *room for parking*

€624,750   CODE EYM

DURAS, DÉPARTEMENT 47

A detached house with two gîtes and a swimming pool; fully restored

£416,500

🛏 7+   📐 10,000m²   *7 kms from town*   *not located on a main road*   *with a garage*

€866,250   CODE EYM

EYMET, DÉPARTEMENT 24

An unusual set of buildings comprising three large detached houses

£577,500

🛏 4   📐 20,000m²   *8 kms from town*   *located in a private lane*   *room for parking and to build a garage*

€1,112,420   CODE LAT

BERGERAC, DÉPARTEMENT 24

A fully-restored, stone watermill with outbuildings, a pool and stables

£742,000

🛏 6   📐 151,800m²   *within 15 mins of town*   *not located on a main road*   *with a garage and carports*

€1,392,970   CODE VEF

NAVARRENX, DÉPARTEMENT 64

A stunning house in rural surroundings; ideal for those seeking a rustic home

£929,000

🛏 8   📐 1,000,000m²   *located in village*   *not located on a main road*   *room for parking*

€3,365,000   CODE DEE

SARLAT, DÉPARTEMENT 24

A 19th-century château, converted into a hotel, with outbuildings to convert

£2,243,500

🛏 15   📐 40,000m²   *within easy reach of town*   *not located on a main road*   *room for parking*

PRICE GUIDE

Builders of new properties in south west France

NEW BUILD IN SOUTH WEST FRANCE
CHARENTES – AQUITAINE – MIDI-PYRENEES

Maisons SIC have been building personalised homes for over 30 years.
From the plot search to handing over the keys our aim is to provide satisfaction and peace of mind.
How reassuring to know you can have a house designed to your requirements, with a ten-year guarantee and at fixed price.
Modern homes are built to a very high standard and Maisons SIC offer you an extensive range of interior fixtures and finishings, tiling and materials.
If you don't feel up to renovating, or just want a maintenance free home, why not consider new build.

**Maisons SIC are present in the UK every fortnight,
please contact us for a meeting
Maisons SIC** - 11, rte de Bordeaux
47400 Tonneins – France
Tel:(0033)553841616 Fax:(0033)553841612
E-mail: contact@maisons-sic.com

www.maisons-sic.com

Dense, verdant forests
Strong southern sun
Rugged mountains

Midi-Pyrenees

Profile 272
Hotspots 274

PRICE GUIDE
€50,000-€100,000 280
€100,000-€200,000 282
€200,000-€500,000 284
€500,000+ 286

Midi-Pyrénées Profile

Getting there

AIR British Airways (0870 850 9850;
www.britishairways.com) flies to Toulouse, as does
Air France (0845 359 1000; www.airfrance.co.uk).
RyanAir (0871 246 0000; www.ryanair.com) flies
from London Stansted into Rodez, **bmibaby** (0870
264 2229; www.bmibaby.com) flies from Cardiff
and the East Midlands into Toulouse, while **British
European** (0870 567 6676; www.flybe.com) flies
into Toulouse.

ROAD The A71/A20 runs from Paris through
Limoges and from there the N20 continues on to
Toulouse. The D938/7 runs to Lourdes and the
N21 continues on from there to Cauterets. From
the Channel ports travel to Le Mans and from
there follow the N138 and N143, then the A20 at
Châteauroux, which takes you to Toulouse.

COACH The **Eurolines** bus service (0870 514
3219; www.eurolines.com) travels from various
cities in the UK to Cahors, Lourdes, Tarbes and
Toulouse.

RAIL The **TGV** service runs from the Gare
d'Austerlitz in Paris through to Toulouse. Contact
Rail Europe (0870 584 8848;
www.raileurope.co.uk) for all the details of local
services. There is a comprehensive network of
local services from Toulouse that operate
throughout the Midi-Pyrénées.

ECONOMY

Traditionally an agricultural area, and despite recent depopulation, this
region's economy has regenerated. Toulouse is the centre for the French
aerospace industry, and there are now many high-tech concerns centred in the
Midi-Pyrénées. Tourism, particularly in Rocamadour and Cahors, has also
added hugely to the economy of the region, and has grown in recent years
due to the increase in budget flights to the area.

BEST/WORST VALUE FOR MONEY

The whole region has experienced an increase in property prices over the last
few years, and the least you can now expect to pay for a habitable property is
150,000 euros. Gers is the most expensive and in-demand *département*, with
interest beginning to expand into the Hautes-Pyrénées. However, there are
still renovation projects to be found, and many good investments.

Traditional, rustic
areas, such as Rodez,
are becoming
increasingly sought
after by foreign buyers

PROFILE

Budget flights to areas such as Averyon has led to the discovery of cheap property hotspots

Toulouse is a very expensive French-centred market, while Aveyron has been opened up to the foreign buyer by budget flights to Rodez and the new A20 motorway. Auch is the capital of Gers, and offers access into the Midi-Pyrénées, but can be pricey. Although in demand, Gers is still a source of reasonably priced period homes, and offers large stone properties with a lot of land and outbuildings which can be targeted as renovation properties or as potential gîtes.

With improved access has come a rise in demand and the inevitable growth in prices

WHERE TO GO FOR WHAT
Averyon is an up-and-coming *département* with a rugged landscape and fairly cheap properties, while Toulouse is ideal for the buyer seeking a metropolis. British buyers have been purchasing property in Toulouse's suburban areas along the *autoroute*. The Hautes-Pyrénées (like the Gers) still offers renovation properties and spacious stone farmhouses, while Cauterets, La Mongie and the northern Hautes-Pyrénées region are the areas to target if you are seeking a property close to the ski resorts.

PROPERTY MARKET
With improved access into the Midi-Pyrénées has come increased interest and an inevitable growth in prices. Demand is currently centred around the Gers *département*, but is spreading into the Hautes-Pyrénées as the Gers becomes increasingly saturated. The Lot, Tarn and Tarn-et-Garonne *départements* have experienced a boom in foreign property sales, and are primarily areas dominated by families and those seeking a retirement home.

Now is an excellent time to invest, as foreign buyers, particularly the British, are discovering the mountainous beauty and Gascon countryside of the area in ever increasing numbers. Huge demand in neighbouring Languedoc-Roussillon has driven property seekers inland, so the Midi-Pyrénées is enjoying increasing interest from international buyers. It has a hugely varied landscape which offers easy access to both the coast and the ski resorts, and is still reasonably priced. However, increased demand means a price boom is likely over the next few years. ■

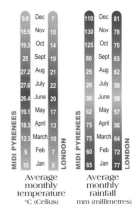

	Average monthly temperature °C (Celius)		Average monthly rainfall mm (millimetres)	
	MIDI PYRENEES	LONDON	MIDI PYRENEES	LONDON
Dec	9.8	7	110	81
Nov	15.5	10	130	78
Oct	19.3	14	125	70
Sept	25	19	80	65
Aug	27.2	21	25	62
July	27.6	22	20	59
June	26.4	20	36	58
May	19.1	17	62	57
April	18.3	13	75	56
March	12.3	10	75	64
Feb	9	7	60	72
Jan	10	6	65	77

Average House Sale Prices

HOTSPOT	2-BED	3-BED	4-BED	5-BED	6/7-BED	8-BED
Bagnères de Bigorre	-	€235K (£155K)	€300K (£200K)	€305K (£205K)	-	-
Cahors/ Rocamadour	€100K (£65K)	€235K (£155K)	-	-	-	€487K (£325K)
Gers/Gascony	€120K (£85K)	€140K (£95K)	€170K (£115K)	€210K (£140K)	€290K (£195K)	€400K (£265K)
Toulouse	€110K (£75K)	-	€425K (£285K)	-	-	-

Midi-Pyrénées Hotspots

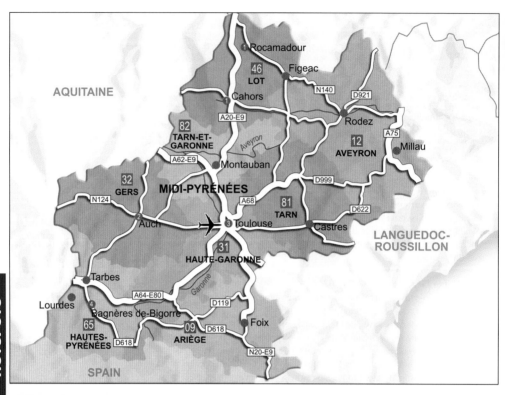

1. Cahors and Rocamadour

ESSENTIALS ■ **POP** 1990: -, 1999: 651,432 ■ **TAXES** Taxe d'habitation 16.77%, Taxe foncière 42.92% ■ **AIRPORT**: Toulouse-Blagnac, BP 103, 31703 Blagnac Cedex, Tel: +33 561 42 44 00, Fax: +33 561 42 45 55

KEY FACTS

SCHOOLS Contact the Rectorat de l'Académie de Toulouse, place Saint-Jacques, 31073 Toulouse, Cedex, Tel: +33 5 61 364000, Fax: +33 5 61 52 80 27, for advice on education

MEDICAL Centre Hospitalier Jean Rougier, 335 rue Prés Wilson, 46000 Cahors, Tel: +33 5 65 20 50 50, Fax: +33 5 65 20 50 51

RENTALS A hugely popular area for tourists, the areas surrounding Cahors and Rocamadour have great rental potential ■ The rental season is guaranteed to last from June to September, with longer term lettings becoming popular in the winter months.

PROS The Lot area has a mild climate during the winter months, and has stunning rural surroundings.

CONS Rocamadour is inundated with coach tours and tourists, which are damaging the natural beauty of the area.

Capital city of the Lot *département* and built on a rocky peninsula, Cahors dates back to 1 BC, and was an important centre during the Middle Ages, proving enticing to Muslim invaders. Pope John XXII, who was born here, founded the University of Cahors in the early 14th-century, which later became the University of Toulouse. Interesting sites are the 12th-century Cathedral of Saint Étienne, notable for its cupolas, the Roman aqueduct ruins and the Pont Valentré, a fortified stone bridge with three towers and seven arches.

Also known for its deep ruby-red wines (the vineyard trail can be followed west of town) Cahors has the biggest property market in the Lot and draws a huge amount of international interest. Prices have increased by approximately 30 per cent in the Midi-Pyrénées area, and Cahors experiences a very high turnover of properties. Nevertheless, the luxurious top-end properties have not been as popular in recent years. Despite which if you are seeking a more exclusive property, prices do range from 100,000 euros to 1,000,000 euros. Prices in the Lot are generally above the national average, but it is possible to find a good range of second homes with land in and around Cahors. Prices start at around 120,000 euros for a renovated property, although there are still one or two ruins available from around 45,000. Twelve miles from the city a typical property costs roughly 640,000 euros. ■

2. Gascony/ Gers

ESSENTIALS ■ **POP** 1990: -, 1999: 172,300 ■ **TAXES** Taxe d'habitation 25.36%, Taxe foncierè 62.13% ■ **AIRPORT**: Toulouse-Blagnac, BP 103, 31703 Blagnac Cedex, Tel: +33 561 42 44 00, Fax: +33 561 42 45 55

Traditionally an agricultural and wine-producing area, Gascony – now known as Gers - is the most rural *département* in France, famed for its preserves, pâtés and particularly foie gras.

The capital Auch is an outstanding Gallo-Roman city on the Saint James of Compostella route, and retains its medieval style, with ochre stone and rose-coloured tiles gracing many old houses around the centre. The cathedral of Saint Mary's was one of the last to be built in France, with its unusual choir stalls and stained glass created by a Gascon artist, Arnaud de Moles. Immediately south of the cathedral, in the tree-filled place Salinis, is the 40-metre high Tour d'Armagnac, which served as an ecclesiastical court and prison in the 14th century. Descending from here to the river is a monumental stairway of 234 steps, with a statue of D'Artagnan, of Three Muskateers fame, gracing one of the terraces.

Auch is the focal point of the Gascony property market and is popular, being regarded as the gateway into the region. Gascony is very popular with the foreign buyer, the majority of whom are British. There is very little cheap property available as Gascony is a wealthy area, but cheaper homes can be found away from Auch in the surrounding rural areas. A two-level townhouse 6 miles from Auch, for example, will start at 50,000 euros, while a haute ville style house costs upwards of 200,000 euros. ■

KEY FACTS

SCHOOLS Contact the Rectorat de l'Académie de Toulouse, place Saint-Jacques, 31073 Toulouse, Cedex, Tel: +33 5 61 36 40 00, Fax: +33 5 61 52 80 27 for advice on education.

MEDICAL Centre Hospitalier, rte Tarbes, 32000 Auch, Tel: +33 5 62 61 32 32.

RENTALS Gascony has always been popular with the British market, and is a popular tourist area ■ The rental season is guaranteed to last from June to September, with 10 weeks of rentals being the least you can expect ■ More people are moving to the area, seeking to set up a holiday rentals business.

PROS Easily accessible from Toulouse, the major airport in the region ■ Property in Gascony is spacious and includes a lot of land, with homes often being extremely luxurious.

CONS Renovation properties do exist, but take longer and more organisation to complete, due to a shortage of artisans and high demand.

3. Toulouse

ESSENTIALS ■ **POP** 1990: -, 1999: 358,500 ■ **TAXES** Taxe d'habitation 26.72%, Taxe foncierè 36.21% ■ **AIRPORT**: Toulouse-Blagnac, BP 103, 31703 Blagnac Cedex, Tel: +33 5 61 42 44 00, Fax: +33 5 61 42 45 55

One of the most vibrant and metropolitan provincial cities in France, Toulouse is dubbed *La Ville Rose*, thanks to its pink-brick buildings constructed from local clay.

Transformed since World War Two into a centre for high-tech industry, the city leads the way in aeronautics, being home to Aérospatiale, the dynamics behind Concorde, Airbus and the Ariane space rocket. The National Space Centre and European shuttle programme are also based here, and Toulouse is the biggest University outside Paris.

Old Toulouse is split by two 19th-century streets, the long north-south rue d'Alsace-Lorraine/rue du Languedoc, and the east-west rue de Metz. Visit Cité de l'Espace to see collections of space artefacts and a life-size model of Mir space station. The Dominican Church of Les Jacobins, which inspired Dali's painting, and the resplendent Renaissance town houses known as *hôtels particuliers*, are also worth a look. Parks include the formal gardens of the Grand-Rond and Jardin des Plantes in the southeast corner of the centre. Don't forget to try the famed *cassoulet*, a hearty casserole made with beans, vegetables, duck, pork and sausage.

There are very few foreign buyers around Toulouse, with the majority being the French people who live and work there, and most foreign buyers live in the suburbs. Being a large city dominated by the French, Toulouse is very expensive, but cheaper properties being found in the surrounding area. A 15th-century windmill, 20 minutes from Toulouse and fully renovated, costs from 328,000 euros. ■

KEY FACTS

SCHOOLS Contact the Rectorat de l'Académie de Toulouse, place Saint-Jacques, 31073 Toulouse, Cedex, Tel: +33 5 61 36 40 00, Fax: +33 5 61 52 80 27 for advice on education.

MEDICAL Hôpital Joseph Ducuing, 15 rue Varsovie, 31300 Toulouse, Tel:+33 5 61 77 34 00.

RENTALS Toulouse is not a holiday rental area but there are more long-term rentals ■ Toulouse's rental market is not directed at foreign holidaymakers, but the local French market.

PROS Tououse is a dynamic and vibrant city, ideal for those who are seeking a metropolitan lifestyle.

CONS Primarily an area dominated by the local French market ■ Most foreign buyers live in the suburbs around Toulouse, especially along the autoroutes ■ Property prices have increased dramatically throughout the Toulouse area.

HOTSPOTS

Midi-Pyrénées Hotspots

4. Bagnères de Bigorre

ESSENTIALS ■ **POP** 1990: -, 1999: 8,423 ■ **TAXES** Taxe d'habitation 27.08%, Taxe fonciere 37.59% ■ **AIRPORT**: Pau-Pyrénées, 64230 Lescar, Tel: +33 5 59 33 33 00

KEY FACTS

SCHOOLS Rectorat de l'Académie de Toulouse, place Saint-Jacques, 31073 Toulouse, Cedex, Tel: +33 5 61 36 40 00, Fax: +33 5 61 52 80 27
MEDICAL Hôpital-Centre Hospitalier Bagnères de Bigorre, 15 rue Gambetta, 65200 Bagnères de Bigorre, Tel: +33 5 62 914111, Fax: +33 5 62 914000
RENTALS The close proximity of the town to the expensive ski resort areas guarantees good rental potential ■ The ski season is guaranteed to generate interest from at least December through to April, and the summer sees activity breaks.
PROS The main ski resort in the Pyrénées is La Mongie-Barage, easily accessible from Bagnères de Bigorre ■ Bagnères de Bigorre is an excellent location only 20 minutes away from the ski resorts.
CONS The area itself is fairly remote and access can be a problem.

At an altitude of 2,877 metres, in the heart of the Pyrénées, this elegant spa town owes its wealth to local grey marble, used to construct the Paris Opera House and the National Assembly. Today, Bagnères produces high-tech railway equipment and has recently seen a boost in slate quarrying.

While enjoying a mild climate, Bagnères draws home buyers with an interest in the nearby intermediate ski resort of La Mongie, which offers access to 64 pistes at lower prices than in Alpine venues. To the south, the Pic du Midi hass splendid panoramas and hiking opportunities over the Pyrénées. Every June the *Fête de la Transhumance* is celebrated with folk singing, films and pageantry, while in July cyclists try their luck on the legendary *Tour de France* passes of Col de Tourmalet and Col d'Aspin. The Saturday morning market offers local specialities such as foie gras, sausages and patisserie. Outdoor activities include an 18-hole golf course, fly fishing in the Adour river or visits to the Grottes de Medous, its spring waters linking two underground cavities.

It is much cheaper to buy in Bagnères de Bigorre than in the expensive ski resorts, with a five-bedroomed chalet located at the base of the Pyrénées costing from 305,000 euros. Those seeking a permanent home tend not to settle in the resorts themselves, due to the expense and the poor weather, and although the town tends to be a mainly French market, it is up and coming with the foreign buyer. Offering competitive prices, a traditional Pyrénéan villa with three double bedrooms is priced from 234,300 euros. ■

USEFUL CONTACTS

Still offering a rural lifestyle, the Midi-Pyrénées is perfect for those seeking an authentic French way of life

PREFECTURE
Préfecture de la Région Midi-Pyrénées
place Saint-Etienne, 1
31038 Toulouse Cedex 09
Tel: +33 5 34 45 34 45
Fax: +33 5 34 45 37 38

LEGAL
Chambre des Notaires de Haute-Garonne
rue Raymond IV, 51

31000 Toulouse
Tel: +33 5 62 73 58 68
Fax: +33 5 62 73 00 91

FINANCE
Direction des Impôts Sud-Pyrénées
Immeuble Le Sully
place Occitane, 1
BP 7164
31072 Toulouse
Cedex 7

Tel: +33 5 34 45 29 41
Fax: +33 5 34 45 29 59

BUILDING & PLANNING
Chambre Régionale de Métiers de Midi-Pyrénées
terrace Chemin Verdale, 59
31240 Saint-Jean
Tel: +33 5 62 22 94 22
Fax: +33 5 62 22 94 30

Union Régionale des CAUE

de Midi-Pyrénées
rue de la Concorde, 39
31000 Toulouse
Tel: +33 5 34 41 39 59
Fax: +33 5 34 41 39 51

EDUCATION
Rectorat de l'Académie de Toulouse
place Saint-Jacques
31073 Toulouse
Cedex

Tel: +33 5 61 36 40 00
Fax: +33 5 61 52 80 27

HEALTH
Caisse Primaire d'Assurance Maladie de Haute-Garonne
boulevard Professeur, 3
Léopold Escande
31000 Toulouse
Tel: +33 5 62 73 80 00
Fax: +33 5 62 73 85 93

HOTSPOTS

Sifex

Established 15 years

Chateaux & Belles Demeures

& Commercial Throughout France

COTES D'ARMOR

Beautiful 18th/19th C. Chateau providing 700m2 of living space. 3 receps, 9 beds, 7 baths. Many original features. Several outbuildings including an old chapel and sacristy. Development potential. 30Ha of land enclosed by walls with an orchard, grassland, a pond and mature trees. A rare and elegant property.

REF: B4-283   *Price: 1,524,490 Euros*

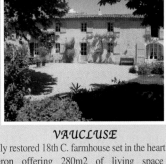

VAUCLUSE

Lovely restored 18th C. farmhouse set in the heart of the Luberon offering 280m2 of living space with independent accommodation in a wing. 3 receps, 5 beds, 2 baths. 1.45 Ha of land. Swimming pool and splendid views of the surrounding countryside. 2km from a village with all amenities. A charming and unspoilt property in a superb setting.

REF: K0-2622   *Price: 1,085,000 Euros*

LOT ET GARONNE

Attractive Quercy stone millhouse. 4 receps, 9 beds, 6 baths. Outstanding surroundings. 25Ha of land comprising a lake, pastures and tree lined hillsides. 3 separate apartments, a miller's house for renovation, large barn, pool. Only 35 minutes from Agen. An exceptionally pretty property.

REF: H2-552   *Price: 880,860 Euros*

VAUCLUSE

Early 17th C. Bastide, beautifully restored by the present owners. Spacious and welcoming. 700m2 of living space 4 receps, 10 beds, 9 baths. Features include a tower, ceilings a la Francaise, stone and provencal tile floors. 0.7Ha of land with olive and fruit trees. Pool. Near Vaqueyras. An outstanding Country House/Hotel.

REF: D7-2165D   *Price; 2,500,000 Euros*

"Entire Site Portfolio featuring selected properties throughout France, with special emphasis on Southern France."

Tel: +44 20 7384 1200   Fax: +44 20 7384 2001

www.sifex.co.uk   Email: french@sifex.co.uk

LIVE IN THE SOUTH BETWEEN
THE ATLANTIC OCEAN AND THE MEDITERRANEAN
IN THE "PAYS DE COCAGNE"

€50–100,000
(£33–66,000)

Still relatively undiscovered, the Midi-Pyrénées offers excellent value for money. Many small stone village properties that can be picked up in relatively good condition for under 100,000 euros, and some may well be habitable, requiring very little improvement.

€27,000   CODE LEB
TRIE-SUR-BAISE, DÉPARTEMENT 65
Requiring complete restoration, a house located in a rural, forested area
£18,000

⬚1 🏠2,000m² 🖼not close to town 🚗not located on a main road
🏠room for parking

€27,500   CODE ABA
SAINT-LARY-SOULAN, DÉPARTEMENT 65
Only five minutes from the ski slopes, a sheep stall to renovate, with views
£18,335

⬚1 🏠10,000m² 🖼within 10 mins of village 🚗not located on a main road
🏠no room for parking

€49,950   CODE AGL
ST.-ANTONIN-NOBLE-VAL, DÉPARTEMENT 74
Located in a beautiful riverside market town, a house requring alot of work
£33,300

⬚2 🏠10,120m² 🖼within 5 mins of village 🚗not located on a main road
🏠room for parking

€66,200   CODE AGL
MONTAUBAN, DÉPARTEMENT 82
A stone village house, habitable, but requiring decoration, with a courtyard.
£44,135

⬚2 🏠with a very small garden 🖼20 mins from town 🚗not located on a main
road 🏠room for parking

€67,075   CODE AGL

MONTAUBAN, DÉPARTEMENT 82

Set in a picturesque river valley, a small ruined mill in need of restoration

£44,715

🛏2 🖼10,120m² 🏠within 5 mins of village 🚫not located on a main road

🏠room for parking

€67,200   CODE VIA

LAUZERTE, DÉPARTEMENT 82

An old stone farm cottage requiring full renovation, in a stunning rural setting

£44,800

🛏3 🖼3,035m² 🏠within 5 mins of village 🚫not located on a main road

🏠room for parking

€76,000   CODE FWY

NR. TOULOUSE, DÉPARTEMENT 31

A small village house requiring some renovation, with outbuildings to convert

£50,665

🛏4 🖼with a garden 🏠within 5 mins of village 🚫not located on a main road

🏠room for parking

€90,555   CODE LEB

TRIE-SUR-BAISE, DÉPARTEMENT 65

A townhouse requiring full renovation, with a second house and courtyard

£60,370

🛏3 🖼with courtyard 🏠within 5 mins of amenities 🚫not located on a main road

🏠room for parking, with a large garage

€90,860   CODE FWY

NR. TOULOUSE, DÉPARTEMENT 31

A village house fully renovated, with a built area of 150m² and a courtyard

£60,575

🛏4 🖼with a courtyard 🏠within 5 mins of village 🚫not located on a main road

🏠room for parking

€91,393   CODE AGL

TOULOUSE, DÉPARTEMENT 82

A fully restored, spacious stone building, offering panoramic country views

£60,930

🛏3 🖼with a garden 🏠2 kms from amenities 🚫not located on a main road

🏠room for parking

PRICE GUIDE

€100–200,000
(£66–133,000)

For 200,000 euros you can expect to secure a habitable character property, with at least four bedrooms and a sizeable garden. There is an abundance of traditional farm properties, and in less popular areas the same price can purchase you a stone-built cottage, with five or more bedrooms.

€100,616

CODE VIA

BOURG DE VISA, DÉPARTEMENT 82

An old stone property with two barns to convert, requiring some renovation

£67,075

🛏4 ▦8,094m² *within 5 mins of village* *not located on a main road* *room for parking*

€101,000

CODE VIA

TOURNON D'AGENAIS, DÉPARTEMENT 46

A substantial stone barn, ideal to renovate and convert into a holiday home

£67,335

🛏4 ▦3,035m² *close to amenities* *not located on a main road* *room for parking*

€112,000

CODE FPP

SAINT-PROJET, DÉPARTEMENT 82

Habitable, but requiring some renovation, this property offers huge potential

£74,665

🛏1 *with a garden* *close to amenities* *not located on a main road* *room for parking*

€118,000

CODE VIA

BOURG-DE-VISA, DÉPARTEMENT 82

An interesting small stone property, with a barn, to be fully renovated

£78,665

🛏n/a ▦2,023m² *close to amenities* *not located on a main road* *room for parking*

€139,000

BOURG DE VISA, DÉPARTEMENT 82

A pretty, renovated village house, located in a hilltop village, with views

£92,665

🛏2 🏡no garden, with a roof terrace 🏞close to amenities

🚫not located on a main road 🏠room for parking, with a garage

€150,000

MIREPOIX, DÉPARTEMENT 09

A village house, in excellent habitable condition, with wonderful rural views

£100,000

🛏3 🏡700m² 🏞within 5 mins of amenities 🚫not located on a main road

🏠room for parking

€152,000

MIREPOIX, DÉPARTEMENT 09

A stunning Pyrenean village house, with stunning views over the mountains

£101,335

🛏3 🏡1,000m² 🏞within 5 mins of amenities 🚫not located on a main road

🏠room for parking, with a garage

€158,000

MIREPOIX, DÉPARTEMENT 09

An attractive stone village house, beautifully restored, with stunning views

£105,335

🛏3 🏡with garden 🏞located in the village 🚫not located on a main road

🏠room for parking

€167,000

BOURG DE VISA, DÉPARTEMENT 82

Two stone cottages and a barn, all to renovate, ideal for a gîte complex

£111,335

🛏5 🏡8,094m² 🏞within 5 mins of village 🚫not located on a main road

🏠room for parking

€195,750

MIRANDOL, DÉPARTEMENT 12

A fully restored, attractive village house, built from stone, with rural views

£130,500

🛏4 🏡with a large garden 🏞within easy reach of town

🚫not located on a main road 🏠room for parking

€200–500,000
(£133–333,000)

A budget of 300,000 euros can secure a stunning mansion or a fully restored, rustic-style cottage, with a swimming pool and extensive grounds. Many properties in this price bracket are fully habitable and offer all modern conveniences.

€243,000   CODE LEB

MARCIAC, DÉPARTEMENT 32

An old rustic farmhouse, with various large outbuildings, ideal for conversion

£162,000

🛏 n/a   📐 7,000m²   🏠 *situated in a small village*   *located on a main road*
room for parking

€247,730   CODE VIA

BOURG-DE-VISA, DÉPARTEMENT 82

A beautifully appointed *maison bourgeoise*, set on the banks of the canal

£165,155

🛏 3   *with a pretty garden*   *located close to amenities*
located on a main road   *room for parking*

€270,174   CODE LAT

GOUTRENS, DÉPARTEMENT 12

Two stone houses, to convert, with exposed wood beams and stone walls

£180,115

🛏 n/a   📐 24,280m²   *close to amenities*   *not located on a main road*
room for parking

€310,000   CODE AGL

PARISOT, DÉPARTEMENT 82

A fully restored cottage, with a swimming pool, ideal for a holiday home

£206,665

🛏 3   *with extensive gardens*   *2 kms from village amenities*
not located on a main road   *room for parking*

€320,200   CODE DAV

NOGARO, DÉPARTEMENT 32

A very secluded, fully restored property, with a gîte and swimming pool

£213,465

⊟5   ▦2,023m^2 ⊞*located close to amenities*   ⊠*not located on a main road*

⌂*room for parking*

€362,232   CODE LAT

LECTOURE, DÉPARTEMENT 32

A restored stone chapel, with beautiful country views, and a converted attic

£241,490

⊟3   ▦1,012m^2 ⊞*near amenities*   ⊠*not located on a main road*

⌂*room for parking*

€365,000   CODE LEB

MARCIAC, DÉPARTEMENT 32

A Gascon farmhouse, with lovely views over the rolling countryside

£243,335

⊟3   ▦2,000m^2 ⊞*close to amenities*   ⊠*located in a quiet country lane*

⌂*room for parking*

€395,880   CODE LAT

PUY L'EVEQUE, DÉPARTEMENT 46

A stone house with a converted barn, ideal for a family holiday home

£263,920

⊟3   ▦20,230m^2 ⊞*close to amenities*   ⊠*not located on a main road*

⌂*room for parking*

€426,800   CODE AGL

VILLEFRANCHE-DE-ROUERGUE, DÉPARTEMENT 09

Situated in stunning countryside, a beautifully renovated rustic property

£284,535

⊟3   ▦20,230m^2 ⊞*within easy reach of town*   ⊠*not located on a main road*

⌂*room for parking*

€450,000   CODE DEE

LOURDES, DÉPARTEMENT 65

This 17th-century house offers a swimming pool and panoramic views

£300,000

⊟5   ▦40,000m^2 ⊞*close to town's amenities*   ⊠*not located on a main road*   ⌂
room for parking

PRICE GUIDE

€500,000+
(£333,000+)

The Midi-Pyrénées offers traditional chalets located in the mountains, as well as the usual châteaux and mansions of the area. Less usual are the turreted castles on sale! As with most regions outside the Cote d'Azur, this price bracket offers extensive properties of great character.

PRICE GUIDE

€530,000   CODE AGL

CASTELNAU MONTRATIER, DÉPARTEMENT 46

A traditional Quercy-style farmhouse, fully renovated, with a swimming pool

£353,335

🛏4 ▣10,120m² 📷5 kms from village and amenities

🚫not located on a main road 🚗with a large parking area and car port

€533,570   CODE DAV

CONDOM, DÉPARTEMENT 32

A stunning stone property, located in a rural position, ideal for a gîte business

£325,715

🛏2 ▣36,420m² 📷within easy reach of town 🚫not located on a main road

🚗room for parking

€580,000   CODE LAT

CASTRES, DÉPARTEMENT 81

A 13th-century manor, in an attractive setting, with huge potential to develop

£386,665

🛏7 ▣27,320m2 📷close to amenities 🚫not located on a main road

🚗room for parking

€690,000   CODE LEB

ARGELES GAZOST, DÉPARTEMENT 65

Set in a unique mountain location with stunning views and a barn to convert

£460,000

🛏7 ▣50,000m² 📷in a secluded location 🚫not located on a main road

🚗room for parking

€780,000

JEGUN, DÉPARTEMENT 32

A traditional Gascon mansion, situated in a secluded rural area, with a lake

£520,000

n/a 45,000m² *in a secluded location* *not located on a main road*

room for parking

€807,000

MONTAUBAN, DÉPARTEMENT 81

An exceptional country estate with a lake, and outbuildings ideal to convert

£538,000

7 505,900m² *within easy reach of town* *not located on a main road*

room for parking, with a large garage

€810,000

PLAISANCE, DÉPARTEMENT 32

A large village property, with lovely traditional features, and a swimming pool

£540,000

n/a 2,000m² *with spacious grounds* *not located on a main road*

room for parking

€1,000,000

LES GETS, DÉPARTEMENT 32

A bar and *chambre d'hote*, with restaurant seating for over 50 people

£666,665

n/a *with garden area* *close to amenities* *not located on a main road*

room for parking

€1,060,000

BOURG-DE-VISA, DÉPARTEMENT 82

Two stone residences, with a barn and swimming pool, fully renovated

£706,665

7 331,800m² *close to amenities* *not located on a main road*

room for parking

€1,450,000

AUCH, DÉPARTEMENT 32

A magnificent 18th-century castle, with summer outbuildings, in a quiet area

£1,110,000

n/a 50,000m² *in a secluded location* *not located on a main road*

room for parking

Beaches and lagoons
Acres of vineyards
Catalan traditions

Languedoc-Roussillon

Profile 290

Hotspots 292

PRICE GUIDE

€20,000-€50,000 296

€50,000-€100,000 298

€100,000-€200,000 300

€200,000-€500,000 302

€500,000+ 306

Languedoc-Roussillon Profile

Getting there

AIR Languedoc-Roussillon has an international airport in Montpellier, and three smaller, but extremely active airports, in Nîmes, Perpignan and Carcassonne. **Ryanair** (0871 246 0000; www.ryanair.com) flies directly from London Stansted into Montpellier, Carcassonne, Nîmes and Perpignan airports. **GB Airways** (0870 850 9850: www.gbairways.com) also flies into Montpellier from Gatwick, while **British Airways** (0870 850 9850; www.britishairways.com) operates from a variety of UK airports to Montpellier and Perpignan (via Paris).
ROAD The A9 runs along the coastline of Languedoc-Roussillon from Nîmes through Montpellier and down to Perpignan. From Paris the A10 leads on to the A20 from Orléans to Toulouse, while the A61 motorway provides access from the west, and the A75 enters from the north. The smaller road networks are well maintained, making for easy access throughout the region.
COACH Eurolines (0870 514 3219; www.eurolines.com) provides coach travel from the UK to Béziers, Carcassonne, Narbonne, Nîmes and Perpignan.
RAIL The **TGV** runs a service between Paris Gare de Lyon and Nîmes, Montpellier and Perpignan, while Motorail operates from Calais to Narbonne. There are Eurostar services between Lille Europe and Perpignan. For more details on local services, contact **Rail Europe** (0870 584 8848; www.raileurope.co.uk).

ECONOMY

A leading centre for the scientific and medical industries as well as for biotechnology, this region is the largest wine-producing area in France. Along with the highest coverage of vineyards in the country, Languedoc has, more recently diversified into advanced technology. Tourism is a major contributor to the economy.

BEST/WORST VALUE FOR MONEY

The large cities of the Languedoc-Roussillon region are extremely expensive places in which to live. For instance, Perpignan is highly fashionable and therefore very costly, and Montpellier — the priciest city in the region — has experienced a 25 per cent increase in property prices over the last five years. The Gard and Hérault *départements* are also expensive and popular, while renovation properties along the coast can cost upwards of 200,000 euros.

Cheaper properties do exist further inland, particularly in the Pyrénées-Orientales *département*, in the far south. Better value can also be found in Aude, which is a cheaper *département* than Gard and Hérault, although in the region prices generally are on the increase and there are few bargain properties around.

The colourful port of Collioure is typical of the popular resorts located on the Spanish border

Languedoc-Rousillon boasts more metres squared of vineyards than any other region

WHERE TO GO FOR WHAT

Céret and Banyuls are attractive towns on the Spanish border offering a Mediterranean climate, and Céret is renowned for being an 'English' town. Perpignan and Montpellier are very exclusive and in demand, and are ideally situated for those seeking a dynamic city environment.

It should be remembered that the south of France is highly expensive and consequently there are very few towns and cities within the Languedoc area that offer cheap property. Those who wish to relocate to the coast will find a great number of coastal resorts to choose from, but you must be prepared to pay a premium for this, as there is also huge demand for coastal villas.

THE PROPERTY MARKET

The popularity of the Côte d'Azur has led to spiralling prices within the area and has driven people to search for other retreats on the western coast. Not yet as popular as the Côte d'Azur, it is predicted that Languedoc will eventually catch up. In the last five years an expansion in the property market has been witnessed with prices doubling, along with increased interest from the British, German and Swiss markets, amongst others. Notably, Uzef on the outskirts of Nîmes is now effectively a British suburb.

The problem with the Languedoc-Roussillon region is the scarcity of property in general, and cheap property in particular. With much of the region being covered in vineyards, there is no room for expansion and property development, but as demand for property is growing continuously, prices are being driven up. Renovation properties are practically non-existent, but throughout Languedoc-Roussillon the real estate market is developing, making this a good time to invest.

NEW BUILDS/TRANSPORT

On the Vermillion Coast some purpose-built resorts have been constructed, but these can be rather less picturesque than the traditional coastal towns. In terms of transport, there has been an increase in budget flights to the region in recent years and this has greatly developed the property market.

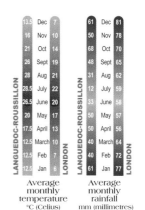

Average monthly temperature °C (Celius)

Average monthly rainfall mm (millimetres)

Average House Sale Prices

HOTSPOT	2-BED	3-BED	4 BED	5 BED	6/7 BED	8-BED
Beziers/Narbonne	€255K (£170K)	€330K (£220K)	€460K (£305K)	€510K (£340K)	-	€855K (£570K)
Carcassonne	€200K (£133K)	€260K (£173K)	€360K (£240K)	€400K (£266K)	-	€800K (£533K)
Banyuls/Céret	€275K (£183K)	€358K (£239K)	€500K (£333K)	€550K (£366K)	-	€1M (£666K)
Montpellier	€300K (£200K)	€390K (£260K)	€540K (£360K)	€600K (£400K)	-	€1.2M (£800K)
Nîmes	€255K (£170K)	€330K (£220K)	€460K (£305K)	€510K (£340K)	-	€855K (£570K)
Perpignan	€250K (£167K)	€350K (£233K)	€450K (£300K)	€500K (£333K)	-	€1M (£666M)

Languedoc-Roussillon Hotspots

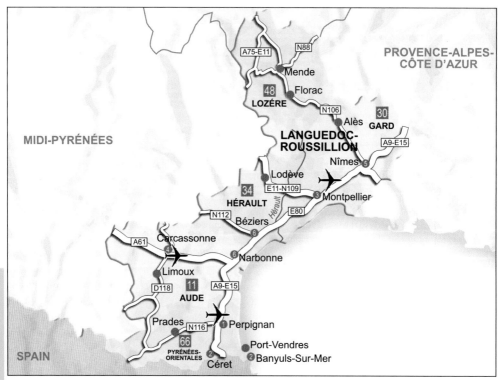

1. Perpignan

ESSENTIALS ▪ **POP** 1990-, 1999: 108,000 ▪ **TAXES** Taxe d'habitation 24.04%, Taxe foncière 33.93% ▪ **AIRPORT** Aéroport Perpignan, avenue Maurice Bellonte, 66000 Perpignan, Tel: +33 4 68 52 60 70, Fax: +33 4 68 51 31 03.

KEY FACTS

SCHOOLS ▪ Contact the Rectorat de l'Académie de Montpellier, 31 rue de l'Université, 34064 Montpellier, Cedex 02, Tel: +33 467 91 49 99, Fax: +33 467 91 50 51 for advice on education.

MEDICAL ▪ Hôpital Maréchal Joffre, 20 av Languedoc, 66046 Perpignan Cedex, BP 4052, Tel: +33 4 68 61 66 33, Fax: +33 4 68 61 68 33.

RENTALS ▪ This is less a recognised area for holiday rentals, as it is more involved with long term rentals for the French market ▪ The area is not a big resort or tourist draw and with very little to offer tourists, it has little rental potential.

PROS ▪ Offering a real variety of surroundings, the town offers proximity to both coast and to the ski slopes ▪ Located only 15 minutes from the Spanish border ▪ The area experiences good weather and very warm winters.

CONS ▪ Perpignan's coastal position make it vulnerable to bombardment by winds from Tunisia, on a similar scale to the Marseille *mistral* ▪ Primarily an industrial city, parts of it are not attractive.

Catalonia's third largest city and the capital of Roussillon, Perpignan lies just 12 miles from Spain's northern border and offers an intriguing blend of the French and Spanish lifestyles. Its golden period was the Middle Ages, when the Majorcan kings held their court here until 1659. With a significant part of the population claiming Spanish ancestry to pre-Civil War times, the Catalan culture is dominant, with road signs and street names displayed in Spanish alongside the vernacular French.

The Place de la Loge, in the renovated and pedestrianised old town, is dominated by the stock exchange building, the Gothic Loge de Mer with Venetian arches, Catalan archways and gargoyles. South of the city, the two-storey Palais des Rois de Majorque with its 13th-century Moorish courtyard, offers one of the best views of Perpignan. A drained moat runs around the palace, which also contains a marble-porched chapel and royal apartments. Sip a glass of locally produced muscat from one of the cafés lining the banks of the Basse, which is more of a canal than a river, criss-crossed with bridges and flower gardens.

The Languedoc-Roussillon region is not as expensive as the Côte d'Azur, and demand for property is rising. Perpignan is primarily a French town where the French live and work, and does not represent a huge market for international buyers. A seven-room villa in Perpignan would cost from 350,000 euros, and a traditional three-bedroom villa approximately 250,000 euros. ▪

2. Southern Roussillon

ESSENTIALS ■ **POP** 1990-, 1999: 13,000 ■ **TAXES** Taxe d'habitation 21.97%, Taxe foncière 36.31% ■ **AIRPORT**
Aéroport Perpignan, avenue Maurice Bellonte, 66000 Perpignan, Tel: +33 4 68 52 60 70, Fax: +33 4 68 51 31 03.

To the southwest of Perpignan, the Roussillon settlements of Céret and Banyuls both enjoy a Mediterranean climate. An ancient town on the river Aude with a Catalan flavour, Céret is known for producing the first cherries in France, which traditionally blossomed in January and were sent to the French President each spring. The pink and russet houses of the old town are grouped around the small bay, filled with small, colourful fishing boats and yachts. Said to be the birthplace of Cubism, Céret was a favourite with Picasso, whose works are on display at the local museum of modern art. Locals remain true to their Catalan roots by hosting regular open-air Sardana dancing and bullfighting.

Ten miles from Perpignan, Banyuls is a pretty village, set amid vine-clad hills, palms and eucalyptus, on the Roussillon plain. A quiet place with no through traffic, Banyuls owns its own wine-making establishment, having long been noted for its sweet port-like red and the Banyuls *Grand Cru*. Villagers say that Banyuls is the sunniest village in Roussillon.

Properties in the area are stone-built and Céret is dominated by the English market. Although Banyuls is not popular with international buyers, anyone buying here would be making a sound investment, as prices have shown a 30 per cent increase over the past two years. A modern villa close to Céret starts at 320,000 euros, while a traditional six-bedroom *mas* close to Banyuls, with 50 hectares of vineyards, costs upwards of 1,180,000 euros. ■

KEY FACTS

SCHOOLS Contact the Rectorat de l'Académie de Montpellier, 31 rue de l'Université, 34064 Montpellier, Cedex 02, Tel: +33 4 67 914999, Fax: +33 4 67 91 50 51 for advice on education.

MEDICAL Centre Hospitalier Spécialisé Léon Jean Grégory, centre de jour La Tuilerie, 7 chem Vivès, 66400 Céret, Tel: +33 4 68 87 38 87.

RENTALS A well-known area with a steady influx of British holiday makers that should ensure a good rental income ■ The rental season lasts from June to September, as the weather is mild and the surroundings attractive ■ Buying to rent in this area is a sound investment.

PROS Properties in the area are built of stone and generally come with a good deal of land ■ The area is well-located close to the border, making Spain easily accessible.

CONS An expensive area, with renovation properties costing from 200,000 euros, while a habitable property starts at 400,000 euros ■ Banyuls can be very isolated in winter, some 40 minutes from Perpignan.

3. Montpellier

ESSENTIALS ■ **POP** 1990:-, 1999: 250,000 ■ **TAXES** Taxe d'habitation 29.58%, Taxe foncière 43.82% ■ **AIRPORT**
Aéroport Montpellier Méditerranée, CS 10 001 - 34137 Mauguio Cedex, Tel: +33 4 67 20 85 00.

The capital of the Languedoc-Roussillion region is a stunning city, sparkling with modern stylish buildings, open squares and fountains. Dating back to the 13th century, Montpellier University is internationally acclaimed for its Faculty of Medicine, which was France's first teaching hospital, numbering Nostradamus among its students.

From its 17th-century mansions with inner courtyards to its new Antigone quarter, and from its neo-classical development of futuristic flats, offices and hotels to its Olympic swimming pool, Montpellier is a must-see location.

Traditionally the heart of Montpellier, the vast 18th-century marble Place de la Comédie is the most lively part of town. Nicknamed '*L'Oeuf*' owing to its curved central roundabout, the ornately sculpted Fontaine des Trois-Graces is at its centre, while cafés and the the well-known statue, *Les Trois Graces*, face the Opéra Theatre — an exact copy of the Paris Opera House. The morning market offers many local specialities and, in particular, north African specialities can be sampled at the Cafeterias Boutonnet or Maquis.

Demand for property in the Montpellier area is ever-increasing, making it more scarce. If you would like to buy a property in central Montpellier, it will carry a 25 per cent premium, as that has been the price increase over the last five years. Villas to renovate are rare in Montpellier, and if you do find one, expect to pay more than 80,000 euros. Instead, try looking in one of the villages just outside the city where a two-storey, renovated 18th-century house costs about 1,000 000 euros. ■

KEY FACTS

SCHOOLS Rectorat de l'Académie de Montpellier, 31 rue de l'Université, 34064 Montpellier, Cedex 02, Tel: +33 4 67 91 49 99, Fax: +33 4 67 91 50 51.

MEDICAL Centre Hospitalier Universitaire, 191 av Doyen Gaston Giraud, 34090 Montpellier, Tel: +33 4 67 33 67 33.

RENTALS Montpellier's coastal location and the fact that Parisians are increasingly drawn to the area guarantees a good rental income

PROS This is a lively and forward-thinking city, with a quarter of its population under the age of 25 ■ Montpellier is an international city which draws a good number of foreign buyers and students alike.

CONS It is estimated that the population of Montpellier will have doubled by 2015, because of its popularity.

Languedoc-Roussillon Hotspots

4. Carcassonne

ESSENTIALS ■ **POP** 1990: -, 1999: 45,000 ■ **TAXES** Taxe d'habitation 22.06%, Taxe foncière 57.15% ■ **AIRPORT** Aéroport de Salvaza, route de Montréal, 11000 Carcassonne Cedex, Tel: +33 4 68 25 04 53, Fax: +33 4 68 71 96 48.

KEY FACTS

SCHOOLS Contact the Rectorat de l'Académie de Montpellier, 31 rue de l'Université, 34064 Montpellier, Cedex 02, Tel: +33 4 67 91 49 99, Fax: +33 4 67 91 50 51 for advice on education.
MEDICAL Hôpital de Carcassonne, route Saint-Hilaire, 11000 Carcassonne, Tel: +33 4 68 24 24 24.
RENTALS This is an extremely popular tourist area, with a rental season lasting from June to September ■ Demand for holiday rentals in the Carcassonne area is very high, and long-term winter lets are an option.
PROS Carcassonne fortress and town represent the second most visited attraction in France, with six million tourists a year ■ The town has many good hotels and restaurants ■ Carcassonne is close to Toulouse, which is easily accessed by flights from the UK.
CONS The climate in Carcassonne is slightly chillier than in other parts of Languedoc because of its proximity to the Black Mountains, and the fact that it is located midway between the Atlantic and Mediterranean climates.■ During the winter months there is very little activity.

As the administrative centre of the Aude *département*, medieval Carcassonne has long enjoyed a reputation as one of the most beguiling UNESCO World Heritage cities in France. Inhabited since the sixth century BC, by the Middle Ages it was the site for the 13th-century Cathar uprising. Carcassonne then became heavily fortified, creating architecture dominated by pointed roofs and double ramparts.

Under the 19th-century architect Viollet-le-Duc, the city's 52 towers and two immense walls were restored to their former glory. In summer the walls and whole courtyards are covered with vines, a perfect place to rest from the sun, surrounded by houses, shops, restaurants and cafés.

Across the river Aude lies the *Ville Basse* (lower town), a typical 13th-century fortified *bastide*. Take a barge past the elegant tree-lined quays of the Canal du Midi, a 200-mile network of navigable waterways linking the Mediterranean Sea to the Atlantic. From June to September, Carcassonne celebrates its rich heritage with a month-long Festival de la Cité in July, crowned with spectacular fireworks on Bastille Day.

Carcassonne boasts a vibrant foreign property market, with interest and demand for property on the increase. Prices are also dictated by the town's excellent location, good weather, and proximity to Toulouse. For example, the price of a three-bedroom town house in Carcassonne starts at 198,000 euros. Best-value properties can be found in the areas north of Carcassonne, where a stone village house with 120 square metres of living space will cost from 167,000 euros. ■

5. Nîmes

ESSENTIALS ■ **POP** 1990: -, 1999: 137,000 ■ **TAXES** Taxe d'habitation 38.22%, Taxe foncière 46.78% ■ **AIRPORT** Nîmes-Garons Aéroport, 30800 Saint-Gilles, Tel: +33 4 66 70 49 49, Fax: +33 4 66 70 91 24.

KEY FACTS

SCHOOLS The only international school in Languedoc is in Montpellier: Rectorat de l'Académie de Montpellier, 31 rue de l'Université, 34064 Montpellier, Cedex 02, Tel: +33 4 67 91 49 99, Fax: +33 46 7 91 50 51.
HOSPITALS Hôpital Caremeau, 246 chemin du Carreau de Lanes, 30029 Nîmes Cedex 9, Tel: +33 4 66 68 68 68.
RENTALS Nîmes offers easy access to the coast and Montpellier, making it good for rental income
PROS Nîmes' proximity to Avignon draws a lot of buyers and tourists to the area ■ Nîmes is one of the biggest tourist attractions in the south of France ■ The city has recently undergone a facelift, with various high-profile architects and designers flocking to offer it vibrancy and modernity ■ There is a healthy demand for property, and many British buyers are moving to this area.
CONS There have been major price hikes due to high demand.

On the border between Provence and Languedoc, Nîmes is capital of the Gard *département* and is best known as the home of denim and for the influence of ancient Rome. The latter's impact is visible in some of the most spectacular ancient remains in Europe. Recently given a hi-tech look by various architects and designers, including Philippe Starck and Norman Foster, Nîmes is bidding to be the city of innovation in today's southern France.

There are many prized ancient landmarks, such as Diana's Temple in La Fontaine Gardens, the Jardin de la Fontaine and the Arènes amphitheatre, now covered with a retractable roof and used to stage bullfights. Twenty minutes from Nîmes lies the Pont du Gard aqueduct, and surrounding Nîmes is the Rhone valley with its gently rolling hills, vineyards and rural towns.

Nîmes' proximity to Avignon draws many buyers, as well as those seeking a rental property in the area. The international demand is great, with the British being particularly drawn to Uzet on the outskirts of Nîmes. Recent price hikes have pushed prices up to Côte d'Azur levels, and this has impacted on the towns and cities that surround Nîmes. Just beyond Nîmes you can purchase a vineyard with 13.75 hectares of vines from approximately 840,000 euros. The Gard *département* is cloaked in chestnut trees and dotted with medieval hamlets, and a renovated property ten minutes from the market town of Uzès would set you back roughly 160,000 euros. ■

6. Beziers-Narbonne

ESSENTIALS ■ **POP** 1990: -, 1999: 119,000 ■ **TAXES** Taxe d'habitation 24.34%, Taxe foncière 45.78% ■ **AIRPORT**
Aéroport Montpellier Méditerranée, CS 10001 - 34, 137 Mauguio Cedex, Tel: +33 467 20 85 00

Located in the Herault *département*, Béziers was already a thriving city when the Romans arrived in 36 BC, and is still an important trade centre for wines and liqueurs. Situated on the river Orb, it is the birthplace of engineer Pierre-Paul Riquet, who designed the Canal du Midi which links the Atlantic to the Mediterranean. The 18th-century arena, known for its bullfights, was designed initially as an opera house, and in August now hosts the four-day, Spanish-style *feria*, a spectacular pageant of music, dancing and fine food. Near the Cathedral is the 19th-century esplanade, and Allées Paul-Riquet, with *allées* running from Place de la Victoire to the gardens of the Plateau des Poètes, and ponds, palm and lime trees specifically created and planted to give it an English flavour.

Narbonne is a medium-sized town which has benefited greatly from tourism, chiefly from the interest in canal holidays which pass through the town's heart, under the Roman bridge. The old town is dominated by its Gothic Cathédrale de Saint-Just et Saint-Saveur. Venture up the north tower for spectacular city views before heading for the Archbishop's Palace, with its permanent art and archaeology museum, or Horreum (underground warehouse).

Béziers is currently one of the cheapest areas in the region, but with the planned A75 motorway, property prices are set to rise. Just 20 minutes from the city, the seaside town of Narbonne-Plage, with its three miles of fine sand, steep gorges and *garrigue* in the protected Clap massif offers cheap property. A beach-front apartment here starts at 118,000 euros. ■

KEY FACTS

SCHOOLS The only international school in Languedoc is in Montpellier: Rectorat de l'Académie de Montpellier, 31 rue de l'Université, 34064 Montpellier, Cedex 02, Tel: +33 4 67 91 49 99, Fax: +33 4 67 91 50 51.
MEDICAL Centre Hospitalier, 2 rue Valentin Hauy, 34500 Beziers, Tel: +33 4 67 35 70 35.
RENTALS Béziers is well located, close to the sea and in a popular part of Hérault ■ Béziers and Narbonne are not popular with the international rental market, but the French like them.
PROS Béziers is currently one of the cheapest areas in which to purchase property ■ It is a developing area that is popular with the foreign market ■ Narbonne is an attractive and peaceful area, close to Béziers and the coast ■ Narbonne is renowned for being excessively windy.
CONS The development of the new A75 motorway will inevitably push up property prices in the area ■ Béziers is primarily a French town and is developing into a major logistical centre. ■ Most British buyers focus on the outskirts, such as Saint-Chinian, Roquebrun, Clermont-l'Hérault and Lamalou-les- Bains.

USEFUL CONTACTS

PREFECTURE
Préfecture de la Région Languedoc-Roussillon
place des Martyrs-de-la-Résistance
34062 Montpellier Cedex
Tel: +33 4 67 61 61 61
Fax: +33 4 67 02 25 38

LEGAL
Chambre des Notaires de l'Hérault
565 avenue des Apothicaires
34000 Montpellier
Tel: +33 4 67 04 10 52
Fax: +33 4 67 52 60 31

Chambre des Notaires des Pyrénées-Orientales
21 boulevard Clémenceau
66000 Perpignan
Tel: +33 4 68 35 14 79
Fax: +33 4 68 35 02 15

FINANCE
Direction des Impôts Sud-Pyrénées
Immeuble Le Sully
1 place Occitane

A region of variety, the Languedoc contrasts rugged mountains with verdant vineyards

BP 7164
31072 Toulouse Cedex 7
Tel: +33 5 34 45 29 41
Fax: +33 5 34 45 29 59

BUILDING & PLANNING

Chambre Régionale de Métiers du Languedoc-Roussillon
L'Orangerie
44 avenue Saint-Lazare
34965 Montpellier

Saint-Dominique
66000 Perpignan
Tel: +33 4 68 34 12 37
Fax: +33 4 68 34 80 90

EDUCATION
Rectorat de l'Académie de Montpellier
31 rue de l'Université
34064 Montpellier
Cedex 02
Tel: +33 4 67 91 49 99
Fax: +33 4 67 91 50 51

HEALTH
Caisse Primaire d'Assurance Maladie de l'Hérault
29 Cours Gambetta
34934 Montpellier
Cedex 9
Tel: +33 4 99 52 53 54

Cedex 2
Tel: +33 4 67 02 68 40

CAUE des Pyrénées-Orientales
11 rue du Bastion

Caisse Primaire d'Assurance des Pyrénées-Orientales
2 rue des Remparts
Saint-Mathieu
66013 Perpignan Cedex
Tel: +33 4 68 35 95 95

€20-50,000
(£13-33,000)

The départements of Aude offer cheaper properties than the southern, coastal regions of the Languedoc. Those looking at a budget of 20,000 to 100,000 euros will find that most properties tend to be small, stone village houses, requiring complete renovation, located in the countryside or around the outskirts of a town.

€44,972   **CODE** CAT

AXAT, DÉPARTEMENT 11

A pretty stone cottage, with a terrace area and a separate dinning room

£29,980

3 • small garden • close to town • not located on a main road • no parking

€42,500   **CODE** CAT

AXAT, DÉPARTEMENT 11

A large, traditional style chalet, located close to the ski slopes and village

£28,333

2 • with small garden • close to town • not located on a main road • with a garage

€76,800   **CODE** CAT

QUILLAN, DÉPARTEMENT 11

A modern property, with a terrace area, rooms to refurbish and a basement

£51,200

2 • with small garden • close to town • not located on a main road • with a garage

€58,000   **CODE** CAT

AX-LES-THERMES, DÉPARTEMENT 09

Located on the border of Ariege and Aude, a fully inhabitable village house

£38,665

3 • with garden • close to town and amenities • not located on a main road • room for parking, with a garage

€50-100,000
(£33-66,000)

*An excellent, habitable second home can be purchased
in the 50,000-100,000 euro range. Ranging from a
townhouse apartment to a semi-detached development
property, the inexpensive nature of Languedoc-Roussillon
when compared with the Cote d'Azur, is obvious.*

€56,595   **CODE** CAC

NARBONNE, DÉPARTEMENT 34

An excellent town apartment located in a historical building in the city centre

£37,730

🛏1 🌳*no garden* 🏙*located in the city centre* 🛣*located on a main road*
🅿*room for parking*

€62,504   **CODE** FWY

NR CARCASSONNE, DÉPARTEMENT 11

An old stone village house in need of modernisation, with stunning rural views

£41,670

🛏2 🌳*no garden* 🏙*within 5 mins of village* 🛣*not located on a main road*
🅿*room for parking, with a garage*

€64,000   **CODE** HAM

LANGUEDOC NATIONAL PARK, DÉPARTEMENT 34

A village house, comprising of three apartments, enjoying a private courtyard

£42,665

🛏3 🌳*with courtyard* 🏙*within 10 mins of village* 🛣*not located on a main road*
🅿*room for parking*

€75,000   **CODE** CAC

PEZENAS, DÉPARTEMENT 34

A semi-detached property, located in a thriving residential development

£50,000

🛏2 🌳$1,000m^2$ 🏙*within 2 mins of amenities* 🛣*not located on a main road*
🅿*uncovered parking area*

€86,700   CODE BUY

NIZAS, DÉPARTEMENT 34

A small, village house, fully renovated, with new furniture and wood floors

£57,800

🛏1 🌳no garden 🏘within 5 mins of village 🛣not located on a main road
🅿no room for parking

€86,895   CODE FWY

CARCASSONNE, DÉPARTEMENT 11

An old village property, fully habitable, with a built area of 80m^2 and a terrace

£57,930

🛏2 🌳a small garden and terrace 🏘within 5 mins of village
🛣not located on a main road 🅿room for parking, with a garage

€86,900   CODE LAT

BERLOU, DÉPARTEMENT 34

A pretty village house with a courtyard, balcony and a 90m^2 living area

£57,935

🛏5 🌳no garden 🏘located in a village with all amenities
🛣not located on a main road 🅿no private parking

€92,993   CODE FWY

CARCASSONNE, DÉPARTEMENT 11

A semi-detached property, consisting of two apartments, requiring some work

£61,995

🛏3 🌳with a small garden 🏘close to amenities 🛣not located on a main road
🅿with on-road parking

€96,042   CODE FWY

HAUTE VALLEY, DÉPARTEMENT 11

A modern house with panoramic valley views, a fully fitted kitchen, and cellar

£64,030

🛏3 🌳with a small garden 🏘within 5 mins of village
🛣not located on a main road 🅿room for parking, with a garage

€99,092   CODE HAM

NR BEZIERS, DÉPARTEMENT 34

A fully renovated house, with exposed stone walls and a fully-fitted kitchen

£66,061

🛏3 🌳775m^2 🏘set in a village with all facilities 🛣not located on a main road
🅿room for parking

€100-200,000
(£66-133,000)

From 100,000 euros upwards, expect properties which are fully habitable and increasingly luxurious. Characterful farmhouses, traditional homes and modern properties are all available within this price bracket. Perks to expect are a garden, garage and proximity to town and amenities.

€105,000   **CODE** HAM

BEZIERS, DÉPARTEMENT 74

A pretty village house in fantastic condition, with a large fitted kitchen

£70,000

🛏4   🌳*no garden*   🚗*15 mins from town*   *not located on a main road*   *with a garage*

€110,000   **CODE** LAT

VIEUSSAN, DÉPARTEMENT 34

A pretty stone property, situated in a quiet rural hamlet, offering lovely views

£73,335

🛏2   *with a garden*   *close to town and amenities*   *not located on a main road*   *room for parking*

€125,000   **CODE** HAM

BÉZIERS, DÉPARTEMENT 34

A renovated village apartment, with a fitted kitchen and air conditioning

£83,335

🛏3   *no garden*   *close to amenities and beach*   *not located on a main road*   *room for parking, with a garage*

€150,900   **CODE** FWY

ABEILHAN, DÉPARTEMENT 34

A fully renovated village house, ready for habitation, extremely spacious

£100,600

🛏2   *with a terrace*   *close to amenities*   *located on a main road*   *room for parking, with a large garage*

€179,000   **CODE** DAV

VIALAS, DEPARTMENT 48

A characterful period farmhouse, with an inner courtyard. Needs renovation.

£119,335

🛏8 ⬜5,860m² 🏠located in a small hamlet 🚫not located on a main road
🅿room for parking

€189,000   **CODE** FRA

LOS GARD, DÉPARTEMENT 30

A detached, 100-year-old property, built from stone with a traditional tiled roof

£126,000

🛏3 ⬜1,000m² 🏠close to amenities 🚫not located on a main road
🅿room for parking

€194,000   **CODE** CAC

PEZENAS, DÉPARTEMENT 34

A charming property, set among the vineyards of Pezenas

£129,333

🛏3/4 ⬜1,200m² 🏠10 mins walk from town 🚫not located on a main road
🅿room for parking, with a garage and carport

€197,000   **CODE** LAT

BEDARIEUX, DÉPARTEMENT 34

A detached modern property

£131,333

🛏4 ⬜with a garden 🏠close to amenities 🚫not located on a main road
🅿room for parking, with a garage

€197,000   **CODE** HAM

BÉZIERS, DÉPARTEMENT 34

A modern property with beautiful views, featuring a terrace and cellar

£131,333

🛏4 ⬜with a garden 🏠close to amenities and beach
🚫not located on a main road 🅿room for parking

€198,000   **CODE** HIF

CORBIÈRES, DÉPARTEMENT 11

A quiet chalet in a habitable state, with striking views and a spacious terrace

£132,000

🛏2 ⬜1,400m² 🏠close to village amenities 🚫not located on a main road
🅿room for parking

€200-500,000
(£133-333,000)

Stunning rural surroundings and a luxurious property with extensive grounds, terraces and a swimming pool can be expected within this price bracket. Alternatively, you could seek a property on the coast or in the popular wine growing areas.

€236,000   **CODE** LAT

NR BEZIERS, DÉPARTEMENT 34

A south facing villa, with a swimming pool, with a modern and stylish interior

£157,335

🛏4   🏠420m^2 🖼*within 5 mins of village*   🛣*not located on a main road*   🏠*room for parking, with a garage*

€237,000   **CODE** HAM

NR BEZIERS, DÉPARTEMENT 34

A beautiful, modern villa, with a swimming pool and fully-fitted kitchen

£158,000

🛏4   🏠996m^2 🖼*within 5 mins of village*   🛣*not located on a main road*   🏠*room for parking*

€245,000   **CODE** VIB

MANERE, DEPARTMENT 66

A detached *mas* property, recently renovated, with traditional oak furniture

£163,335

🛏4   🏠1,200m^2 🖼*within 5 mins of village*   🛣*not located on a main road*   🏠*room for parking*

€245,600   **CODE** AIF

CARCASSONNE, DEPARTMENT 11

A farm to renovate, ideal for a self-catering cottage, with a 600m^2 living space

£163,735

🛏-   🏠3,000m^2 🖼*only 20 kms from town*   🛣*not located on a main road*   🏠*room for parking*

€289,000   **CODE** BUY

PUIMISSON, DÉPARTEMENT 34

A renovated property, enjoying all mod cons, with a well manicured garden

£192,665

🛏8   🌁1,500m^2 🖼within 5 mins of the city centre

🖼not located on a main road   🏠room for parking, with a garage

€293,300   **CODE** AIF

MINERVOIS, DÉPARTEMENT 11

A lovely house, with 140m^2 of living space and a swimming pool

£195,535

🛏4   🌁1,300m^2 🖼located close to village   🖼not located on a main road

🏠room for parking, with a garage

€296,408   **CODE** HAM

NR BEZIERS, DÉPARTEMENT 34

A beautifully built, modern villa, with a large veranda and swimming pool

£197,605

🛏6   🌁1,750m^2 🖼located on the edge of the village

🖼not located on a main road   🏠room for parking

€321,000   **CODE** AIF

CARCASSONNE, DÉPARTEMENT 34

A beautiful house in a rural location with stunning views and a pool

£214,000

🛏-   🌁3,000m^2 🖼close to village amenities   🖼not located on a main road

🏠room for parking

€330,000   **CODE** AIF

CARCASSONNE, DÉPARTEMENT 11

A luxurious property, this house resides in a peaceful location, with a lake

£220,000

🛏-   🌁17,000m^2 🖼20 kms from town   🖼not located on a main road

🏠room for parking

€350,633   **CODE** AIF

NIMES, DÉPARTEMENT 30

A luxurious village house, with a swimming pool, and several terraces

£233,755

🛏3   🌁1,300m^2 🖼located in a village with all commodities

🖼not located on a main road   🏠room for parking, with a garage

PRICE GUIDE

€352,050 **CODE** VEF

NR ARLES-SUR-TECH, DÉPARTEMENT 66

A stunning, stone-built property

£234,700

🛏 5/6 🏠 2,000m² 📷 within 5 mins of village 🚫 not located on a main road

🏠 room for parking, garage for 3 cars

€360,050 **CODE** VEF

CANET PLAGE, DÉPARTEMENT 66

An attractive bungalow, with a swimming pool and views over the vineyards

£240,035

🛏 - 🏠 with large garden 📷 within 5 mins of village and beach

🚫 not located on a main road 🏠 room for parking

€389,500 **CODE** LAT

MINERVOIS, DÉPARTEMENT 11

A character property located in this popular wine growing area, with a pool

£259,665

🛏 5 🏠 2,023m² 📷 within 5 mins of amenities 🚫 not located on a main road

🏠 room for parking, with a garage

€405,000 **CODE** AIF

CARCASSONNE, DÉPARTEMENT 11

A luxury property located in an exclusive village, with a fitted kitchen

£270,000

🛏 4 🏠 3,850m² 📷 within 5 mins of town 🚫 not located on a main road

🏠 room for parking, with a garage

€420,200 **CODE** LAT

BEZIERS, DÉPARTEMENT 34

A beautiful villa with swimming pool, offering lovely views and stunning interior

£280,135

🛏 3 🏠 2,023m² 📷 close to amenities 🚫 not located on a main road

🏠 room for parking

€425,580 **CODE** AIF

MINERVOIS, DÉPARTEMENT 11

Well-appointed, a stone-built, country house, with a 400m² living space

£283,720

🛏 6 🏠 1,200m² 📷 located in the heart of the village

🚫 not located on a main road 🏠 room for parking

REAL **LIVES** • REAL **HOMES** • REAL **FRANCE**

french
magazine

STOP
DREAMING OF A PLACE IN THE SUN!

No.1
FOR BUYING AND LETTING
OVER 120 PAGES OF PROPERTY INSIDE

Find your **DREAM FRENCH HOME** in the biggest and best homes and property magazine

PLUS!
The finest in French travel, food, wine, renovation stories and advice

REAL LIVES • REAL HOMES • REAL FRANCE

french magazine

ISSUE 17 APRIL/MAY 2004 £3.50

Run to the hills
Discover the idyllic Midi-Pyrénées region

No.1 FOR PROPERTY & HOLIDAYS

Nantes
Make a detour to the gateway to the West

Real life stories
Renovating a Charente farmhouse
Starting a wine business in Calais
A Provence villa gets a makeover

HOOKED ON FRANCE!

GREAT NEW FEATURES
● Your queries answered by the experts ● Notes from a small village ● French icons: the 2CV ● Reportage from Armagnac country ● French kitchen: smelly cheeses ● Etiquette explained

Gone fishing in the Mayenne

ON SALE AT ALL GOOD NEWSAGENTS

€500,000+
(£333,000+)

As with most regions, 500,000 plus euros is what you would expect to pay for a historical building or château. Vast grounds, some with vineyards, lakes, or even outbuildings. Ideal for a gîte complex, all 500,000 plus properties offer these attractions.

€650,000   CODE HIF

CARCASSONNE, DÉPARTEMENT 11

A renovated house, fully habitable, offering a swimming pool and terrace

£433,335

🛏3 🏠180,000m² *close to amenities* *not located on a main road*
room for parking, with a garage

€723,600   CODE FRA

CARCASSONNE, DÉPARTEMENT 11

Two modern country houses and apartments, located in a stunning valley

£482,400

🛏4 🏠50,000m² *close to town amenities* *not located on a main road*
room for parking, with a large garage

€826,000   CODE AAA

AIGUES MORTES, DÉPARTEMENT 30

A stunning *mas* property, built from stone, with vineyards in the grounds

£550,665

🛏4 🏠4,600m² *close to amenities* *not located on a main road*
room for parking

€848,000   CODE FRA

SAINT-PONS-DE-THOMIERES, DÉPARTEMENT 34

A luxurious 19th-century traditional property, only one hour from the coast

£565,335

🛏10 🏠3,427m² *close to towns amenities* *not located on a main road*
ample room for parking

€990,000 — **CODE** VIB

RIVESALTES, DÉPARTEMENT 66

A renovated property, enjoying mature gardens and featuring vineyards

£660,000

🛏5 📐12,140m^2 🏪close to amenities 🛣not located on a main road
🅿room for parking

€1,300,000 — **CODE** VIB

FITOU, DÉPARTEMENT 11

A 10th-century château, comprising of a two apartments. Potential to convert

£866,665

🛏n/a 🌳with extensive grounds 🏪close to amenities 🛣not located on a main
road 🅿room for parking

€1,365,000 — **CODE** FRA

MONTPELLIER, DÉPARTEMENT 34

Three stone houses dating back to the 17th-century, with original features

£910,000

🛏n/a 📐60,700m^2 🏪close to amenities 🛣not located on a main road
🅿room for parking, with a garage

€1,417,500 — **CODE** VIB

LAUDIES, DÉPARTEMENT 66

A gîte complex, with five self-catering apartments, and a house to renovate

£945,000

🛏n/a 📐5,000m^2 🏪close to town 🛣not located on a main road
🅿room for parking

€1,900,000 — **CODE** DAV

MONTPELIER, DÉPARTEMENT 34

A unique 19th-century, Italianate property, in excellent condition

£1,266,665

🛏7 📐84,000m^2 🏪close to town 🛣not located on a main road
🅿room for parking

€3,201,500 — **CODE** DEE

NR AVIGNON, DÉPARTEMENT 30

An historic 12th-century château, situated amongst vineyards, with a pool

£2,134,335

🛏6 📐346m^2 plus a 600m^2 courtyard 🏪close to amenities
🛣not located on a main road 🅿room for parking

PRICE GUIDE

Endless sandy beaches
Glamourous and lavish
Lavender and olives

Côte D'Azur, Provence and Corsica

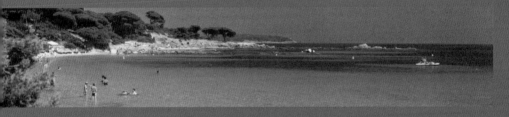

Profile 310

Hotspots 312

PRICE GUIDE

€20,000-€100,000 320

€100,000-€200,000 322

€200,000-€500,000 324

€500,000+ 328

Côte d'Azur, Provence and Corsica Profile

Getting there

AIR Ryanair (0871 246 0000; www.ryanair.com) offers flights from Stansted to Nîmes (two and a half hours from Nice). **British Airways** (0870 850 9850; www.britishairways.co.uk) operates to Marseille and Nice via Heathrow. **easyjet** (0871 750 0100; www.easyjet.com) serves Nice, Marseille and Toulon from Gatwick. Flights are available from **British Midland** (0870 607 0555; www.britishmidland.com) to Nice from East Midlands. **GB Airways** (0870 850 9850; www.gbairways.com) flies to Toulon from Gatwick. **Flybe** (0870 889 0908; www.flybe.com) serves Nice, Toulouse and Bergerac from Southampton. **Jet2** (0870 737 8282; www.jet2.com) operates flights to Nice from Leeds and Bradford. **Air France** (0845 359 1000; www.airfrance.co.uk) flies into Figari and Calvi on Corsica via Orly Airport. **British Midland** (0870 607 0555; www.flybmi.co.uk) operates chartered flights to Ajaccio in Corsica on Sundays, via Thompsons. **SEA** Southern Ferries/SNCM (0207 491 4968; www.sncm.fr) operates between Nice and Marseille to Calvi, Bastia, Ajaccio and Propriano in Corsica. **ROAD** The A6 gives a direct route from Paris to Lyon, then the A7 to Orange and Avignon links to the A8 for Cannes and Nice. On leaving Paris, the A1 joins the A6, via the N412/A1 junction. At junction A9, the A6 joins the A6/E15 to Villefranche. At the Villefranche junction, join the A46, and the A42/E611 at the A42 junction. This links back to the A46, via the A43 junction. Take the A7/E15 to Aire de Mornas-Village from the A46. Then take its junction with the A9 on to the A7/E714, then the A8/E80 via the junction with the A8 at A8-E80. This road leads into Nice-centre. To reach Aix-en-Provence from Paris: from the A46 join the A42/E611 at the A42 junction. From here join the N346, then the A46 at the A43/A46 junction. This links to the A46, which leads to the A7/E15. At the A9 junction join the A7/E714, then the A8/E80 towards Nice. This joins the D10 at junction 29, leading directly into Aix-en-Provence. **COACH** Eurolines (0870 580 8080; www.eurolines.com) operates services to Toulon, Toulouse, Cannes and Marseille, Antibes, Fréjus, Grasse, Nîmes, Marseille, Saint-Tropez and Nice. **RAIL** TGVs (www.tgv.com) operate from Paris and Lille to Aix-en-Provence and Marseille, and **Rail Europe** (0870 584 8848; www.raileurope.co.uk) runs lines from London Waterloo to Aix-en-Provence, Cannes, Antibes, Marseille, Nice, Nîmes and Toulon.

THE ECONOMY

The Côte d'Azur's Mediterranean climate, beaches and international kudos have created a tourist-based economy in Cannes, Saint-Tropez and Nice, which in turn has encouraged a thriving property buying and rental market, both for permanent movers and second-home buyers. Fuelled by international investment, a seemingly boundless property market has grown up, world renowned for famous rental tenants during Cannes' International Film Festival. In addition, a vibrant software industry has emerged at La Gaude.

Corsica, too, is reliant on its idyllic position and beaches for a tourist-based economy, while engaging in some agricultural activity as well. Provence's coastal villages, and vineyards, provide a mix of tourism and industry, while Marseille is home to France's biggest port.

BEST/WORST VALUE FOR MONEY

A rising star with low prices, Briançon offers a two-bedroom stone cottage in Rosans from 20,000 euros and a five-bedroom house in Ancelle for 100,000 euros. Town houses in the Beuch Valley start at 20,000 euros. Strong rental markets in and around Aix-en-Provence, particularly in Le Tholonet, ensure that a property costing 180,000 euros can attract 13,500 euros in rentals per month. Six miles from town, villages like Saint-Marc-Jaume, can secure a rental income of 670 to 2,000 euros/month from a cheap property, while Sainte-Maxime and Draguignan in the Var offer cheaper homes than the cities, yet afford a profitable summer rental season.

Popular with select holidaymakers, Corsica's clement climate guarantees a

Tourism is big business in Nice, and consequently many locals have cashed in, particularly via rentals

rental season from May until the end of October, while the exclusive nature of the island and its restricted number of holidaymakers adds to its appeal. Maussane, Pont Royal and Les Baux form a popular tourist triangle with high prices, but the busy rental market can justify a costly investment. Mougins, Menton and Juan-Les-Pins offer less space for more money, proving that villas can be as expensive inland as on the coast, (from 70,000 euros to 470,000). High changeover fees asked by locals for the upkeep of holiday properties in Saint-Rémy can make an unprofitable rental market for one-home, buy-to-let owners. Barcelonnette's château-style properties have a limited winter rental period and limited accessibility.

WHERE TO GO FOR WHAT
This region is dominated by buy-to-let homes, and those movers who wish to let their property should head for Aix-en-Provence and Marseille. Cannes is one to be missed for those who long for peace and quiet, as for many people, packed roads and hordes of tourists have robbed the town of its sparkle.

PROPERTY PRICE TRENDS
A proven success story for buying to let, Cannes has a year-round rental market. Foreign and French purchasing power has pushed prices up, and local first-time buyers have been priced out of the market. Up to 50 euros per square metre can be secured from a rental property per month, within Boulevard de La Croisette and Rue d'Antibes prime areas, and a yield of nine to 11 per cent was recently achieved on 100,000-euro properties. Cheaper properties exist in Nice's Riquier borough, a favourite with locals, and a thriving long-term rental market exists. Saint-Tropez's market has plateaued, and although a property will hold its value, prices do not have the same potential to rise as in Cannes.

NEW TRANSPORT PLANS
The region is to become even more accessible via extensions southwards from the existing TGV station at Nîmes, linking Marseille, Béziers and Perpignan to a route that will terminate in Barcelona by 2020.

The Côte d'Azur guarantees the foreign buyer a good return on their investment

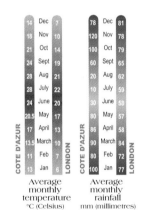

Average monthly temperature °C (Celsius)

Average monthly rainfall mm (millimetres)

Average House Sale Prices

HOTSPOT	2-BED	3-BED	4-BED	5-BED	6/7-BED	8-BED
Aix-en-Provence	€200K (£135K)	€890K (£595K)	€1.6M (£1.1M)	-	-	-
Antibes	€2M (£1.5K)	-	€2M (£1.5K)	-	€3.5M (£2.5M)	-
Briançon	€230K (£155K)	-	-	-	-	€1.4M (935K)
Cannes	-	€350K (£235K)	-	€2.5M (£1.5M)	-	-
Marseille	€1.5M (£1M)	-	-	-	-	-
Nice	-	-	€500K (£335K)	€500K (£335K)	€750K (£500K)	-
Porto Vecchio	€270K (£180K)	-	-	-	-	-
Saint-Tropez	€615K (£410K)	-	€1M (£666K)	€2M (£1.5M)	€2.5M (£1.5M)	-
Toulon	-	€600K (£400K)	-	-	-	-
Var département	-	-	-	-	-	-
Vaucluse	-	€300K (£200K)	-	-	-	-

Cote d'Azur, Provence and Corsica Hotsp

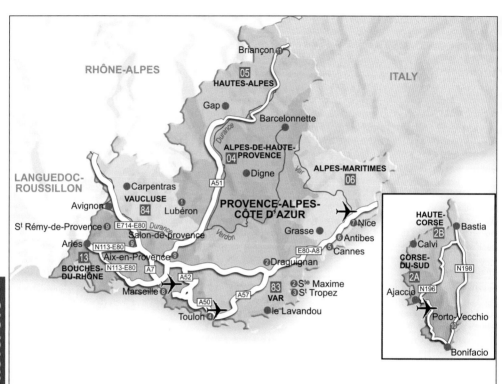

1. Vaucluse: (Lubéron)

ESSENTIALS ■1990: 467,075, 1999: 499,685, ■ **TAXES** Taxe d'habitation:-, Taxe foncière:- ■ **AIRPORT**
Aéroport d'Avignon, 141 allée de la Chartreuse, 84140 Montfavet; Tel: +33 4 90 81 51 51.

KEY FACTS

SCHOOLS The nearest school is the International Bilingual School of Provence, petite route de Bouc Bel Air 500, 13080 Luynes; Tel:+33 4 42 24 03 40.
MEDICAL Centre Hospitalier du Pays d'Apt, ave Marseille, 84400 Apt. ■ Hôpital, ave Georges Clémenceau 119, 84300 Cavaillon; Tel:+33 4 90 78 85 00.
RENTALS Rental income in Lubéron is in the region of 1,500 euros per week during July and August ■ Average rental prices for a long-term let throughout the year for a two-bedroom apartment is 540 euros per month ■ On average a three-bedroom house costs 800 euros per month to rent.
PROS The region is easily accessed by the A7 motorway. Cavaillon connects to the N7 and Marseille is directly served ■ There is a growing community of British and other foreign nationals.
CONS Houses are very expensive: from Cavaillon to Gordes they cost about 1,500 euros per square metre.

This region has long been an escape for well-to-do Parisians, Dutch and British, with buyers attracted by the older properties that are frequently found within easy reach or walking distance of villages. Visitors and incomers are drawn by traditional Provençal houses, or *mas,* with beguiling views, and by the abundant Provençal architecture with its arches, exposed stone walls, open fireplaces, spacious rooms, warm colours and terracotta. Mediterranean vegetation and olive trees add to the attraction. Village houses with balconies, terraces and small courtyards invite the residents to dine al fresco and enjoy the Mediterranean climate.

The best-value properties are to be found to the north of the Vaucluse at Bollène (a town famed in the past for its troglodyte inhabitants) the Côtes du Rhône village of Visan and Sault to the east. Although these areas are supposedly less chic, with a less developed infrastructure, they are a gateway to the serene beauty of the high plateau. The Sault countryside was also selected in 1992 as one of the 20 World Heritage Sites to be protected by UNESCO.

Prices are predicted to drop a little. The whole *département* is extremely expensive, but there are certainly cheaper properties to be found in the north of the area. Lubéron with its mountain villages offers spectacular views of the countryside, and renovation *mas* or *bastide* cost from 300,000 euros. ■

2. Inland Var (Draguignan, Sainte-Maxime)

ESSENTIALS ■ **POP** 1990: 32,851, 1999: 34,814 ■ **TAXES** Taxe d'habitation: 23.63%, Taxe foncière: 29.12%
■ **AIRPORT** Aéroport de Toulon Hyères, boulevard de la Marine, 83400 Hyères Tel: +33 825 01 83 87.

Recently blighted by forest and heathland fires which destroyed homes and forced the evacuation of more than 9,000 people, the Var property market suffered too, experiencing a decline in interest. However, as one of the areas first discovered by the British, the Var remains a highly popular area, offering prices under 150,000 euros, while renovation properties are rare. Inland Var is blessed with vineyards and olive groves, spectacular lavender plantations and acres of sunflowers.

This *département* is well situated between the mountains and the sea, with medieval hilltop villages offering a quieter lifestyle than Saint-Tropez. The superb climate with more than 300 days of sunshine each year is another bonus. Skiers are within easy reach of les Arcs, with its TGV station providing a good connection to the rest of Europe. Draguignan, the former capital, is a large commercial town with many museums, while the towns of Lorgues and Brignoles have excellent markets. The village of Fayence is the hang-gliding capital of Europe, while Le Muy, a traditional Provençal town, has a huge selection of food shops and one of the best markets in southern France.

Prices have stabilised, with best value buys found far north around Aups, a town on the edge of the Alps which is famous for its truffle market. Other areas to consider include Lac Saint-Croix, the largest man-made lake in Europe, at the foot of the Gorges du Verdon. ■

KEY FACTS

SCHOOLS Mougins School, avenue Dr. Maurice Donat 615, Font de l'Orme, BP 401, 06251 Mougins Cedex, Tel +33 4 93 90 15 47; www.mougins-school.com ■ International School of Nice, avenue Claude Debussy 15, 06200 Nice, Tel: +33 4 93 21 04 00, www.isn-nice.org.

MEDICAL Centre Hospitalier de Draguignan, route Montferrat, 83300 Draguignan, Tel: +33 4 94 60 50 00.

RENTALS Very good in the summer ■ Average rental prices for the long-term let of a three-bedroom apartment are 650 to 680 euros ■ A three-bedroom house costs about 910 euros per month ■ Houses are more popular for lets, with a two-bedroom house costing 1,100 euros per week.

PROS Affordable prices. This is not a touristy town, and the inhabitants are local ■ The town is pretty, with Provençale architecture and atmosphere, and situated 50 miles from Nice ■ A good climate.

CONS Not directly on the coast ■ Property prices have increased.

3. Saint-Tropez

ESSENTIALS ■ **POP** 1990:-, 1999: 17,012 ■ **TAXES** Taxe d'habitation: 15.58%, Taxe foncière: 18.22% ■ **AIRPORT** Aéroport International Saint-Tropez La Mole; Tel: +33 4 94 54 76 40.

Nestling at the foot of the Massif de Maures, Saint-Tropez still retains its tiny squares and rich pastel-coloured houses that first beguiled Guy de Maupassant in the 19th century. Although the mass arrival of tourists causes the town to suffer traffic congestion in the summer, it has not deterred the international jet-set, who take up residence in multi-million dollar yachts along the waterfront. There is an excellent fruit, vegetable and fish market at the Place aux Herbes and the famous brasseries Le Gorille and Sénéquier are not to be missed.

One new type of property for sale is to be found at the Golf Country Club de Gassin. This is a completely purpose-built development, with high levels of security and private access to a beach, golf club and marina. For buyers looking for the traditional, the villas have farmhouse-style doors and unpolished marble features. In recent years the market has hit a plateau after the previous steep price-hike, and consequently it has become difficult for property owners to make money back from initial investments. There are approximately 60 villas and 73 town houses on the development, many of which are still being built or are selling at prices of between 613,000 euros and 2,280,000 euros.

As Saint-Tropez is in great demand, there is the potential in general for many buyers to make a good profit from renting out their properties. A two-bedroom apartment costing 180,000 euros could rent for 1,150 per week in July and August, dropping to 500 euros a week in April or October. ■

KEY FACTS

SCHOOLS Nearest: Mougins, Nice and Luynes, as listed.

MEDICAL Hôpital de Saint-Tropez, avenue Foch, 83990 Saint-Tropez, Tel: +33 4 94 47 58 08.

RENTALS Average to excellent (short-term), depending on location and furnishings. ■ More of a summer/short-term letting market. ■ Average prices are 690 euros per week for a studio apartment, while a one-bedroom apartment costs 1,000 euros per week and a two-bedroom apartment is 2,000 euros.

PROS If you buy a property here it will hold its value ■ Very many private villas are available. ■ Sainte-Maxime is in a quiet location, right next to Saint-Tropez, and has a traditional harbour. ■ Extensive golfing facilities are available at Sainte-Maxime.

CONS You cannot buy property here unless you possess one million euros ■ Without a huge bank balance it will not be possible to spread your investment, as in Cannes and have the potential for cross-letting a property ■ Some think Saint-Tropez has been overrun by tourists and 'international's' and become slightly tawdry as a result.

HOTSPOTS

Côte d'Azur, Provence and Corsica Hotsp

4. Toulon

ESSENTIALS ■ **POP** 1990:170,167, 1999: 166,442 ■ **TAXES** Taxe d'habitation: 26.87% , Taxe foncière: 34.54%
■ **AIRPORT** Aéroport de Toulon Hyères, boulevard de la Marine, 83400 Hyères; Tel: +33 8 25 01 83 87.

KEY FACTS
SCHOOLS Nearest is Luynes (55 miles), Mougins
(75 miles) and Nice (95 miles), as listed.
MEDICAL Centre Hospitalier Intercommunal Toulon-
La Seyne-sur-Mer, avenue du Colonel Picot 1208,
83000 Toulon; Tel: +33 4 94 61 61 61;
www.ch-toulon.fr
RENTALS Average rental prices for a long-term let
throughout the year are 530 euros per month for a
two-bedroom apartment ■ A two-bedroom house
costs an average of 850 euros per month ■
Average short-term lets during the summer are 450
euros a week for a two-bedroom apartment, rising to
950 euros for a three-bedroom house.
PROS Ouerse and Pierre-Sieu are excellent
locations to buy a vineyard, which can be bought for
less than the price of a flat in London
■ Calculated in terms of the size and privacy of its
property, vineyards begin at 1.5 million euros ■
Toulon has an excellent Mediterranean climate.
CONS Destroyed in World War II, Toulon has been
rebuilt and is not an authentic Provençal town ■
There is no price ceiling for vineyards.

While Toulon centre is not considered a hotspot, the Mont
Faron area offers impressive views of the city's port and
bay. Expect to find houses painted in Provençal pastel
shades, with the stone door and window frames integrated
into the façades. Close by, the fortified town of Hyères
(13 miles from Toulon) is considered a desirable location
thanks to its position at the foot of the Maures hills, bordered by the
Mediterranean. Offering 14,000 hectares of protected scenery and water
sports facilities, Hyères is consistently awarded the European Blue Flag for
its marina and beaches. The old town features fine examples of
12th-century architecture, including the Château Saint-Bernard and the
Tour de Saint-Blaise, built by the Knights Templar. Toulon's naval legacy
remains a fascinating draw for visitors, with the National Maritime
Museum recounting the city's seafaring past. The bustling Provençal
market that is one of largest in the region.
   Toulon is not regarded as the most desirable area by foreign property
buyers. Predominantly catering for its local inhabitants, expect Toulon to
be a typical French city rather than displaying the glitz and glamour found
further south. In consequence, the market experiences a rapid turnover
of property driven by the local French population. Prices are expensive,
though affordable compared to those on the French Riviera. An
average three-bedroom property in the area would set you back around
600,000 euros. ■

5. Cannes

ESSENTIALS ■ 1990: 69,363, 1999: 68,214 ■ **TAXES** Taxe d'habitation: 26.02%, Taxe foncière: 26.53%
■ **AIRPORT** Aéroport Cannes-Mandelieu, 06150 Cannes-La Bocca, LFMD, Tel: +33 4 89 88 98 28

KEY FACTS
SCHOOLS Nearest: Mougins (4 miles), Nice (20
miles) and Luynes (95 miles), as listed.
MEDICAL Centre Hospitalier de Cannes, avenue
des Broussailles 13, 06400 Cannes, Tel: +33 4 93
69 70 00, www.hopital-cannes.fr
RENTALS Rentals, both short and long-term, are
highly lucrative ■ For short-term lets, the excellent
weather gives Cannes excellent rental potential ■
During the Cannes Film Festival those who own
property have no limits on what they can charge ■
Long- term lets can yield from 720 to 1,400
euros a month.
PROS Nice's posh relation, so there are many
more amenities on offer ■ The rarity of new
building developments enables a property to retain
its value, creating a thriving rental market ■
Excellent weather.
CONS Properties are extremely expensive, selling
from 1,500 euros to 20,000 euros per square metre
■ There are not many native, first-time buyers
because of tight planning regulations ■ Villas can
range from 400,000 euros plus; there is no ceiling.

Glitzy Cannes combines history, beautiful architecture,
ornate palace-style hotels, well-heeled holidaymakers and
its world-renowned film festival. The price of property in
Cannes has been rising fast, but that hasn't deterred British
buyers, who are prepared to shell out for a place with
sunshine and sophistication. In terms of the European
summer rental market, the French Riviera is the most popular area for
holidaymakers — even more than Spain, Greece and Italy — so buying to
rent on the Riviera is an excellent investment.
   Summer rental prices on the Riviera are very expensive due to the limited
length of the season, with prices varying from 660 euros for a studio to 4,800
euros for a four-bedroom house. The cheapest property would be a third floor
studio in the centre of Cannes, which would sell for 60,000 euros. A modern
studio property in a quieter area of Cannes, with private swimming pool, would
fetch 89,000 euros. A two-bedroom apartment with swimming pool costs
roughly 235,000 euros. Le Cannet is a popular area, located outside of Cannes,
where a two-bedroom roof-top apartment can cost 281,000 euros. A villa will
set you back 2,440,000 euros. Three miles inland from Cannes lies the hilltop
village of Mougins, where Picasso made his home. Famous for its picturesque
narrow lanes, gastronomy and superb coastal views, and a renovated three-
bedroom 18th-century village house would cost 350,000 euros. ■

6. Antibes

ESSENTIALS ■ **POP** 1990: 70,688, 1999: 73,383 ■ **TAXES** Taxe d'habitation: 20.65%, Taxe foncière: 25.73%
■ **AIRPORT** Aéroport Nice-Cote d'Azur, 06281 Nice Cedex; Tel: +33 8 20 42 33 33, www.nice.aeroport.fr

Antibes has proved an attractive location to buyers mesmerised by its setting, its stunning views and long hours of sunshine. Famous for its international jazz festival, the military citadel Fort Carré and the magnificent old town, Artists and writers have long chosen to live here, and famous names include Picasso and Graham Greene. Residents can enjoy the international flavour created by visitors, who have their pick of 48 beaches, from small coves to sheltered, family-friendly bays.

These foreign buyers are not expressing a preference for any particular style, although the traditional Provençal villa is still selling strongly. The secluded area of Cap d'Antibes, set just outside of the centre of town, which has retained some woodland despite the rise in property development, is extremely expensive. A luxuriously appointed villa here, with private swimming pool and six bedrooms or more, can cost upwards of 3,620,000 euros. Property prices are rising faster in Cap than anywhere else in the Côte d'Azur.

The best value properties are to be found inland from Antibes, towards Mougins, Valbonne and Biot, where properties are located north of the motorway and are consequently less expensive. Due to its proximity to Nice and the A8, the town of Villeneuve-Loubet has proved particularly successful with the overseas property market, and for a one-bedroom studio here buyers can expect to pay 150,000 euros. ■

KEY FACTS
SCHOOLS The nearest schools are Mougins (6 miles) and Nice (12 miles), as listed.
MEDICAL Centre Hospitalier d'Antibes, Route Nationale 7, 06600 Antibes Juan les Pins; Tel: +33 4 92 91 77 77, www.ch-antibes.fr
RENTALS Most rentals are short-term ■ An average rental price for a long-term let throughout the year would be 860 euros for a two-bedroom apartment ■ A house with three bedrooms costs approximately 1,270 euros per month ■ On average, a two-bedroom apartment can command 580 euros per week during peak season.
PROS A real town with a strong community, there is always activity here ■ The property market is stable, making for a safe investment ■ Popular with yachting enthusiasts, it has an extensive infrastructure, and the N98, A8 motorway and D5 roads run directly into town.
CONS The property market has a high rate of turnover, while villas and houses are only ever on the market for a very short length of time ■ Prices for a four-bedroom villa in a good locale can start from 2,000,000 euros.

7. Nice and area

ESSENTIALS ■ **POP** 1990: 345,674, 1999: 345,892 ■ **TAXES** Taxe d'habitation: 24.88%, Taxe foncière: 29.17%
■ **AIRPORT** Airport Nice-Cote d'Azur, 06281 Nice Cedex, Tel: +33 820 42 33 33, www.nice.aeroport.fr

In Nice location is paramount, with Nice West being a popular choice due to its proximity to the airport, and more land available to build on. Other hotspots include Mont Boron, with superior views over town and sea. Although within walking distance of the town and Villefranche, this is one of the most exclusive spots on the Côte d'Azur. The port, fortress, old town, and coastline all contribute to the beauty of the village, which dates back to 130 BC. The best value properties here can be found north of the railway. Old Nice is favoured for its charm, with its flower markets, restaurants and pedestrian zones creating an attractive environment within the centre of town.

Nice is an expensive area, yet the boroughs can yield cheaper properties. Potential buyers are mostly interested in second homes, choosing properties with a swimming pool and sea views. Brand new homes are in demand, and villas frequently offer a choice of colours, tiles and layout before being finished. These residences are full of charm - they feature *belle époque* and *art deco* interiors, and are built with small balconies. Resales have increased steadily in the entire Nice area, at around eight per cent per annum, but in specific areas it has doubled and even tripled over the last three years. New building projects are increasing at 14 per cent per annum and almost half of these are bought as weekend or second homes. ■

KEY FACTS
SCHOOLS Nearest is Mougins, as listed.
MEDICAL Centre Hospitalier Universitaire. The hospital has four establishments: ■ Archet: +33 4 92 03 55 55 ■ Cimiez: +33 4 92 03 44 44 ■ Pasteur: +33 4 92 03 77 77 ■ Saint Roch: +33 4 92 03 33 33; www.chu-nice.fr
RENTALS Excellent for long and short-term lets, rental is big business for the native population, and this is an ever-popular summer destination ■ Long-term lets for a two-bedroom apartment is 800 euros per month annually ■ A three-bedroom apartment costs an average of 920 euros per month ■ Average short-term lets range from 600 euros per week for a two-bedroom apartment, to 2,200 euros a week for a four-bedroom house in peak season.
PROS Nice has excellent transport networks ■ As an international hotspot, Nice has undeniable glamour ■ Miild, sunny winters and gentle summer breezes.
CONS The area is packed during summer ■ Very expensive and unlikely to generate huge rental yields as villas are expensive.

HOTSPOTS

Côte D'Azur, Provence and Corsica Hotsp•

8. Marseille

ESSENTIALS ■ **POP** 1990: 800,550, 1999: 807,071 ■ **TAXES** Taxe d'habitation: 29.64%, Taxe foncière: 25.99% ■ **AIRPORT** Aéroport Marseille Provence, BP 7 Aéroport, 13727 Marignane Cedex, Tel:+33 4 42 14 14 14

KEY FACTS

SCHOOLS Nearest is Luynes (14 miles), as listed.
MEDICAL Hôpital Sainte Marguerite, bd de Sainte
Marguerite 270, 13009 Marseille, Tel: +33 4 91 74
40 00 ■ Hôpital Salvador, bd de Sainte Marguerite
249, 13009 Marseille, Tel: +33 4 91 74 40 00 ■
Hôpital de la Timone, rue Saint Pierre 264, 13005
Marseille, Tel: +33 4 91 38 60 00
RENTALS Excellent, year-round rental potential ■
There is a very good student rentals market, while
July and August attract holidaymakers ■ The
average rental price for a long-term let throughout
the year is 600 euros a month for a two-bedroom
apartment ■ Average short-term lets for a two-
bedroom apartment per week are 600 euros, and
820 euros a week for a two-bedroom house.
PROS Marseille's image is much improved ■ Money
spent on improvments has attracted foreign buyers
■ Toulon is within easy reach of the city.
CONS Marseille used to have a rather unflattering
image and this can linger; the city has only recently
managed to shake off this image inland.

A melting pot of nationalities with a rich cultural heritage,
Marseille is associated with the golden age of maritime
prosperity in the late 19th century. With historic links to the
shipping industry, France's oldest city is now being revitalised
thanks to regeneration and investment projects in many of its
districts, with the aim of creating a southern gateway to
Europe. Marseille is also the second largest city in France, offering fine
architecture, museums like the Musée de Marseille focusing on a Greco-Roman
past, and the greatest concentration of theatres per head of population. Along the
Vieux Port at Place Thiars, you will find trendy cafes, bars and restaurants,
while early risers might like to visit the fish market, to source the ingredients for
that local speciality, *bouillabaisse*. Ferries run regularly between the Vieux Port
and the Château d'If, the island prison setting for Alexandre Dumas' *The Count
of Monte Cristo*.

Marseille's considerable regeneration has helped the foreign property market
get back on its feet. There are more than 100 *quartiers*, many with their own
village life, while the upmarket 8th district offers modern 18 metre square two-
bedroom studios in a modern apartment block from 50,000 euros. If you're
looking for a coastal village try Ensuès-la- Redonne, 12 miles west of Marseille.
Looking out over the sea, this combines beautiful bays and deep rocky inlets
which extend all along the coast, with the city forming a backdrop. A modern,
three-bedroom villa here has a starting price of 1,600,000 euros. ■

9. Aix-en-Provence and Saint-Rémy-de-Provence

ESSENTIALS ■ **POP** 1990: -, 1999: 146,874 ■ **TAXES** Taxe d'habitation: 18.25%, Taxe foncière: 17.85% ■ **AIRPORT** Aéroport Marseille Provence, BP 7 Aéroport, 13727 Marignane Cedex; Tel: +33 4 42 14 14 14.

KEY FACTS

SCHOOLS Nearest is Luynes, as listed.
MEDICAL Centre Hospitalier, 2 ter, ave Indié et Denis
Pelissier, 13210 Saint Rémy-de-Provence; Tel: +33 4
32 60 02 85.
RENTALS Offering excellent rental potential ■ A
studio apartment can be let for around 350 euros a
month. ■ In Le Thalonet a house costing around
405,000 euros can be let for about 30,000 euros a
month ■ Average rental prices for the long-term let of
a two-bedroom apartment is 1,100 euros per month
■ For the Saint-Rémy triangle, short-term average
lets cost about 530 euros for a two-bedroom
apartment per week and 900 euros a week for a two-
bedroom house.
PROS The large student population makes for healthy
rentals ■ Aix-en-Provence is more desirable than the
Var, as all amenities are found in the town ■ An
average studio costs from 105,000 euros ■ This area
avoids the busy summer tourist season.
CONS Studio apartments are in very short supply
■ Fewer vineyards available than in the Var, though
these avoids the summer tourism madness of
the coastal towns ■ The Saint-Rémy triangle is
very expensive.

Dating back to Roman times and loved by the painter Paul
Cézanne, Aix-en-Provence is well known for its impressive
monuments and cultural heritage. The old town, in the centre
of Aix, is ringed by a circle of boulevards and squares, while
the main street, Cours Mirabeau, is lined with trees, terrace
cafés, bookshops and spectacular fountains, earning it a
reputation as the most beautiful in southern France. Some 45 miles from Aix
and surrounded by lush green, perfumed valleys, St Rémy's ancient streets –
such as Rue Carnot, which is an ideal stop for local crafts – are lined with
beautifully restored old houses.

This area is very expensive and there is a restricted amount of land available
for development. In the village of Venelles, perched on a rock four miles from
Aix, quality properties and beautiful scenery have attracted buyers to homes. A
typical four-bedroom south-facing property costs about 375,000 euros. Saint-
Victoire offers a more rural environment in which a renovated property costs
about 480,000 euros. The market town of Saint-Rémy-de-Province is much
sought after for its properties, particularly by celebrities and others who
appreciate its unhurried pace of life. It is therefore one of the most expensive
places in Provence in which to buy. In Saint-Rémy prices start at 890,000 euros
for a *maison de maître*, while a luxury four-bedroom 19th-century stone
farmhouse starts at 1,650,000 euros. ■

10. Corsica - Porto-Vecchio

ESSENTIALS ■ **POP** 1990: 9,307, 1999: 10,536 ■ **TAXES** Taxe d'habitation: 23.83%, Taxe foncière: 17.38% ■ **AIRPORT**
Ajaccio Airport, 20090 Ajaccio Cedex, Tel: +33 4 95 23 56 56, www.ajaccio.aeroport.fr

Blessed by breathtaking mountain scenery, alpine volcanic lakes and more than 600 miles of dramatic coastlines, Corsica is frequently described as the 'Scented Isle' as the aroma of its *maquis* and forests perfume the air. The principal towns are Ajaccio (where Napoleon was born in 1769), Bastia, Sartène and Bonifacio. French is the official language of Corsica, but many native locals speak Corsican (Corsu).

Located at the end of a sheltered gulf, the port of Porto-Vecchio is currently the most popular area of Corsica, and its marina is one of the island's most prominent ferry links, connecting the city to mainland France and Italy. Porto-Vecchio has a maze of narrow streets lined with exclusive shops and stylish boutiques, fashionable restaurants and lively bars. The resort is best known for its beaches, such as the Palombaggia and Cala Rossa, which are some of the best known in the whole of Corsica

Corsica is not a popular market for foreign buyers seeking to relocate. The market is dominated by the locals; while short-term holiday rentals dominate the island's property market, many locals cash in on the busy summer months and invest in rental properties. Property is expensive, and this reflects the island's exclusive nature and atmosphere. Traditional properties vary from white stone villas with red-roof tiling to the Provençal terracotta-based villa. Expect to pay around 100,000 euros for a two-bedroom air-conditioned apartment, and approximately 270,000 euros for a two-bedroom villa with swimming pool. ■

KEY FACTS

SCHOOLS nearest: Nice, as listed.
MEDICAL Hôpital, route Santa Mariza, 20169 Bonificio, Tel: +33 4 95 73 95 73 ■ Centre Hospitalier Notre-Dame de la Miséricorde, avenue Impératrice Eugénie 27, 20000 Ajaccio, Tel: +33 4 95 29 90 90 ■ Centre Hospitalier Général, Rte royale, 20200 Bastia, Tel: +33 4 95 59 11 11.
RENTALS Rental income is excellent in the summer months, ranging from 2,000 euros to 10,000 euros a week depending on a property's facilities. A property with an outside pool has a season from May till the end of October ■ More of a short-term/summer market, with average rental prices ranging from 950 euros a week for a two-bedroom apartment to 1,100 euros a week for a two-bedroom house.
PROS Beautiful beaches and close proximity to Bonifacio and Bastia.
CONS The main pitfall of living or buying to let in Corsica is the difficulty and expense in reaching the island ■ Limited access and flight times have an obvious impact on rental potential ■ To preserve the island's beautiful lush greenery, direct flights are limited. Paris, Nice and Marseille offer direct flights.

HOTSPOTS

11. Briançon and surrounding Alpine resorts

ESSENTIALS ■ **POP** 1990: -, 1999: 11,487 ■ **TAXES** Taxe d'habitation: 23.15%, Taxe foncière: 57.23% ■ **AIRPORT**
Aéroport de Turin, Tel: +39 1 15 67 63 61, www.turin-airport.com

Europe's highest town, Briançon, is the largest settlement in the Serre Chevalier area, a grouping of Hautes-Alpes ski resorts in the Guisane valley linked by 77 lifts and 155 miles of runs. The area is well known for its Mediterranean climate, offering 300 days of sunshine per year, excellent skiing and local traditions. Serre Chevalier has 111 runs, and its popular villages include Chantemerle (1,080 metres and Villeneuve (1,120 metres), both located near the ski lifts. Villeneuve is a 10-minute ride from Chantemerle, the largest of the villages, with an attractive centre.

Monêtier-les-Bains (1,200 metres) has more rustic charm, being a typical Savoyard village with minimum development, in keeping with local styles. It has also been a spa town for hundreds of years, and you can still take the waters. The villages are not very far apart and are well served by the local bus service.

Briançon enjoys a beautiful setting with hilltop fortifications and old town. Its steep streets, many shops and restaurants create a lively ambience beside the 18th-century ramparts. However, the town is not fully served by ski buses, which can result in long walks for skiers to and from the ski lifts.

A renovated four-bedroom country house a 15-minute drive from Briançon, starts at 193,000 euros. In Monêtier-les-Bains, a two-bedroom apartment at the heart of the village costs approximately 230,000 euros. ■

KEY FACTS

SCHOOLS Nearest: Nice (130 miles), Mougins (175 miles) and Luynes (150 miles), as listed.
MEDICAL Centre Hospitalier, ave Adieu Daurelle 24, 05 05 Briançon Cedex; Tel: +33 4 92 25 34 56).
RENTALS Excellent rental potential, with the season lasting all year. ■ There is potential for four months' ski rental and three months' summer rental. ■ On average, long-term lets for a two-bedroom apartment is 550 euros per month. ■ Short-term lets during the summer average between 520 euros a week for a studio apartment and 580 euros for a two-bedroom apartment.
PROS Aspres and Serres village houses range from 52,000 euros to 1,000,000 euros. ■ Property is excellent value for money and many French are opting to buy in this area, instead of purchasing a ski lodge and summer home ■ The south coast is only two hours' drive away. ■ Opportunity for almost year-round rental.
CONS The cold climate can be discouraging.

Useful Contacts

Many parts of the Cote d'Azur are extremely expensive, and popular with tourists, making for a healthy rentals market

PREFECTURES
Préfecture de la Région
Provence-Alpes-Côte d'Azur
boulevard Paul-Peytral 2
13282 Marseille Cedex 20
Tel: +33 4 91 15 60 00
Fax: +33 4 91 15 61 90

Préfecture de Corse
parc Belvédère 9
BP 229
20179 Ajaccio Cedex
Tel: +33 4 95 29 99 29
Fax: +33 4 95 21 32 70

LEGAL
Chambre des Notaires
des Bouches-du-Rhône
boulevard Périer 77
13008 Marseille
Tel: +33 4 91 53 49 67
Fax: +33 4 91 81 24 84

Chambre des Notaires

des Alpes-Maritimes
rue du Congrès 18
06000 Nice
Tel: +33 4 93 87 94 30
Fax: +33 4 93 87 76 51

Chambre des Notaires
de la Corse du Sud
cours Grandval 2
20000 Ajaccio
Tel: +33 4 95 51 31 36
Fax: +33 4 95 21 04 24

FINANCE
Direction des Impôts
Sud-Est Réunion
rue Roux de Brignoles 23
13281 Marseille Cedex 6
Tel: +33 4 91 13 82 01
Fax: +33 4 91 37 92 69

BUILDING AND PLANNING
Chambre Régionale de
Métiers Provence-Alpes-Côte

d'Azur
L'Orangerie
avenue Saint-Lazare 44
34965 Montpellier Cedex 2
Tel: +33 4 67 02 68 40
Fax: +33 4 67 79 50 08

Chambre Régionale de
Métiers de Corse
Chemin de la Sposata
20090 Ajaccio
Tel: +33 4 95 23 53 00
Fax: +33 4 95 23 53 03

CAUE des Bouches-du-
Rhône
rue Montgrand 35
13006 Marseille
Tel: +33 4 91 33 02 02
Fax: +33 4 91 33 42 49

CAUE de Haute-Corse
bis rue de l'Annonciade 2
20200 Bastia

Tel: +33 4 95 31 80 90
Fax: +33 4 95 31 54 80

EDUCATION
Rectorat de l'Académie
d'Aix-Marseille (Bouches-du-
Rhône, Vaucluse, Alpes-
Haute-de-Provence, Hautes-
Alpes)
place Lucien-Paye
13621 Aix-en-Provence
Cedex 1
Tel: +33 4 24 88 88
Fax: +33 4 42 26 68 03

Rectorat de l'Académie
de Nice (Alpes-Maritimes,
Var)
avenue Cap-de-Croix 53
06181 Nice Cedex
Tel: +33 4 93 53 70 70
Fax: +33 4 93 53 72 44

Rectorat de l'Académie de

Corse, BP 808
boulevard Rossini
20192 Ajaccio Cedex
Tel: +33 4 95 50 34 08
Fax: +33 4 95 51 27 06

HEALTH
Caisse Primaire d'Assurance
Maladie des Alpes-Maritimes
rue Roi Robert Comte 48
de Provence
06100 Nice
Tel: +33 4 92 09 40 00
Fax: +33 4 92 09 43 43

Caisse Primaire d'Assurance
Maladie d'Ajaccio, BP 910
boulevard Abbé Recco
Quartier Les Padules
20702 Ajaccio Cedex 9
Tel: +35 4 95 23 52 00
Fax: +33 4 95 20 64 74

€20-100,000
(£13-66,000)

The high demand for property on the Cote d'Azur means that bargains are a rarity. For under 100,000 euros it is possible to purchase a small, modern property, but in popular, in-demand areas such as Nice and other coastal resorts, this amount will only stretch to a one-bedroom apartment.

PRICE GUIDE

€43,000 CODE CAC

NICE, DÉPARTEMENT 06

A small ground floor studio in excellent condition, close to parkland

£28,665

🛏1 🪟with a 7m^2 terrace 🚌close to amenities 🚫located on a main road 🚗no private parking

€61,000 CODE CAC

NICE, DÉPARTEMENT 06

A fourth-floor studio, with an open plan kitchen and mountain views

£40,665

🛏1 🪟no garden 🚌located in the centre of town 🚫located on a main road 🚗no private parking

€76,000 CODE CAC

NICE, DÉPARTEMENT 06

A renovated studio apartment, located in an extremely popular area of Nice

£50,665

🛏1 🪟no garden, with balcony 🚌in town centre 🚫located on a main road 🚗parking spaces to rent nearby

€83,886 CODE IMO

NARBONNE, DÉPARTEMENT 11

An airy apartment with lovely views over the canal, enjoying a balcony

£55,924

🛏1 🪟with 7.4m^2 balcony 🚌close to amentites 🚫located on a main road 🚗no private parking

€100-200,000
(£66-133,000)

If an hour inland from the coastal resorts, villa
ces drop dramatically, and a villa for renovation
n fall within the 200,000 euros price bracket.
herwise, the choice is restricted to little more than
wo-bedroom apartment.

€100,000   CODE CAC

LA GARDE FREINET, DÉPARTEMENT 83

A charming mezzanine apartment, newly decorated and with a fitted kitchen

£66,665

🛏1 🌳*with a shared garden and pool* 🏪*within 5 mins of amenities*

🛣*not located on a main road* 🅿*room for parking*

€102,500   CODE HAP

NICE, DÉPARTEMENT 06

Close to the harbour and offering stunning views, an apartment requiring work

£68,335

🛏1/2 🌳*no garden* 🏪*close to all amenties* 🛣*not located on a main road*

🅿*no room for parking*

€105,930   CODE HAR

MOUGINS LE HAUT, DÉPARTEMENT 06

Set in a development, with tennis and swimming facilties, a studio apartment

£70,620

🛏1 🌳*with a terrace* 🏪*close to all amenities* 🛣*not located on a main road*

🅿*with private parking*

€117,386   CODE EJC

LE LUC-EN-PROVENCE, DÉPARTEMENT 83

An 18th-century Provençal house with a roof-top terrace and lovely views

£78,260

🛏3 🌳*2,000m^2* 🏪*within walking distance of amenities*

🛣*not located on a main road* 🅿*no private parking*

PRICE GUIDE

€138,000 — CODE HAP

NICE, DÉPARTEMENT 06

An apartment development, located in a desirable location, with open terraces

£92,000

🛏 1/4 🪴 with a balcony or terrace 🛒 close to all amenities

🛣 not located on a main road 🚗 with private parking

€146,800 — CODE HAP

NICE, DÉPARTEMENT 06

A small apartment, located on the third floor of a quiet, characterful building

£97,865

🛏 1 🪴 with no garden 🛒 close to all amenities 🛣 not located on a main road

🚗 no private parking

€155,000 — CODE HAR

CANNES, DÉPARTEMENT 06

An apartment set within a golfing development, well located near the beach

£103,335

🛏 2 🪴 with a garden and a terrace 🛒 close to all amenities

🛣 not located on a main road 🚗 with room for parking

€160,000 — CODE CAC

NICE, DÉPARTEMENT 06

An apartment with panoramic views from the terrace, ideal for family holidays

£106,665

🛏 1 🪴 with 8m^2 terrace 🛒 in town centre 🛣 located on a main road

🚗 no private parking, a garage can be purchased for extra cost

€164,650 — CODE HAR

CAVAILLON, DÉPARTEMENT 84

A town house, perfect for a second home, with a mature garden and balcony

£109,765

🛏 3 🪴 500m^2 🛒 within 5 mins of amenities 🛣 not located on a main road

🚗 room for parking

€168,000 — CODE AZU

AJACCIO, DÉPARTEMENT 2A

An apartment offering stunning views over the coastline from its 7m^2 terrace

£112,000

🛏 3 🪴 no garden 🛒 located in the town centre 🛣 located on a main road

🚗 room for parking, with a garage

€168,100   CODE CAC

NICE, DÉPARTEMENT 06

A charming apartment, located in the heart of Nice, and tastefully renovated

£112,065

⊟3 🏵no garden 🖼located close to amenities 🖼not located on a main road
🏠no private parking, room to park on the street

€170,500   CODE HAR

NICE, DÉPARTEMENT 06

Set on the top floor of a bourgeois-style building, a well-located modern flat

£113,665

⊟1 🏵no garden 🖼within 5 mins of amenities 🖼located on a main road
🏠no private parking

€176,000   CODE HAR

AVIGNON, DÉPARTEMENT 84

A spacious villa property, offering double glazing, located on the fourth floor

£117,335

⊟3 🏵no garden 🖼within 5 mins of amenities 🖼not located on a main road
🏠room for parking, with a secure car park

€187,650   CODE IMO

SAINT-RAPHAËL, DEPARTMENT 74

Houses on this development enjoy 50m^2 of living space and a balcony

£125,100

⊟2 🏵with shared gardens 🖼close to town amenities
🖼not located on a main road 🏠no private parking

€194,500   CODE HAP

NICE, DÉPARTEMENT 06

An apartment, recently refurbished, spacious and airy, set on the fourth floor

£129,665

⊟1 🏵no garden 🖼close to all amenities 🖼not located on a main road
🏠no room for parking

€197,640   CODE HAR

LUBERON, DÉPARTEMENT 84

Located in a rural area, a modern villa with stunning views

£117,335

⊟2 🏵729m^2 🖼within 5 mins of amenities 🖼not located on a main road
🏠room for parking, with a garage

PRICE GUIDE

€200-500,000
(£133-333,000)

A traditional farmhouse in a good state of repair should fall under the 500,000 euros mark, while coastal penthouse apartments can equal this price. In less popular coastal resorts comfortable properties with sea views can be had for less than 500,000 euros, as well, but areas around Nice and St-Tropez with sea views are still not readily affordable.

€210,000 — CODE DEE

SAINT-TROPAZ, DÉPARTEMENT 83

An apartment located in an 18th-century Provençal mansion, in a rural area

£140,000

⊟3 🚫no garden 🖼within 5 mins of village 🚫not located on a main road

🏠room for parking

€230,000 — CODE HAM

MERCANTILE NATIONAL PARK, DÉPARTEMENT 06

A mansion, located on the edge of the national park, ideal for a rural retreat

£153,335

⊟9 🏞35,000m² 🖼within 5 mins of village 🚫not located on a main road

🏠room for parking, with two garages

€252,000 — CODE LAT

MALLEMORT, DÉPARTEMENT 13

A housing development, located on a golf course, with landscaped gardens

£168,000

⊟3/4 🌳with garden 🖼close to development amenities

🚫not located on a main road 🏠Each house features a garage

€315,000 — CODE FRA

SAINT-RÉMY-DE-PROVENCE, DÉPARTEMENT 13

A stunning villa, situated within easy reach of this popular area, with a pool

£210,000

⊟2 🏞850m² 🖼within 5 mins of town 🚫not located on a main road

🏠room for parking

€325,000   CODE HAM

CLANS, DÉPARTEMENT 06

A modern villa, enjoying a luxurious garden area planted with olive trees

£216,665

🛏6 ▦2,279m² 📍located on the edge of the village

🚫not located on a main road 🅿room for parking, with a car port and garage

€325,000   CODE HAM

ENTREVAUX, DÉPARTEMENT 04

A stone villa, enjoying a balcony and terrace area, built in the 19th century

£216,665

🛏6 ▦40,000m² 📍near to town and amenities 🚫not located on a main road

🅿room for parking, with a garage

€330,000   CODE FRE

NICE, DÉPARTEMENT 06

A village house, located close to all amenities, offering a separate studio flat

£220,000

🛏2 ▦no garden, with balcony and terrace 📍within 5 mins of town

🚫located on a main road 🅿with on-road parking

€342,000+   CODE LAT

NICE, DÉPARTEMENT 06

A new villa development, with a shared swimming pool, close to the beach

£228,000+

🛏3/4 ▦400m² 📍20 mins from town 🚫not located on a main road

🅿Each villa comes with a garage

€356,620   CODE VEF

SERRES, DÉPARTEMENT 05

Located in a stunning valley overlooking the mountains, a villa with pool

£237,745

🛏5 ▦with large garden 📍within 5 mins of village 🚫not located on a main road

🅿room for parking, with a garage

€357,000   CODE HAM

TOURETTE-SUR-LOUP, DÉPARTEMENT 06

A Provençal stone property, with grounds boasting olive trees. With views

£238,000

🛏3 ▦1,600m² 📍close to village amenities 🚫not located on a main road

🅿room for parking, with a garage

PRICE GUIDE

€380,000 CODE LAT

VALBONNE, DÉPARTEMENT 06

A modern villa, set in a private development, with a fitted kitchen and terrace

£253,335

🛏3 🏵with a small garden 🚗within 5 mins drive of town centre

🚫not located on a main road 🏠room for parking, with a garage

€381,122 CODE FRA

ROQUESTERON, DÉPARTEMENT 06

A detached property, habitable, with splendid views over the southern Alps

£254,080

🛏3 🏵20,000m² 🚗3.5 kms from town and amenities

🚫not located on a main road 🏠room for parking

€381,123 CODE HAM

NR NICE, DÉPARTEMENT 06

An impressive detached 19th-century stone property, in excellent condition

£254,082

🛏3 🏵17,500m² 🚗close to village 🚫not located on a main road

🏠room for parking

€402,800 CODE EJC

LA MOTTE, DÉPARTEMENT 83

A superb 19th-century village property with a swimming pool and terrace

£268,535

🛏5 🏵with garden 🚗10 mins drive from town 🚫not located on a main road

🏠room for parking

€421,000 CODE AZU

PORTO-VECCHIO, DÉPARTEMENT 2A

An attractive and modern property, comprising of three separate villas

£280,665

🛏10 🏵with a large garden 🚗close to amenities 🚫not located on a main road

🏠with private parking and electric gates

€423,550 CODE VEF

SERRES, DÉPARTEMENT 05

A truly unique Provençal farmhouse, in a rural setting, with mountain views

£282,365

🛏4 🏵12,000m² 🚗close to town and amenities 🚫not located on a main road

🏠room for parking

€450,000 — CODE FRE

ISOLA, DÉPARTEMENT 06

Located in this popular ski resort, these properties offer excellent amenities

£300,000

⊟2 ⌂no garden ▨within 5 mins of resort amenities ▨not located on a main road ⌂room for parking

€457,000 — CODE FRA

SISTERON, DÉPARTEMENT 04

A luxurious villa, plus two-bedroom gite, set close to the mountains and coast

£304,665

⊟3 ⌂$3,437m^2$ ▨within 5 mins of village ▨not located on a main road ⌂room for parking

€468,628 — CODE EJC

LA LONDE, DÉPARTEMENT 83

A coastal villa, with panoramic views over the sea and countryside

£312,420

⊟3 ⌂with garden ▨close to amenities ▨not located on a main road ⌂room for parking

€474,000 — CODE FRA

MARIGNANE, DÉPARTEMENT 13

A totally renovated 19th-century farmhouse, close to the beach

£316,000

⊟3 ⌂$1,400m^2$ ▨within 5 mins from local amenities ▨not located on a main road ⌂room for parking

€487,800 — CODE DAV

SALERNES, DÉPARTEMENT 83

A recently constructed villa, in a rural area, with a swimming pool

£325,200

⊟5 ⌂$2,600m^2$ ▨2 kms from town ▨not located on a main road ⌂room for parking, with a garage

€499,000 — CODE EJC

ST PAUL DE VENCE, DÉPARTEMENT 06

A penthouse apartment with a spacious terrace and views of the coast

£332,665

⊟3 ⌂with large garden ▨within 5 mins of village ▨not located on a main road ⌂room for parking

PRICE GUIDE

€500,000+
(£333,000+)

Along the Nice and Saint-Tropez coastline the sky's the limit for villa prices, and upwards of 500,000 euros can secure anything from a luxurious penthouse apartment to a superbly restored 18th-century mansion, or a stunning modern villa. Most offer a private swimming pool and many can be built to order.

€686,000   CODE EJC
LE THORONET, DÉPARTEMENT 83
Fine restoration of an 18th-century mill house, with swimming pool
£457,335
🛏4 🏠2,000m² 🚗within 5 mins of town, only 10 mins from Nice
🛣not located on a main road 🏠room for parking, with a garage

€690,000   CODE EJC
ANTIBES, DÉPARTEMENT 06
A luxurious town house located in the centre of town, with a swimming pool
£460,000
🛏5 🏠2,023m² 🚗in town centre 🛣not located on a main road
🏠room for parking, with a garage for two cars

€731,755   CODE DEE
HYÈRES, DÉPARTEMENT 83
An 11th-century residence with turret, this property offers unparalleled views
£487,835
🛏6 🏠200m² 🚗within 2 mins from amenities 🛣located on a main road
🏠room for parking, with a garage

€823,224   CODE DEE
GAP, DÉPARTEMENT 04
Set in a protected area overlooking the Ubabye valley, an 18th-century house
£548,815
🛏2 🏠70,000m² 🚗50 kms from town 🛣not located on a main road
🏠garage for four cars

€965,000 CODE EJC

AUPS, DÉPARTEMENT 83

A stone-built country house with three cottages to renovate in the grounds

£643,335

🛏5 ⬚2,000m² 🏡close to the village ⊘not located on a main road

🚗room for parking, with a large garage

€976,000 CODE AZU

COGGIA, DÉPARTEMENT 2A

A modern villa with panoramic sea views, offering a living area of 181m²

£650,665

🛏4 ⬚2,500m² 🏡close to town amenities ⊘not located on a main road

🚗room for parking, with a garage for two cars

€980,000 CODE LAT

TOURRETTES-SUR-LOUP, DÉPARTEMENT 06

A south-facing villa, comprising of two apartments, with views over the coast

£653,335

🛏5 ⬚2,023m² 🏡near all amenities ⊘not located on a main road

🚗room for parking

€990,000 CODE FRE

VALBONNE, DÉPARTEMENT 06

A charming Provençal family villa, set in a private estate, offering sea views

£660,000

🛏n/a ⬚with large gardens 🏡within 5 mins of village ⊘not located on a main

road 🚗room for parking

€1,067,000 CODE DAV

FAYENCE, DÉPARTEMENT 83

A fully restored stone property, with a covered terrace and a swimming pool

£711,335

🛏6 ⬚2,872m² 🏡within 5 mins of village ⊘not located on a main road

🚗room for parking

€1,180,000 CODE DAV

LE GARDE FREINET, DÉPARTEMENT 83

A fully restored stone property with a separate apartment and swimming pool

£786,665

🛏4 ⬚5,300m² 🏡within 5 mins of village ⊘not located on a main road

🚗room for parking, with a garage

PRICE GUIDE

€1,260,000   CODE LAT

CANNES, DÉPARTEMENT 06

A private development comprising of five villas, with views over Cannes bay

£840,000

4   1,500m^2 close to town amenities   located on a private road

each villa includes a garage

€1,400,000   CODE LAT

SAINT-MAXIMIN-LA-SAINTE-BAUME, DÉPARTEMENT 13

An 18th-century mansion, with an adjoining apartment, and mountain views

£933,335

4   10,120m^2 within driving distance of amenities

not located on a main road   room for parking

€1,450,000   CODE DAV

SALERNES, DÉPARTEMENT 83

A restored stone property, in a rural location, with four outbuildings to convert

£966,665

3   350,000m^2 close to town amenities   not located on a main road

room for parking

€3,354,000   CODE DAV

SAINT-PAUL-DE-VENCE, DÉPARTEMENT 06

A magnificent stone villa, with landscaped gardens and views over the coast

£2,236,000

4   2,600m^2 within walking distance of town   not located on a main road

room for parking, with a double garage

€4,268,500   CODE LAT

VENCE, DÉPARTEMENT 06

A Provençal-style stone property, with a guest house, tennis courts and pool

£2,845,665

7   10,000m^2 close to amenities   not located on a main road

room for parking, with a garage

€6,400,000   CODE LAT

SAINT-TROPEZ, DÉPARTEMENT 83

A magnificent Italianate mansion, with two pools and a separate apartment

£4,266,665

9   8,094m^2 within 5 mins of village   not located on a main road

room for parking

PRICE GUIDE

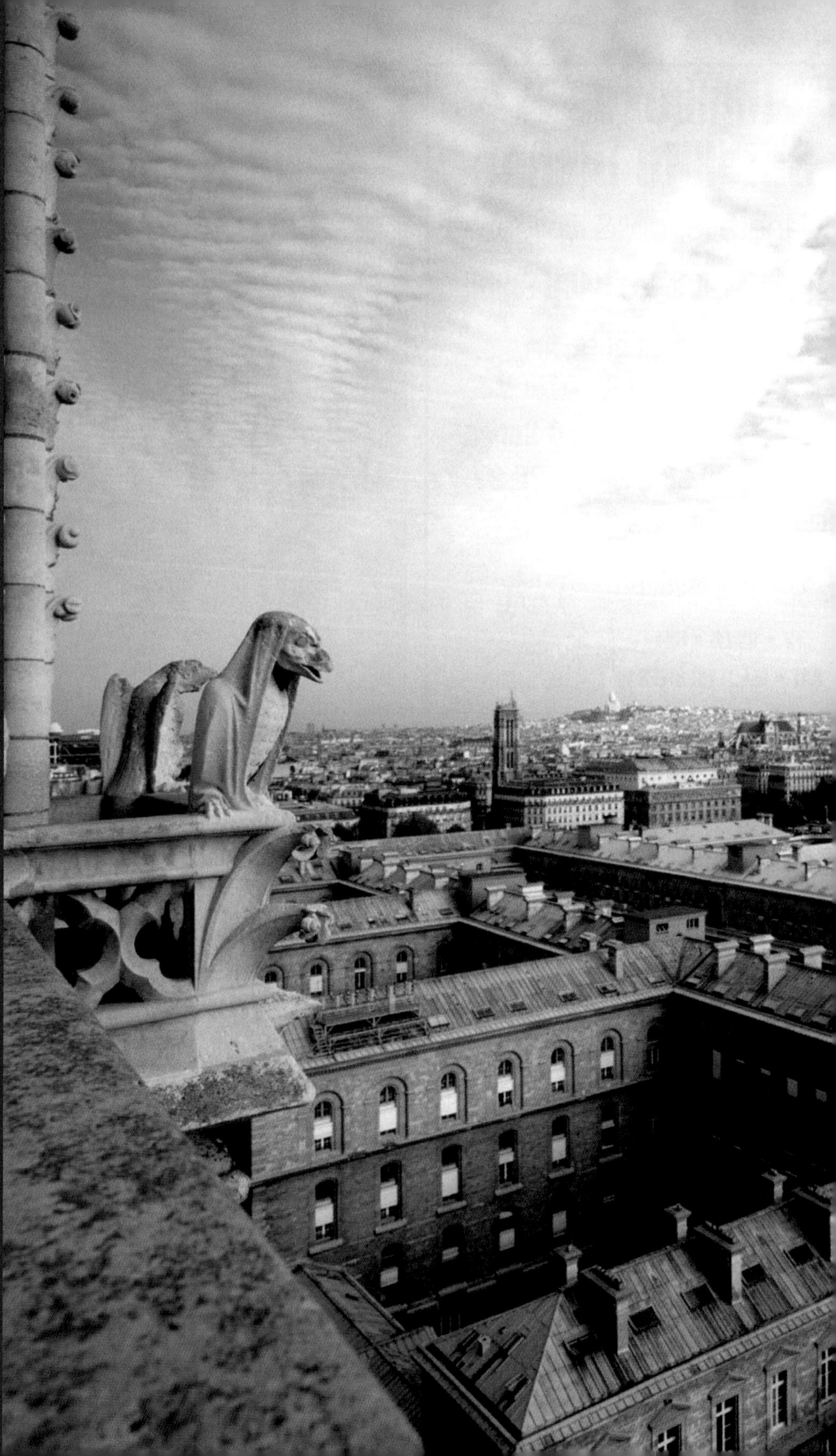

FELIX STENSSON/ALAMY

Average Lettings matrices
Directory of Contacts
Index To Agents

Buyer's Reference

REFERENCE

Average House Price Matrix 334
Average Flat Price Matrix 337
Average Letting's revenues 340

USEFUL INFORMATION
Glossary Of Useful Terms 343
Directory of Contacts 346
Index To Agents 358
Index 366
Index To Advertisers 370

Prices can vary dramatically
across the various
arrondissements of Paris

House sale prices

SUB REGION	2-BED	3-BED	4 BED	5 BED	6/7 BED	8-BED
1er	€500K (£333.5K)	€750K (£500K)	€1.06M (£1M)	-	-	€2M (£1.5M)
2ème	€500K (£333.5K)	€750K (£500K)	-	€960K (£640K)	-	€2M (£1.5M)
3ème	€500K (£333.5K)	€750K (£500K)	€1.06M (£1M)	-	-	€2M (£1.5M)
4ème	€500K (£333.5K)	€750K (£500K)	€1.06M (£1M)	-	-	€2M (£1.5M)
6ème	€305K (£203.5K)	-	-	-	-	-
7ème	-	-	-	-	-	-
8ème	-	-	-	-	-	€3.2M (£2M)
16ème	€600K (£400K)	-	-	-	-	-
17ème	€600K (£400K)	-	-	-	-	-
Agen	€100K (£66K)	€210K (£140K)	€350K (£233.5K)	€500K (£333.5K)	€680K (£453.5K)	€1M (£666K)
Aix-en-Provence	€200K (£133.5K)	-	€554K (£369.5K)	€647K (£431.5K)	€890K £595K)	€1.6M (£1.1M)
Amiens	€188K (£125K)	€367K (£244K)	€433K (£289K)	€438K (£288.5K)	€454K (£302.5K)	-
Angers	€120K (£80K)	€210K (£140K)	€210K (£140K)	-	€355K (£235K)	-
Antibes	€2M (£1.5M)	-	€2M (£1.5M)	-	€3.5M (£2.5M)	-
Archachon	€96.5K (£64.5K)	€235K (£156.5K)	€265K (£176.5K)	€427K (£284.5K)	€562.5K (£375K)	-
Auvergne lakes	-	-	-	-	-	-
Auxerre	-	-	-	-	-	-
Avranches	€75K (£50K)	€98K (£65.5K)	€113K (£75.5K)	€215K (£143.5K)	€225K (£150K)	€240K (£160K)
Bagneres/Bigorre	-	-	-	-	-	-
Bayonne	-	-	€266K (£177.5K)	-	€502K (£334.5K)	€644K (£429.5K)
Beaujolais	€175K (£115K)	-	-	-	-	-
Bergerac	-	-	-	€338K (£225.5K)	€400K (£266.5K)	-
Besançon	-	-	€225K (£150K)	€260K (£170K)	€350K (£233K)	-
Beziers-Narbonne	€255K (£170K)	€330K (£220K)	€460K (£306.5K)	€510K (£340K)	-	€855K (£570K)
Biarritz	€120K (£80K)	-	-	-	€375K (£250K)	-
Bordeaux	-	€170K (£113.5K)	€265K (£176)	€288.5K (£192.5K)	€375K (£250K)	-
Brest	€105K (£70K)	€120K (£80K)	€150K (£100K)	€225K (£150K)	€255K (£170K)	€375K (£250K)
Briançon	€230K (£153.5K)	-	-	-	-	€1.4M (£933K)
Caen	€113K (75.5K)	€128K (£85.5K)	€165K (£110K)	€210K (£140K)	€300K (£200K)	€375K (£250K)
Cahors/Rocam	€100K (£66.5K)	-	-	-	-	€1M (£666K)
Cannes	-	€350K (£233.5K)	-	€2.5M (£1.5M)	-	-
Cap Ferret	-	-	€265K (£176.5)	-	€375K (£250K)	-
Carcassone	€200K (£133.5K)	€260K (£173.5K)	€360K (£240K)	€400K (£266.5K)	-	€800K (£533.5K)
Céret Banylus	€275K (£183.5K)	€358K (£238.5K)	€500K (£333.5K)	€550K (£366.5K)	-	€1M (£666K)
Châlons	-	€100K (£66.5K)	€175K (£116.5K)	€210K (£140K)	€210K (£140K)	-
Chamonix	-	-	-	€120K (£80K)	€120K (£80K)	-
Charente	€115K (£76.5K)	€150K (£100K)	-	€240K (£160K)	€650K (£433.5K)	-
Charleville-Méz	-	€120K (£80K)	€122K (£81.5K)	€154K (£102.5K)	€170K (£113.5K)	€244.5K (£163K)

SUB REGION	2-BED	3-BED	4 BED	5 BED	6/7 BED	8-BED
Châtellerault	-	€94K (£62.5K)	€101.5K (£67.5K)	€129.5K (£86.5K)	€270K (£180K)	-
Clermont-Ferrand	-	€110K (£73.5K)	€170K (113.5K)	€225K (£150K)	-	-
Corrèze	€105K (£70K)	-	€158K (£105.5K	-	-	-
Côte d'Or	€120K (£80K)	€150K (£100K)	€200K (£133K)	€300K (£200K)	-	-
Courchevel	€120K (£80K)	€120K (£80K)	€120K (£80K)	-	-	-
Deauv/Trouville	€120K (£80K)	€135K (£90K)	€189K (£126K)	€233K (£155.5K)	€315K (£210K)	€450K (£300K)
Dieppe	-	-	-	-	€238K (£158.5K)	-
Dijon	€110K (£73.5K)	-	-	-	-	-
Dinan	-	-	€208K (£138.5K)	-	-	-
Dinard	€128K (£85.5K)	€150K (£100K)	€315K (£210K)	€240K (£160K)	€315K (£210K)	€375K (£250K)
Dordogne	€100K (£66.5K)	€210K (£140K)	€350K (£233.5K)	€500K (£333.5K)	€680K (£453.5K)	€1M (£666K)
Épernay	-	-	€190K (£126.5K)	€230K (£153.5K)	-	-
Gers/Gascony	€120K (£80K)	€140K (£93.5K)	€170K (£113.5K)	€210K (£140K)	€290K (£193.5K)	€400K (£266.5K)
Grenoble	-	€120K (£80K)	-	€120K (£80K)	€190K (£125K)	-
Guingamp	€113K (£75.5K)	€135K (£90K)	€120K (£80K)	€150K (£100K)	€180K (£120K)	€225K (£150K)
Hesdin	€148K (£98.5K)	€115K (£76.5K)	€150K (£100K)	€400K (£266.5K)	€500K (£333.5K)	€600K (£400K)
Honfleur	€96K (£64K)	-	-	-	-	-
Ile-de-Ré/ La Roch	€175K (£116.5K)	€185K (£123.5K)	€215K (£143.5K)	-	-	-
Inland Calvados	€95K (£63.5K)	€257K (£171.5K)	€253K (£168.5K)	€450K (£300K)	€450K (£300K)	€543K (£362K)
Lake Annecy	-	€300K (£200K)	€360K (£240K)	-	€1.5M (£1M)	-
Lake Geneva	€120K (£80K)	€120K (£80K)	€120K (£80K)	-	-	-
La Roche Posay	-	-	-	-	-	-
Le Mans	€92K (£61.5K)	-	€123.5K (£82.5K)	€161.5K (£107.5K)	€198K (£132K)	€334K (£222.5K)
Le Portes/Soleil	€220K (£146.5K)	-	€395K (£263.5K)	€1.5M (£1M)	-	-
Les Menuires	-	-	-	-	-	-
Le Touquet	€180K (£120K)	€225K (£150K)	€300K (£200K)	€525K (£350K)	€600K (£400K)	€900K (£600K)
Lille	€148K (£98.5K)	€115K (£76.5K)	€150K (£100K)	€400K (£266.5K)	€500K (£333.5K)	€600K (£400K)
Limoges	€75K (£50K)	€120K (£80K)	€170K (£113.5K)	€225K (£150K)	€300K (£200K)	€500K (£333.5K)
Lons-le-Saunier	-	€110K (£73.5K)	€130K (£86.5K)	-	€200K (£133.5K)	€210K (£140K)
Lorient	€105K (£70K)	€120K (£80K)	€150K (£100K)	€225K (£150K)	€255K (£150K)	€375K (£250K)
Lot-et-Garonne	-	-	-	-	-	-
Lyon	-	€183.5K (£122K)	€282K (£188K)	€297.5K (£198.5K)	€462K (£308K)	€880K (£586.5K)
Marseille	€249.5K (£166K)	€250K (£166.5K)	€280.5K (£187K)	€409.5K (£273K)	€465K (£310K)	€700K (£466.5K)
Megève	-	-	€2.2M (£1.5M)	-	-	-
Méribel	-	-	-	-	-	-
Metz	-	€215K (£143.5K)	€200K (£133.5K)	-	€350K (£233.5K)	-
Montpellier	€300K (£200K)	€390K (£260K)	€540K (£360K)	€600K (£400K)	-	€1.2M (£800K)
Montreuil	€148K (£98.5K)	€334K (£222.5K)	€355K (£236.5K)	€355K (£236.5K)	€500K (£333.5K)	€600K (£400K)

HOUSES

House sale prices

SUB REGION	2-BED	3-BED	4 BED	5 BED	6/7 BED	8-BED
Morbihan	€113K (£75.5K)	€128K (£85.5K)	€165K (£110K)	€203K (£135.5K)	€300K (£200K)	€450K (£300K)
Morvan	€75K (£50K)	€100K (£66.5K)	€135K (£90K)	€165K (£110K)	-	-
Nancy	-	€230K (£153.5K)	€260K (£173.5K)	-	-	-
Nantes	€200K (£133.5K)	-	€350K (£233.5K)	-	-	-
Nice	-	-	€500K (£333.5K)	€500K (£333.5K)	€750K (£500)	-
Nîmes	€255K (£170K)	€330K (£220K)	€459K (£306K)	€510K (£340K)	-	€855K (£570K)
Orléans	€200K (£133.5K)	-	€335K (£223.5K)	-	€425K (£283.5K)	-
Perpignan	€250K (£166.5K)	€350K (£233.5K)	€450K (£300K)	€500K (£333.5K)	-	€1M (£666K)
Poitiers	€100K (£66.5K)	€160K (£106.5K)	€180K (£120K)	€395K (£263.5K)	-	-
Porto Veccio	€270K (£180K)	-	-	-	-	-
Quimper	€120K (£80K)	€168K (£112K)	-	€185K (£123.5K)	€215K (£143.5K)	€406K (£270.5K)
Reims	€45K (£30K)	€160.5K (£107K)	-	€201K (£134K)	€261.5K (£174.5K)	-
Rennes	-	€120K (£80K)	-	€354.5K (£236.5K)	-	€565K (£376.5K)
Rouen	€113K (75.5K)	€128K (£85.5K)	€165K (£110K)	€210K (£140K)	€400K (£266.5K)	-
Saint-Malo	€75K (£50K)	€98K (£65.5K)	€128K (£85.5K)	€165K (£110K)	€210K (£140K)	€300K (£200K)
Saint Rémy	-	-	-	-	-	-
Saint Tropez	€1M (£666K)	-	€2.5M (£1.5M)	-	-	-
Sarlat	-	-	-	-	-	-
Saumur	-	€138K (£92K)	€138K (£92K)	€193K (£128.5K)	€213K (£142K)	€299.5K (£199.5K)
Somme Valley	-	-	-	-	-	-
Strasbourg	-	-	€250K (£166.5K)	€300K (£200K)	€600K (£400K)	-
Toulon	-	€154K (£102.5K)	€259K (£172.5K)	€340K (£226.5K)	-	€620.5K (£413.5K)
Toulouse	€43K (£28.5K)	€181K (£120.5K)	€223.5K (£149K)	€277.5K (£184.5K)	€366K (£244K)	€427.5K (£285K)
Tourraine	€120K (£80K)	-	€365K (£243.5K)	-	-	-
Tours	€120K (£80K)	€131K (£87.5K)	€173K (£115.5K)	€186K (£124K)	€281K (£187.5K)	€296K (£197.5K)
Val d'Isere	-	€250K (£166.5K)	-	€3M (£2M)	-	-
Vallée des Lacs	-	-	-	-	€350K (£233.5K)	-
Var	-	-	-	-	-	-
Vaucluse	-	€300K (£200K)	-	-	-	-
Vendée	€135K (£90K)	€165K (£110K)	€200K (£133.5K)	€235K (£156.5K)	-	-
Versailles	€385K (£256.5K)	-	€686K (£457.5K)	-	-	€1.5K (£1M)
Vichy	-	-	€400K (£266.5)	€400K (£266.5)	-	-
Vosges	-	-	€195K (£130K)	€125K (£83.5K)	€200K (£133.5K)	-

Apartment sale prices

SUB REGION	STUDIO	1-BED	2/3-BED	4/5 BED	6/7 BED	8-BED
1er	€200K (£133.5K)	€380K (£253.5K)	€590K (£393.5K)	€1.6M (£1M)	-	€1.5M (£1M)
2ème	€200K (£133.5K)	€400K (£266.5K)	€802K (£534.5K)	€802K (£534.5K)	-	-
3ème	€200K (£133.5K)	€330K (£220K)	€1.2M (£800K)	€1.2M (£800K)	€900K (£600K)	€2.9M (£1.9M)
4ème	€200K (£133.5K)	€400K (£266.5K)	€750K (£500K)	€1.2M (£800K)	-	-
6ème	€155K (£103.5K)	€400K (£266.5K)	€740K (£493.5K)	€2M (£1.5M)	€1.8M (£1.2M)	€2.9M (£1.9M))
7ème	€205K (£136.5K)	€440K (£293.5K)	€888K (£592K)	€1.5M (£1M)	€2.5M (£1.5M)	€4.1M (£2.7M)
8ème	€200K (£133.5K)	€400K (£266.5K)	€1.5M (£1M)	€2M (£1.5M)	€1.5M (£1M)	-
16ème	€200K (£133.5K)	€425K (£283.5K)	€1.5M (£1M)	€1.5M (£1M)	€2M (£1.5M)	€2.3M (£1.5M)
17ème	€200K (£133.5K)	€425K (£283.5K)	€559K (£372.5K)	€1.5M (£1M)	€2M (£1.5M)	€2.3M (£1.5M)
Agen	€30K (£20K)	€66.5K (£44.5K)	€122K (£81.5K)	€168K (£112K)	€250.2K (£166.8K)	-
Aix-en-Provence	€105K (£70K)	€219K (£146K)	€540K (£360K)	€577.8K (£385.2K)	€900K (600K)	-
Amiens	-	€97K (£64.5K)	€137K (£91.5)	€180K (£120K)	-	-
Antibes	€150K (£100K)	€183K (£122K)	€337K (£224.5K)	€480K (£320K)	-	-
Auvergne lakes	€86K (£57.5K)	-	€209K (£139.5K)	€383K (£255.5K)	-	-
Bay of Archachon	€86K (£57.5K)	€108K (£72K)	€234K (£156K)	€377K (£251.5K)	€459K (£306K)	-
Beaujolais	-	-	€86K (£57.5K)	-	-	-
Besançon	-	€69.7K (£46.5K)	€78K (£52K)	€137K (£91.5K)	€150K (£100K)	E614K (£409.3K)
Bergerac	-	-	-	€80K (£53.5K)		
Beziers-Narbonne	€50K (£33.5K)	€80K (£53.5K)	€125K (£83.5K)	€180K (£120K)	€290K (£193.5K)	€350K (£233.5K)
Biarritz	€120K (£80K)	-	€239.5K (£159.5K)	€343.5K (£229K)	€377K (£251.5K)	-
Bordeaux	€124K (£82.6K)	€126K (£84K)	€222K (£148K)	€222K (£148K)	€367K (£244.6K)	-
Caen	€26K (£17.5K)	€66K (£44K)	€112K (£74.5K)	€212K (£141.5K)	-	-
Cannes	€600K (£400K)	€600K (£400K)	€700K (466.6K)	-	€1M (£666K)	
Cap Ferret	-	€80K (£53.5K)	€120K (£80K)	€150K (£100K)	€200K (£133.5K)	-
Carcassone	-	€80K (£53.5K)	€120K (£80K)	€150K (£100K)	€200K (£133.5K)	-
Céret & Banylus	-	€80K (£53.5K)	€120K (£80K)	€150K (£100K)	€200K (£133.5K)	-
Chamonix	-	-	€600K (£400K)	-	-	-
Charleville-Méz	-	-	-	€108K (£72K)	€168K (£112K)	-
Châtellerault	-	-	-	€140K (£93.5K)	-	-
Clermont-Ferrand	-	€68K (£45.5K)	€154.5K (£103K)	€189K (£126K)	-	-
CorrÈze	-	-	€200K (£133.5K)	€300K (£200K)	-	-
Courchevel	-	-	€600K (£400K)	-	-	-
Dieppe	-	€78K (£52K)	€109K (£72.5K)	€185K (£123.5K)	-	-
Dijon	€49K (£32.5K)	€60K (£40K)	€130K (£86.5K)	€145K (£96.5K)	-	-
Deauv/Trouv	€61.4K (£40.9K)	€147K (£98K)	€162.5K (£108.5K)	€300K (£200K)	-	-
Dinan	€52.5K (£35K)	-	€106K (£70.5K)	-	-	-
Dinard	€52.5K (£35K)	€106K (£70.5K)	€168K (£112K)	€214K (£142.5K)	-	-
Épernay	-	-	€360K (£240K)	-	-	-

Apartment sale prices

SUB REGION	STUDIO	1-BED	2/3-BED	4/5 BED	6/7 BED	8-BED
Golfe du Morb	€50K (£33.5K)	€70K (£46.5K)	€112K (£74.5K)	-	-	-
Grenoble	-	-	€169.5K (£113K)	€219K 9 (£146K)	-	
Guingamp	€40K (£26.5K)	€70K (£46.5K)	€110K (£73.5K)	-	-	-
Honfleur	€35K (£23.5K)	-	€103K (£68.5K)	€265K (£176.5K)	-	
Ile-de-Ré/ La Roch		€70K (£46.5K)	€106.5K (£71K)	€165.5K (£110.5K)	€304K (£202.5K)	€327K (£218K) -
Lake Annecy	-	€150K (£100K)	€265K (£176.5K)	-	-	
Le Mans	€37K (£24.5K)	€81.5K (£54.5K)	€85.5K (£57K)	-	-	-
Les Portes/Soleil	-	€380K (£253.5K)	€380K (£253.5K)	-	-	-
Le Touquet	€120K (£80K)	€128K (£85.3K)	€225K (£150K)	-	-	-
Lille	€50K (£33.5K)	€68K (£45.5K)	€170K (£113.5K)	-	-	-
Limoges	€47K (£31.5K)	€50K (£33.5K)	€83K (£55.5K)	€122K (£81.5K)	-	-
Lorient	-	-	€92.7K (£61.8K)	€124.9K (£83.3K)	€149K (£99.3K)	-
Lyon	€60K (£40K)	€138K (£92K)	-	-	-	
Marseille	€61K (£40.5K)	-	€189.5K (£126.5K)	-	-	
MegÈve	€130K (£86.5K)	€220K (£146.5K)	€220K (£146.5K)	-	-	
Méribel	€130K (£86.5K)	-	€600K (£400K)	€600K (£400K)	-	-
Metz	-	€62.5K (£41.5K)	€72.5K (£48.5K)	-	-	
Montepellier	-	€80K (£53.5K)	€120K (£80K)	€150K (£100K)	€200K (£133.5K)	-
Montreuil	-	€89.7K (£59.8K)	€144.2K (£96.1K)	€299K (£199.3K)	€381K (£254K)	€425K (£283.3K)
Nancy	€40.1K (£26.7K)	€67.7K (£45.1K)	€109K (£72.6K)	€178.7K (£191.1K)		
Nantes	€71.6K (£47.7K)	€147.5K (£98.3K)	€263.8K (£175.9K)	-	-	
Nice	€76K (£50.5K)	€198K (£132K)	€250K (£166.5K)	€280K (£186.5K)	-	
Nîmes	-	-	€125K (£83.5K)	€217K (£144.5K)	€220K (£146.5K)	-
Perpignan	€38K (£25.5K)	€50K (£33.5K)	€80K (£53.5K)	€120K (£80K)	-	-
Poitiers	€30K (£20K)	€80K (£53.5K)	€150K (£100K)	-	-	-
Porto Veccio	-	-	-	-	-	-
Reims	€57.7K (£38.5K)	€91K (£60.6K)	€150K (£100K)	€290.5K (£193.7K)	-	-
Rennes	-	-	€145K (£96.6K)			
Rouen	-	-	€46.5K (£31K)	€68.6K (£45.7K)		
Saint Malo	€35K (£23.5K)	-	-	-	-	-
Saint Tropez	-	€135K (£90K)	€210K (£140K)	€610K (£406.5K)	-	-
Saumur	-	-	€66.5K (£44.5K)	€85K (£56.5K)	-	-
Somme Valley	€133K (£88.5K)	€136K (£90.5K)	€192K (£128K)	-	-	-
Strasbourg	-	€140.9K (£93.9K)	€202.3K (£134.8K)	-	-	-
Toulon	-	€98K (£65.3K)	€159.6K (£106.4K)	€484K (£322.6K)	-	-
Toulouse	€71K (£47.5K)	€95.5K (£63.5K)	€179K (£119.5K)	-	-	-
Var	-	-	€128K (£85.5K)	-	-	-
Vendée	-	€87K (£58K)	€179K (£119.5K)	-	-	-

Letting prices

SUB REGION	2-BED	3-BED	4 BED	5 BED	6/7 BED	8-BED
1er	€2.1K (£1.4K)	-	-	-	-	-
2ème	€3K (£2K)	-	-	-	-	-
3ème	€1.5K (£1K)	-	-	-	-	-
4ème	€2.5K (£1.5K)	€5K(£3.5)	-	-	-	-
6ème	€2.5K (£1.6K)	€3K (2K)	€3K (2K)	-	-	-
7ème	€3.5K (£2.3K)	€6K (£4K)	-	-	-	-
8ème	€4.5K (£3K)	€4.5K (£3K)	-	-	-	-
16ème	-	€4.5K (£3K)	€7K (£4.5K)	-	-	-
17ème	€2K (£1.5K)	€5.5K (£3.5K)	-	-	-	-
Agen	-	-	-	-	-	-
Aix-en-Provence	€585 (£390)	€845 (£563)	€845 (£563)	€2.4K (£1.6K)	€2.4K (£1.6K)	-
Amiens	-	-	-	-	-	-
Angers	€570 (£380)	€655 (£436)	€656 (£438)	-	€890 (£593)	€660 (£440)
Antibes	€590 (£395)	€975 (£650)	€815 (£543)	-	€2.5K (£1.6K)	€2.5K (£1.6K)
Arcachon	-	-	-	-	-	-
Auvergne Lakes	-	-	-	-	-	-
Auxerre	€670 (£446)	-	€670 (£446)	-	€1.2K (£800)	€1.2K (£800)
Avranches	€405 (£270)	-	-	-	-	€600 (£400)
Bagnerres/Bigorre	-	-	-	-	-	-
Bayonne	€412 (£275)	€900 (£600)	-	-	€1.2 (£800)	€1.6K (£665K)
Beaujolais	€115 (£77)	€1.5K (£1K)	€1.5K (£1K)	€1.5K (£1K)	€1.5K (£1K)	-
Bergerac	-	-	-	-	-	-
Besançon	-	-	-	-	-	-
Beziers/Narbonne	-	-	-	-	-	-
Biarritz	€415 (£276)	€900 (£600)	-	-	€1.2 (£800)	€1.6K (£1K)
Bordeaux	€485 (£325)	-	-	-	-	€2,011K (£1,340K)
Brest	-	-	-	-	-	-
Briançon	€600 (£400)	€1.1K (£730)	€1.5K (£1K)	€1.3K (£865)	€1.5K (£1)	-
Caen	€542 (£362)	-	€1,148 (£766)	-	€600 (£400)	€934 (£623)
Cahors/Rocam	-	-	€700 (£466)	€700 (£466)	€700 (£466)	€900 (£600)
Cannes	€800 (£534)	€985(£656)	€1.5K (£1K)	€1.6K (£1.1K)	€1.6K (£1.1)	€2K (£1.3K)
Cap Ferret	€415 (£276)	€900 (£600)	-	-	€825 (£550)	€2K (£1.3K)
Carcassone	-	-	-	-	-	-
Céret Banylus	€640 (£426)	€805 (£536)	€865 (£576)	€1.5K (£1K)	€1.5K (£1K)	€1.7K (£1.1K)
Châlons	-	-	€220 (£146)	€360 (£240)	-	-
Chamonix	€1.3K (£865)	€1.3K (£865)	€1.3K (£865)	-	-	€2.1K (£1.4K)
Charente	€525 (£350)	€570 (£380)	€670 (£446)	-	€670 (£446)	€1.3K (£865)
Charleville-Méz	-	-	€200 (£154)	€250 (£167)	-	-

Letting prices

SUB REGION	2-BED	3-BED	4 BED	5 BED	6/7 BED	8-BED
Châtellerault	€400 (£267)	€500 (£333)	€500 (£333)	-	€710 (£473)	€1.6K (£1.1K)
Clermont-Ferrand	€175 (£117)	€175 (£117)	€325 (£216)	€200 (£133)	€200 (£133)	-
Corrèze	€200 (£133)	-	€450 (£300)	€450 (£300)	-	-
Côte d'Or	€550 (£366)	-	€670 (£446)	-	€830 (£555)	-
Courchevel	€450 (£300)	-	€450 (£300)	€450 (£300)	€450 (£300)	-
Deauville/Trouville-		€675 (£450)	-	-	-	€1.5K (£1K)
Dieppe	€300 (£200)	€430 (£287)	€750 (£500)	-	-	€1.1K (£730)
Dijon	€670 (£446)	-	€670 (£446)	-	€1.2K (£800)	€1.2K (£800)
Dinan	€375 (£250)	-	-	-	-	-
Dinard	-	-	-	-	-	-
Dordogne	€995 (£633)	€810 (£540)	€810 (£540)	-	€800 (£533)	€1.3K (£865)
Épernay	-	€215 (£145)	€305 (£203)	€360 (£240)	-	-
Gers/Gascony	€400 (£265)	€470 (£315)	€585 (£390)	€1.5K (£1K)	€1.5K (£1K)	€2K (£1.3K)
Grenoble	€165 (£110)	-	-	-	-	-
Guingamp	-	-	-	-	-	-
Hesdin	-	-	-	-	-	-
Honfleur	€450 (£300)	€540 (£360)	-	€805 (£536)	-	-
Ile de Ré/La Roch	€385 (£256)	€585 (£392)	€495 (£330)	€805 (£537)	€1K (£665)	€1.6K (£1.1K)
Inland Calvados	-	-	-	-	-	-
Lake Annecy	€1.5(£1K)	€920 (£614)	-	-	-	-
Lake Geneva	-	€825 (£550)	€825 (£550)	€1.6K (£1.1K)	€1.6K (£1.1K)	€1.6K (£1.1K)
La Roche-Posay	-	-	-	-	-	-
Le Mans	-	€655(£436)	-	-	-	-
Les Portes	€830 (£555)	€1.1K (£735)	€880 (£587)	€990 (£660)	€1.6K (£1.1K)	€1.7K (£1.2K)
Les Menuires	€1.5K (£1K)	-	-	-	-	-
Le Touquet	-	-	-	-	-	-
Lille	-	-	-	-	-	-
Limoges	€190 (£126)	€190 (£126)	-	-	-	-
Lons-le-Saunier	-	-	-	-	-	-
Lorient	€600 (£400)	€600 (£400)	€600 (£400)	-	-	-
Lot-et Garonne	-	-	-	-	-	-
Lyon	-	-	-	-	-	-
Marseille	€700 (£466)	€910 (£606)	€1.2K (£800)	€1.2K (£800)	€1.2K (£800)	-
Megève	€750 (£500)	-	-	-	-	-
Méribel	€1.5 (£1K)	-	-	-	-	-
Metz	-	-	-	-	-	-
Montpellier	-	-	-	-	-	-
Montreuil	-	-	-	-	-	-

SUB REGION	2-BED	3-BED	4 BED	5 BED	6/7 BED	8-BED
Morbihan	€320 (£213)	-	€385 (£256)	€1.5K (£1K)	-	€1.8K (£1.2K)
Morvan	€670 (£445)	-	€670 (£445)	-	€1.2K (£800)	€1.2K (£800)
Nancy	-	-	-	-	-	-
Nantes	-	€655(£436)	-	-	-	-
Nice	€685 (£456)	€850 (£567)	€945 (£630)	-	€950 (£633)	€1.6K (£1.1K)
Nîmes	-	-	-	-	-	-
Orléans	-	-	-	-	-	-
Perpignan	-	-	-	-	-	-
Poitiers	-	-	-	-	-	-
Porto Veccio	-	-	-	-	-	-
Quimper	-	-	-	-	-	-
Reims	-	€215 (£143)	€305 (£203)	€360 (£240)	-	-
Rennes	-	-	-	-	€345 (£230)	-
Rouen	-	€565 (£376)	-	-	-	-
Saint-Malo	€580 (£387)	-	€600 (£400)	-	-	-
Saint Rémy	-	-	-	-	-	-
Saint Tropez	€885 (£590)	€770 (£514)	€770 (£514)	-	€1.4K (£935)	€1.8K (£1.2K)
Sarlat	-	-	-	-	-	-
Saumur	€570 (£380)	€660(£440)	€660(£440)	-	€890 (£595)	€660 (£440)
Somme Valley	-	-	-	-	-	-
Strasbourg	-	-	-	-	-	-
Toulon	€900 (£600)	€950 (£634)	€1.4K (£935)	-	-	-
Toulouse	-	-	€1.3K (£865)	€1.3K (£865)	-	-
Tourraine	€590 (£393)	€660(£440)	-	-	-	€1.3K (£865
Tours	€590 (£393)	€660(£440)	-	-	-	€1.3K (£865)
Val d'Isere	-	-	-	-	-	-
Vallée des Lacs	-	-	-	-	-	-
Var	€700 (£467)	€815 (£544)	€1.5K (£1K)	-	€2.1K (£1.4K)	€2.1K (£1.4K)
Vaucluse	€845 (£563)	€980 (£653)	€940 (£626)	€1.3K (£865)	€1.5K (£1K)	€1.7K (£1.2K)
Vendée	€365 (£245)	€655(£436)	€720 (£480)	-	€720 (£480)	€1.5K (£1K)
Versaille	-	-	-	-	-	-
Vichy	-	-	-	-	-	-
Vosges	-	-	-	-	-	-

LETTING

Glossary

A Glossary of useful terms and phrases relating to legal and financial aspect of purchasing a house, and the property market

A

acompte nm
deposit

acte nm
deed

* **acte authentique**
deed; conveyance

* **acte authentique de vente**
conveyance

* **acte de vente**
conveyance

agent immobilier nm
estate agent

architecte nmf
architect

artisan nm
builder; skilled craftsman

assurance multirisques habitation nf
comprehensive household insurance

B

bail nm
lease

bastide nf
Provençal country house

bâtiment nm
building

C

caisse nf
office; fund

* **caisse primaire d'assurance maladie**
state health insurance centre

carte nf
card; permit

* **carte de séjour**
residence permit

* **carte grise**
car registration document

* **carte professionelle**
professional licence

cave nf
cellar

caveau nm
small cellar

centre des impôts nm
local tax office

certificat nm
certificate

* **certificat de conformité**
certificate of compliance

* **certificat d'urbanisme**
planning permission certificate

chambre nf
bedroom; chamber

* **chambre des notaires**
chamber of notaries

* **chambre de(s) métiers**
chamber of trade

* **chambres d'hôte**
bed and breakfast; bed and breakfast rooms

chauffage nm
heating

clause nf
clause

* **clause pénale**
penalty clause

* **clause suspensive**
get-out clause

* **clause tontine**
survivorship clause

colombage nm
half-timbering

compromis de vente nm
sales contract

conservation des hypothèques nf
land registry

contrat nm
contract

* **contrat de réservation**
reservation contract for a property still to be constructed

cotisation nf
contributions

contribution sociale nf
social charge

copie authentique nf
certified copy

copropriété nf
co-ownership

* **charges de copropriété**
maintenance/service charges for flats

* **immeuble en copropriété**
block of flats

cuisine nf
kitchen

D

demande de prêt nf
loan application

département nm
administrative area

dépendance nf
outbuilding

dépôt de garantie nm
deposit

domicile nm
place of residence;home

droit nm
right; duty; law

* **droit de préemption**
right of first refusal

* **droits de succession** inheritance tax

* **droit de timbre**
stamp duty

duplex nm
maisonette

E

eau de la ville nf
mains water

en propriété libre adv
freehold

expert immobilier nm
valuer

expertise nf
valuation; survey

F

ferme nf
farm; farmhouse

fermette nf
small farmhouse

fosse septique nf
septic tank

G

gendarmerie nf
police station

géomètre nm
land surveyor

grange nf
barn

grenier nm
attic

H

hypothèque nf
mortgage; remortgage

I

immobilier nm
property

impôt nm
tax

* **impôt sur les plus-values**
capital gains tax

* **impôt sur le revenu des personnes**

"Finance your dream."

or How to acquire property in France.

You're interested in buying property or a home in France? If so, we are the ideal partner you've been looking for. Who could be better placed than Entenial - the leading French financial institution specializing in real-estate and asset financing - to offer you the help you need to make your dream come true?

We'll design a financing solution perfectly tailored to your resources and your desires, and guide you with a sure hand through the legal labyrinth of buy property in France.

Our most heartfelt wish is to be able to say:
"Welcome to your new home!"
So, don't hesitate any longer! It's easy to make contact and start getting better acquainted…

For mortgages tailored to yc future home in France, send us an e.mail at:

international@entenial.com

THE FRENCH BANK SPECIALIZING IN REAL-ESTATE AND ASSET FINANCIN

Entenial

A credit institution licensed as a bank (Paris Trade and Companies Register 562 064 352) – A French limited company (société anonyme) with a share capital of €180,218,856 – Head office : 16, rue Volney – 75008 Paris –
Entenial's loans are governed by the provisions of French law and, in particular, articles L312-1 and seq. of French Consumer Law. Borrowers enjoy a 10-day right-to-cancel period.
If the sale of the property is subject to securing a loan, and if no financing is granted, the vendor is required to return all deposits paid.

physiques (IRPP)
income tax
indivision nf
joint ownership
L
location nf
letting; rented accommodation
longère nf
longhouse or long barn

M
mairie nf
town hall
maison nf
house
* maison bourgeoise
upmarket period house
* maison de campagne
country cottage
* maison individuelle
detached house
* maison jumelée
semi-detached house
* maison de maître
classic mansion-style house
mandat nm
power of attorney
manoir nm
country manor
mas nm
stone farmhouse

N
notaire nm
notary (the lawyer who oversees the
conveyancing)

0
occupant nmf
occupier
offre nf
offer; bid

P
parcelle de terre nf
plot of land
pavillon nm
typical modern house
permis de construire nm
planning permission
pierre nf
stone

* en pierre
built of stone
* pierre de taille
sandstone; limestone
pigeonnier nm
dovecote
plan nm
plan; outline
* plan cadastral
official record of site boundaries
* plan d'occupation des sols
local authority plan outlining
the area's planning restrictions
préfecture nf
administrative offices of the local
state representative
prélèvement automatique nm
direct debit
prêt nm
loan
* prêt immobilier
mortgage
* prêt immobilier à taux fixe
fixed-rate mortgage
* prêt immobilier à taux variable
variable-rate mortgage
*** prêt immobilier sans
capital différé**
repayment mortgage
promesse de vente nf
sales agreement

R
rectorat nm
local education authority

S
salle nf
room
* salle à manger
dining room
* salle de bain
bathroom
* salle d'eau
shower room
salon nm
sitting room
séjour nm
living room
société civile immobilière (SCI) nf
property-holding company
sous-seing privé nm
private agreement

surface habitable nf
living space
système d'écoulement des eaux nm
drainage

T
taxe nf
tax
* taxe d'habitation
residential tax
* taxe foncière
property ownership tax
* taxe sur la valeur ajoutée (TVA)
VAT
* toutes taxes comprises (TTC)
VAT included
titre nm
title deed
toit nm
roof
toiture nf
roofing
tout-à-l'égout nm
mains drainage
type (T) nm
(followed by a number) a property with
a given number of main rooms
* T4
four-room flat

U
usufruit nm
lifetime interest

V
villa nf
detached modern house
vendre v
to sell
* à vendre
for sale
vendeur nm
seller
vente nf
sale
* vente aux enchères
auction
versement nm
payment
volet nm
shutter

The Directory

ACCOUNTANTS

A E A Antipolis Experts Associes
(French equivalent to Chartered Accountant)
Bastille de la Mer, Batiment C,
6062 Route de Nice,
06600 Antibes
Tel: +33 4 92 91 87 81

Arthur D Little France
50 avenue Gauteur
75017 Paris
Tel: +33 1 55 74 29 00

Blevins Franks Group Limited
Barbican House
26-34 Old Street
London EC1V 9QQ
Tel: 020 7336 1000

Coopers & Lybrand
32 rue Guersant
75017 Paris
Tel: +33 1 56 57 56 57

Ernst & Young
Tour Ernst & Young
11 allée de l'Arche
92037 Paris la Défense Cedex
Tel: +33 1 46 93 60 00

Factofrance Heller
Tour Facto
18 rue Hoche
92988 Paris La Défence Cedex
Tel: +33 1 46 35 70 00

Inter Audit
21 bis rue Lord Byron
75008 Paris
Tel: +33 1 43 59 58 73

PKF (Guernsey) Limited
PO Box 296,Suites 13 & 15,
Sarnia House
Le Truchot, St Peter Port
Guernsey GY1 4NA
Tel: 01481 727927

Price Waterhouse

Tour AIG
34 place des Corolles
92908 Paris la Défense Cedex
Tel: +33 1 56 57 58 59

ARCHITECTS

A4 Architects Associes
64 Cours le Rouzic
33100 Bordeaux
Tel: +33 5 56 32 33 66

Adrian Barrett
(Design and Construction Consultant)
Lower Road, Churchfields
Salisbury SP2 7PN
Tel: 01722 333583
www.adrian-barrett.co.uk

Cedric Mitchell
22a Hill Street
Haverfordwest
Pembrokeshire SA61 1QE
Tel: 01437 762244

David Martyn Architects
rue des Martyrs
24210 La Bachellerie
Tel: +33 5 53 50 57 82

Graham Price
16 Place Mazarin
53500 Ernée
Tel: +33 2 43 05 40 06
pricegraham@aol.com

Iain Stewart
8 rue Pailleron
69004 Lyon
Tel: +33 4 78 30 01 92

James Matthews
71 Hornsey Lane Gardens
London N6 5PA
Tel: 020 8347 5970

Louis Sorridente
808 rue de la Colle
06570 Saint Paul de Vence
Tel: +33 4 93 32 58 26

Pierre M Weingaertner

Le Mas des Couestes
Route de St Canadet
13100 Aix en Provence
Tel: +33 6 60 55 29 74

PSI Sarl
(Chartered Building Surveyor)
Mas Agora
Place Jules Ferry
84440 Robion
Tel: +33 4 90 76 60 65

Robert Lyell Architects
4 Allée des Maronniers
11300 Limoux
Tel: +33 4 68 31 25 66

BANKS AND FINANCIAL ADVISORS

Abbey National
Les Arcades de Flandre
70 rue Saint Sauveur
59046 Lille Cedex
Tel: +33 3 20 18 18 18

Anthony & Company
(Overseas Tax Advisers)
11 Villantipolis
473 route des Dolines
06560 Valbonne
Tel: +33 4 93 65 76 24

AXA Mutuelles Unis
William Gérard
5 avenue Tournelli
06600 Antibes
Tel: +33 4 93 34 64 10

Banque Scalbert Dupont
9 rue Royale BP 179
62103 Calais Cedex
Tel: +33 3 21 19 11 77

Barclays France Champs Elysees
6 Rond Point des
Champs Elysees
75008 Paris
Tel: +33 1 44 95 13 80

Britline Credit Agricole
15 esplanade Brillaud de

Lujardière
14050 Caen Cedex
Tel: +33 2 31 55 67 89

Charles Hamer
87 Park Street
Thame
Oxfordshire OX9 3HX
Tel: 01844 218 956

Conti Financial Services
(Overseas Mortgage Advisers)
204 Church Road
Hove, Sussex BN3 2DJ
Tel: 01273 772811

Dun & Bradstreet International
55 avenue de champs pierreux
92012 Nanterre
Tel: +33 141 37 50 00

Eurogroupe
Tour Areva
92084 Paris la Défence Cedex
Tel: +33 1 47 96 63 90

Fralex
4 Wimpole Street
London W1G 9SH
Tel: 020 7323 0103

French Mortgage Connection
(French Legal Advisers)
20 Park Road Fordingbridge
Hampshire SP6 1EQ
Tel: 01425 653408

HSBC
Private Bank France
Head office
20 place Vendôme
F-75001 Paris
Tel: +33 1 44 86 18 61

John Siddall International
(Financial/Investment Advice)
Parc Innolin, 3 rue du Golf
33700 Bordeaux-Merignac
Tel: +33 5 56 34 75 51

Kevin Sewell Mortgages

(Investments/Mortgages)
7a Bath Road Business Park
Devizes
Wiltshire SN10 1XA
Tel: 01380 739198

MFS Partners
(Independent Financial
Advisers)
Grovesnor House
47 Alma Road
Plymouth
Devon PL3 4HE
Tel: 01752 664777

Porter & Reeves
5 rue Cambon
75001 Paris
Tel: +33 1 42 61 55 77

Simone Paissoni
22 avenue Notre Dame
06000 Nice
Tel: +33 4 93 62 94 95

Templeton Associates
(Mortgage Brokers)
3 Gloucester Street
Bath
BA1 2SE
Tel: 01225 422282

**BUILDERS AND
DECORATORS**
A Neal
Ombrabols
12700 Capdenac Gare
Tel: +33 5 65 64 81 54

Brittany Renovations
(Renovation, Heating,
Construction, Decorating)
4 Langedraou
22580 Plouha
Tel: +33 2 96 20 38 11

Central Construction
115 City Road
Norwich NR1 2HL
Tel: 01603 762804

D Cheeseman

(Carpentry & joinery)
Rouffignac
46600 Montvalent
Tel: +33 5 65 32 56 11

Espace Immobilier
15 bld de La Liberté
BP 51 34701 Lodève Cedex
Tel: +33 4 67 96 42 32

Gedimat
Brunel Freres
ZA La Petrole
127 rue Curie BP116
34400 Lunel
Tel: +33 4 67 71 16 22

John Rainforth
Les Puits Neufs
84300 Cavaillon
Tel: +33 4 90 76 28 01

Keith Beaseley & Associates
Les Moellons
4 rue des Noyers
La Bonniere
17250 Geay
Tel: +33 5 46 95 37 02

Le Sabot Bleu
Place de la République
11260 Esperanza
Tel:+33 4 68 74 23 60

Magon Home Improvements
(Interior Decoration and
Renovation Work)
12 rue Corneille
78220 Viroflay
Fax: +33 1 30 24 71 48

Heritage Renovation
(Septic Tanks, General
Building, Sandblasting,
Electrics)
1 rue de Moulin
17470 Contré
Tel: +33 5 46 33 32 04

First Realty
(Property Developers)
111 Avenue Victor Hugo

75784 Paris Cedex 16
Tel: +33 1 46 26 23 26

Mark LaTour
11220 Rieux en val
France
Tel: +33 4 68 24 02 94
www.diyinfrance.com

**Societe Cevenole de Travaux
Publics**
(Ground Works)
Cartels
34700 le Bosc
Tel: +33 4 67 44 13 18

Welby
La Bénardais
22100 Léhon
France
Tel: +33 2 96 87 57 37

BUILDING PLANNING
**Fédération Nationale des
CAUE (FNCAUE)**
20-22 rue du Commandeur
75014 Paris
www.fncau.asso.fr
(This national association of
*conseils d'architecture,
d'urbanisme et de
l'environnement de Paris*
(CAUE)
Tel: +33 1 48 87 70 56

BUILDING SUPPLIES
Brico Lots
Le Jonco
16400 La Couronne
Tel:+33 5 45 67 42 84

CICO Chimney Linings
The Street
Westleton
Saxmundham
Suffolk IP17 3AG
Tel: 01728 648608

CAR HIRE
Alamo
Brassmill Lane
Bath

BA1 3JE
Tel: 0870 599 3000

Autos Abroad
Weldon House
Corby Gate Business Park
Priors Haw Road
Corby Northants NN17 5JG
Tel: 0870 066 7788

Avis
The Victoria Building
Harbour City
Salford Quays
Manchester
M5 2SP
Tel: 0870 6060100

Car Hire Ware House
11 Snowbell Road
Kingsnorth
Ashford
Kent TN23 3NF
Tel: 01233 500464

Easy Autos
1 High Street
Twyford
Reading
RG10 9AB
Tel: 0870 054 0200

Eurodrive Car Rental
Navigation Yard
Chantry Bridge
Wakefield
WF1 5PQ
Tel: 0870 160 9060

Europcar UK Ltd
Europcar House
Aldenham Road
Bushey
Watford WD23 2QQ
Tel: 01923 811000

Hertz Car Hire
23 Broadwater Road
Welwyn Garden City
Hertfordshire
AL7 3BQ
Tel: 01707 331433

Holiday Autos House
Pembroke Broadway
Camberley
Surrey GU15 3XD
Tel: 0870 400 0056

Holiday Wheels
Flightform House
Halifax Road
Cressex Business Park
High Wycombe
Bucks
HP12 3SN
Tel: 01494 751515

Nova Rent-a-Car
1 Castle Street
Portaferry
BT22 1NZ
Tel: 028 4272 8189

Regent Car Rental
Tel: 01273 821777
Fax: 01273 821999
res@regent-res.demon.co.uk

Skycars International
Monument House
215 Marsh Road
Pinner
Middlesex HA6 3A
Tel: 0870 789 7789

The Car Hire Group
Weldon House
Corby Gate Business Park
Priors Haw Road
Corby
Northamptonshire N17 5JG
Tel: 0870 758 9945

CARPENTERS
Robin Pacey
Leur Vras
2 Heut Pennar Guer
29620 Guimaec
Tel: +33 2 98 67 67 50

Stuart Cook
Valley House
Burne
Bickington

Devon
TQ12 6PA
Tel: 01626 824749

CHAMBERS OF COMMERCE
Assemblée des Chambres Françaises de Commerce et d'Industrie (ACFCI)
45 avenue d'Iléna
BP 3003
7573 Paris Cedex 16
Tel: +33 1 40 69 37 00
www.acfci.cci.fr

Paris Chamber of Commerce and Industry
Bourse De Commerce
2 Rue De Viarmes
75001 Paris
Tel: +33 1 53 40 48 05
www.ccip.fr

CURRENCY EXCHANGE
CA Britline
15 esplanade Brillaud
de Laujardière
14050 Caen
Cedex
Tel: +33 2 31 55 67 89

Currencies4Less
160 Brompton Road
Knightsbridge
London SW3 1HW
Tel: 020 7228 7667

Currency UK
1 Battersea Bridge
London
SW11 3BZ
Tel:020 7738 0777

Halewood International Foreign Exchange
59-60 Thames Street
Windsor
Berkshire SL4 1TX
Tel: 01753 859159

MoneyCorp
2 Sloane Street

Knightsbridge
London SW1X 9LA
Tel: 020 7235 4200

Tom Wells
Le Moulin à Vent
16380 Charras
Tel: +33 5 45 23 05 09

ESTATE AGENTS AND DEVELOPERS
Fédération Nationale des Agents Immobiliers (FNAIM)
129 rue du faubourg Saint-Honoré
75047 Paris Cedex 08
Tel: +33 1 44 20 77 00
www.fnaim.fr

Agences-immobilieres.com
www.agences-immobilieres.com

Fédération Nationale des Promoteurs Constructeurs
106 rue de l'Universite
75007 Paris
Tel: +33 1 47 05 44 36
www.fnpc.fr

Fédération of Overseas Property Developers, Agents and Consultants (FOPDAC)
Lacey House
St Clare Business park
Holly Road
Hampton Hill
Middlesex TW12 1QQ
Tel: 020 8941 5588
www.fopdac.com

EXHIBITIONS AND SEMINARS
Buying Your Dream Home in France
(Workshops/Seminars in the South West)
20 High Street, Honiton
Devon EX14 1PU
Tel: 01404 47830
www.homebuyingfrance.co.uk
Homes Overseas Exhibitions
(28 exhibitions each year, held

in the UK, Scandinavia and Ireland)
207 Providence Square
Mill Street
London SE1 2EW
Tel: 020 7939 9888

UNIBAEL
(Office space)
5 Boulevard Malesherbes
75008 Paris
Tel: +33 1 53 43 73 05

World of Property/ Focus on France
(Three exhibitions each year in the UK)
1 Commercial Rd
Eastbourne
East Sussex BN21 3XQ
Tel: 01323 726040

Vive La France
(Annual Show)
Grand Hall, London Olympia
Jan 21 - 23
Tel: 0870 902 0444

International Property Show
(Shows held throughout the year in London, Bristol and Manchester)
Fax: 01962 736596

Brittany Central
Moulin de Kerlautre
56160 Lignol
Tel: +33 2 97 27 02 96

GOVERNMENT BODIES
Department of Social Services Overseas Branch
EU Office
Benton Park Road
Longbenton
Newcastle-Upon-Tyne
NE98 1ZZ

France Embassy
58 Knightsbridge
London SW1X 7JT
Tel: 020 7073 1000

Buying abroad?

Before jumping in with both feet, talk to us

If you are buying a property in France, Moneycorp can help you to make the most of your hard-earned capital. Exchange rates directly affect the Sterling amount that you will pay for your property and by speaking to us, we can save you money.

We have been helping people convert currency since 1979. Our friendly, expert staff won't baffle you with jargon, but will guide you to the most competitive exchange rates available and protect you from adverse currency fluctuations. What is more, with Moneycorp, there's no commission charge for our service and no obligation to buy your currency from us.

Contact us now on +44 (0) 20 7808 0500 to find out how Moneycorp can save you money.

Don't let foreign exchange be an afterthought

MONEYCORP
Commercial Foreign Exchange

2 Sloane Street Knightsbridge
London SW1X 9LA UK
+44 (0) 20 7808 0500
www.moneycorp.com

www.ambafrance-uk.org

**French Chamber of
Commerce**
21 Dartmouth Street
London SW1
Tel: 020 7304 4040
www.ccfgb.co.uk

**HOUSE INSPECTION,
GARDENING AND
CLEANING**
Azur Security
497 route de Nice
06560 Valbonne
Tel: +33 4 93 12 18 79

Brittany Home Care Service
4 Oakfields
Walton-on-Thames
Surrey KT12 1EG
Tel: 01932 247681

Charente Caretakers
Chemin de la Perche
16170 Vaux-Rouillac
Tel: +33 5 45 96 56 41

Chevalier Conservation
(Cleaning and Restoring
Carpets and Rugs and
Antiques)
64 bld de la Mission-Marchand
92400 Courbevoie
Tel: +33 1 47 88 41 41

Entreprise Christian Audibert
La Selle d'Andon
06750 Andon
Tel: +33 4 93 60 20 01

Marine Security
41 Burnley Road
Newton Abbott
Devon TQ12 1YD
Tel: 01626 365282

Vendée Rendez-vous
Le Vicariat
32 rue de la Venise Verte
85420 Oulmes
Tel: +33 2 51 52 49 09

INSURANCE
Agence Eaton
(Continent Assurances)
BP 30 1 Parc Doarel Molac
56610 Arradon
Tel: +33 2 97 40 80 20

Agençe Tredinnick
(Household, Health, Travel and
Mortgage Insurance)
12 Rue Dupy
16100 Cognac
Tel: +33 5 45 82 42 93

Andrew Copeland Group
230 Portland Rd
London SE25 4SL
Tel: 020 8656 2544

Anglo-French Underwriters
25 rue de Liege
75008 Paris
Tel: +33 1 44 70 71 00

Aviva
52 rue de la Victoire
Paris 75009
Tel: +33 1 55 50 55 50

Cabinet F X Bordes
11 rue des Desportés
BP 05, 24150 Lalinde
Tel: +33 5 53 61 03 50

**Chubb Insurance Company
of Europe**
16 avenue Matignon
75008 Paris
Tel: +33 1 45 61 73 00

Agence Tredennick
12 rue Dupuis
16100 Cognac
Tel: +33 5 45 82 42 93

Eric Blair
33 Bld Princesse Charlotte
BP 265 MC
98005 Monaco Cedex
Tel: +37 7 93 50 99 66
(Monaco)

Europ Assistance
Sussex House
Perrymount Road
Haywards Heath
West Sussex RH16 1DN
Tel: 01444 442800
(or)
1 promenade de la Bonnette
92633 Gennevilliers
Tel: +33 1 41 85 85 85

**European Benefits
Administrators**
28 rue Momogador
75009 Paris
Tel: +33 1 42 81 97 00

**Lark Insurance Broking
Group**
(Home Insurance)
Wigham House
Wakering Road
Barking Essex IG11 8PJ
Tel: 020 8557 2300

Lloyds of London
4 rue des Petits Peres
75002 Paris
Tel: +33 1 42 60 43 43

**London & European Title
Insurance Services Ltd**
5th Floor Minerva House
Valpy Street
Reading RG1 1AQ
Tel: 0118 957 5000

Matthew Gerard TIS Ltd
(Travel Insurance)
MG House
7 Westminster Court
Old Woking
Surrey GU22 9LQ
Tel: 01483 730900

Saga Services Ltd
(Holiday Home Insurance)
The Saga Building
Middelburg Square
Folkestone Kent CT20 1AZ
Tel: 01303 771111

London and European
Minerva House
Valpy Street
Reading RG1 1AQ
Tel: 0118 957 5000

Tyler and Co
12 rue de la Paix
75002 Paris
Tel: +33 1 42 61 63 31

Woodham Group Ltd
Plas Kenrhos, Burry Port
Carmarthenshire SA16 0DG
Tel: 01554 835252

INTERIOR DESIGN
Art Projet
16 bis rue Segurane
06300 Nice
Tel: +33 4 93 89 50 89

Chaix Decoration
8 rue Paul Deroulède
06000 Nice
Tel: +33 4 93 88 52 02

Darty
(TV and Hi-Fi Equipment,
Household Appliances)
129 avenue Galliéni
93140 Bondy
Tel: +33 1 48 02 32 32

Home Comforts
Chez Deschamps
Route de Medillac
16210 Chalais
Tel: +33 5 45 98 00 97

Hestia-Domus Decoration
11 boulevard Carnot
06000 Nice
Tel: +33 4 93 56 10 43

Ikea (Marseille)
Tel: +33 8 25 82 68 26
Ikea (Paris)
Tel: +33 8 25 82 68 26
Interior's Design
151 avenue Francis Tonner
06150 Cannes

Tel: +33 4 92 19 49 79

La Chaise de Provence
1 rue Saint-Pierre
13005 Marseilles
Tel: +33 4 91 47 98 96

La Poterie Sourdive
Le village
26270 Cliousclat
Tel: +33 4 75 63 05 69

Les Toiles de Mayenne
(Interior Decoration, Fabrics)
9 rue Mézière
75006 Paris
Tel: +33 1 45 48 70 77

Loft
(Interior Designers)
25-27 rue de la Buffa
06000 Nice
Tel: +33 4 93 16 09 09

Manuel Canovas
(Interior Decoration, Fabrics)
223 rue Saint-Honoré
75001 Paris
Tel: +33 1 58 62 33 50

Manufacture des Lauriers
Avenue de la Foux
83670 Varages
Tel: +33 4 94 77 64 79

Mondo
(Japanese mattress specialist)
85 bld Beaumarchais
75003 Paris
Tel: +33 1 48 04 04 02

Raineri Decoration
16 rue Biscarra
06000 Nice
Tel: +33 4 93 80 27 89

Sharlyn Interiors
Saddlers House
High St, Bloxham
Oxon OX15 4LU
Tel: 01295 721666

Shogun
71 avenue des Ternes
75017 Paris
Tel: +33 1 40 68 07 61

Societe des Ocres de France
BP 18
526 avenue Victor Hugo
84401 Apt Vaucluse Cedex
France
Tel: +33 4 90 74 63 82

Souleiado
39 rue Proudhon
13150 Tarascon
Tel: +33 4 90 91 08 80

Madame Taillardat
44 avenue Marceau
75008 Paris
Tel: +33 1 47 20 1712

**Urbann Home Design
(CINNA)**
Angle 123 rue d'Antibes
06400 Cannes
Tel: +33 4 93 68 32 20

Woodstock Fires Ltd
3 Station Road
Heathfield
East Sussex
TN21 8LD
Tel: 01435 868686

KITCHEN SUPPLIES
Ceiling Racks
GNU Ltd
The Old Bakery
Pontesbury
Shrewsbury SY5 ORR
Tel: 01743 792900

Cuisine & Cuisinier
1570 chemin Saint Bernard
06220 Vallauris
Tel: +33 4 92 95 37 37

Godin
(Stoves & Hobs)
Sarl Bauris & Fils
764 route de Grenoble

06200 Nice
Tel: +33 4 93 08 11 08

Mr Pine
The Old Sorting Office
Maple Road
Bramhall
Stockport SK7 2DH
Tel: 0161 439 0055

Old Image
451 Gloucester Road
Horfield
Bristol BS7 8TZ
Tel: 0117 975 4434

Woodstock Fires Ltd
(Delivers to FR/UK)
3 Station Road
Heathfield
East Sussex TN21 8LD
Tel: 01435 868686

LANGUAGE SERVICES
**Accelerated Learning
Systems**
50 Aylesbury Road
Aston Clinton, Aylesbury
Bucks HP22 5AH
Tel: 01296 631177

Accent Francais
7 rue de Verdun
34000 Montpellier
Tel: +33 4 67 58 12 68

Accents of America
9 rue Casimir Delavigne
75006 Paris
Tel: +33 1 44 07 05 05

Accord
14 bld Poissonnière
75009 Paris
Tel: +33 1 55 33 52 33

Actilangue
2-4 rue Alexis Mossa
06000 Nice
Tel: +33 4 93 96 33 84

Alliance Francaise

101 bld Raspail
75270 Paris Cedex 06
Tel: +33 1 42 84 90 00

British Institute in Paris
9-11 rue de Constantine
75007 Paris
Tel: +33 1 44 11 73 73

**Centre de Pratique de
Langues Etrangeres**
58 rue de l'Hopital Militaire
59000 Lille
Tel: +33 3 28 53 00 28

Clac
10 Shelford Park Avenue
Great Shelford
Cambridgeshire CB2 5LU
Tel: 01223 240340
www.clac.org.uk

CFILC
7 rue Duvergier
75019 Paris
Tel: +33 1 40 05 92 42

**Département des Etudiants
Etrangers**
Centre de Francais
Langue Etrangere
Universite Charles de
Gaulle/Lille II BP 149
59653 Villeneuve-d'Ascq Cedex
Tel: +33 3 20 41 60 00

CPFP
Tel: +33 1 53 16 15 34

Ecole des 3 Ponts
Château de Matel
42300 Roanne
Tel: +33 4 77 71 53 00

Ecole Yvelines Langues
2a rue Ducastel
78100 Saint Germain en Laye
Tel: +33 1 30 61 02 08

Eurotalk Limited
315-317 New Kings Road
London SW6 4RF

LANGUAGE

Tel: 020 7371 7711

French Language Courses
Alexandra and John
Waddington
16110 La Rochefoucauld
Tel: +33 5 45 63 53 07

**ICT (Intermediare
Consultante Traduction)**
Castel Briasse
La Briasse
19310 Ayen
Tel: +33 5 55 25 21 66

ICL-Clarife
67 bld Vauban
59800 Lille
Tel: +33 3 20 57 92 19

Janet O'Brian
La Croix Lagrise
35120 Cherrueix
Tel: +33 2 99 80 86 55

La Cardere
Institut de la Langue Francaise
71580 Frontenaud
Tel: +33 3 85 74 83 11

Language in Provence
L'Oustalet
Fontaine de Guby
84490 Saint Saturnin
Tel: +33 4 90 75 56 47

**Language Studies
International**
350 rue Saint Honoré
75001 Paris
Tel: +33 1 42 60 53 70

Lutece langue
31 rue Etienne Marcel
75001 Paris
Tel: +33 1 42 36 31 51

**OISE Intensive Language
Schools
(French courses in Paris)**
OISE House
Binsey Lane

Oxford OX2 OEY
Tel: 0845 601 1157

Paris Langues
30 rue Cabanis
75014 Paris
Tel: +33 1 45 65 05 28

Promolangues
8 rue Blanche
75009 Paris
Tel: +33 1 42 85 19 45

LEGAL EXPERTS
Conseil Supérieur du Notariat
31 rue du Général Foy
75008 Paris
Tel: +33 1 44 90 30 00
www.notaires.fr

LETTING SPECIALISTS
French Magazine
Cambridge House South
Merricks Media Ltd
Henry Street
Bath BA1 1JT
Tel: 01225 786851

French Life
Kerry House, Kerry Street
Horsforth Leeds LS18 4AW
Tel: 0870 444 8877

Meon Villas
Meon House
College Street
Petersfield GU32 3JN
Tel: 01730 230200

Quality Villas
46 Lower Kings Road
Berkhampstead
Hertfordshire HP4 2AA
Tel: 01442 870055

Something Special
Field House
Station Approach
Harlow, Essex CM20 2EW
Tel: 020 8939 5137

Vacances en Campagne

Manor Courtyard
Bignor, Pulborough
West Sussex RH20 1QD
Tel: 01798 869461

Est Paul Gee
(Kitchens, Cookers Central
Heating)
Centre Commercial
32410 Castera-Verduzan
Tel: +33 5 62 68 12 48

PET TRANSPORTATION
Airpets Oceanic
Willowslea Farm
Spout Lane
Stanwell Moor
Staines
Middlesex
TW19 6BW
01753 685571

Animal Airlines
35 Beatrice Avenue
Manchester
Lancashire
M18 7JU
0161 2234035

Animal Inn
Dover Road
Ringwould
Deal
Kent
CT14 8HH
01304 373597

**Chilworth Pet
Exports/Chilworth Kennels**
Lordswood Lane
Chilworth
Southampton
SO16 7JG
02380 766876

Pet Travel Services
24 Cruston Street
Dunfermline
Fife
KY12 7QW
01383 722819

Skymaster Air Cargo
Room 15
Building 305
Cargo Terminal
Manchester Airport
M90 5PY
0161 4362190

**The Dog House International
Kennels and Cattery**
Camino De La Sabatera 5
Teulada/Moraira
Alicante, Spain
+34 965 741302

Transfur
19 Dean Close
Salisbury Green
Southampton
SO31 7TT
01489 588072

PROPERTY SEARCH
Brittany Properties
2 rue de la Boissiere
22810 Belle
Isle en Terre
Brittany
France
Tel: +33 2 96 43 09 94
e-mail: sales@
brittanyproperties.com

**Charente-Maritime French-
Home-Service**
Tel: +33 5 46 94 48 59
rsayner@club-internet.fr

Devon International
2 Impasse de La Source
ZA Secterur Gare
13770 Venelles
Tel: +33 4 42 54 68 58

French Discoveries
92 Oxford Road
Mosely B13 9SQ
Tel: 0121 4491155

Homes in Real France
3 Delgany Villas
Plymouth PL6 8AG

Tel: 01752 771777
sales@hirf.co.uk

La Foncière Charentaise Sarl
14 bis Grande Rue
16140 Aigre
Tel: +33 5 45 21 78 38

Live France Group
Pavail
32100 Condom
France
Tel: +33 5 62 28 02 64
www.livefrancegroup.com

London Paris Dream Home
Flat 19
St Gabriel's Manor
25 Cormont Road
London SE5 9RH
Tel: 020 7820 1337
www.parisdreamhome.com

Property Centre
42 California Road
Longwell Green
Bristol BS30 9XL
Tel: 0870 444 2078
www.overseasproperties.com

The Mediterranean Property Agent
26 High Street
Sevenoaks Kent TN13 1HX
Tel: 01732 451144
www.tmpa.co.uk\

South Loire Property Search
La Gouarie
Bossay sur claise 37290
Indre et Loire
France
Tel: +33 2 47 94 44 20
www.southloire
propertysearch.com

REMOVALS AND HAULAGE

Anglo French Removals
Invicta Works
Farleigh Lane
Barming Maidstone
Kent NE16 9LX

Tel: 01622 679004

Armishaws
3 Alfred's Way
Wincanton Business Park
Wincanton
Somerset BA9 9RT
Tel: 01963 34065

Associated Moving Services
1,2 & 3 Pelham Yard
High Street, Seaford
East Sussex BN25 1PQ
Tel: 01323 892934

Bishop's Move Group
Harcourt Street
Off Southern Street
Manchester
Lancashire M28 3GN
Tel: 0845 666 3322

Bradshaw International
Centrepoint
Marshall Steven's Way
Westing House Road
Trafford Park Manchester
M17 1PP
Tel: 0161 877 5555

Brookfields
Cesncoch
Nr Welshpool
Powys
SY21 OAQ
Tel: 01938 810 649

Burk Bros
Burk Bros Trading Estate
Foxs Lane
Wolverhampton
West Midlands WV1 1PA
Tel: 01902 714555

Callington Carriers
International Removers
Valentine Road
Callington
Cornwall PL17 7DF
Tel: 0157 938 3210

Cotswold Carriers

Warehouse No.2
The Walk, Hook Norton Rd
Chipping Norton
Oxon
OX7 5TG
Tel: 01608 730500

David Dale Removals
Dale House
Forest Moor Road
Harrogate HG5 8LT
Tel: 01423 867788

Ede Bros
Nightless Copse,
Rusper Road, Capel
Dorking, Surrey RH5 5HE
Tel: 01306 711293

Eardley's Removals and Storage
Unit 2 First Avenue
Crewe CW1 6BG
Tel: 01270 588225

Farrer & Fenwick Removals
Bridge House
Bridge Street
Walton-on-Thames
Surrey KT12 1AL
Tel: 01932 253737

F&N Worldwide Removals
Unit 14, Autumn Park
Dysart Road Grantham
Lincolnshire NG31 7DD
Tel: 01476 579210

Franklins Removals Ltd
112 Streetly Lane
Sutton Coldfield
B74 4TB
Tel: 0121 353 7263
www.franklinsremovals.com

French Connexion
The Old Vicarage
Leigh, Sherborne
Dorset DT9 6HL
Tel: 01935 872222

Greens Removals Ltd

Tomo Industrial Estate Creeting
Road
Stowmarket
Suffolk IP14 5AY
Tel: 01449 613053

H AppleYard & Sons
Denby Way
Hellaby Industrial Estate
Rotherham
Yorkshire S66 8HR
Tel: 01709 549718

Hambleton Removals and Storage
Capp House
96d South End
Croydon CRO 1DQ
Tel: 020 8686 1197

Henry's Table
Newnham Court Farm
Bearsted Road
Maidstone Kent
ME14 5LH
Tel: 01622 734211

Homeship ASM (International Transport/ Removal/Shipping)
Garenor Tour D, BP 360
93616 Aulnais sous Bois Cedex
Tel: +33 1 48 65 21 61

Home to Home
UK Head Office
Units W1 & W2
Hazel Road Woolston
Southampton
SO19 7GB
Tel: 0800 783 4602

Henry Johnson Ltd.
(Customs and Shipping Agent)
5 rue Jacques Kablé
75018 Paris
Tel: +33 1 46 07 94 39

Kidds Services
International House
Kidd Park Cliff Road
Hornsea, Hull
East Yorkshire

REMOVALS

HU18 1JB
Tel: 0800 252220

David Powell
The Elephant House
Deykin Avenue
Birmingham B6 7BH
Tel: 0121 326 6008

Langdon Removals Bristol
163 South Liberty Lane
Bristol
BS3 2TL
Tel: 0117 963 7404

Lawlers Removals & Storage
Wreakes Lane
Dronfield S18 1PN
Tel: 0114 275 1020

Martell's International Removers
Charlwood Road
East Grinstead RH19 2HG
Tel: 01342 321303

Metro Removals
Orion Way
Kettering
Northants N15 6NL
Tel: 01536 519696

Monarch UK & Internatonal Movers
Grove Barns
North Road
South Ockendon RM15 6SR
Tel: 0800 954 6474

The Personal Moving Service Ltd
Tel: +33 2 33 35 31 80
barry@tpmsl.com
www.tpmsl.com

Reflex Move
Castlegate Business Park
Old Sarum
Sailsbury SP4 6QX
Tel: 01722 414350

Richman-Ring Ltd

Eurolink Way
Sittingbourne
Kent
ME10 3HH
Tel: 01795 427151

Simpsons of Sussex
Units 1-3 Ditchling Common
Industrial Estate
Burgess Hill, Hussocks
Sussex BN6 8SL
Tel: 0800 027 1958

TBA
2 Strawberry Hill
Bloxham, Banbury
Oxon OX15 4NW
Tel: 01295 720902

Trans Euro Worldwide Movers
47 Route Principal du Port
92238 Gennevilliers Cedex
Tel: +33 1 34 48 97 97

APRP
Chemin des Chaudronniers
94310 Orly
Tel: +33 1 48 92 34 15

White and Company
23 Invincible Road
Farnbrough
Hampshire GU14 7QU
Tel: 01252 541674

SOLICITORS AND LEGAL ADVISORS

James Bennett & Co Solicitors
Nightingale House
Brighton Road, Crawley
West Sussex RH10 6AE
TEL: 01293 544044

Blake Lapthorn
(Solicitors)
Holbrook House
14 Great Queen Street
London WC2B 5DG
Tel: 020 7430 1709

Rothera Dowsons
2 Kayes Walk
Off Stone Street
The Lace Market
Nottingham NG1 1PZ
Tel: 0115 910 0600

French Mortgage Connection
20 Park Road, Fordingbridge
Hampshire SP6 1EQ
Tel: 01425 653408

Fox Hayes
(Solicitors)
Bank House
150 Rounday Road
Leeds LS8 5LD
Tel: 0113 209 8922

John Howell & Co
(International Lawyers)
The Old Glassworks
22 Endell Street
Covent Garden
London WC2H 9AD
Tel: 020 7420 0400

Kingsfords
(Solicitors)
5/7 Bank Street
Ashford
Kent TN23 1BZ
Tel: 01233 624545

Liliane Levasseur-Hills
69 Pullman Lane
Godalming
Surrey GU7 IYB
Tel: 01483 424303

MB Law
King Charles House
King Charles Croft
Leeds LS1 6LA
Tel: 0113 242 4444

Mortgages for Business
London Office
53-55 High Street
Sevenoaks TN13 1JF
Tel: 01732 471600

Pannone & Partners
(Solicitors)
123 Deansgate
Manchester M3 2BU
Tel: 0161 909 3000

Philip Winter-Taylor
wintertaylors@aol.com

Pretty Solicitors
Elm House
25 Elm Street
Ipswich
Suffolk IP1 2AD
Tel: 01473 232121

Riddell Croft & Co
(Solicitors)
27 St Helen's Street
Ipswich, Suffolk IP4 1HH
Tel: 01473 384870

Russell-Cooke
2 Putney Hill
London SW15 6AB
Tel: 020 8789 9111

Sean O'Connor & Co
(Bilingual Solicitors)
2 River Walk
Tonbridge, Kent TN9 1DT
Tel: 01732 365 378
seanoconnorco@aol.com354

Simone Paissoni
(In France for France)
22 avenue Notre Dame
06000 Nice
Tel: +33 4 93 62 94 95
spaissoni@magic.fr

Stephen Smith Solicitors
(France Limited)
161 Cemetery Road
Ipswich IP4 2HL
Tel: 01473 437186

Taylors
The Red Brick House
28-32 Trippet Lane
Sheffield S1 4EL
Tel: 0114 276 6767

Thrings Townsend
(Solicitors)
Midland Bridge
Bath BA1 2HQ
Tel: 01225 340000

Turner & Co
(Solicitors)
59 Charlotte Street
St Paul's Square
Birmingham
B3 1PX
Tel: 0121 200 1612

Trevor Bennett & Co.
144 Knutsford Road
Wilmslow
Cheshire
SK9 6JP
Tel: 01625 586937

VEF (UK) Ltd.
(Legal services & French
Property services)
4 Raleigh House
Admirals Way
London E14 9SN
Tel: 020 7515 8660

SURVEYORS
AlpineSpace Ltd
BP 43
74400 Argentière
Tel: +33 4 50 54 22 81

Burrows-Hutchinson
11 rue du Parc
56160 Ploerdut
Tel: +33 2 97 39 45 53

Curchod & Co.
54 Church Street
Weybridge, Surrey KP13 8DP
Tel: 01932 823630

James Latter
(Expert Immobilier)
Couvrigny
14700 Saint Pierre du Bû
Tel: +33 2 31 90 17 70

PSI Sarl

Mas Agora
Place Jules Ferry
84440 Robion
Tel: +33 4 90 76 60 65

Smith-Woolley & Perry
Chartered Surveyors
130 Sandgate Road
Folkstone CT20 2BW
Tel: 01303 226622

SWIMMING POOLS
A B Piscines Ltd
11 Rue André Pichon
24340 Mareuil
Tel: +33 5 53 56 68 87

Bakewell Pools Ltd.
38 Bagley Wood Road
Kennington
Oxford OX1 5LY
Tel: 01865 735205

Claire Pernod-Fantini
119 bd Sadi Carnot
06110 Le Cannet
Tel: +33 4 92 99 01 00

Clearwater Swimming Pools
Ltd
The Studio
81 Langley Close
Headington
Oxford OX3 7DB
Tel: 01865 766112

Christal Pools
139 Enville Street
Stourbridge
West Midlands DY8 3TD
Tel: 01384 440990

JW Green Swimming Pools
Ltd
Regency House
88a Great Brick Kiln Street
Graiseley
Wolverhampton WV3 0PU
Tel: 01902 427709

London Swimming Pool
Company

138 Replingham Road
London SW18 5LL
Tel: 020 8874 0414

Peter Joyce Poolstore UK Ltd
Monks Brook House
Nutburn Road
North Baddesly
Southampton
SO52 9BG
Tel: 0845 128 4373

Piscines du Canal
Michel Roques
56 av Foch
34500 Béziers
Tel: +33 4 99 43 08 69

Transaqua
60 Couers Reverseaux
1700 Saintes
Tel: +33 5 46 97 25 84
www.transaqua-piscines.com
transaqua@wanadoo.fr

TELEVISIONS
Big Dish Satellite
Mouriol Milhaguet
87440 Marvel
Tel: +33 5 55 78 72 98
www.bigdishsat.com

French-Help
32140 Chelan
Tel: +33 5 62 66 08 25

Susat UK
37 Spencer Mews
London W6 8PB
Tel: 0845 451 3133

TV5 (UK) Medialink
King's House
Bristol BS99 5HR
Tel: 0117 954 9189

TV5 (France)
19 rue Cognacq-Jay
75007 Paris Cedex 07
Tel: +33 1 44 18 55 55

UBALDI

272 avenue de la Californie
06002 Nice
Tel: +33 4 93 18 80 88

TOURISM
Maison de la France
178 Piccadilly
London W1J 9AL
Tel: 090 6824 4123
www.franceguide.com

TRAVEL – AIR
Air France
Terminal 2
London Heathrow Airport
Hounslow
Middlesex
TW6 1ET
Tel: 0845 0845 111
Tickets:
10 Warwick Street
London
W1B 5LZ

Aurigny Air Services
Southampton International
Airport
Southampton
Hampshire
SO18 2NL
Tel: 01481 822886
Bookings:
Ayline House
Alderney Airport
Alderney
Guernsey
Channel Islands
GY9 3AJ
aurigny.com

Britannia Airways Ltd.
London Luton Airport
Luton
Bedforshire LU2 9ND
Tel: 0870 6076757/
01582 424155

British Airways Travel Shops
213 Picadilly
London W1J 9HQ
Tel: 0845 6060747

British Midland
Cargo Building
552 Shoreham Road East
Hounslow
Middlesex TW6 3EU
Tel: 0870 2400203
bmicargo.com

EasyJet Airline Plc.
Easyland
London Luton Airport
Bedfordshire LU2 9LS
Tel: 0870 600 0000
www.easyjet.com

FlyBe
Jack Walker House
Exeter International Airport
Exeter EX5 2HL
Tel: 0871 7000123

Genie Travel
60 Lansdowne Street
Hove Sussex
Tel: 01273 770453

Lyddair
London Ashford Airport
Lyddair
Kent
TN29 9QL
Tel: 01797 320000

Ryanair
Dublin Airport
County Dublin
Tel: 0871 246 0000

TRAVEL – COACH
Eurolines
52 Grosvenor Gardens
Victoria
London SW1W OAU
Tel: 0870 808080

TRAVEL – RAIL
Euro Tunnel
Contacts Centre
St Martin's Plain
Cheriton Parc
Folkestone
Kent, CT19 4QD

Tel: 0870 5353535

Eurostar (Head Office)
Eurostar House
Waterloo Station
12 Lower Road
London SE1 8SE
Tel: 0870 518 6186

Eurostar (Customer Services)
3rd Floor, Kent House
81 Station Road
Ashford, Kent TN23 1AP
Tel: 0870 518 6186

Rail Europe Ltd
34 Tower View
Kings Hill
West Malling
Kent ME19 4ED
Tel: 0870 584 8848
www.raileurope.co.uk

SNCF
23 avenue de la Porte
d´Aubervilliers
75018 Paris
Tel: +33 8 91 36 20 20

TRAVEL – SEA
Brittany Ferries
Milbay Docks
Plymouth
Devon PL1 3EW
Tel: 0870 536 0360

Condor Ferries Ltd.
Condor House
New Harbour Road
South Hamworthy
Poole
Dorset BH15 4AJ
Tel: 0845 345 2000

Ferries to France
Barclays Bank Chambers
65 High Street
Tring HP23 4 AB
Tel: 0870 011 2499

Ferry Savers
International Life

Leisure Ltd
Kerry House
Kerry Street
Horsforth
Leeds LS18 4AW
Tel: 0870 990 8492

France Canterbury
29/30 Palace Street
Canterbury
Kent CT1 2DZ
Tel: 01227 454508

Hoverspeed Ltd
International Hoverport
Dover
Kent
CT17 9TG
Tel: 0870 524 0241

Irish Ferries
Corn Exchange Building
Brunswick Street
Liverpool, L2 7TP
Tel: 0870 5171717

Norfolkline
Norfolk House
South Osborne Way
Off Western Access Road
Immingham Dock
North East Lincs DN40 2QA
Tel: 01469 570900

P&O Portsmouth
Peninsular House
Wharf Road
Portsmouth
Hampshire PO2 8TA
Tel: 0870 242 4999

P&O Ferries
Channel House
Channel View Road
Dover Kent CT17 9TJ
Tel: 01304 863000

Seafrance
Whitfield Court
Honeywood Close
Whitfield
Dover Kent CT16 3PX

Tel: 01304 828300

UTILITIES
Electricité de France (EDF)
(Information)
Tel: +33 0 58 13 70 00
www.edf.fr

Gaz de France
23 rue Philibert Delorme
75840 Paris Cedex 17
Tel: +33 1 47 54 20 20
www.gazdefrance.com

WEB HOSTING
Financial Systems Limited
www.frenchpropertylinks.com
dfs@financialsystems.co.uk

Sam Mooney
(Web Design)
11220 Riex En Val
France
Tel: +33 4 68 24 02 94
www.fortheloveofwork.com

Stickland Web Studio
83 North Trade Road
Battle, East Sussex TN33 0HN
Tel: 01424 775021
www.sticklandweb.co.uk
mike@sticklandweb.co.uk

For a full list and contact details of all the Estate agents featured in this guide turn to page 222

UTILITIES

Index of Agents

Key to the three-letter codes identifying the agents, based both in Britain

CODE	NAME AND ADDRESS	CONTACT DETAILS
AAA	**Alpine Apartments Agency** Hinton Manor, Eardisland Leominster, Herefordshire HR6 9BG	**Tel: 01544 388234**
ABA	**Abafim** 97 rue Maréchal Foch 65000 Tarbes, France	**Tel: +33 5 62 34 54 54**
AGL	**Agence l'Union** 19 Place de la Halle 82140 Saint Antonin Noble-Val Tarn et Garonne, France	**Tel: +33 5 63 30 60 24**
AHB	**A House in Brittany** 1 Windsor Road, Worthing West Sussex, BN11 2LU	**Tel: 01903 202272**
AIF	**Aude Immo Futur** 4 rue de Verdun 11000 Carcassonne, France	**Tel: +33 4 68 71 23 70**
AIM	**Aims International** Le Bourdonne 53640 Le Horps, France	**Tel: +33 2 43 04 26 99**
ALZ	**Allez Français** La Moinerie 79500 Paizay Le Tort, France	**Tel: +33 5 49 27 01 22**
AZU	**Azur Properties** Villa Azur Corniche Superieure Saut du Loup F-83380 Les Issambres Sainte Maxime France	**Tel: +33 6 89 15 50 62**
BPS	**Burgundy Property Specialists** Les Roches 21320 Mont St Jean France	**Tel: +33 3 80 84 35 21**

and France, whose properties are featured in the Price Guide

CODE	NAME AND ADDRESS	CONTACT DETAILS
BUD	**Burgundy Discovery** www.burgundydiscovery.com	**Tel: +33 3 85 49 51 34**
BUR	**Burgundy 4 U** 6 Place Carnot 21200 Beaune France	**Tel: +33 3 85 98 96 24** www.burgundy4u.com
BUY	**Buy French Property** 204 Southampton Road Ringwood, Hampshire BH24 1JG	**Tel: 01425 479541**
CAC	**Coast and Country** 71 rue de Tournamy 06250 Mougins, France	**Tel: +33 4 92 92 47 50**
CAT	**Cather Castles** Le Caussigne 11230 Rivel, France	**Tel: +33 4 68 69 35 61**
CBR	**CB Richard Ellis** 65 av Victor Hugo 75116 Paris, France	**Tel: +33 1 45 02 35 02**
DAV	**David King Associates** 76 Gosberton Road London SW12 8LQ	**Tel: 0702 094 0020**
DEE	**Demeures de France** 41 rue Barrault 75013 Paris, France	**Tel: +33 1 44 17 95 40**
DEV	**Devon International** 16 rue Pasteur 55700 Stenay, France	**Tel: +33 3 29 80 69 75**
EJC	**EJC French Property** Chemin de Repenti 83550 Vidauban, France	**Tel: +33 4 94 99 72 00**

AGENTS

Index of Agents

CODE	NAME AND ADDRESS	CONTACT DETAILS
EQU	**Equinoxe Immobilier** 6 rue Gambetta 24000 Périgueux, France	**Tel: +33 5 53 08 40 69**
EYM	**Eymet Immobilier** 7 rue du Temple 24500 Eymet, France	**Tel: +33 5 53 74 50 40**
FDC	**French Discoveries Charente** 11 rue de la Gare 16260 Chasseneuil, France	**Tel: 0871 717 4164**
FFF	**First for French Property** 69 Wealden Way Haywards Heath West Sussex RH16 4DD	**Tel: 01444 451250**
FON	**Fonciere Charentaise** 14 bis Grande rue 16140 Aigre, France	**Tel: +33 5 45 21 78 38**
FPP	**French Property Shop** Elwick Club Churchroad, Ashford Kent TN23 1RD	**Tel: 01233 666902**
FRA	**Francophiles** Barker Chambers, Barker Road Maidstone, Kent ME16 8SF	**Tel: 01622 688165**
FRE	**FRE Conseil Patrimoine** 52 bd Victor Hugo 06000 Nice, France	**Tel: +33 4 97 03 03 33**
FWY	**French Ways** Les Grandes Masures 35420 Monthault, France	**Tel: +33 2 99 98 06 89**
GEO	**George V** Chemin des Salines14800 Saint-Arnault, France	**Tel: +33 1 55 12 15 62**

CODE	NAME AND ADDRESS	CONTACT DETAILS
GRM	**Groupe Mobilis** 41 rue Francois 75008 Paris	**Tel: +33 1 47 20 30 00**
HAM	**Hamilton Estate Agents** 2 Burges Close, Thorpe Bay Essex SS1 3JW	**Tel: 01702 294691**
HAP	**Hamptons International** European Department 168 Brompton Road Knightsbridge London SW3 1HW	**Tel: 020 7589 8844**
HAR	**Harrison Stone** PO Box 41, Petworth West Sussex GU28 OYZ	**Tel: 01798 342776**
HEX	**Hexagone France Ltd** Webster House 24 Jesmond Street Folkestone, Kent CT19 5QW	**Tel: 01303 221077**
HIF	**Homes in Real France** 3 Delgany Villas Plymouth, Devon PL6 8AG	**Tel: 01752 771777**
HOM	**Homefinder** 23 place du Marché 23300 La Souterraine France	**Tel: +33 5 55 63 59 41**
IMO	**Imoinvest** 15 rue Henri Bocquillon 75015 Paris, France	**Tel: +33 1 44 25 92 32** Mob: +33 6 62 41 06 06
ISM	**Immobilier Saint Michel** 10 rue Saint Michel 14000 Caen, France	**Tel: +33 2 31 34 55 55**

Index of Agents

AGENTS

CODE	NAME AND ADDRESS	CONTACT DETAILS
JBF	**JB French Houses** 12 The Friary, Friary Close Selsey, Portsmouth, PO5 2LS	**Tel: 02392 297 411**
LAF	**L'Affaire Française** 25 Grand Rue, 16200 Jarnac, France	**Tel: +33 5 45 81 76 79**
LAT	**Latitudes** Grosvenor House, 1 High Street Edgware, Middlesex HA8 7TA	**Tel: 020 8951 5155**
LEB	**Le Bonheur** My French Property Quartier Cutorte, rue du Vieux Bourg Larreule, 65700, France	**Tel: +33 5 62 96 94 27**
LEG	**Leggett Immobilier** Le Bourg 24340 La Rochebeaucourt France	**Tel: +33 5 53 56 62 54** Mob: +33 6 07 80 06 21
LUC	**Lucien Voillequin Immobilier** 10 rue Jean-Roussat BP 98, 52204 Langres Cedex France	**Tel: +33 3 25 87 05 28**
MPS	**Mediterranean Property Search** 1 Copplestone Road Budleigh Salterton Devon EX9 6DS	**Tel: 01395 442689**
MOR	**Moret Real Estate** 17 rue Thiers 90000 Belfort, France	**Tel: +33 3 84 28 18 73**
MUR	**Muret Immobilier** rue du Puits de L'Appent 16560 Coulgens, France	**Tel: +33 5 45 70 32 74**
PAP	**Papillon Properties** Les Broux, 86400 St-Gaudent France	**Tel: +33 5 49 87 45 47**

CODE	NAME AND ADDRESS	CONTACT DETAILS
PFI	**PFI International** Leatherhead, Surrey	**Tel: 01372 378414**
SIF	**Sifex** 1 Doneraile Street London SW6 6EL	**Tel: 020 7384 1200**
SIG	**Sirguey Immobilier** rue du Château 68640 Waldingheffen, France	**Tel: +33 3 89 07 77 17**
SIP	**Simply Burgundy** Brionnais, France www.simplyburgundy.com	**Tel: +33 4 77 64 23 84**
SLP	**South Loire Property Search** La Gouarie Bossay Sur Claise 37290 Indre, France	**Tel: +33 2 47 94 44 20**
SOU	**Souillac Country Club** Lachapelle-Auzac 46200 Souillac, France	**Tel: +33 5 65 27 56 00**
VEF	**VEF** 4 Raleigh House, Admirals Way London E14 9SN	**Tel: 020 7515 8660**
VIA	**Vialex International** rue Messager 47470 Beauville France	**Tel: +33 5 53 95 46 24**
VIB	**Vibo Immobilier** BP18, 33 RN9 11510 Fitou, France	**Tel: +33 4 68 45 69 19**
VOS	**Vosges Mountain Properties** 100 Chemin de la Blanche Femme Le Grand Valtin 88230 France www.vosgesproperties.com	

AGENTS

Acknowledgments

BRITTANY
Frances McKay and Dorethee
Nachez Francophiles
(01622 688165)
Peter Robinson
French Magazine
(01706 364046)
Alison Durbid Maison Selecte
(0871 717 4283)
Jeremy Waldron
Brittany Travel (01920 412012)
Ian Fowler Aims International
(+33 2 43 04 26 99)
Sylvia-Moore Direct Properties
Adam Harrison Harrison Stone
(01798 342776)
Currie French Properties
(01223 576084)
Anja Davies La Boursaie
(+33 2 31 63 14 20)

NORMANDY
Frances McKay and Dorethee
Nachez Francophiles
(01622 688165)
Currie French Properties
(01223 576084)
Jean-Bernard Le Fur
JB French Property
(02392 297411)
Anja Davies La Boursaie
(+33 2 31 63 14 20)
Roger French Discoveries
Normandy (01308 717174162)

NORD-PAS-DE-CALAIS
Frances McKay and Dorethee
Nachez Francophiles
(01622 688165)
Success Immobilier
(+33 3 21 04 58 46)
Christine Hilton La Residence
(01491 838485)
Carolyn Cohen Latitudes (0208
9515155)

ILE-DE-FRANCE
Catherine Godet
Christine Roquelaure,
Roquapart Paris Rentals
(+33 1 46 22 15 12)
Claire Waddy
French Magazine
(01300 348353)
David King

David King Associates
(07020 940020)
Gregory Chidiac
The French Embassy
(0207 0731030)
Dianne Falls
French Magazine
(0208 969 4663)
Nancy Rudick
French Magazine
(+33 1 51 87 43 86 53)
George Cumming
Groupe Mobilis
Ghoncheh Haery
PPC Conseil Patrimonie
(+33 1 42 66 00 88)
DEE Demeures de France
(+33 1 44 17 95 40)
Guy Fraissinet
Agence IB
(+33 1 42 97 13 06)
Agence Paris Seine
Immobilière (+33 1 45 44
66 00)
Agence CB Richard Ellis
Résidentiel (Agence du 16ème)
(+33 1 45 02 35 02)
Agence de l'assemblée
(+33 1 45 55 05 05)
Agence Immobilière Etude
Doumer (+33 1 45 03 03 45)
Monsieur Tiberghien Agence
Wagram (+33 1 47 64 44 77)
Acta Immobilier
(+33 1 40 41 15 40)
Cabinet Vermeille
(+33 1 39 49 97 97)
Servissimo
(+33 1 43 29 03 23)
Institut d'aménagement et
d'urbanisme de la région Ile
De France Médiatheque
(+33 1 53 85 79 17)

CHAMPAGNE ARDENNE
Office de Tourisme de
Charleville-Mézières
(+33 3 24 55 69 90)
Monsieur Laurant Rogez
Office de Tourisme de
Champagne-Ardenne
(+33 3 24 55 69 90)
Interhome (+33 1 53 36 60 00)
Immobilier Nouvelle
Génération
(+33 3 24 56 37 37)

Loisirs Accueil Ardennes (+33
3 24 56 00 63)
Corinne Lambert
Gîtes de France Ardennes
(+33 3 24 56 89 65)
Mlle Schlick (The City Council)
Mairie de Charleville-Meziéres;
(+33 3 24 33 89 05)
Immo-France
(+33 3 24 33 32 86)
Agence Immobilière Sefac
(+ 33 3 24 33 06 05)
Gîtes de France Ardenne
(+33 3 24 56 89 65)
Office de Tourisme de Reims
(+33 3 26 77 45 00)
France No.1 Immobilier
(+33 3 26 85 10 60)
Pierre Lacreuse Laforêt
Immobilier (+33 3 26 77 97 97)
Office de Tourisme d'Epernay
(+33 3 26 53 33 00)
Michelle Immobilier
(+33 3 26 55 99 99)
Primmo Immobilier
(+ 33 3 26 55 00 22)
Cabinet Reims Agence
(+33 3 26 40 06 97)
Office de Tourisme de
Châlons-en-Champagne
(+33 3 26 65 17 89)
Champagne Immobilier
+33 3 26 65 03 11)
Patrick Quiquener
Euro Conseil Immobilier
(+33 3 26 21 12 77)
Cabinet Jacquet Immobilier
(+33 3 26 21 77 77)
Gîtes Ruraux
William Pearson
Marina Properties
(01273 818819)
Office de Tourisme de
Strasbourg
(+33 3 88 52 28 28)

ALSACE, LORRAINE AND
FRENCH-COMTÉ
Office de Tourisme de
Strasbourg (+33 3 88 52 28 28)
Moselle Comité de Tourisme
(Gîtes de France)
(+33 3 87 37 57 69)
Immo Conseil
(+33 3 88 61 20 76)
Immobilière Claude Rizzon

(+33 3 88 77 40 40)
Agence Guy Hoquet
immobilière des Contades
(+33 3 88 24 11 72)
Loc'Vacances
(+33 2 98 53 44 74)
Chalets Label Nature
(+33 3 88 78 11 39)
Office de Tourisme de Metz et
Nancy (+33 3 87 55 53 76)
Century 21 (+33 3 87 65 39 29)
Monsieur Cimino; Agence
Saint Louis (+33 3 87 18 42 69)
Immo Metz
(+33 3 87 56 92 92)
Office de Tourisme de Nancy
(+33 3 83 35 22 41)
Immobilière Claude Rizzon
(+33 3 83 15 68 68)
Agence Duroc Gestion et
Ventes Immobilieres
(+33 3 83 36 74 31)
Sogiler (+33 3 83 35 00 75)
Interhome (+33 1 53 36 60 00)
Cabinet Trilogie
+ 33 3 81 81 85 85
Immobilière Comtoise
(+33 3 81 81 06 33)
Immo Group
(+33 3 81 53 35 35)
Office de Tourisme de
Besançon (+33 8 20 32 07 82)
Office de Tourisme de France
de Doubs (+33 3 81 82 80 48)
Maison de la Franche Comté
(+33 1 42 66 26 28)
Jura Comité de Tourisme
(+33 3 84 87 08 87)
Office de Tourisme de
Clairvaux-les-Lacs
(+33 3 84 25 27 47)
Office de Tourisme des
Rousses (+33 3 84 60 02 55)
Office de Tourisme de Haut
Jura Morez (+33 3 84 33 08 73)
Office de Tourisme de Lons-
le-Saunier (+33 3 84 24 65 01)
Office de Tourisme de Saint
Claude (+33 3 84 60 40 38)
Office de Tourisme de Dole
(+33 3 84 72 11 22)
Laf̂oret Immobilier
(+33 3 84 86 19 90)
Sogeprim (+33 3 84 87 20 70)
Immovision 39
(+33 3 84 24 48 78)

INDEX

Clairvaux Phima Relations
Conseil Immobilier
(+33 3 84 85 18 34)
Century 21 (+33 3 84 60 00 72)
Office de Tourisme de Metz
(+33 3 87 55 53 76)
Prima Relations Conseil
Immobilier (+33 3 84 85 18 34)
I. D. Immobilier
(+33 3 87 18 12 12)

THE LOIRE
Office de Tourisme de
Touraine Amp Loire
Immobilier Bishop and Co
(01332 747474)
Currie French Properties
(01223 576084)
Demeures de France
(+33 1 44 17 95 40)
Carol Whyte Sinclair Overseas
(+01525 375319)
PPC Conseil Patrimonie
(+33 1 42 66 00 88)
Ian and Jo Buchanan French
Magazine (+33 2 41 82 62 69)
John Carter PIF (Properties In
France) (0121 744 0820)
Joseph Reveliere Agence
Transimmo (+33 241 89 16 94)
Beth Edgell VEF (UK) Ltd
(0207 5171036)
Sarzerac de Forge Immobilier
(+33 5 45 95 64 92)
Solis Immobilier
Toit pour toi
Jean-Marie Desailly
(http://www.frenchpropertylinks.c
om)
Office de Tourisme du Mans
(+33 2 43 28 17 22)
Philip Waddingham
 South Loire Property Search
(+33 2 47 94 44 20)
Comité départemental de
Tourisme de la Sarthe
(+33 2 43 40 22 50)
Peter Elias Allez France (0871
7174176)
Devon International
(07966 366106)
George and Valerie Atlantic
Locations (01752 252 567)

BURGUNDY

Benjamen Haas Burgundy4u

POITOU-CHARENTES
French Discoveries
Liz Oliver Francophiles
Hilary Mirrey; French Magazine
(01539 623215)
David King Associates
(020 8673 6800)
Mr Mellone French Magazine
(+33 6 07 99 59 69)
Annie Christie French
Magazine (+33 251 69 66 07)
David Barnes Les Granges Sarl
(+33 5 46 59 77 41)
Paul Owen Marketing Director,
VEF (UK) Ltd (0207 5171036)
Sarzerac de Forge Immobilier
Toit Pour Toi
Penny Zoldan Latitudes (0208
9515155)
San Martell immobilier
(+33 5 49 85 57 09)
Solis Immobilier
(+33 5 45 32 31 16)
Ken Hulse Charente Homes
(+33 5 45 89 12 09)

LIMOUSIN & AUVERGNE
Office de Tourisme de Vichy
(+33 4 70 98 71 94)
Actice (+33 4 70 98 46 70)
Agence de l'Europe
(+33 4 70 32 80 83)
Century 21 (+33 4 70 30 12 50)
Sarl Agence Lagrue
Martin Kemsley LAF L'Affaire
Francaise (+33 5 55 78 67 15)
Office de Tourisme de
Limoges (+33 5 55 34 46 87)
Office de Tourisme de
Clermont-Ferrand
(+33 4 73 98 65 00)
Lawrence Brown English Today
(+33 55 77 53 35)
Limoges Mairie
(+33 5 55 45 64 08)
Curries French Property
(01223 576 084)
Wilma Van Den Berg Van den
Berg Immo (+33 5 55 25 28 00)
Demeures de France
(+33 1 44 17 95 40)
Jonathan Pugh MER Groupe
Mercure (+33 5 61 21 52 01)
with local agent Xavier de la

Chaise
Association de Gîtes de
France (+33 5 55 77 09 57)
Immo2000 (+33 5 55 77 27 32)
Auvergne Immobilière
(+33 4 73 93 55 06)
Adi Immobilier
(+33 4 73 29 47 47)
Chauval Transactions
(+33 4 73 25 57 55)
Cabinet Charberet
(+33 4 73 25 57 55)
Jacquelien Diender Auvergne
France Homes
(+33 4 73 88 80 52)
Marc Gotteur Agence Sagat
(+33 4 73 79 60 40)
Agence Boits et Forests
(+33 5 55 23 25 64)
Agence Immo19
(+33 5 55 24 49 43)
Carine Duflot France Limousin
Immobilier (+33 5 55 73 17 66)
Beth Edgell VEF (UK) Ltd
(0207 5171036)
Office de Tourisme de Vichy
(+33 4 70 97 33 33)
Limoges Chamber of
Commerce

RHÔNE-ALPS
Zigi Davenport; Alpine
Apartments Agency
(01544 388234)
Combotte Immobilier
Susan Offen Thorncliffe
Properties
Pierrick Parnaud
(parnaud@regiondeurbanedely
on.fr)
Beth Edgell VEF (UK) Ltd
(0207 5171036)
Sixième Sers Immobilier
Vesta 2000

AQUITAINE
Roger Windsor L'Affaire
Francaise
Vanessa Hayden Eymet
Immobilier (+33 5 53 36 01 60)
Madeline Action Habitat
Mike Ridding and Ludovic
Hanks Souillac Country Club -
(Dordogne).

Michelle VEF (UK) Ltd
MIDI-PYRENÉES
Patrick-Abafim Midi Pyrenees
Property
Charles Smallwood Agence
l'Union
Michelle VEF (UK) Ltd
Edward Landau; My French
Property (Le Bonheur)

LANGUEDOC ROUSSILLON
Patrick Verhaeghe AB Real
Estate (Estate-pv@ab-real-
estate.com)
Dorethee Nachez Francophiles
(01622 688165)
Harrison-Stone
Beth Edgel VEF (UK) Ltd
(0207 5171036)
Freddy Rueda Agence
Immobilière (+33 4 67 36 34 28)

PROVENCE, NICE AND
CÔTE D'AZUR
Harrison-Stone
Beth Edgell VEF UK
(0207 5171036)
Patrick Verhaeghe AB Real
Estate (Estate-pv@ab-real-
estate.com)
Olivier Morvan Hamptons
International (Riviera office)
Concept Vision Immobilier
Agence du Soleil
Agence Otonello
Agence immobiliere Cabinet
Delval
Agence Azur France
Bienvenue Consulting
Acanthimmo
Agence Immobiliere Cezanne
Simply Corsica
Sarah Francis, Sifex
Patrick Bras
PPC Conseil Patrimonie
Hideaways France (+01539
442435)
Marie Kerstenne@something
special.co.uk
Agence Centre Croisiere
Penny Zoldan, Latitudes (0208
9515155)
Nicolle Anderson, Simply
Travel
Susan Offen Thorncliffe
Properties

INDEX

Index

The following abbreviations have been used in the 'property price bands' section of this index: bp: budget pr

A
Accountants 346–7
Agen 259
Air routes 22–3, 24
Airports 22, 23, 221
Aix–en–Provence 310, 311, 316
Ajaccio 317
Allier 221
Alsace: 151–165
Hotspots 154–156
Prices see under property Price bands
profile
Useful contacts 157
Ambilou 169
Amiens 102, 103, 105
Ancelle 310
Angers 168, 169, 171
Angling:
Fishing Lakes of the Somme
Valley 106
Haut–Doubs 156
Angoulême 201, 203, 205
Annecy 234, 235, 236
Antibes 315
Apartments:
Besançon 156
Chamonix 238
Clermont–Ferrand 222
Dijon 191
Lake Annecy 236
Lyon 241
sale prices 337–8
Trois Vallées 238
Val d'Isère 238
Aquitaine: 255–269
Hotspots 258–60
Prices see under property price bands
Price bands
Profile 256–7
Useful contacts 261
Arcachon 256–7, 258
Ardennes 137
Atnac–Pompadour 222
Attestation de vente 38
Auch 273, 275
Aude 290, 294
Aups 313
Autun 187
Auvergne: 22, 23, 221–2
Hotspots 221, 221–2
Prices see under property price bands
Profile 219–220
useful contacts 223
Auxerre 187, 190
Auxois 187
Avenue de Clichy (Paris) 119
Avenue George V (Paris) 119
Avenue Montaigne
(Paris) 119
Avesnois 106

Aveyron 272–3
Avignon 294
Avranches 87
Alpes d'huez 240

B
Bagnères de Bigorre 276
Banking 40
Banyuls 291, 293
Barcelonette 311
Barn conversions 29
Bastia 23, 317
Batignolles (Paris) 119
Baud 62, 65
Baugé 168, 169
Bayonne 257, 260
Beaches:
Aquitaine 260
Brittany 65, 66
Charente 205
Corsica 310, 317
Côte d'Azur 314
Ile de Ré 204
Languedoc–Roussillon 293
Loire 169, 170
Nord–pas–de–Calais 106
Normandy 84, 86
Beaujolais area 234, 242
Beaune 188
Business case study 54–5
Belfort 157, 235
Bellac 203
Belleville Valley 239
Bergerac 23, 259
Besançon 152, 153, 156, 235
Besse–en–Chandesse 219, 222
Beuch Valley 310
Béziers 22, 295
Biarritz 257, 260
Biot 315
Boating/sailing: see water sports
Bogny–sur–Meuse 139
Bollène 312
Bonifacio 317
Bordeaux 23, 205, 257, 260
Boubers–sur–Canche 106
Bouc Bel Air 310
Boulogne 23
Brest 62, 66
Briançon 310, 317
Brignoles 313
British ghettos 21
Brittany: 61–79
Hotspots 64–8
Prices see under property price bands
Profile 62–3
Transport plans 63
Useful contacts 68
Brive 23, 219
Budget airlines/flights 22–3,

24, 175, 273
Builders, French or British? 47
Building conversions 47–8
Building land, shortages 235,
238, 239
Building supplies 347
Burgundy: 185–199
Hotspots 188–190
Prices see under property price bands
Profile 186–7
Useful contacts 190
Bussière Poitevine 203
Buying and selling: 24–5
10 steps to buying 39
10 tips for buyers 42
Buying at auction: 38
Case study 52–3
Checks and pitfalls 28–9
Completion 38–9
Contracts: 37–8
Hidden costs 34–5, 47, 50
Legal process 37–40
Private sales 38
Steps to buying 32–51
Prices see under property price bands
Buying guide:
Apartment sale prices 337–8
House sale prices 334–6
Letting prices 339–341

C
Caen 82, 86
Cahors 272, 274
Cala Rossa 317
Calais 102, 103
Cannes 310, 311, 314
Canoeing see water sports
canoeing, Fishing Lakes of the
Somme Valley 106
Cap d'Antibes 315
Cap Ferret 258
Capital gains tax 25
Carcassonne 23, 294
Carnac 67
Carpenters 348
Carte d'immatriculation 54–5
Carte de séjour de
ressortissant de l'Union
41, 42, 54
Cauterets 273
Céret 291, 293
Certificat d'urbanisme 29, 46
Chablais region 237
Chalets, Rhône–Alps 235, 237,
239, 240, 241
Châlons–en–Champagne 138,
139, 141
Châlons–sur–Marne see
Châlons–en–Champagne
Chalus 219

Chambers of commerce 348
Chambéry 235
Chamonix 234, 235, 238
Champagne–Ardenne: 137–49
Hotspots 140–1
Prices see under property price bands
Profile 138–9
Useful contacts 142
Champs Elysées 119
Chandelais 168
Chantemerle 317
Charente 13, 202, 203,
Charente–Maritime 202, 203–4
Gîtes as investment 203
Charleroi, airport 23
Charleville–Mézières 138, 139,
140
Chartreuse Regional Park 240
Chassagne–Montrachet 188
Châteaux:
Dordogne 259
Loire 169, 171, 173
Châtellerault 202, 205, 206
Chaudanne 238
Chauvigny 202, 203
Chinon 169
Cities, rental properties
48–9, 119
Clairvaux (Jura) 152
Clermont–Ferrand 22, 218,
219, 220–1
Tram service planned 219
Clichy 119
Coach travel 357
Coastal regions:
Aquitaine 256–58, 260
Brittany 62–4, 65–7
Côte d'Azur/Provence
/Corsica 310–11, 313–16
Languedoc–Roussillon
291, 295
Loire 169, 170
Normandy 84–5, 86–7
Poitou–Charentes 204
Coastal resorts:
Arcachon 256–7, 258
Biarritz/Bayonne 257, 260
Corsica 317
Côte d'Azur 313–16
Deauville 84
Dieppe 87
Golfe du Morbihan 67
Ile de Ré/La Rochelle 204
Le Touquet Paris Plage 104
Narbonne–Plage 295
Rental properties 26, 310–11,
313, 314
Trouville 85
Vendée Coast 169–70
Cognac 202, 203, 205

low to medium price; mhp: medium to high; tr: top of range. Bold page numbers indicate hotspot profiles.

Collogne–la–Rouge 222
Combloux 237
Commercial opportunities, business case study 54–5
Consumer Protection Act (UK, 1987) 50–1
Cornouaille coast 66
Corrèze 218 219, 222
Corse–du–Sud 317
Corsica: 23, 317
Prices see under property price bands
Profile 310–11
Useful contacts 318
Côte d'Azur:
Prices see under property price bands
Profile 310–11
Useful contacts 318
See also Provence
Côte d'Émeraude 79
Côte d'Or 186–7, 188
Côtes–d'Armor 62, 67
Côtes du Rhône 312
Courchevel 235, 238, 239
Crime areas, Paris 119
Croisette 239
Cross–country skiing:
Haut–Jura 156
Megève 237
The Vosges 155
Currency exchange 348

D
Data Protection Act (UK, 1998) 27
Deauville 82, 83, 84
Department of Social Security (UK), information on healthcare and pension rights 43
Developers 35, 48
Dieppe 82, 87
Dijon 187, 189, 235
Dinan 63, 64
Dinard 63, 64
Directory 346–57
Dordogne: 13, 21, 256–7, 259
Letting/rental properties 26, 48
Doubs 156
Draguignan 310, 313
Drainage 28–9
Duingt 236

E
E106, medical cover 43
E111, health form 42
E121, pensioners' health form 43
Ebreuil 222
Education 44–5
Ensuès–la–Redonne 316

Épernay 138, 139, 141
Estate agents: 24–5, 34, 37, 50, 65, 348
Index of 362–3
Étretat 85
Euros, purchasing 50
Eurostar 22
Evian–les–Bains 237
Exchange rates 12
Exhibitions and developers 348

F
Farmhouses:
Burgundy 189
Loire 171, 172
Lot–et–Garonne 259
Midi–Pyrénées 273
Fayence 313
Fécamp 85
Fermettes, Champagne–Ardenne 139
Ferries 23
Finance: 32–51
Tips 51
See also buying and selling
Finistère 63, 66
Fishing see angling
Fishing Lakes of the Somme Valley 106
Flaine 235
France:
Official map 18–19
political and economic trends 20–1
Population shifts 21
Regions with map 16–17
Transport developments 22–3
Franche–Comté: 151–65
Hotspots 156
Prices see under property price bands
Profile 152–3
Useful contacts 157
Furniture, import into France 40–1
Futuroscope 26, 205

G
Gard 21, 290, 294
Gascony see Gers
Gers 272, 273, 274, 275
Gîtes as investment:
Charente–Maritime 203
Loire 169
Metz 153
Uzerche 219
Glossary 343–5
Golf 205
Golf Country Club de Gassin

313
Golfe du Morbihan 62, 63, 65, 67
Gorges du Verdon 313
Grenoble 234, 235, 240
Guingamp 67
Guisane Valley (Hautes–Alpes) 317

H
Hang gliding 313
Haut–Doubs: 156
Winter sports 153
Haut–Jura: 156
Outdoor pursuits 156
Haute–Savoie 24, 237
Hautes–Alpes 317
Hautes–Pyrénées 272–3
Healthcare 42–3
Hérault 290, 295
Hesdin 103, 104, 106
Honfleur 83, 85
Horse racing 205
Horse riding:
Auvergne 221
Burgundy 189
Hotspots:
Alsace 154, 155
Aquitaine 258–60
Brittany (Bretagne) 64–8
Burgundy 188–90
Franche–Comté 156
Ile–de–France 120–5
Languedoc–Roussillon 292–5
Limousin & Auvergne 220–2
Loire 170–3
Lorraine 155
Midi–Pyrenees 274–6
Nord–pas–de–Calais & Picardy 104–6
Normandy 84–8
Poitou–Charentes 204–6
Household goods, import into France 40–1
How to use the book 14
How to use the guide 58–9
Hyères 314

I
Ile de la Cité 120
Ile–de–France: 20, 117–34
Hotspots 120–5
Prices see under property price bands
Profile 118–19
Useful contacts 126
See also Paris
Arrondissements:
Ile d'Oloron 202
Ile de Ré 202, 203, 204
Ile–Saint–Louis (Paris) 122

Insurance: 350
Against title defects 39
Household insurance 40
Interior design 350

J
Juan–les–Pins 311

K
Kitchen supplies 351

L
La Bourbole 221
La Clayette 234, 242
La Clusaz 235
La Creuse 219
La Daille 240
La Fleche 169
La Gaude 310
La Mongie 273, 276
La Roche sur Yonne 169, 170
La Roche–Posay 205
La Rochelle 23, 202, 203, 204
La Sable d'Or 170
La Souterraine 220
La Tania 239
Lac Saint–Croix 313
Lake Annecy 234, 236
Lake Geneva 237
Language services 351–2
Languedoc–Roussillon: 21, 289–307
Hotspots 292–5
Prices see under property price bands
Profile 290–1
Useful contacts 295
Le Cannet 314
Le Hameau des Ours 237
Le Lude 169
Le Mans 168–9, 172
Le Marais (Arrondissement 3) 122
Le Marais (Arrondissement 4) 118, 122
Le Muy 313
Le Praz 239
Le Quesnoy 106
Le Tholonet 310
Le Touquet 103
Le Touquet Paris Plage 104
Leaseback schemes 28
Legal experts 352
Legislation, regarding rental properties 27
Les Arcs 313
Les Batiments de France register 173
Les Baux 310–11
Les Chavannes 241
Les Gets 235, 241

Les Menuires 239
Les Minimes marina (La Rochelle) 204
Les Portes du Soleil 241
Les Rousses, ski resort Developments 153, 156
Les Sables d'Olonne 169, 170
Les Thermes, spa 237
Letting agents/companies 26, 50
Levallois 119
Lille 102, 103, 105
Limoges 23, 218–20
Limousin: 13, 22, 23, 217–31
Hotspots 220, 222
Prices see under property price bands
Profile 218–19
Useful contacts 223
L'Isle Jordain 203
Listed buildings 47
Location accession 40
Loire: 167–82
Hotspots 170–3
Prices see under property price bands
Profile 168–9
Rental properties 26
Useful contacts 173
Lons–le–Saunier 155, 158
Lorgues 313
Lorient 62, 65
Lorraine: 151–65
Hotspots 155
Prices see under property price bands
Profile 152–3
Useful contacts 157
Lot 273, 274
Lot-et-Garonne 256, 257, 259
Lubéron 312
Lyon 234–5, 241, 242

M
Maçon 234–6
Magazines, advertising or finding homes 24, 26
Manche 87
Manche peninsula 82, 83
Marseille 23, 310, 311, 316
Maussane 310–11
Medical care 43
Megève 234, 237
Menton 311
Méribel 235, 238–9
Mont d'Or leisure resort 156 ski resort developments 155, 219
Metz 152, 153, 155
Meursault 188
Midi–Pyrenees: 271–87
Hotspots 274–6
Prices see under property price bands
Profile 272–3
Useful contacts 276

Mill houses, Auxerre 190
Monêtier–les–Bains 317
Mont d'Arbois 237
Mont Blanc 234, 237, 238
Mont Chéry 241
Mont–Dore, ski resort 219, 221
Mont–Saint–Michel 87
Montmartre (18éme Arrondissement, Paris) 118
Montmélian 235
Montmorillon 203
Montparnasse (14éme Arrondissement, Paris) 118
Montpellier 23, 290, 293
Montreuil 103, 104, 106
Morbihan 62, 63, 65, 67
Mortgage raising (prêt immobilier) 36–7
Morvan 187, 189
Morzine 235, 241
Mougins 311, 314, 315
Moulins 221
Mulhouse 235
Multipropriétés 35, 39–40

N
Nancy 152, 153, 155
Nantes 23, 168, 169, 171
Narbonne 295
Neuilly 119, 124
Nice 23, 310, 311, 315
Nîmes 291, 294
Noise zones 27
Nord–pas–de–Calais & Picardy: 101–15
Hotspots 104–6
Prices see under property price bands
Profile 102–3
Useful contacts 107
Normandy: 81–98
Hotspots 84–8
Prices see under property price bands
Profile 82–3
Useful contacts 88
Notaires:
Contacts 37–8
Conveyancing 39
Fees 34–5, 50

O
Océanopolis (Brest) 66
Opal coast 103, 106
Orléans, hotspot 172
Ormaret 237
Orne 83
Outdoor pursuits:
Auvergne 221
Burgundy 189
Champagne–Ardenne 141
Haut–Jura 156
Lake Annecy 236
Midi–Pyrénées 276
Rental properties 26, 48

Vosges 152, 155
See also ski resorts
Ownership, legal aspects 39–40
P
Palombaggia 317
Pantin, property rentals 26
Parcay les Pins 169
Paris: 118–19
Hotspots 120–5
Letting properties 26, 48, 50
Métro service 22
Prices see Ile–de–France, prices
profile 118–19
Useful contacts 126
1éme Arrondissement 119, 120
2éme Arrondissement 119, 121
3éme Arrondissement 122
4éme Arrondissement 122
5éme Arrondissement 119
6éme Arrondissement 119, 123
7éme Arrondissement 119, 123
8éme Arrondissement 119, 124
9éme Arrondissement 118, 119
14éme Arrondissement 118
16éme Arrondissement 118, 119, 124
17éme Arrondissement 119, 125
18éme Arrondissement 118
19éme Arrondissement 119
20éme Arrondissement 119
Pau 257
Pays Yonnais 170
Périgeux 259
Périgord 259
Perpignan 23, 290, 291, 292
Pet passports 41
Pet transportation 352
Picardy see Nord–pas–de–Calais:
Plan local d'urbanisme 34
Planning permission, renovations and building works 46–7
Poitiers 202, 203, 205
Poitou–Charentes: 201–15
Buying case study 52–3
Hotspots 204–6
Prices see under property price bands
Profile 202–3
Rental properties 203
Useful contacts 206
Wildlife reserves 205–6
Pont Royal 310–11
Pontarlier 156
Port Ripaille 237
Porto–Vecchio 317
Preyerand 239

Properties:
Finding the right one 32
Letting 26–7, 48–51
See also rental properties
maintenance 48
Moving in 40–1
New builds 32–4, 48
See also buying and selling
property fairs/exhibitions 24
Property market:
Commercial 13
Residential 12–13, 21
Property price bands 13
bp Alsace, Lorraine & Franche–Comté 158–9
bp Aquitaine 262–3
bp Brittany 70–1
bp Burgundy 192–3
bp Champagne–Ardenne 144–5
bp Côte d'Azur/Provence /Corsica 320–1
bp Ile–de–France/Paris 127
bp Languedoc–Roussillon 296–9
bp Limousin & Auvergne 224–5
bp Loire 176–7
bp Midi–Pyrénées 280–1
bp Nord–pas–de–Calais & Picardy 108
bp Normandy 90–1
bp Poitou–Charentes 208
bp Rhône–Alps 244–5
lmp Alsace, Lorraine & Franche–Comté 160–1
lmp Aquitaine 264–5
lmp Brittany 72–3
lmp Burgundy 194–5
lmp Champagne–Ardenne 146–7
lmp Côte d'Azur/Provence /Corsica 322–3
lmp Ile–de–France/Paris 127
lmp Languedoc–Roussillon 300–1
lmp Limousin & Auvergne 226–7
lmp Loire 178–9
lmp Midi–Pyrénées 282–3
lmp Nord–pas–de–Calais & Picardy 110–11
lmp Normandy 92–3
lmp Poitou–Charentes 210–11
lmp Rhône–Alps 246–7
mhp Alsace, Lorraine & Franche–Comté 162–3
mhp Aquitaine 266–7
mhp Brittany 74–7
mhp Burgundy 196–8
mhp Champagne–Ardenne 146–7
mhp Côte d'Azur/Provence /Corsica 324–7
mhp Ile–de–France/Paris 128–9
mhp Languedoc–Roussillon 302–4

mhp Limousin/Auvergne 228–30
mhp Loire 180–1
mhp Midi–Pyrénées 284–5
mhp Nord–pas–de–Calais & Picardy 112–13
mhp Normandy 94–5
mhp Poitou–Charentes 212–13
mhp Rhône–Alps 248–50
tr Alsace, Lorraine & Franche–Comté 164–5
tr Aquitaine 268–9
tr Brittany 78–9
tr Burgundy 199
tr Champagne–Ardenne 150–1
tr Côte d'Azur/Provence /Corsica 328–30
tr Ile–de–France/Paris 130–4
tr Languedoc–Roussillon 306–7
tr Limousin & Auvergne 231
tr Loire 182
tr Midi–Pyrénées 286–7
tr Nord–pas–de–Calais/Picardy 114–15
tr Normandy 96–8
tr Poitou–Charentes 214–5
tr Rhône–Alps 252–3
Property search 352
Property-holding companies 37
Provence: 21, 309–30
Hotspots 312–17
Prices see under property price bands
Profile 310–11
Rental properties 26, 48
Useful contacts 318
PTZ (prêt à taux zéro) 12
Puligny–Montrachet 188
Puy de Sancy 219
Puy–l'Eveque 274
Puyicard 310
Pyrénées–Atlantique 257
Pyrénées–Orientales 290

Q
Quimper 66

R
Rabies, vaccinations 41
Rail travel 357
Railways, developments 22
Reberty 239
Reims 23, 138, 139, 141
Removals and haulage 353–4
Rennes 62, 65
Renovation Projects:
Aquitaine 257
Burgundy 189
Franche–Comté 152–3
Grenoble 240
Languedoc–Roussillon 291
Limousin & Auvergne 218–20
Loire 169, 172, 173

Midi–Pyrénées 272–3
Normandy 85, 87
Planning permission 46–7
Provence 312
Rental properties:
contracts 50–1
Côte d'Azur/Provence 310–11, 313, 314
Legislation regarding 27
Limousin & Auvergne 219
Locations 26, 48–9
Loire 169, 172
Lorraine 153
Managing lets 50–1
Operating as a business 51
Poitou–Charentes 203
Ski resorts 26, 48, 50, 153, 219, 239
Tenants 49–50
Winter rentals 153, 219
see also gîtes as investment; properties, letting rente viagière 40
Résidence de tourisme status 28
Resident's permit see carte de séjour
Retirement, in France 42, 43, 187, 257, 273
Rhône 233
Rhône–Alps: 233–53
Hotspots 236–242
Prices see under property price bands
Profile 234–5
Useful contacts 242
Roads, developments 22
Rocamadour 272, 274
Rodez 273
Roquebrune–sur–Argens 310
Rosans 310
Rouen 82, 86
Roussillon (southern) 293
Ryanair 22–3, 257

S
Saint–Claude 156
Saint–Cloud 119
Sainte Foy 238, 240
Saint–Germain (7éme Arrondissement, Paris) 119, 123
Saint–Germain–des–Prés (6éme Arrondissement, Paris) 119, 123
Saint–Gervais 237
Saint–Malo 63, 64
Saint–Marc–Jaume 310
Saint–Martin 204
Saint–Pierre–de–Chartreuse 240
Saint–Pol–sur–Ternoise 103
Saint–Rèmy–de–Provence 311, 316
Saint–Savin 203
Saint–Tropez 310, 311, 313
Sainte–Marie 204
Sainte–Maxime 310, 313
Saintes 202, 203

Sarlat 259
Sartène 317
Sarthe 172
Saulieu 189
Sault 312
Saumur 168, 169, 171
Savoie 24
Sea routes 23
Sea travel 356
Seine–Maritime 83, 86
Septic tanks 28–9
Serre Chevalier 317
Seven Valleys area (Nord–pas–de–Calais) 103, 106
Ski resorts: 24, 26
Auvergne 219, 221
Construction developments 155, 235
Franche–Comté 153, 156
Hautes–Alpes 317
Les Arcs 313
Midi–Pyrénées 257, 273, 276
Rental properties 26, 48, 50, 153, 219, 239
Rhône–Alps 234, 235, 237–41
see also outdoor pursuits; winter sports
Social security:
Benefits 43–4
Registration for 42–3
Solicitors and legal advisors 353–4
Spas 222, 237, 276
St Nazaire 169
Strasbourg 23, 152, 153, 154
Surveyors 356
Surveys 356, 50
Swimming pools 29, 170, 171, 236, 257, 259, 315, 356

T
Talloires 234, 235, 236
Tarare 234, 242
Tarn 273
Tarn–et–Garonne 273
Tax breaks 34
Taxation: 45–6, 51
Capital gains 25, 46, 51
Income tax 45, 51
Inheritance tax 46, 51
Property taxes 45
Social charges 46, 51
Wealth tax 45, 51
Televisions 356
Tenants:
Contracts 50–1
In rental properties 49–50
TGV links 22, 24, 235, 311, 313
Thonon–les–Bains 234, 237
Toulon 23, 314
Toulouse 23, 272–3, 275, 294
Touraine 169, 173
Tourist attractions 26
Tours 168, 169, 173, 202
Trade Descriptions Act 50

Trocadéro (Paris) 119
Trois Vallées 235, 238, 239, 240
Trouville 82, 83, 85
Tulle 219
Turenne 222

U
User groups 35, 39–40
Utilities, connection to 40
Uzef 291
Uzerche 219, 222
Uzès 294

V
Val d'Isère 234, 235, 238, 240
Valbonne 315
Vallée des Lacs 156
Vallèe de la Marne 139
Vannes 67
Var 310, 313
VAT 34
Vaucluse (Lubéron) 312
Vendée Coast 169, 170
Vermilion Coast 291
Versailles 119, 125
Verzy 139
Vézelay 189
Vichy 219, 221, 222
Villefrance (Côte d'Azur) 315
Villefranche–sur–Saône 234, 242
Villeneuve 317
Villeneuve–Loubet 315
Visan 312
Vosges, the 155
Outdoor pursuits 152, 155
Watersports:
Besançon 156
Fishing Lakes of the Somme Valley 106
Haut–Doubs 156
Ile de Ré/La Rochelle 204
Lake Allier 221
Lake Annecy 236
Limousin & Auvergne 219
Morvan Regional park 189
Poitiers and area 205
Web hosting 357
Websites:
Advertising or finding homes 24, 26, 35, 40
New builds 34
Wildlife reserves, Poitou–Charentes 204, 205
Wine tours, business case study 54–5
Winter sports: 99
Haut–Doubs 153
Rhône–Alps 234, 235, 237–41
see also ski resorts
Working in France, EU and non–EU nationals 42
Y
Yonne 189

The Index to Advertisers

An index of advertisers, listing all the companies and Estate Agents who advertised in the guide

Escape Currencies	p.4.	Century 21	p.216
VEF (UK)	p.6	L'Affaire Francaise	p.216
Halewood	p.15	Armishaws	p.232
Denise Duncanson	p.60	Perigord Weekend	p.232
A House In Brittany	p.60	Transaqua	p.232
Josselin Immobilier	p.60	ERA ACPI Immobilier	p.243
Breton Homes	p.69	PFI International	p.243
Aims International	p.80	Burrow Hutchins	p.243
Immobilier St Michel	p.80	Liliane Levasseur Hill	p.243
French Discoveries	p.80	Currencies4less	p.251
Homes In Real France	p.89	Grandchamp Immobilier	p.254
Bonne Vie Holidays	p.89	Waterside Properties	p.254
A Home In Normandy	p.89	Legett Immobilier	p.254
Condor Ferries	p.99	Herman De Graaf	p.254
Sea France	p.100	Maison SIC	p.270
Ouicanhelp	p.109	Sifex	p.277
Success Immobilier	p.109	La Maison Du Bonheur	p.278
Properties In France	p.109	Vialex	p.278
Barclays	p.116	Action Habitat	p.278
Conseil Patrimoine	p.135	Le Bonheur	p.278
David King & Associates	p.135	Bruyère Immobilier	p.279
Escape Currency	p.135	Le Moulin De La Mer	p.288
Agence Immobilière	p.136	Harrison Stone	p.297
Ideal France	p.136	Vibo Immobilier	p.297
Francophiles	p.136	Rural Retreats	p.297
The French Property Shop	p.136	French Magazine	p.305
Currencies Direct	p.149	Conseil Patrimoine	p.308
Blue Homes	p.150	Leonie Lelievre	p.308
Agence Transimmo	p.166	Lavender Homes	p.308
M&M International	p.166	French Property Finder	p.319
LRP Associates	p.175	Lord & Sons	p.319
Agence Vallée	p.175	Couleurs De France	p.331
South Loire Property Search	p.175	Finninger and Helbach	p.331
Immocommerce	p.183	Leggett Immobilier	p.331
Burgundy4u	p.184	Professe	p.331
French Magazine	p.184	La Meridienne International	p.342
Caxtons	p.191	Entenial	p.344
Muret Immobilier	p.200	Moneycorp	p.349
LA Fonciere Charentaise	p.200	Exclusive Healthcare	p.355
Souillac Country Club	p.207	Agence Eaton	p.355
Papillon Properties	p.207	Siddalls	p.371

INDEX TO ADS